KING OF THE MOB

Rocco Perri and the Women Who Ran His Rackets

JAMES DUBRO
ROBIN F. ROWLAND

VIKING

VIKING

Penguin Books Canada Ltd, 2801 John Street, Markham, Ontario,
Canada L3R 1B4
Penguin Books Ltd, 27 Wrights Lane, London W8 5TZ (Publishing &
Editorial) and Harmondsworth, Middlesex, England (Distribution &
Warehouse)
Viking Penguin Inc., 40 West 23rd Street, New York, New York 10010, U.S.A.
Penguin Books Australia Ltd, Ringwood, Victoria, Australia
Penguin Books (N.Z.) Ltd, 182-190 Wairau Road, Auckland 10, New Zealand

First published by Penguin Books Canada Limited, 1987

Copyright © James Dubro and Robin F. Rowland, 1987

Printed in Canada

Canadian Cataloguing in Publication Data
Dubro, James, 1946 —
King of the mob: Rocco Perri and the women who ran his rackets
ISBN 0-670-81533-0

1. Perri, Rocco. 2. Crime and criminals — Ontario — Hamilton
— Biography. 3. Distilling, Illicit — Ontario — Hamilton — History.
4. Narcotics dealers — Ontario — Hamilton — Biography.
I. Rowland, Robin F. II. Title.

HV6248.P45D83 1987   364.1'33'0924   C87-093553-4

For Ron Haggart, Peter Herrndorf,
Bill Macadam and Barry Morgan
with gratitude

CONTENTS

CAST OF PRINCIPAL CHARACTERS

Rocco Perri's Gang
Brassi, Antonio "Tony"
Bordanaro, Calogero "Charlie"
Carboni, Rosario "Ross"
D'Agostino, James "Jimmy"
D'Agostino, Domenic
DiPietro, Frank (a.k.a. LaPietro)
Gogo, Sidney
Italiano, Nazzareno "Ned"
Longo, Domenic
Longo, Frank
Moranda, Tony
Moranda, Pat "Patsy"
Newman, Annie (Annie Perri)
Papalia, Antonio "Tony"
Perri, Rocco "Roc"
Roma, Tony
Romeo, Frank
Romeo, Joe
Romeo, Mike
Rossi, Frank (alias Ross)
Rossi, Tony (alias Ross)
Sacco, James
Sacco, Peter "Black Pete"
Serge, Mike
Starkman, Bessie "Bess"
   (Bessie Perri)
Sullivan, Jim
Sylvestro, Frank (Sylvester)

The Law
Bell, Charles W., MP, lawyer
Crocker, Joseph, Hamilton police
Goodman, Ernest, Hamilton police
Hammond, Edward, OPP
Jelfs, George F., magistrate
Miller, John, OPP
O'Reilly, Michael, lawyer
Stringer, William, OPP
Whatley, William, Hamilton police
   chief
Zaneth, Frank, RCMP

Others
Armaly, David, customs officer
Curwood, James, rounder
Goldhart, Milt, bootlegger
Hatch, Harry, distiller
Leo, Jesse, Rocco's mistress
Magaddino, "Don" Stefano, Buffalo
   godfather
Perri, Mike, Rocco's brother
Routledge, Olive, Rocco's mistress
Sacco, Domenic, Chicago mobster
Scaroni, Domenic, godfather
Serianni, Joe, gang leader
Sottile, Joe, Niagara Falls, NY, boss
Taglerino, John, Black Hand boss
Taglerino, Sam, bootlegger

Police files and media reports from the time period covered in this book contain many variant spellings of names. Individuals even used different spellings of their own names. To avoid confusion, one spelling has been chosen for each name and will be used throughout this book. See the index for variant spellings.

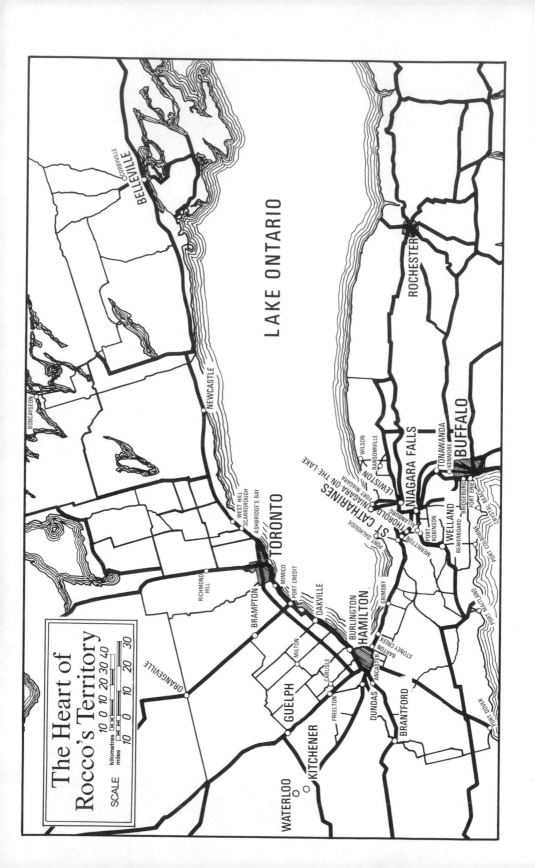

The Heart of
Rocco's Territory

SCALE

kilometres 10 0 10 20 30 40
miles 10 0 10 20 30

LAKE ONTARIO

BELLEVILLE
CORBYVILLE

BOBCAYGEON

NEWCASTLE

RICHMOND HILL

WEST HILL
SCARBOROUGH
ASHBRIDGE'S BAY

TORONTO

MIMICO
PORT CREDIT

BRAMPTON

OAKVILLE

MILTON

ORANGEVILLE

GUELPH

CARLISLE

FREELTON

KITCHENER

WATERLOO

DUNDAS

ANCASTER

BRANTFORD

BURLINGTON
HAMILTON
BARTON

STONEY CREEK

GRIMSBY

PORT DOVER

ROCHESTER

WILSON

RANSOMVILLE

LEWISTON
PORT NIAGARA

NIAGARA-ON-THE-LAKE

ST. CATHARINES

THOROLD
ALLANBURG

MERRITTON

PORT DALHOUSIE

PORT ROBINSON

WELLAND

BEAVERBOARD

PORT COLBORNE

PORT MAITLAND

NIAGARA FALLS

TONAWANDA
KENMORE

BUFFALO

BRIDGEBURG
FORT ERIE

CRYSTAL BEACH

A MOB FUNERAL

FRIDAY, AUGUST 15, 1930

Bessie Starkman's casket, bronze and steel with silver trim, rested on a carved catafalque in the centre of the long drawing room at 166 Bay Street South, Hamilton, headquarters of the mob in southern Ontario.

The casket was open, the woman's fine features cold, as if chiselled from stone. Her hair was covered in pure white silk and her body was wrapped in a white-silver shroud, all covered in a white veil. Above the casket was a fine net of white silk lace. At the head of the casket was a silver candelabrum with three long, flickering tapers.

On the white ceramic mantle were the gold-framed photographs of Bessie's two daughters as children. Three wreaths were at the foot of the coffin. Word had been sent out that no flowers were wanted — it was to be a simple Orthodox Jewish burial service. A wall tapestry of an Egyptian goddess hung near the casket.

Prohibition, in Canada and the United States, had brought riches and fame to Bessie and her common-law husband Rocco Perri, who had begun bootlegging out of their kitchen in 1916. The press had hinted that it was Bessie who was behind the cocaine and morphine trafficking in Ontario.

1

It was said that Rocco's influence had reached into the Cabinet in Ottawa.

Bessie was more than just a mistress to Rocco Perri, self-proclaimed "King of the Bootleggers." She was Rocco's Queen, his second-in-command, the financial brains of the gang. It was said openly that Bessie ran the Perri mob. She had power, money and some measure of respect, for without respect she could not command — and command she did. Rocco had ignored the Mafia rule that a woman had no place in the mob. Bessie had been his right hand from the beginning.

A gang funeral like those in Chicago and New York was not what Hamilton had been expecting, and certainly not that weekend. The eyes of the world were on Hamilton for quite a different reason. On Saturday, August 16th, the best athletes from eleven nations were to gather in the city for the first British Empire Games.

Stores and businesses were draped in patriotic red, white and blue. The Union Jack flew from many homes, while others displayed the flags of the eleven competing nations. Viscount Willingdon, Governor General of Canada, was to open the games with Prime Minister R. B. Bennett at his side.

At first, no rabbi or synagogue was willing to bury Bessie. One reason given was that she had deserted the Jewish faith when she ran away to live with Rocco, a Catholic, seventeen years earlier. But by the afternoon of August 15th, Rocco had found a burial place, in Ohev Zedek Cemetery, on a lonely country road behind the brow of Hamilton mountain. Rocco had paid $2,000 for a plot at the back of the cemetery. Ohev Zedek, which means, ironically, "Lovers of Justice," was a dreary place that summer afternoon, its grass yellowed by the sun. The small wooden building reserved for the burial service was drab and paint-blistered.

All day Friday, mourners arrived at the Perri home. Police and reporters noted cars from Buffalo, Montreal, Chicago, Detroit and Toronto pulling up and parking on Bay Street. Well-groomed guards, Italian and Jewish, watched as thousands filed past the open casket. The guards turned away the curious and politely welcomed the invited.

At the head of the casket there was now a pillow of orchids, roses and gladioli, with a ribbon of gauze displaying the gold inscription, "To my wife," and a card, "with love from Rocco." Other wreaths now surrounded the casket and great loose bundles of roses lay nearby. Gang tradition had superseded Orthodox custom.

Two of Perri's young cousins, Pat and Tony Moranda, collected the cards. "We want to send cards of thanks to all who sent these wreaths," they said.

On Saturday morning, fifteen thousand people witnessed the opening ceremonies of the British Empire Games. Thousands more across North America listened to them on the radio. The vice-regal party arrived to a fanfare of trumpets, followed by a parade of athletes.

But gangland still dominated the day's news reports. In its five o'clock edition that afternoon, the Toronto *Star* headlined, "PERRI PUTS $5,000 PRICE ON SLAYERS' HEADS"; "EMPIRE'S FINEST YOUTH BATTLE FOR SUPREMACY" took second place. All the papers carried details about the next day's funeral. The Hamilton *Herald* speculated that the ceremony would be on the scale of those held for Dion O'Banion, the Al Capone rival who had been gunned down in his Chicago flower shop in November 1924.

Bessie's murder on the evening of Wednesday, August 13, had been as sensational as O'Banion's. She had been hit at point-blank range with two blasts from a shotgun as she got out of her car at the Perri mansion. But while O'Banion's murder had a clear motive — his war with Al Capone — the reasons for Bessie's murder remained a mystery.

Her casket, however, was no secret. It cost $3,000. Brown Brothers, the Hamilton establishment's funeral home, described it as "bronze silver steel, full couch length, of state design with silver extension handles." They said it was one of the finest and costliest made, similar in design to the one Rudolf Valentino was buried in and much like those "obtained for many New York gangsters."

Rocco issued an open invitation for the public to

attend. He hired all the available Hamilton taxis for members of the Italian community and for others who did not have their own cars and who wanted to be part of the procession.

By late Saturday, Rocco had found a rabbi to officiate at the funeral — Isadore L. Freund, of Goldsboro, North Carolina, former rabbi at Anshe Sholem Synagogue in Hamilton, who was in the city to visit friends.

Sunday, August 17th, was one of those oppressively humid late summer days so common in southern Ontario. The Perri house opened at 6:30 that morning. By mid-morning, a line snaked across the lawn, up the stairs and into the drawing room where Bessie lay. A floral crucifix, sent by a thoughtless mourner, had been given a place of honour on the casket. A Jewish relative spotted it and hid it behind another bouquet. By the casket was a triangle of flowers built above a wreath and in the centre of the triangle was a clock, its hands set at 11:35, the time Bessie was shot to death. It was from "Leo and friends, Guelph."

At one o'clock, an hour before the funeral, Fred Griffin arrived. A top reporter from the Toronto *Star*, he had originally been in Hamilton to cover the Games. He couldn't get in the front door because of the long line of mourners, so he went around to the back of the mansion. There, the garage where the shooting had taken place was filled with the curious. He pushed his way through the crowd and knocked on the kitchen door, the same door Bessie had been reaching for when she was shot.

The bright white kitchen was full of men and women, Italians and Jews. Many of them were ordinary, hard-working people, relatives of Rocco or Bessie. Others were gangsters, Rocco's relatives from Calabria or Jewish mobsters who controlled bootlegging operations in Toronto. There were the pallbearers, six young men in tuxedos, black bow ties, white shirts and grey silk gloves.

Rocco's cousin, Mike Serge, had been released for the day on orders of Attorney General W. H. Price from a three-month jail sentence for illegal possession of alcohol — everyone said Mike had taken the rap for Rocco in the case. He was there with his escort, a Sheriff's Officer.

The chief mourners were Rocco Perri; Bessie's daughters, Mrs Gertrude Maidenberg and Mrs Lilly Shime, and their husbands; Rocco's niece, Mrs Stallrini, from Detroit; Joe Serge and his wife; Joe and Mike Romeo and their wives; and Frank Catanzrite.

In a sitting room there were the Jewish women, wearing black. In the dining room, almost blocked from view by flowers, there were more women in black — the Italians.

Griffin walked to the front drawing room where the coffin was almost hidden in flowers as the last sightseers passed the casket. There were at least a hundred wreaths. Two lines of chairs formed a corridor between banks of flowers. As Griffin watched, a young man lifted the veil to get a closer look at Bessie. The guard in the room said roughly, "Don't do that," grabbed the man by his arm and shoved him out the door. Moments later the doors were closed.

Outside, the sidewalks had filled. Traffic had been jammed since just after noon. Rocco sent some of his men out to push the crowd back from the door and to stop others from trying to climb in the open windows. "Get the police," Rocco told someone.

At 1:30 P.M. a detachment of uniformed officers appeared. They were under the command of Deputy Chief Ernest K. Goodman. By then, the Italian men outside on the verandah and inside the door were holding back the throng that was surging up steps, trying to enter the house. Police and gangsters together drove the crowd away with a great deal of scuffling, shoving and shouting.

Meanwhile, in the sitting room, Gertrude Maidenberg had collapsed in the heat and had been carried to another room to recover. Just before two o'clock, Rabbi Freund arrived. He was a young bespectacled man wearing a blue suit and a grey fedora.

Rocco entered the crowded drawing room, followed by

Bessie's daughters and their husbands. "Where's Rocco's hat?" someone asked, and a hat was found for him. The Jewish mourners, following custom, were already wearing hats. Some of the Italian men grabbed hats and put them on while others stood bare-headed.

The two daughters, moaning softly, took one last look at their mother and then sat down in the nearby chairs. Rocco stood at the casket, his hands on its side. His shoulders shook. He stood silently for a moment and then sat down. Someone turned on the chandelier above the casket, flooding the room with brilliant white light.

"The heat was almost unbearable," Griffin wrote.

The coffin was closed and Bessie's picture turned towards the wall.

Rabbi Freund began to read, "I will lift up mine eyes unto the hills...." A clock chimed two and below in the basement, the Perris' German Shepherd began to bark. There was fresh shouting from outside and Charles Shapiro, the undertaker, went out to quiet down the crowd. A police officer yelled, "Order, order, order," as if he were in court, but the crowd was not in a solemn mood. They laughed, they jostled, they shouted. The reporters noted the crowd was not made up of only Italians and Jews; there were "Anglo-Saxons" there, as well. Spectators from around the Empire who had been in Hamilton for the Games mingled with "every known bootlegger, gambler, petty crook and racketeer in the district," and jostled curious onlookers from Toronto, the Niagara Peninsula, Buffalo and Chicago. The crowd was estimated to be several thousand strong. Fights broke out among the spectators. Marmaduke Slack reported to the police that his pocket had been picked and he had lost his wallet containing $15 and his streetcar tickets home.

The funeral service going on inside was a simple one. There was no cantor and there was no eulogy. It concluded as Rabbi Freund said, "Peace be to Bessie Perri, who has gone to eternity."

Rocco, his head buried in his hands, sobbed. "Yes, she is gone." He took both daughters by the arm, told them to be brave, and walked with them to the rear of the house.

Outside, the police and Perri's men had cleared a narrow path across the front lawn to the hearse. Rocco had ordered ten cars for the flowers. Five were parked nearby, the others were stuck in traffic a block away. Several thousand faces watched 166 Bay Street South, people stood on sidewalks, trampled lawns, climbed onto the funeral cars and clambered onto the roofs of verandahs.

When the doors opened, "there was an animal sound from the crowd, a kind of anticipatory, 'Ah!' like the sound of a mob at a Mexican bullfight."

The crowd surged and the police had to fight to keep the path open as, first, the flowers were carried out, leaving petals scattered on the walkway. Twenty minutes later the cars were piled high with wreaths and bouquets, and the casket was brought out, its bronze and silver shimmering in the afternoon light. Watching the entire proceeding was sixty-two-year-old Senior Inspector John Miller of the Ontario Provincial Police, the province's most experienced detective, who had been assigned by Attorney General W. H. Price to head the murder investigation.

Rocco Perri and the two daughters came next, as police and seven or eight swarthy bodyguards pushed and shoved their way through the restive crowd to the curbside and their car. As the mob cut off the rest of the mourners, Perri's men pushed their way through to rescue the black-clad women, who were in danger of being crushed. Half a dozen people swarmed onto the hearse and had to be pulled off bodily by Perri's guards.

It was half an hour before all the mourners had reached their cars. By then the procession had begun to inch its way through the crowd, escorted by a single motorcycle officer, towards the main streets of Hamilton, which were still decorated with the Union Jacks and red, white and blue bunting of the previous day's ceremonies.

The six blocks surrounding the house were jammed with cars. Rocco, Gertrude and Lilly rode together in one car, its windows curtained. At Herkimer Street the cortege was held up. The crowd pressed against the hearse and the cars. As the procession climbed through the "Jolley Cut" (the mountain access road) and turned onto the Caledonia Road to the cemetery, a distance of four and a half miles, the crowd was three and four deep. The trip took over an hour.

On the steeply sloping access road the hearse broke down and the sheriff's officer escorting Mike Serge came to the rescue with his heavy-duty car and a tow rope. But even then the car and hearse had to stop every few minutes to adjust the tow.

Another crowd had been waiting at Ohev Zedek cemetery since early morning. Cars filled the nearby fields. The cemetery, "not much bigger than a good-sized back yard," was surrounded with a wooden picket fence. Its gate was closed, but the crowd had broken down part of the fence at the back, squeezed through and swarmed among the simple stones of the cemetery. A single traffic officer had the daunting task of trying to keep the entrance free for the funeral cortege. The total number of spectators at the funeral of Bessie Perri was later estimated at 25,000.

The ten flower cars crawled past the gate, then slowly found their way back to the city, where the flowers were stored in an empty shop on King Street, to be sent on to the city's hospitals the next day.

The Holy House was a small frame building at the side of the cemetery. In the Orthodox ceremony, the body would be removed for ritual washing.

Inside, the Italians crossed themselves, but they were not sure what else to do and allowed the Jewish mourners to take charge. Rabbi Freund read a brief prayer and then the casket was carried out. Griffin reported that an argument broke out as the casket was opened. Someone shouted, "Get it out here." Then, according to Griffin, the pallbearers took up the casket and moved out into the mob before Rabbi Freund could read the prayer. There was no ritual washing.

Griffin reported on the scene outside: "There was loud shouting, around the grave there was literally a fight as people struggled to get close. There was pushing and shoving...the angry shouts of men...the cries of women being pushed and hurt.... There were no police present. It was a free-for-all of morbid curiosity.... The sun beat down, torridly. The little graveyard seemed hot as a blast furnace. There was not a breath of wind."

Away from the graveside, a carelessly thrown cigarette started a fire that swept through the dry grass. Fifty men and boys were diverted from the spectacle to stop the blaze that threatened the parked cars and a child sleeping in one of them. The fire was stopped in time.

"Rocco Perri and his friends fought their way to the graveside just as the casket, fixed in the lowering apparatus, had sunk flush to the level of the ground," Griffin continued. Just at that moment, Rocco Perri swayed and seemed to faint. He pitched forward and almost fell into the grave. Bodyguards pulled open his collar and shirt, then battered the crowd back so he could get some air. "Finally they got him to the car and got him in. There he lay back exhausted. Thus he stayed while the body of Bessie was eventually lowered."

Some of the crowd had turned and followed Rocco to the car while others pressed in on Lilly Shime and Gertrude Maidenberg, who also collapsed under the strain.

Griffin wrote: "A little Englishman started shouting, 'Give the ladies air,' and went slightly berserk, flailing with his fists." But the little man did manage to clear some room for the women and their husbands, and the bodyguards took the two daughters away from the graveside.

Neither Rocco nor Bessie's daughters were present as Rabbi Freund read a prayer in Hebrew. A "Pillow of Life," a white bag containing some earth, was placed in the casket under her head. Then the coffin was lowered into the ground. Orthodox custom had called for a plain wooden coffin. As a compromise, the ornate bronze and silver casket was lowered into a frame of wood, and a wooden lid was placed over it. Men began to shovel earth into the grave.

"May peace come to Bessie Perri," someone said at the graveside. It was over.

The bodyguards pushed, shoved and punched their way through the crowd, escorting the mourners back to the cars, which edged their way back toward Hamilton, back to 166 Bay Street South.

The funeral of Bessie Perri marked the end of an era, the decade when Canada was the home of the rumrunners who supplied the thirsty United States and their often equally parched fellow countrymen with forbidden liquor. The era had been launched by an idealism that equated temperance with liberty and had ended with mobsters, businessmen, bureaucrats and statesmen co-operating in the criminal endeavour of supplying liquor to millions of people who wanted a drink. It had ended in murder, and during the years of the Great Depression, many would look back at the cocky little King of the Bootleggers and his consort with nostalgia.

CHAPTER 1

WHEN BOOKIES MADE HOUSE CALLS:
ROC AND BESS AT WORK AND PLAY

By the mid-1920s, Rocco and Bessie were on top of the world. They were grossing well over a million dollars a year — about two million dollars a month in today's currency and they had established the business system they were to follow until Bessie's death. The bootlegging business was booming, as were gambling, bookmaking, loansharking and the drug trade. Rocco made the deals and Bessie handled the money, but both ran the gang. Of course, there were expenses — maintaining fleets of cars, paying hirelings and suppliers, wholesale bribery of officials. One of Rocco's biggest deals was made with the Hatch family. On December 28, 1923, Harry Clifford Hatch, the ambitious and foul-mouthed general manager of Corby's, and his brother Herbert had put together a deal worth $1.5 million to purchase the old Gooderham's distillery in Toronto from the founding families, the Gooderhams and the Worts.

Rocco had begun making regular purchases from Gooderham's in 1924. In April or May of 1925 he walked into the offices of Gooderham & Worts in Toronto to pay for a shipment in person and he was ushered into the offices of Herbert Hatch and Larry McGuinness. Their firm, Hatch & McGuinness Ltd. was officially a sales agent for Gooderham & Worts. In reality, Hatch & McGuinness was the front that kept Gooderham & Worts respectable: they made the deals with bootleggers such as Rocco Perri on behalf of the firm.

It is not known whether Rocco ever met the president, Harry Hatch. Herbert Hatch and McGuinness were Harry's insulation. Asked later if he ever met Harry Hatch or did business with him directly, Rocco replied, "I don't remember."*

That particular day Rocco had a complaint. He was a regular customer, but Gooderham & Worts was also selling to John B. ("Ben") Kerr, a small-time but ambitious Hamilton bootlegger. A deal was struck and Perri got a monopoly for Hamilton — Kerr ended up working for him. Officially, of course, the liquor would be sold for export to the United States. Larry McGuinness told Rocco that he needed someone in the United States to place the orders. Rocco gave him the name of Joe Penna, from Wilson, New York, on the south shore of Lake Ontario. In reality, the orders would come direct from Bessie. (For Rocco's real export trade to the United States, orders would be placed through his partner Jim Sullivan from Fort Erie.) Rocco also made deals for liquor that others ordered for shipment to the U.S. He arranged for Hatch & McGuinness to take orders from Dominic Sacco in Chicago, Sacco's brother Nino in Buffalo and Rocco Pitsimenti from Mulberry Street in New York's Little Italy.

As well as the export business to New York and Chicago, from which he must have taken a cut, Rocco controlled most of the bootlegging in Hamilton, Guelph and Brantford.

OPP Inspector Albert Boyd reported, "Mrs Perry appears to be head of all Hamilton activities" and it was Bessie who did the business with Gooderham & Worts in Toronto, with Seagram's in Waterloo, with the Kuntz Brewery in Kitchener and the Hiram Walker distillery in Windsor. She usually began the week by placing an order to Gooderham's on Monday morning. Then she would collect the weekend's

---

*Did Harry Hatch meet Rocco? The official transcript of the Royal Commission on Customs and Excises in 1926 shows Hatch answering, "Yes," but newspaper transcripts have Hatch answering "No" to that question.

take, from bootlegging or from the liquor and gambling at the roadhouses, from the bookies.

On the day of an order — she called between three and five times a week — Bessie would telephone Lionel L. Sinclair, the manager of the Gooderham & Worts shipping department, with an order for about 125 cases. She had a $20,000 line of credit with them. (Both Herbert Hatch and Larry McGuinness did visit the Bay Street mansion to collect money. Almost all the officials of distilleries and breweries denied the Perris ever visited their establishments but William Wetlings, the sales manager for the Taylor and Bate brewery in St Catharines in the early 1920s, later remembered that Rocco Perri was a frequent visitor to the brewery and that Bessie was there at least once. It is likely, therefore, that both Rocco and Bessie also visited their other suppliers.)

At Gooderham's, Sinclair would call the Postal Telegraph Co. in Niagara Falls, New York and send a telegram to himself, from Joe Penna, Wilson, New York, "confirming" the order. Then he would fill out an order form and take it to an excise officer where he would swear an oath that it was a genuine export order. Rocco's boats — either his big boat, the *Atun*, capable of carrying between six hundred and seven hundred cases and doing twenty knots, or Jim Sullivan's *Miss Ontario* or the chartered *Kitty, Onaway, Elmo* or *Mary* — would make their way from Hamilton or other ports to either the Gooderham's dock in Toronto or the nearby Canada Steamship Lines wharf.

The loading of the boat would be supervised by a customs officer. He kept one copy of the B-13 export form, sent one copy to the customs office on Wellington Street in Toronto and handed the rest to the "captain" of the boat. The boat would leave in the late afternoon and would usually put in at one of the docks in Hamilton, at a beach in Oakville or at an abandoned brickyard beside Joe Burke's Lakeview Inn in Port Credit.

Rocco was usually nearby, watching the operation to make sure everything went smoothly. Sometimes there were problems. In December 1926, for example, OTA officers received the tip that the *Atun* would be bringing in a load at a dock at the foot of MacNab Street in Hamilton, where Rocco had tied up another speedboat and a dinghy. That night a well-lit dredging barge was also tied up to the MacNab Street dock, so the *Atun* darted back into the darkness and tied up at another dock. But it was too late. They had been seen. Fifty-nine years later, just before he died in 1985, one of the OTA officers, Charlie Wood, recalled how that night they came upon three men loading whisky into a Reo truck and a Studebaker. One got away, but they arrested Joe Sullivan and Patsy Lasconi. Then Rocco came out of the darkness and asked to speak to the officer in charge, Bob Bryen. Perri took Bryen down the dock and "made him an offer, which was refused," Wood said. (There were no witnesses to the offer, so Perri was not charged.)

Once the whisky or gin was loaded into the trucks and cars, it was taken to secret warehouses around the city or trucked to Rocco's contacts in Guelph or Brantford. One of the warehouses was the then empty house at 27 Railway Street, next door to Frank Romeo's house at number 25. From there the liquor would be distributed to the hotels, roadhouses and blind pigs.

Rocco and Bessie Perri permitted senior members of the gang, like Mike Romeo, Rosario ("Ross") Carboni and Charlie Bordonaro, to operate on their own. Bessie would advance them cash to purchase beer from the local Grant's Spring Brewery, which they then sold to wholesale and retail customers. They would pay Bessie back the advance plus a portion of the profits.

Bank records also showed that Bessie trusted Romeo and Carboni to take large amounts of cash to the bank on her behalf and sometimes cash large cheques.

The Mascia brothers, who ran a Hamilton grocery store, would order direct through Bessie, calling her up with an order for Gooderham & Worts rye or Seagram's whisky. It would be delivered, depending on stock available, anytime from a half-hour to a day later. Louis Mascia then wrote a cheque out to Bessie. As for beer, Mascia bought it direct from Grant's Spring with little pretence that it would be exported.

Small-time Hamilton bootleggers, such as the Gobia family who ran a small blind pig on Mulberry Street, sold liquor and "strong beer." They got their supplies from Frank Romeo, Mike Romeo's cousin. In Ontario the legal alcohol content of a drink was 2.2 percent, and in 1925, the legal limit was raised to 4.4 percent. "Strong beer" was 9 percent and, officially, was manufactured by the breweries "for export," but it kept finding its way back into Ontario. Rocco Perri was well known and liked among the small bootleggers of Hamilton. Mrs Gobia was quoted by an undercover investigator as saying she knew and liked Rocco, who had done "several good favours" for her.

Despite his denials, from the beginning Rocco had also dealt in moonshine. Counterfeit liquor labels had been found in his Hess Street grocery in a 1919 raid, and beginning in 1924, Rocco and other Ontario bootleggers were buying redistilled denatured alcohol from local boss Joe Sottile in Niagara Falls, New York, who ran a giant distilling plant in an abandoned theatre. Denatured alcohol was the ethyl alcohol used in industry to which poisons such as methyl or wood alcohol, carbolic acid, formic acid, formaldehyde or acetone were added to give it an unpleasant taste and smell. It was common practice throughout the United States during Prohibition to redistill the denatured alcohol and sell it as liquor.

To obtain the redistilled denatured alcohol from Sottile, Perri traded Canadian whisky and beer. Once the alcohol was delivered, some of Rocco's men used it to counterfeit real liquor. Gin was made by adding oil of juniper. Scotch was made by adding caramel and a trace of creosote to give a smoky flavour. Bourbon and rye were made of a combination of redistilled alcohol, caramel and prune juice. For slightly better quality, the bootleggers would cut the genuine whisky with the alcohol to make four bottles out of three.

Everything for the bootlegger: *This price list, seized in an OPP raid in 1926, shows just how open and flagrant was the counterfeiting of labels of premium brands of liquor during Prohibition in the United States and Canada.*

SCOTCH	per dozen
Black & White 5ths & pts.	30¢
Ushers Green Stripe	32
Sandy MacDonald 5ths & pts.	32
Peter Dawson 5ths & pts.	32
John Dewar 5ths & pts.	30
White Horse 5ths & pts.	33
King George 5ths & pts.	30
Watson No. 10	35
Johnny Walker Red 5ths & pts.	30
Johnny Walker Black 5ths & pts.	30
Old Smuggler 5ths & pts.	30
Teachers Highland Cream	32
Bullock & Lade (B & L)	35
Ambassador 5ths & pts.	30
Perfection	30
Gold Thimble 5ths & pts.	33
Black Rod 5ths & pts.	30
King William	35
John Haig	35
Robert McNish-Doc. Spec.	40
Haig & Haig	30
Lawson	20

CARTON PACKAGES	per dozen
Glen Moray	55¢
Royal George	55
Long John with metal corks	65
Old Parr	55
Old Smuggler Double Dimple	55
Old Smuggler Pinch with caps	55
H. & S.	55
Old Orkney	55
V.O.B.	55
Ambassador Pinch with caps	55
Gold Thimble Pinch	55
Aberlour-Glenlivet	55
Argyle	60
Robertson Perfection	75

WINES AND CORDIALS	per dozen
Duff Gordon Sherry	33
Martini & Rossi Ital. Ver.	45
Benedictine	70
Sauterne Haut de Lizi	35
Sauterne-Calvet	30

Above prices are subject to change without notice.

Pint Aluminums, Non-Refillable Fitments, Corking Machines, Capping Machines for Tinfoil Caps

Prices above quoted are for 100 Dozen of a brand 10¢ per dozen extra in smaller quantities.

TO BE USED FOR NON-ALCOHOLIC PURPOSES.

Tel. Canal 4426

THE PERFECT TINFOIL CO. INC.

Importers and Wholesale Dealers in Bottlers Supplies

487 Broadway New York, N.Y.

Avail yourself of our open order department.

Champagne was a mixture of alcohol, cheap Niagara white wine, cider, sugar and compressed carbon dioxide. Only the best customers got the real thing.

The redistilled alcohol was smuggled into Canada in tins of one and five U.S. gallons, either hidden under coal and industrial coke trucked across the border at Niagara or brought by boats returning from dropping the "good stuff" on the U.S. shore. Perri bootlegger Charles Bordonaro, who kept a grocery and butcher shop on MacNab Street in Hamilton, had a "wine cellar" excavated under his sidewalk, where he kept the bottles of good Canadian whisky, gin and brandy, the tins of U.S. alcohol and the counterfeit labels for making up the new product.

Rocco had two close allies in Toronto. One was Joseph Burke, the owner of the Port Credit Lakeview Inn roadhouse. Port Credit was often Rocco's railhead for whisky from the Seagram's and Hiram Walker distilleries, which was loaded into boats at the abandoned brickyard beside the roadhouse. The other was Mike Bernardo, who bought beer from the National Brewery in Montreal on Bessie's behalf, had it shipped by rail to Port Dalhousie where it was loaded into boats, most of it going east to New York, the rest west to Hamilton. Bernardo was also the "agent" for boats that brought imported liquor — real scotch, French brandy, schnapps and European wine — from the warehouses of the French islands of St Pierre and Miquelon. The boats were small enough to make it through all the St Lawrence canals, but large enough to carry profitable loads into Ontario, where it was not only forbidden by prohibition, but was also "duty free," since no federal taxes had to be paid on the illicit goods. From Ontario, the rest of the liquor found its way into western New York or along the Welland Canal (in Rocco's territory, of course) to Detroit and Chicago.

The money flowed through Bessie, who kept the books for Rocco and handled the day-to-day business. She had accounts in the name of either Bessie Perri or Bessie Stark-man in Hamilton branches of the Imperial Bank, Standard Bank, the Bank of Commerce, the Bank of

Montreal and the Royal Bank, as well as four accounts in Toronto and more in Buffalo. An OPP inspector would later say that Rocco had his own account in the Bank of Buffalo, officially for payment of orders of "olive oil and macaroni." During a 1927 investigation, it was estimated that she had $869,000 in the seven Hamilton accounts alone. The Perris never paid more than a pittance in taxes nor were they ever prosecuted. In other ways, however, they did make something of a contribution to society: as Bessie noted in a famous interview with Dave Rogers of the *Star,* they often gave large amounts of money to religious charities, both Catholic and Jewish.

One of the Perris' competitors, a small-time bootlegger named Mildred Sterling, who called herself "the Queen of the Bootleggers" told undercover investigators about Bessie and Rocco:

> Bessie, a Jewish woman, who is Rocco's wife, is the brains of the works and also has plenty of money. Of course, Rocco is no dummy, but he had nothing when he married Bessie. She gave him his start and today he is a millionaire. ..."
>
> Rocco Perri and his strong men have the town scared to death....The law have nothing on Perri, but he has plenty on the big fellows in this town, as every individual knows, how abrupt [*corrupt?*] these officials have been, but they still will not open up on Perri; otherwise the Hamilton newspapers would not be large enough for publication of the names of those uncovered.... Rocco can get anything done. All he has to do is flash the high ball and the works are in; that is why Rocco has been getting away with lots of trouble.

While Bessie was at Hamilton on the phone to the distillers, Rocco would be making his rounds in Toronto, Hamilton and the Niagara region. He took a special interest in his gambling and bookmaking empire.

In 1923, Ernest Hemingway, then a reporter for the Toronto *Star*, described the betting system in southern Ontario. He estimated that at least 10,000 people patronized the bookmakers in Toronto alone, playing about $100,000 a day. "For years Toronto has been known all over the world as the biggest betting town in North America." Wires from the local tracks, such as Woodbine, and from tracks all over North America, found their way into the bookmakers' hangouts. At the time Toronto bookies paid out a maximum of $15 for a win on a two-dollar bet, meaning a 200 to 1 shot would pay just $30 for the two-dollar investment.

Large bets, (the limit on bets in those days was usually less than $5,000) and heavy action was laid off to larger bookmakers in Montreal. "Key operators in Toronto at present are commission men. They work on the basis of two and one-half percent commission on the bet. Eighty percent of these commissions are placed in Montreal," Hemingway reported.

In those days bookies made house calls. The "agents," Hemingway called them, either worked one office building, or each day visited offices, factories, stores and even homes.

In one aspect of his story, Hemingway was wrong. He reported that the days of the giant bet, of the thousands of dollars dropped at a track, had ended with Ontario's 10.5 percent tax at the track and the pari-mutuel machines. What he didn't know was that in New York, Arnold Rothstein was systematizing the lay off system across North America, that along with Prohibition, the mob was organizing the continent for bettors.

Perri's gambling territory extended throughout a forty-mile arc centred in Hamilton. The bookies — then called "handbook men" — either worked the phones (much of the business being done on long distance to outlying towns and farms) or worked as newsdealers or hotel desk clerks to deal with walk-in customers who laid bets.

One of Perri's handbook agents specialized in collecting bets from women gamblers. It was probably Bessie's suggestion. For the upper class, the agent would dispatch a runner to the ladies' homes, so they could place their bets without their husbands' ever knowing.

The top bettors in the Niagara region had a direct line to Perri, although one of his "personal staff" actually answered the phone. (At one point the book was actually run out of the attic of 166 Bay Street South.) Customers, one 1925 report said, were "often in such a position that [*they*] dare not squeal for fear of losing a high position, social standing or bank credit." The report adds, "Naturally the handbook man finds out all about the financial resources of such clients," a direct link to the loansharking that goes hand in hand with gambling. It also hints at the source of Perri's political influence in the region.

Rocco's agents were also active in Hamilton's steel mills and manufacturing plants: "the handbookmen do not sit back and wait for business," the report noted.

Once the morning's business was done, if he wasn't tracking one of his shipments, Rocco would join the afternoon sidewalk social conversation in Little Italy, watch a game of bowls or drop in at a pool hall at Murray and James streets in Hamilton.

The Perri mansion at 166 Bay Street South was open to his relatives, friends and followers. His brother, Mike Perri, lived there for a time, and Bessie's daughters stayed there on occasion. Perri, an excellent cook, liked to put together big Italian dinners. There was always a dog in the house and Rocco could be seen walking it in the neighborhood.

The Perris' evenings were quiet. They stayed at home relaxing, listening to the radio or playing cards with Rocco's close cousins, the families of Mike and Joe Serge. When they went out it was to homes of other senior gang members like Frank DiPietro or Frank Sylvestro. They were an openly affectionate couple. Bessie and all his friends called him "Roc." He called her "Bess."

They also had a house on North St. in St Catharines, a house in Thorold and an apartment building in Windsor, all rented out.

After Warner Brothers released *Little Caesar*, starring Edward G. Robinson, in January 1930, the press dubbed Rocco "Canada's Little Caesar." In some ways, he fitted the description. He liked exclamatory ties, "fashionable race track outfits" and custom-tailored business suits. He was suave, immaculate, unperturbed. Rocco was a product of a verbal culture; he was articulate but had trouble reading and writing English. He was cocky, had a wide grin, tossed off wisecracks, smoked big cigars when relaxed and puffed on endless cigarettes when he was nervous.

Bessie dressed in expensive dresses and jewellery worth thousands of dollars, which she wore every day. She was bright, witty and petite, with a soft voice and manner that hid a woman who was sharp and tough inside, someone who figured all the odds and all the angles. Rocco loved to give her thick wads of cash and Bessie loved to spend it, going on shopping sprees in Toronto and New York. Roc and Bess were a perfect match.

At least once a week, they visited Toronto together in their big Marmon limousine. For Rocco it was a time to see associates in the Ward. Although Jewish bootleggers had most of the Toronto market, the Italians did a good business there, too. Old-time residents of Walton Street in the Ward remember Perri arriving to make deliveries of "olive oil" and other products to the Italian storekeepers and handing out quarters to kids who crowded around the big, black car. Perri loved children.

Sometimes Rocco would head off for a business meeting with the Italiano family on Dundas Street West or he would make a "social call" on the Wortzman brothers on Beverley, the biggest Jewish bootleggers in Toronto. Rocco finally would drop in on a gambling den on Dundas Street East or some of the smaller gambling joints and blind pigs in the Ward and in Little Italy along Clinton Street, probably keeping an eye on connections — and the competition.

Bessie used the Toronto visits to visit her daughters, Lilly and Gertrude. When they were small and lived with their father, Harry Tobin, on William Street (now St. Patrick Street), Bessie would wait outside the McCaul Street school until the girls got out of class, and then she would greet them with hugs and gifts. When they were teenagers, it was Bessie who paid for their private schooling, while Harry Tobin ran a pawnshop on York Street. Bessie later said that she never once telephoned his house. Her daughters would call her and she would then meet them by arrangement. She told a friend that her moments with her daughters made up for all the trouble she had with her legal husband.

In the mid-1920s, both Gertrude and Lilly were frequent visitors to the house at 166 Bay Street South. When Gertrude married, it was Bessie who helped the young couple get a start in life — and she doted on her first grandchild, Gertrude's son, Stanley Maidenberg.

Neither did Rocco neglect his own two daughters, whom he had had by his mistress, Olive Routledge. An OPP surveillance report from 1926 said that Rocco visited the Routledge farm in Musclow every so often, "and outfitted the whole family." What exactly happened to the money isn't clear. Rocco was often generous but the OPP also noted that the Routledge farm house was "a rather dilapidated hovel."

Rocco, who loved to drive sporty cars, was a travelling man. Into the early 1920s, he kept his cover as a macaroni salesman as he travelled to Sudbury, North Bay and Ottawa. But most of his journeying took place in the sphere of his influence; Toronto and the Niagara Peninsula. He was frequently seen in St Catharines, then the base of the D'Agostino brothers; in Niagara Falls, headquarters for Jimmy Sacco; and in Welland, Thorold and Merritton. But his trips were not only for business: at different times Rocco had girlfriends in Sudbury and Niagara Falls.

Rocco would also cross into the United States — when he could get past the United States immigration authorities — to meet with allies south of the border. There was Joe Sottile at the Third Ward Political Club on Thirteenth Avenue, the front for the distilling operation in Niagara Falls, New York; the Niagara Falls Calabrian ally, Joe Serianni, who was involved both in bootlegging Canadian booze from the border into Ohio and in operations such as mail robberies. Rocco also dropped in on his New York and Chicago customers and mob allies from time to time.

Rocco Perri did not become the King of the Mob in southern Ontario without ruthless street smarts and charisma. He maintained his leadership by insuring that he had the respect necessary for a mob leader while depending on Bessie's advice and financial ability.

Athough the core of Rocco's gang were fellow Calabrians, he employed talent from many ethnic groups: Ukrainians, Jews, Irish, Greeks, French Canadians and British Canadians. His was the first truly multicultural mob in Canada.

Although Bessie was arrogant at times and kept a close watch on the purse strings, she also had some leadership ability. She was strong enough to give orders to the Italian members of Rocco's gang, who for the most part had a grudging respect for her. Still, she never forgot that Rocco was the boss.

The middle years were the height of the Roaring Twenties, when the same Cuba-bound, liquor-laden boat could leave Ontario four times a day, when the music of the jazz age crackled on the radio. Southern Ontario had its own vaudeville circuits, and on Saturday nights the Loew's Wintergarden on Yonge Street was filled with crowds who had come to see the latest Canadian and American stars. In ten years Rocco and Bessie had risen from the mud of the Welland Canal to become King and Queen of the Bootleggers, from being poor immigrants to enjoying the status of celebrities, from receiving labourer's wages to a million dollars a year.

CHAPTER 2
THE LAND OF OPPORTUNITY

Rocco Perri was born in the village of Plati about twenty kilometres inland from the east coast of Calabria, the toe of the Italian boot, on December, 27, 1887. The name Plati means "flat," and the village had been poor for centuries, depending largely on its numerous olive groves for its slender income. Plati dates back to the pre-Roman settlement of Magna Grecia. By the nineteenth century it had also become known for its brigands.

In the nineteenth century Calabria was a land of villages perched on rocky peaks, peasants struggling to scrape together a living on poor soil and plagued by earthquakes. It was also patriarchal and authoritarian. Harsh circumstances produced a tough, proud people. "Often all they really have is their honour; an insult touches any sense of superiority they have," a police intelligence officer born in Calabria says.

The bandit tradition gave rise to the Calabrian N'Dranghita, or Honoured Society, which adopted and adapted the traditions of the Neapolitan Camorra and the Sicilian Mafia, and produced a crime family headed by a patriarch and consisting of relatives and friends from the same village. A man's word of honour was crucial; the head of the family commanded absolute obedience. The rule of silence was enforced by death.

To this day Plati is known as a *casa madre*, or mother house of the Honoured Society. Secret reports from both the Ontario Police Commission and the Italian *Carabinieri* reveal that Mafia members in towns such as Locri, Siderno, San Luca and Grotteria, while independent, are closely allied with Plati. Mobsters from Plati control most of the drug trade in Australia, but their profits are deposited in banks in Locri. The modern Siderno group has cells in Toronto, New York, Albany, Chicago, Connecticut and Naples, Florida. Family names that would have been familiar to Rocco Perri — Sergi, D'Agostino, Papalia — are still active in Calabria today.

At the turn of the century, hundreds of thousands left southern Italy and emigrated to America; sometimes whole villages would pack up and go. According to his application for Canadian naturalization, filed in 1921, Rocco Perri arrived in Boston on board the *S.S. Republic* in April 1903 and headed for New York. At the time he could have settled in one of the two Italian neighbourhoods in New York: downtown in Little Italy or uptown in East Harlem. For most of the immigrants, the American dream soon evaporated in the slums of the growing industrial cities. The sixteen-year-old Rocco Perri probably got his first exposure to crime in New York.

Rocco, who was not always truthful in court, would later testify that he left New York sometime in 1904. Nothing is known of what he did from then until May 1908 when he entered Canada from White Mountain, Vermont. He lived in Montreal for about six months, and then, according to his citizenship papers, went on to Parry Sound, where he stayed for three years. Rocco may have had relatives in Parry Sound; two men, F. Perri and his son, A. Perri, were killed by a rockburst on a Canadian National Railways cut at Key Harbour near Parry Sound on December 3, 1907.

According to his citizenship papers, Rocco then lived in Trenton for about six months before moving to Hamilton. However, in the spring of 1912, he was known to be working as a labourer in Toronto's Ward — the area bounded on the south by Queen Street, on the east by Yonge, on the north by

College and on the west by University Avenue. It was there that he met Bessie Starkman.

Besha (Bessie) Starkman was born in Poland on April 14, 1889. Her parents, Shimon (Sam) and Gello (Gloria) Starkman, were among the thousands of destitute East European Jews who arrived in Toronto at the end of the nineteenth century. They were fleeing the pogroms of Russia and the poverty of the east and hoping for a new promised land.

The Starkmans settled in the Ward, which was home for the Jews who worked in the garment industries, the Italian labourers, pedlars, grocers and musicians, the Irish and the few Chinese permitted into Canada at the time. East of Yonge Street at Parliament Street was Cabbagetown, then known as the largest Anglo-Saxon slum outside of London.

It was to the Ward that most poor immigrants came, just north of the city's two main railway stations: Union Sation at the Esplanade and Simcoe Street and the Great Western Station at the entrance to Yonge Street. Originally called St John's Ward, its name was quickly shortened. The first boarding houses appeared in the 1870s; by 1887 it was officially condemned as an overcrowded slum, but little was done to improve conditions.

If Rocco worked in Parry Sound, he was perhaps like many Italian labourers who went north in the spring to work on the railways or canals or in the mines, returning to the boarding houses of the Ward for the winter.

Most of the Jews in the Ward found jobs in its garment industry. The Toronto city directory for the period shows the few Starkmans as either operators or clerks for the T. Eaton department store and catalogue chain, in the company's manufacturing complex beside its downtown Toronto flagship store. Hundreds of the city's Jews worked in the poor conditions at the Eaton plant.

No part of the Ward was exclusive. It was poor and density was high. In 1911, the medical officer of health reported that 108 houses in the Ward, all occupied, were unfit for human habitation. The houses were surrounded by sweatshops, yards full of rags, open privies. By 1900, the

Jews and Italians who could afford it had already moved out of the district.

In 1907, Harry Tobin, twenty-three, born in Russia and now a driver for a bakery, was living in a boarding house at 2 Foster Place, a tiny sidestreet jutting east from Elizabeth Street. On December 15, 1907, he married Besha Starkman, who was then eighteen. By 1911, the Tobins had moved to 63 Chestnut Street in the heart of the Ward and taken in a boarder, Samuel Menkin, who had a barber shop at 63½ Chestnut. During these years two daughters, Lilly and Gertrude, were born.

For three months in 1912, the Tobins had a new boarder — twenty-four-year-old Rocco Perri. According to one version of the first meeting between Bessie and Rocco, she encountered the rag-clad young man and simply invited him home, since he needed a place to stay.

Rocco — soft-spoken, good looking, five-foot-four, with a dark complexion, brown eyes and black hair — was perhaps a little lonely. He wooed and won the auburn-haired, vivacious and intelligent Bessie Tobin away from her husband. Years later the Toronto *Star* romanticized the episode in a story about Harry Tobin published at the time of Bessie's funeral:

> For a while they were happy. Then she started to be absent. For a while he wondered. Around the corner was the reason. A strong, square-shouldered Italian immigrant swinging a pick had attracted her. People told him. He didn't believe. Hadn't he two nice babies? One afternoon he went out on business. He came back. His wife had gone. Another Italian immigrant was swinging a pick around the corner. Two babies sat on the floor crying.

Rocco and Bessie appeared together for the first time in 1913 in St Catharines. They arrived with no money and no friends. Rocco got a job as a labourer, working on the enlargement of the Welland Canal.

The project brought in scores of labourers who settled in St Catharines on Lake Ontario, at Port Colborne on the shore of Lake Erie and at Thorold and Welland between the lakes. Many of the labourers were Italian, and in the years to come the area from the Welland Canal to the U.S. border along the Niagara River was the centre of organized crime in the region.

Rocco laboured at the canal for about a year, in shoes, it is said, that were so thin that they did little to protect his feet from the sand and mud of the canal. Rocco and Bessie were very much in love, living together in a hovel, both dressed in rags. Some of the Italians shunned them because Bessie was Jewish. According to the legend that grew up later, Bessie sometimes went without food to provide for Rocco. Another story suggests Bessie did not like the rough conditions of the area and left Rocco for a few months until love drew her back.

In August 1914, Europe was plunged into the First World War. Rocco was suddenly out of a job; funding for the Welland Canal project had been cut. But by then he had a friend. "Don" Filippo Mascato gave Rocco an occasional, part-time job in his bakery. The "baker" gets a passing and unexplained mention as the "notorious Filippo Mascato" years later in a secret Ontario Provincial Police report. It is through Mascato that Rocco probably got his introduction to the workings of the underworld in Canada.

During this period Bessie and Rocco had a child who died soon after birth.

Around this time, Mascato decided to return to Italy. He closed the bakery and Rocco was once more unemployed. His next job, again as a labourer, was in the quarries of the Canada Crushed Stone Company in the village of Dundas near Hamilton.

By 1916 Rocco and Bessie Perri were living in Hamilton at 157 Caroline Street North. Rocco was now working as a part-time travelling salesman for the Superior Macaroni Company, but most of his fellow, non-British immigrants were in a different line of work.

Hamilton in those days was growing into Canada's primary steel-manufacturing centre. With newly developed electric power from Niagara Falls and with the impetus of the war, Hamilton, by 1915, had come out of a slump.

Factories worked around the clock, manufacturing armaments and other supplies for the war. Since many of the city's English and Scottish immigrants had joined the Canadian Expeditionary Force, it was largely Hamilton's other immigrants who powered the war industries. Among them were the Italians, whose numbers had tripled to 5,000 between 1911 and 1918. Most of them were single male labourers. But they were not very welcome in Hamilton, which had been 91 percent British in 1911 and still considered itself to be British. The city directory did not even record the names of non-British immigrants. An "Italian" was recorded at some addresses. Restrictive covenants in deeds forbade sales to "foreign-born Italians, Greeks or Jews" as well as "negroes, Asiatics, Bulgarians, Austrians, Russians, Serbs, Rumanians, Turks and Armenians."

The boom of the war years did not mean an increase in the standard of living; working men's wages remained about the same while rents went up 60 percent and available rental accommodation actually declined. Wartime inflation pushed up other costs. There was labour unrest in Hamilton in the spring of 1916, with strikes at the car shops of the Toronto, Hamilton and Buffalo Railway, and at the Steel Company and Dominion Steel Foundries.*

It was not a life attractive to a young, ambitious couple like Rocco and Bessie Perri. What they needed was an opportunity.

Organized crime had existed in Canada since French bootleggers first sold brandy to the Indians at Louisbourg in 1657. Later, at the end of the nineteenth century, the Dominion was a land of opportunity for gangs like the English family of Ed Johnson, who counterfeited a million dollars' worth of Canadian and U.S. currency, and the gang of Scottish freebooters who terrorized eastern Ontario and northern New York. In the late 1890s Ontario's provincial detective service had its hands full trying to stop a central

---

*For more detailed information about the social history of Hamilton, see John C. Weaver's excellent *Hamilton: An Illustrated History.*

Ontario 'barn burning for insurance' racket. It was run by the Ballard brothers, sons of a black American and his Irish Canadian wife. David Ballard, a slight man, the brains of the mob, forced farmers in Dufferin County to overinsure their barns. If anyone refused, Ballard's giant brother and enforcer, James, visited the farmer and threatened to burn the farmer's house with his family inside. The Ballards were helped by insurance adjusters who would gain large commissions when the barn was rebuilt and reinsured.

When the police prepared to round up the gang after the death of a young farmer in a barn fire, all justices of the peace in the area but one were afraid to sign the arrest warrants — and that one, it turned out, was actually on Ballard's payroll.

The Ballard gang used all the tactics that also made the Italian Black Hand infamous during the first years of the century. Extortion, fraud, threats, corruption of officials and co-operative businessmen were not the inventions of criminal Italian immigrants.

The Black Hand, however, became the newspaper code word for Italian organized crime. The first Black Hand extortion appears to have occurred in Brooklyn, New York, in August 1903, when a shopkeeper received an extortion note signed "Mano Nera," or Black Hand. The extortionists were independent local crooks led by a Calabrian named Annunziato Cappiello. The New York *Herald* covered the case and gave the term "Black Hand" to the world. Most often, it was used to refer to any one of the gangs that were forming in the streets of American cities. Occasionally it actually had a connection with the transplanted Mafiosi of the old country. There had been news stories about the Mafia in Sicily and the Camorra in Naples, but the catchy term Black Hand became the most common news peg for the next twenty years. The first transplanted Mafiosi arrived in the United States in the years before the Civil War, and the Mafia came to public attention several decades later with the murder of New Orleans police chief David Hennessy in 1890 and the rise of the first Sicilian criminals on the New York waterfront in the same year.

In Canada, in 1904, a royal commission investigated the activities of Antonio Cordasco, the "King of the Workers," a Montreal-based labour agent, or *padrone*, who controlled most of the temporary Italian workers in Canada.

Cordasco led a parade through the streets of Montreal in January 1904. After two of his foremen presented Cordasco with a crown designed like that of the King of Italy, his followers paid their respect to the don by kissing his hand. A month later, Cordasco was honoured again, this time with a banquet. By summer, however, Deputy Minister of Labour William Lyon Mackenzie King and the royal commission appointed to inquire into the immigration of Italian labourers were actively investigating Cordasco.

The word *padrone* was not used in Italy as such. In North America at the turn of the century it was used to describe the go-between who acted for the new Italian immigrant to North America (most often a temporary worker who intended to return home) and the established society. The *padrone* was the godfather of his charges. He provided services. His agents in Italy hired the labourer and got him his steamship ticket. In North America, the *padrone* got the labourer a job. For the employer he put together a work gang that could be sent to a construction site, gangs led by the *padrone's* men, the *sub-bossi* and *caposquadri*.*

In Canada, these work gangs went north to work in the bush for the Canadian Pacific and Grand Trunk railways during the summer. If the labourer wanted to return home during the winter, the *padrone* sold him the steamship ticket. If the labourer stayed in Toronto or Montreal, he often lived in a *padrone*-run boarding house — a dark, overcrowded, squalid place — and paid exorbitant rents.

Many of the *padroni* ran post offices and Italian-language newspapers, outfitters, grocery stores and saloons. Toronto's *padrone* was Albert Dini, Cordasco's chief rival. He opened an office on York Street in 1901 and provided labour gangs for the Grand Trunk Railway. For Italian labourers in Toronto,

---

*For a fascinating account of the *padrone* system, see Robert F. Harney's titles in the bibliography.

Dini furnished rooming houses and postal and banking services. After a 1908 earthquake, it was to Dini, rather than the Italian consul, that Calabrians and Sicilians went for help in reaching relatives. And it was quite possibly Dini who had hired Rocco.

The network of *padroni* was, for the first few years, a monopoly, providing labour where it was needed throughout North America, recruiting in Italy and Switzerland and maintaining contacts in cities across North America. Some of these men were relatively honest, helping out people from the old country.

Cordasco, however, provided those services for a steep price. Testimony at the royal commission showed that the Canadian Pacific Railway, through its "special services" department, had granted Cordasco a monopoly in hiring Italian workers for the CPR across Canada. It was Cordasco's reward for helping to break a strike in 1901.

The "King of the Workers" had a piece of every transaction. He charged a registration fee of one dollar for each workman and five dollars for each foreman. At the same time, the CPR paid him a dollar a head for each man hired. He also controlled the provisioning of work gangs, making up to a 150 percent profit on cans of sardines and old, mouldy bread.

The workers signed letters authorizing the CPR to pay their wages directly to Cordasco. His "bank" sent money home to Italy, but Cordasco took his cut. He made loans to foremen so they could pay the registration fees for his work gangs.

Cordasco was the organizer, the ultimate go-between. His *sub-bossi* organized the work gangs, his *caposquadri* were the foremen. Italian organized crime groups were organized later along the same lines, with boss, underboss and *caporegieme* or *capodecima*.

John (a.k.a. Joseph) Taglerino brought the Black Hand to Canada in 1906. In that year, a Hamilton grocer by the name of Salvatore Sanzone began receiving Black Hand extortion letters. He would receive the letters for the next three years.

In late 1908, the first official notice of Black Hand extortion in Ontario came in Fort Frances, a wilderness town in the northwestern part of the province. On December 7, 1908, Nicholas Bessanti and an Italian who used the name Joe Ross called on a baker named Louis Belluz. Bessanti and Ross handed a Belluz a letter. Written with red ink in Italian, the letter demanded $100. If Belluz did not pay, the letter said, his buildings would be burned and he would be killed. (The extortionists were apparently not sure of Belluz's ability to pay. A secret memo to the attorney general "Re Italian Society in Fort Frances" reveals that the Black Hand letter contained a postscript saying that the extortionists would accept $50.) Belluz took the letter to the police, the Black Hand members were warned and they did not follow up on their extortion attempt.

In May 1909, Bessanti, his common-law wife (a Métis woman named Aggie Gordon) and a Frank Dusanti were charged with housebreaking and theft by Kenneth D. Campbell, the Ontario Provincial Police constable in Fort Frances. During the interrogation Aggie Gordon voluntarily told Campbell how the Black Hand gang operated. Bessanti then told what he knew. They said the gang had been formed by two men, Frank Tino and Frank Muro, who had forced a number of the Italian immigrants in Fort Frances to join the society, paying a $25 entry fee. Bessanti could only afford to pay $10, which was accepted. Bessanti went on to relate:

> In joining the Society we took a solemn oath that we would obey our leader's orders: would rob, burn, kill as he directed, that we would protect one another from the hands of the law, to disobey these orders we would expect to be punished by death or otherwise decided upon by the Society. The Society met every Saturday night in the west end of a freight shed and there they decided what to do to raise money.

About sixteen Italian men in the area were forced to join, but it seems that only four, including Bessanti, took part in any criminal activity. One man, Angeline Satoria, stood up to the extortionists and refused to join. Having failed in Fort Frances, Tino and Muro moved on to Port Arthur and later Duluth, Minnesota, where they were rounded up and deported to Italy.

Meanwhile, in the fall of 1909, the Black Hand gang in Hamilton found themselves before the courts. Salvatore Sanzone, recipient of its letters for three years, had complained to the police. John Taglerino, who ran an "Italian boarding house" and store on Sherman Avenue North and who was later named boss of the gang, was charged along with Joseph Courto, Carmelo Colombo, Ernesto Speranza, Sam Wolfe and Ralph Rufus.

Rufus and Courto turned King's evidence. Rufus claimed that Taglerino had ordered him to write the letters threatening Sanzone. Courto told the court that Ernesto Sparanza had written the first letter, again on the orders of Taglerino. Courto said that he had been forced into the extortion attempt because he owed Taglerino money. When the extortion attempt failed, the gang decided to hold up Sanzone's store. Courto said he went to the grocer to warn him of the impending hold-up.

The police were waiting on Dundas Street at the time that the hold-up was to occur and picked up three gang members, who were charged with extortion. Taglerino was later charged with conspiracy to utter a threatening letter, and he and the three henchmen were convicted.

As the police probed and the newspapers headlined the Black Hand across North America, a new opportunity for the organized criminal was appearing on the horizon. The Temperance movement was gathering strength, pressing for bone-dry Prohibition across the continent. The movement was to provide a means of gaining wealth for a new class of gangster, who would have to be smarter than the crude extortionist, who would need the organizational skills of a *padrone* and the charisma of a bandit chieftain.

Rocco and Bessie filled the bill — and the opportunity for their entry into big-time crime came on Saturday, September 16, 1916. On that day at seven o'clock in the evening, the hotel bars closed and the Ontario Temperance Act (OTA) became law.

The act, introduced in 1916 as a temporary wartime measure by Conservative Premier William Hearst, a temperance advocate and pillar of the Methodist church, made possession of liquor or beer outside one's home illegal. The homeowner was permitted to retain a "cellar supply," but it was illegal to sell a drink; the government closed bars, taverns, clubs and liquor stores. Alcohol could be sold for sacramental, industrial, artistic, scientific and medicinal purposes by licensed distillers, brewers and wholesalers. Doctors could issue prescriptions for it. The OTA permitted the manufacture of native wines in "limited quantities." In fact, Niagara wines with as much as 20 percent alcohol were sold throughout the Prohibition era, and 30,000 permits were issued to those who wanted to make wine at home.

On the morning of Friday, September 15, 1916, liquor stores in Hamilton were doing a rush business. Profits for these legal establishments had been $1,000 a day during the preceding week. When the stores opened at eight o'clock Saturday morning, some of them already had lineups. The hotels began to run out during the day. All the old beer stocks in Hamilton were exhausted by 6:45 P.M., and some hotels began to sell the new temperance beer, which contained only 2.2 percent alcohol. By then most of the celebrants were too far gone to notice the difference. But at seven o'clock the doors closed.

On Monday, September 18, the *Spectator* estimated that selling liquor in Hamilton was a five million dollar business. Thirty-three taverns and sixteen liquor stores closed. Three private clubs had their licences terminated.

Rocco and Bessie Perri got into the booze business at once. According to the Perri legend, it was Bessie's brains and drive combined with Rocco's connections that got them started.

During Prohibition, bootlegging was carried on courtesy of the Canadian Royal Mail. It was legal, in any province governed by Prohibition, to order liquor from another province. The Prairie provinces, which had gone dry first, developed the idea of ordering "by mail" from other provinces. In Ontario, those who could afford it, and bootleggers like Rocco, ordered their stock from Quebec, which was not dry. Soon the licensed distilleries and breweries found a simple way around the OTA. They sent agents to Quebec. A customer placed his order with the Quebec agent, who then supplied the booze from stock "on hand" at the brewery around the corner from the customer.

This ad for the Kuntz Brewery shows open defiance of the Ontario Temperance Act. It appears in the book, A History of the Catholic Church in Waterloo County, *published in 1916.*

Kitchener Public Library

It was the late winter of 1917 when Rocco and Bessie first came to the attention of the police. A man came to Detective Ernest Goodman to complain that after visiting a prostitute at 157 Caroline Street North and paying her a two-dollar fee, he had been robbed of the rest of his cash.

Goodman, along with Detective Jack Cameron and the complainant, visited the house and interviewed Bessie and Rocco in the kitchen. (Bessie told the cops her name was "Rose Cyceno." The surname was probably an anglicization of

"Sussino," the name Rocco would use later, and which was most likely his mother's name.) In the end Goodman had to report that the prostitute involved was not in the house. She may actually have left or the complainant may have lost his courage. The man promised to meet the police later, but didn't show up at the appointed time. Goodman merely reported that 157 Caroline Street was a disorderly house and recommended that it be watched.

Italian organized crime had entered the prostitution field in North America. It brought in as much, if not more money than extortion. The immigrant man, often alone, living in crowded boarding houses, was not respectable enough to appeal to young Canadian women and did not have the money to support a wife from the old country in the traditional manner. Prostitutes were in demand. Italian criminals were involved in prostitution rings in Chicago, Philadelphia, Boston, Milwaukee, Denver and San Francisco in the years before U.S. Prohibition. It was prostitution that established the foundation for organized crime that was to grow up under Prohibition, providing a forbidden service that could be used to corrupt the authorities.

In a 1911 "exposé" of prostitution, *Fighting the Traffic in Young Girls or War on the White Slave Trade: a Complete and Detailed Account of the Shameless Traffic in Young Girls,* the author, Ernest Bell, claimed that "...there is more white slave trafficking in Hamilton than any other city its size in the whole of America — not Canada, but America." Bell's information came from the report of two "female detectives" hired when the YWCA discovered "parents are beginning to get afraid to send their daughters to the city, where they know temptation exists at the railway station."

The police watched the house on Caroline Street North and raided it during the early hours of March 9, 1917. Among the raiders was a lanky thirty-two-year-old probationary plainclothesman named Joseph Crocker, an immigrant from Cornwall who had arrived in Hamilton in 1910 and joined the police force on May 14, 1913. Bessie was charged with keeping a disorderly house because it was she, and not Rocco, who was the registered owner of the house.

She again gave her name as Rose Cyceno. A young woman named Mary Ashley was charged with being an inmate. Seven men were found in the house at the time. Three men gave their address as 15 Railway Street. Railway Street was a centre of mob activity in Hamilton in those early days and still is today. As for Rocco, the court record showed that he was a macaroni salesman and was away on the road.

The case went before Police Magistrate George Frederick Jelfs the next morning. Magistrate Jelfs, a twenty-four-year veteran of the bench, was already a legendary figure in the city. Born in Sherborne, Dorset, in 1853, he had arrived in Hamilton on his eighteenth birthday. First a clerk for the city solicitor, Jelfs was appointed the third police magistrate in Hamilton's history in 1893. Throughout his career he strove to bring both the dignity and the eccentricity of the British bench to Hamilton. He believed passionately in British concepts of justice.

Jelfs looked like a judge. The *Spectator* described him as "a fine-looking gentleman, clean shaven and with iron grey hair — always close cut." Despite his aristocratic demeanour, Jelfs was often sympathetic to immigrants confused by the justice system. He was known for showing clemency to young offenders during those years when children were still tried in adult courts. But he took a tough stance against the hardened cons.

Jelfs infuriated lawyers. They called him "erratic" because they could never predict what he would conclude. He would decide every case on what he considered its merits. Sometimes, when a poor man could not afford a lawyer, he used his judicial power to make sure a case was made for the defence.

The prosecutor in the Rose Cyceno case that morning in March was Deputy Police Chief David Coulter, an Ulsterman who had joined the force in 1878, then rose through the ranks to detective, inspector and then deputy.

"Rose Cyceno" was called to the witness box by Coulter. She claimed that Mary Ashley was just a tenant and that she had no knowledge of any illicit activity. When asked to identify the woman in the prisoner's box as her tenant, Bessie smiled.

"I don't know," she said, "but I'll see."

She trotted over to the dock and made a close examination of the suspect. After almost two minutes she returned to the witness box.

"Yes, that's her," she said. She then told Coulter that Mary Ashley had been boarding with her for three weeks. When she had discovered Mary's occupation — "a woman of the town" — Bessie claimed she had ordered her tenant to leave.

Five years later Rocco had to explain the same events when he applied for Canadian citizenship. In it, Rocco said that Mary Ashley was a boarder who was visited several times a week by her young fiancé.

> The night of the raid, there were eight [sic] friends or acquaintances in the house besides my wife and myself. With these people, the young girl, Mary Ashley, had nothing to do. They were in the house in a social way upon my wife and myself. Some policemen, including Probationers Plain Clothes Men Crocker, Chamberlain and Young, raided my house. In spite of everything we could tell them they insisted upon laying a charge against my wife of keeping a disorderly house. These men, as well as myself, swore upon oath, that they were only there for the purpose of a social call upon my wife and myself and they had nothing to do with the young girl. The Police Magistrate, however, on learning that the young girl and the young man who called upon her, as above described, had been found together, refused to believe anything in my wife's defence.... If my wife and I had known that there was anything improper going on between the young man and the young girl, we would not have allowed her in the house.

Of the found-ins, Bessie said, "These men were my friends who came to visit me."

"How long have you been here?" asked Coulter.

"About seven weeks," Bessie said.

"My, what a lot of friends you have made in seven weeks!" Coulter exclaimed.

"They came from Toronto and Montreal and London. I ran a store in Toronto."

"Very popular?" concluded Coulter.

Jelfs ruled that the defence was "too thin," and convicted everyone involved. Bessie was fined $50 or two months, Mary got $20 or one month and the seven found-ins were charged $5 each. The story was the lead item in the Hamilton *Spectator* court report the next day.

Of course, Bessie's men "from Toronto, Montreal and London" were not simply friends. They were the core of the organization that Rocco and Bessie were building. They ordered whisky "by mail" from Quebec and bought moonshine from the basement stills of Hamilton's Little Italy. They sold it for fifty cents a glass, part of an "entertainment package" offered to the boarding house immigrant, which also included prostitution and gambling services. Rocco took his cut. Bessie kept the accounts. On December 1, 1916, she had opened an account in a Hamilton branch of the Bank of Toronto. They were coming up in the world.

That summer Rocco and Bessie were able to hire a yacht that sailed out into Lake Ontario for parties far away from the prying eyes of the Hamilton police.

Late on the evening of Sunday, December 23, 1917, another development helped Rocco and Bessie's business. Robert Borden's government gave Canadians a Christmas present. Nationwide prohibition was declared, not by Act of Parliament, but by use of the draconian War Measures Act. Effective on Christmas Eve, importation of liquor into Canada was banned. The order-in-council claimed that the recent federal election had given the government "an unmistakable mandate for the vigorous prosecution of the war.... It is beyond question that the use of liquor affects adversely the realization of this purpose."

Transportation of liquor within Canada was banned as of April 1, 1918, and the date of a manufacturing ban was to be proclaimed later. The regulations were to remain in effect until twelve months after the war ended. But there was one key exemption. For constitutional reasons the War Measures decree did not affect areas that voted to remain wet. In Quebec, local option had made Trois Rivières, Quebec City, St Hyacinthe and Hull dry. But Montreal and Sherbrooke remained wet, and the decree would not affect those two cities until they, too, voted to be dry.

Then an order-in-council outlawing the manufacture of spirits with greater than 2.5 percent alcohol was proclaimed on March 11, 1918, and became effective twenty-one days later, on April 1st. The federal government had outlawed the mail order system. But again there were exceptions. The manufacture of native wines in Ontario and the manufacture of beer in Quebec was permitted to continue until December 31, 1918. There was by then a provincial prohibition law in Quebec that was to come into effect on May 1, 1919, along with the War Measures decree. As for Montreal, it would remain the "one great wet spot" — at least until May, 1919.

So most of Canada was now "bone-dry," the envy of temperance workers south of the border still campaigning for total prohibition. But Rocco Perri and bootleggers across the country were doing a roaring business and the daily court dockets filled with BOTAs (Breaches of the Ontario Temperance Act).

South of the border, on August 1, 1917, the Senate approved the Eighteenth Amendment to the constitution, outlawing the "manufacture, sale or transportation of intoxicating liquors" within the United States. The House of Representatives had approved the amendment on December 17, 1917. Now three-quarters of the states had to ratify the amendment.

Late in 1917, Rocco and Bessie bought a grocery store at 105 Hess Street North, and they moved the old business to the new address. On March 25, 1918, Bessie — "Rose Cyceno" — was again charged with keeping a house of ill-fame. In this case, the charges were dismissed. The little booze they had sold to the customers at Caroline Street now became more important. Rocco was selling the whisky at fifty cents a glass, across the counter of his store.

On May 18, 1918, Rocco Perri appeared under his own

name in a Hamilton court for the first time, charged with "neglect to return to the scene of an accident" three weeks before.

Arthur Carscallen, a chauffeur, charged that Rocco had refused to give his name and address after a collision in Hamilton. Rocco told the chauffeur, whose car was seriously damaged, to take down the licence number.*

Peter Florin, Rocco's witness, was cross-examined by Deputy Chief Coulter. Florin had to admit that he had no steady job and had recently been fined under the "anti-loafing" act.

"I have no faith in what such a man as you would say in the witness box," Magistrate Jelfs told Florin.

Norman Kay, Rocco's lawyer, tried to countercharge Carscallen with also leaving the scene, but that failed. Rocco was found guilty and was fined $20.

Not until New Year's Day 1919 did police attention again focus on Rocco Perri's activities. Two hours into the New Year, Hamilton constables Robert Smith and Walter McLean heard three shots and saw a man run out of an alley across Hess Street and disappear down Cannon Street. Hearing the sounds of a noisy party, Smith and McLean arrived at Rocco's store and house at 105 Hess Street North. The partyers, all evidently Italian, denied having heard shots. Then one of the guests told the two cops that there was a man lying in a snowbank outside.

In the alley Smith and McLean found a man moaning in pain. They picked him up and carried him into the kitchen. Smith went outside again and found a fedora hat. Returning, Smith was told that the wounded man was Tony Martino, who boarded at 16 Murray Street West, and that the hat belonged to him. McLean called an ambulance, which took Martino to hospital.

Rocco told Duty Detective Reginald Shirley that his name was Rocco Sussino and that so many people had

---

*In the fall of 1918, Carscallen, aged 19, and by then a taxi driver, died of what today is called "sudden acute cocaine intoxication." He collapsed and died several hours after taking cocaine for just the second time.

turned up at his place he could not keep track of them all. The house was searched, no weapons were found and Shirley reported "there was no evidence of disorderly conduct." Shirley then went to the hospital at 6 A.M. Martino had died at 5:30.

A coroner's jury was gathered on New Year's Day to view the body, and then the inquest was adjourned for ten days. The dead man was identified as Tony Martino, twenty-seven years old, a quiet man who had come from Italy five years before, leaving a wife in his native village. He worked at the International Harvester plant and lived in a boarding house with a large number of Italian guests.

Three detectives questioned Rocco and Bessie the next day at the store. It was then that Detective Shirley saw the fedora and remembered a man he had seen frequently in court, a man who used to pinch his grey fedora and pull its brim down in front of his face. The man's name was Alberto Naticchio. The detectives showed the hat to Smith, who recalled finding it beside the body.

The police went on to visit a crowded boarding house at 104 Caroline Street North, run by Harry and Elizabeth Corruzo. A man was lying on one of the beds when Shirley entered Naticchio's room, followed by the Corruzos' curious little daughter. On the wall beside another bed was a studio photograph of three men in cowboy costumes. Shirley asked the boarder, who was one of the men in the photograph, if the man in the middle was Alberto Naticchio. The man said he didn't know. The little girl grabbed the photograph and piped up that it was a man who lived in the house but who had then gone away.

On Saturday, January 4th, Rocco and Bessie came forward with information. They told the detectives they were now sure that the hat belonged to Alberto Naticchio.

Rocco had delayed as long as he could, as he had helped Naticchio flee to the United States. Naticchio was a bootlegging member of Rocco's gang and it was good business to get him out of the country.

If Rocco hoped that his "co-operation" would stop the police investigation, he was wrong. That evening, the police raided his store. As the store was registered in his name, Rocco was charged with breaching the Ontario Temperance Act. He appeared in court on Monday January 6th.

The Hamilton *Herald* reported the case:

Rocco Perri Sussino, grocer, 105 North Hess Street must have bathed in booze, washed his teeth with it, used it for shaving, gargled his throat with it, shampooed his raven locks with it and utilized it as a massage.

The OTA tax on the toilet water Sergeant May and Constables Coburn and Goddard found on Rocco's premises Saturday night amounted to $1,000.

There were eighteen quarts of "ski" under a bed in the living apartments above the store, a gallon can of alcohol in an upstairs kitchen, a partly filled bottle and glass in the downstairs kitchen, two dozen "dead soldiers" in the bathroom, a hundred gallons of wine in the cellar and a bunch of whisky labels and seal of a Canadian distillery...

"It looks to me as if the prisoner had been trafficking in liquor to a large extent. I'm not sure he shouldn't be held on a charge of fraud because he had those labels in his possession," remarked [Magistrate Jelfs].

Norman Kay, Rocco's lawyer, argued that the liquor was cellar stock because it was in a private house and Rocco "had to go outside in the back yard to get from the store to the house upstairs."

"No living apartments can be private with a store in the same building," replied Jelfs, who found Rocco guilty, fined him $1,000 and confiscated the liquor. Bessie paid the fine. The case marks the first public indication that Rocco was a major bootlegger. Whisky labels and seals were in his basement. His customers were likely paying fifty cents a glass for a dwindling stock of good Canadian whisky that had been cut with moonshine grain alcohol and water. The usual cut was making four bottles out of three.

Four years later, Rocco would tell his version of the case in his affadavit:

One night on returning from an entertainment to which my wife and I had gone, I found a number of Policemen in my place, raiding it for liquor. I protested and pointed out that what I had was in my private premises and I was entitled to keep it, but one of the Policemen claimed to have found a small bottle in the kitchen [shop is crossed out]. This was true, as my wife, who had been serving behind the counter in the store had been suffering from tooth ache and for relief had been carrying a small bottle with a little liquor in it, into the [store] kitchen and there used it and left the bottle...they seized whatever was in my private dwelling house and laid a charge against me.

The following Thursday, January 9th, fifty people, almost all of them Italian, crowded into the police court to hear the inquest into Martino's death. Martino's best friend since boyhood, Domenic Racco, was called to the stand. He told how he accompanied Martino in the ambulance.

Racco had asked Martino, "Who shot you?"

"I don't know," Martino had told his friend. "Leave me alone," were his last words.

Rocco "Sussino" was the next witness. He told the inquest that he had known Martino, who often came over to his place, for five or six months. Rocco said he did not know there had been a shooting until the police arrived; he had heard the shots but only thought someone was fooling around.

Bessie was the next witness. "Pretty, stylish," the *Herald* called her. She told the inquest that she, too, had known Martino, that he had not been at the party and that she had recognized him as the police had placed him on the kitchen table.

Rocco was recalled.

"Was there a man put out of your house that night who was drunk or partly drunk?" asked S.F. Washington, Hamilton's veteran Crown attorney.

"I didn't put anybody out, but I told a couple of friends of mine to go home because they were drunk," Rocco replied.

"Did they go together?"

"No, one went at a time."

"How long before the shooting did they go?"

"About ten or fifteen minutes."

"Do you remember their names?"

"No, I know so many people."

The Corruzzos and their boarders were called. They told how Naticchio fired shots out of the house at midnight; the boarders and Detective Shirley all identified that grey fedora.

Then it was for Dr Hopkins, the coroner, to sum up. "I have never in all my experience seen such equivocation and lying as that displayed by the witnesses this evening," he said. "It appears they were trying to tell as little as possible."

The jury was out for sixteen minutes. It returned with the verdict that "Martino came to his death from a bullet fired from a revolver and we believe that the man, Alberto Naticchio, mentioned in the evidence was the man who fired the fatal shot."

The next morning a wanted poster was issued, complete with the silly cowboy picture of Naticchio in the stetson and bandanna, and the offer of a $100 reward. Police sources told the Hamilton *Herald* that the killing was a case of mistaken identity, that Naticchio, confused by drink and darkness, had mistaken Martino for someone else, a man against whom he probably had a grudge. They were probably right about the grudge, but it's unlikely that Naticchio didn't know who he was killing.

Rocco Perri had learned a lesson. He got himself a new lawyer, one with better connections than Norman Kay. The lawyer was Michael J. O'Reilly, a big, red-haired Irishman, counsel for the local Catholic diocese and a prominent member of the Liberal party.

O'Reilly appealed Rocco's BOTA conviction. He had the local licence inspector, a man named Sturdy, visit Hess Street. Sturdy agreed with Rocco's contention that the liquor was in a private home and thus was "cellar stock." The appeal court ordered the liquor returned and Rocco got back $700 of the $1,000 fine, the rest going to court costs and lawyer's fees.

In March 1922, Detective Joe Crocker brought Alberto Naticchio back to Hamilton from western Pennsylvania, an area similar to Hamilton that needed Italian labourers. The Mafia had followed the demand. Naticchio worked as a machine helper in a coal mine until someone spotted the reward poster. Under "rigid" questioning he admitted that he had fled from Hamilton the night of the shooting, but claimed that a man named Tony Latriano was the guilty party, and that Latriano had forced him to leave Hamilton because he had witnessed the shooting.

At the preliminary hearing in April, Rocco was a Crown witness. He said he had heard the shots but thought they were part of the celebrations.

"Do you know this man, Tony Latriano?" asked the new Crown attorney, George W. Ballard.

"I might know him, but not by that name," Rocco said.

Bessie said she had also heard the shots but paid no attention.

At the trial in October 1922 Rocco was questioned by Naticchio's lawyer, Charles W. Bell (who at that time also represented the Perris). Now he had a new story to tell. A mystery man named Tony, dressed in a soldier's uniform, had appeared. No one knew the man's surname, but Rocco suggested it might have been "Lobriano."

In three different appearances, Rocco gave three versions of what had happened on that New Year's Eve. But Rocco and everyone else got their stories straight when it counted at the trial. The mystery man created enough reasonable doubt that there was no case. The judge directed a verdict of not guilty.

As for Alberto Naticchio, he went back to work for Rocco. An RCMP intelligence report in 1926 listed him as a senior member of the Perri mob.

CHAPTER 3

THE OTHER WOMAN

In 1919, bootlegging was thriving in Ontario. The distillers and brewers, forbidden by the War Measures Act to manufacture intoxicating beverages, turned to soft drinks such as O'Keefe's Ginger Ale. It left the field wide open for bootleggers.

To ethnocentric policemen and reporters in those years, the word "Italian" became synonymous with "bootlegger." It wasn't true, of course. For the rich of Toronto's Forest Hill and Rosedale, obtaining liquor was as simple as calling the agent for a distillery and arranging for some remaining stock to be delivered. For the English and Irish in Cabbagetown, there was the local version of poteen. Italian and Jewish bootleggers competed for business in the Ward and beyond. There were a dozen *koiratorpia*, illegal drinking dens that sold alcohol and homemade beer, among the Finnish boarding houses on Widmer Street. The Hungarian immigrants had their private social clubs, which were fronts for bootleggers.

Sometime in 1919, Rocco Perri became a "traveller" for the Superior Macaroni Company. It was a perfect cover. He travelled the province from Hamilton to Toronto and as far away as North Bay, arranging liquor sales for his customers, many of them small Italian grocery stores — which also bought his macaroni and olive oil.

Rocco controlled most of the liquor — genuine, cut or homebrewed — being sold in the Hamilton area. Some small-time competitors did operate in Hamilton, but most of them were too small for Rocco to worry about.

Comfortably established in the bootlegging business, Rocco had turned to adventures of a different kind. Sometime in 1918 he met and pursued a young farm woman named Olive Routledge, who had come to Hamilton from Musclow in rural Hastings County. Olive had gone to high school in nearby Bancroft and had lived on the family farm with her parents, Mr and Mrs George W. Routledge, until she was thirty. In 1917, she moved to Hamilton and took a job at the Chipman, Holton Knitting Company.

Reports differ as to how their first meeting took place. She told her father that she had met him while they were both staying at the same boarding house. Later, it would be said she had met Rocco at one of his summer parties on a yacht in Lake Ontario. He told her his name was Rocco Ross. According to letters Olive sent back to her aging parents, she kept steady company with Rocco. The charming, generous young Italian — Rocco and Olive were the same age, each born in 1887 — courted the woman and soon she came to the belief that they would be married. She had no inkling of the existence of Bessie Starkman. As for Bessie, in the beginning she knew nothing. Rocco's travels provided a cover for that, too.

Olive "returned his affections," as the press reported, and in 1918 she was pregnant. Her parents believed she had married Ross and Olive kept up the pretence. She returned to Musclow claiming to be a married woman and gave birth to a daughter she named Autumn. Olive asked "Rocco Ross" to marry her. He refused, but said he would pay for the support of the child.

Olive was heartbroken and angry. She left Hamilton for St Catharines, where she tried to support herself and the child by working as a maid.

In the spring of 1919, Premier William Hearst tightened up the Ontario Temperance Act, making alcohol sales a government monopoly, outlawing advertising and limiting a doctor's stock to ten gallons. He called a provincial election and a referendum on the Ontario Temperance Act for October 20, 1919.

Meanwhile, south of the border, on January 14, 1919, Nebraska had become the thirty-sixth state to ratify the Eighteenth Amendment to the American Constitution. A year later, on January 16, 1920, it would be unconstitutional in the United States to manufacture, sell or transport intoxicating liquors.

In the Ontario campaign the wets had no one to vote for. Several Conservatives stood for individual liberty but the party policy was dry. So was Liberal policy, even though the party's leader, Hartley Dewart, opposed the Liberal prohibition platform. Both Liberals and Conservatives were fighting against a surge in the popularity of a third party, the United Farmers of Ontario (UFO).

In June, Dewart accused J.A. Ayearst, the chief licence inspector, of taking kickbacks from private detectives employed to help enforce the OTA. Dewart said Ayearst diverted some of the money the detectives received from their agencies and deposited it in a special bank account. (Ayearst was later cleared by a public inquiry).

On October 8th, Dewart charged that the Tories were trying to buy the Jewish vote in Toronto's Ward by distributing five thousand bottles of *vishnick*, a form of cherry brandy that was 62 percent alcohol. The Hearst forces lamely said that *vishnick* was for sacramental purposes and therefore legal.

The United Farmers of Ontario under Ernest Drury had forty-five candidates elected. The Tories retained just twenty-five seats, Hearst and most of his Cabinet even losing their own ridings. The Liberals remained the official Opposition, with twenty-nine seats.

As for the OTA referendum, the Prohibitionists declared that all "right-thinking people" would vote straight "no" to all of its four questions. Anyone who disagreed was in league with liquor interests and the devil. Prohibition did, indeed, win — by an overwhelming majority, 406,676 to 246,683. In rural areas, the pro-prohibition vote was ten to one, but the cities voted wet. The UFO formed a coalition with the Labour party and took office. W.E. Raney was named attorney general. One of the few lawyers in the UFO, Raney was an active member of the Dominion Alliance for the Total Suppression of the Liquor Traffic, an organization thirteen years older than the powerful American Anti-Saloon League. He was determined to stop alcohol consumption in Ontario.

Raney had a fight on his hands. In early 1919 Quebec had voted to allow the sale of light beer, cider and wine, forestalling the provincial prohibition that had been scheduled to begin on May 1st. Montreal was still "the one big wet spot" and it was well stocked. Manufacture and transport of liquor were illegal but booze from Quebec was finding its way into Ontario and also into the United States: the United States had declared "wartime prohibition" on June 19, 1919, seven months after the end of the war.

After the Eighteenth Amendment was ratified, Congressman Andrew Volstead of Minnesota sponsored, and Wayne Wheeler, of the Anti-Saloon League actually wrote, the American enforcement measures. The law set the "intoxicating" level of alcohol at 0.05 percent. Domestic possession of alcohol was permitted in the Volstead Act and native wines and ciders were exempt to protect the grape and apple farmers. The Volstead Act passed the House 287 to 100 and the Senate by voice vote on October 1919, overriding Woodrow Wilson's veto.

On December 27, 1919, police and Internal Revenue agents in Worcester, Massachusetts, discovered and seized a load of liquor in a shipment of hay. It was the first official interception of Canadian alcohol, carried out three weeks before the United States was to go "bone-dry." On January 16, 1920, the Eighteenth Amendment and the Volstead Act came into effect.

Meanwhile, back in Canada, on January 1, 1920, the War Measures Act decree expired. It was legal once more to manufacture liquor anywhere in Canada, legal to transport it between provinces and legal to send it out of the country.

The mail order business roared back to life. American railroad companies organized weekend jaunts from New York to Montreal, and it didn't take long for Ontario to present American customers with a new version of the old mail order system. It worked simply. An American customer would write or telephone a Canadian distillery or brewery with an order. The only problem was shipment, but the American customer soon found that there were plenty of willing bootleggers to make deliveries. Rocco used his Calabrian connections with the Scaroni brothers of Guelph and Joe Serianni, their friend across the border in Niagara Falls, New York. And another contact arrived in Niagara Falls in 1919 or 1920: Giuseppe Sottile also known as Joseph Henry, an Italian American of Sicilian descent.

Officially, all the liquor and beer was sold for export to the United States. In fact, right from the beginning some of Rocco's boats turned around to the Ontario shore and the liquor and beer was "reimported" to Canada and sold to customers in Hamilton, Guelph and across southern Ontario. Two then secret reports, one from the U.S. Border Patrol and the second from the U.S. Customs, would later describe how liquor was sent to the U.S. Loads were cleared from Toronto, Hamilton, Cobourg, Belleville, Port Colborne, Port Dover and Port Stanley. A favourite spot for smugglers was the tiny village of Bridgeburg, Ontario, where the railway bridge spanned the Niagara River to Black Rock, New York, the entry point to Buffalo. As the U.S. Border Patrol would later report:

> ...those engaged in the smuggling business along this particular section of the border are mostly old expert rivermen of the hardened criminal class who are ceaselessly active in their calling and who are likewise practically devoid of fear. They are always ready to face the dangers of a storm-lashed or ice-filled river, with its treacherous currents, at any time a profitable cargo for their craft is available and if cornered by officers will not hesitate to fight...The numerous islands in the upper Niagara River offer a conspicuous example as to the need for motor boat equipment [for law enforcement]. These several islands, which extend from the City of Buffalo to Niagara Falls, form an effective screen for river smugglers and serve as excellent hiding places and relay stations for their contraband cargoes.

It took just six months for the United States to complain. On July 23, 1920, "high officials of the Royal Canadian Mounted Police" told the New York *Times* that while the RCMP were doing everything in their power to stop infraction of Canadian federal law, "it is really for the American authorities to see that liquor does not cross the imaginary line 3,000 miles long...." That simple statement from the New York *Times'* RCMP source summed up what was to be Canadian federal policy for years to come.

Just seven days later, Rocco Perri made his only entry on the police blotter in 1920. A Hamilton police file card with Perri's record notes: "1920 July 30th. Allow a ferocious dog to be at large. Fined $50.00 and dog ordered to be destroyed."

By now Rocco and Bessie were taking steps to increase their influence. They sold the Hess Street grocery store and bought a nineteen-room mansion at 166 Bay Street South, in the centre of an upper-middle-class neighbourhood, but strategically close to Little Italy in the city's north end.

When Bessie closed her account in the Bank of Toronto on October 11, 1919, it contained $25,000. A couple of days later, she opened two new accounts, both in the name of Bessie Starkman, one in a branch of the Imperial Bank and the second in a branch of the Standard Bank. Rocco and Bessie filled the mansion with oriental rugs, a $2,000 piano, a billiard room and a well-equipped modern kitchen, where Rocco indulged his passion for cooking. Years later, his friends would remember the gourmet meals he cooked and served.

The Perris also built a secret wine cellar under the basement floor of the mansion. The vault was carefully hidden, the ground was cool and it was perfect for hiding the stocks of liquor that were delivered to the mansion. It remained hidden until long after the era of Rocco Perri and was discovered only by accident in October 1957 when a small boy fell through the floor of the run-down house.

Some time after the Perris moved to 166 Bay Street South in 1920, police raided the mansion and found fifteen cases of whiskey in the garage. Rocco was not charged. He was able to prove that the garage was leased to man named Tony Morano. Morano was fined $500. A mob boss is almost always insulated by his men. The story of Tony Morano would be repeated in years to come. It was always the other guy who took the rap for Rocco Perri.

In the same year, Rocco reconciled with Olive Routledge. She returned to Hamilton, and began once again to see "Rocco Ross." She dared not return home to Musclow, where people would wonder why she did not live with her husband. The fact that her lover would not marry her was putting greater and greater strain on her mind. Olive still knew nothing of Bessie and she appealed to Rocco to "play square" with her. Instead, Rocco gave Olive money. He was often generous, and was willing to support the child. Olive believed that it wasn't enough, and she continued to look for work that could help her support herself and her child. By late 1920, she was pregnant with Rocco's second child.

Bessie had her own domestic problems to handle. She still cared a great deal about her two daughters, Lilly and Gertrude, now young schoolgirls in Toronto, but Harry Tobin treated Bessie as if she was dead. In order to see her two girls, Bessie would have to drive from Hamilton to Toronto to make surreptitious visits, meeting the girls as they left school in the afternoon.

On October 20, 1920, British Columbia voted to allow the sale of liquor in government stores. The president of the British Columbia Prohibition party blamed it all on women; he said that they had misunderstood the ballot. *The New York Times,* with the perspective of distance, reported that British Columbia's largely British population "had never taken kindly to Prohibition." Six days later Alberta, Saskatchewan, Manitoba and Nova Scotia all voted to continue prohibition. (But Regina, Winnipeg and Halifax voted solidly wet and had their share of blind pigs [booze cans].)

In February 1921, Rocco took Olive Routledge to St Catharines and checked her into hospital. There she gave birth to their second daughter, Catharine. When Olive's parents travelled to the city hospital to see their daughter and the grandchild, they asked for Mrs Ross, only to discover that their daughter was registered under the name Mrs Perry. In all the excitement, the Routledges forgot to ask why their daughter's "husband" went by two names.

Meanwhile, Ontario was preparing for yet another referendum on prohibition. Premier E. C. Drury was under heavy pressure to stop the mail order system. Late in 1920, UFO member F. G. Sandy had introduced a bill that made it an offence for anyone to transport, deliver or receive liquor for consumption within Ontario. The law was to take effect the day after a referendum outlawed the interprovincial liquor trade.

On April 18, 1921, the drys won the referendum by just 166,385 votes, a drop from their last margin of victory. Hamilton had one of the largest wet votes in the province, each ward voting for booze by a large majority — but Wentworth County, surrounding Hamilton, voted dry. The government announced that importation from Quebec would end on July 19th. The Sandy Act, forbidding transport, would become law on the same day. Quebec then announced that after May 1st it would sell liquor only to bona fide residents in Quebec. Then, in August, an incident took place which skewed the effects of the dry vote. Police at Sandwich, Ontario, near Windsor, seized a load of beer belonging to the British American Brewing Company, which was being loaded into a speedboat for transport to Wyandotte, Michigan. The beer was seized as "liquor in transit for use in the province in contravention of the Ontario Temperance Act."

On August 10th, James Haverson, K.C., the lawyer who helped write the Ontario Temperance Act, appeared before Windsor Magistrate W. E. Gundy to defend the brewery. Haverson argued that the breweries were not obliged under federal law to obtain export licences. He emphasized that the OTA said nothing about the export of liquor.

Gundy, in considering his decision, was facing a different constitutional situation from that of his U.S. counterparts. The British North America Act which had established

Canada in 1867, had contained a key phrase granting "shop, saloon, tavern and auctioneer licences" to the provinces for the raising of provincial or local revenue. Nevertheless, the federal government had claimed jurisdiction over liquor by passing the Canada Temperance Act (also known as the Scott Act) in 1878. It was a local option law, allowing for individual municipalities to decide by referendum whether they would be wet or dry. Some areas of Canada remain dry to this day under the Canada Temperance Act. All liquor sales, unless permitted by the Scott Act, were illegal.

Three decisions of the British Privy Council, then the highest court, clarified federal-provincial jurisdiction. In 1882, the Judicial Committee of the Privy Council ruled the federal government could pass general temperance laws under the "peace, order and good government" clause of the BNA Act. The following year, it upheld the right of the provinces to pass legislation on liquor matters of a local nature as long as the laws did not interfere with interprovincial trade. In 1896, in a case between the governments of Ontario and Canada, it ruled that the province had the right to restrict the sale of liquor as long as those provincial restrictions did not interfere with federal jurisdiction. It meant the federal government could control the manufacture and transport of alcohol, while the provinces could control its local consumption.

Gundy ruled in favour of the British American Brewing Company and released the beer, which went to Wyandotte that afternoon. In his written decision, Gundy noted that the beer had been purchased in the United States for shipment to Michigan, that the proper invoices had passed Customs and that the boat had all the necessary clearance papers. There was no question of failure to comply with export regulations nor was there any question of the bona fides of the company. Ontario had simply prohibited the importation of liquor and the manufacture, transport or sale of liquor for consumption within Ontario. None of these laws, Gundy wrote, had changed pre-prohibition liquor laws. The Privy Council had established that provincial law could not interfere with the export trade.

A decision of a police magistrate, the lowest court in Canada, is normally not binding on other judges, but *Rex* vs. *British American Brewing Company* was never appealed because Magistrate Gundy had not interpreted a law. He had merely found that there was no law prohibiting the export of liquor. The case stood right across the country, awaiting action by the House of Commons, action that did not come. The Conservative government of Arthur Meighen was too busy gearing up for the election that was to be held in December 1921.

Now it was lawful in Canada to manufacture, sell and transport liquor, beer and wine for export, even though it was still illegal to sell within certain provinces, including Ontario. The new Liberal government of William Lyon Mackenzie King would leave the loophole open for years. That is how a police magistrate doomed Prohibition in both Canada and the United States.

Late in the summer of 1921, Rocco had driven Olive and the children to the Routledge family homestead near Musclow. Olive's mother, an invalid, was overjoyed at their arrival. The old lady still believed her daughter was legally married to Rocco Ross. Rocco stayed for a couple of weeks, and then returned to Hamilton after a phone call about "business of an imperative nature" — probably the Gundy decision.

In November 1921, Rocco made a routine application for naturalization as a Canadian citizen, filling out a form in which he stated that he had been born in Plati, Italy, had arrived in Boston on the *Republic* and that he had lived for the past six years in Hamilton, and in Trenton for two years before that. He signed the application "Rocco Perry." He was told to appear in court for a citizenship hearing on March 8, 1922. The results would hardly be what Rocco expected.

Also in November, S. F. Washington, Hamilton's veteran Crown attorney, resigned to be replaced by George W. Ballard, who, according to later police reports, was not as effective as his predecessor.

At Queen's Park, the UFO attorney general, W. E.

Raney, was becoming increasingly frustrated with bootlegging in Ontario. He had tried, and failed, to find a way around Magistrate Gundy's decision. Bootleggers were also doing a roaring business within the province and that was clearly illegal. On November 30th, after a magistrate imposed the maximum fine allowed under the OTA ($1,000), assistant Crown attorney J. C. McRuer told the court that bootleggers were making $19,000 a week in Toronto. Roadhouses, taverns long the new network of paved highway beyond municipal boundaries, were also springing up. One of the first, biggest and best was the Lakeview Inn in Port Credit, twelve miles west of Toronto. Joe Burke ran the hotel and ordered some of his booze from Rocco Perri. Other supplies were ordered directly from the breweries and distilleries, via the small-boat route from Toronto's dockyard, through the Western Gap and across Lake Ontario to Port Credit. In January 1921, OTA enforcement officers raided the Lakeview Inn. Under a trapdoor, the police found an icehouse filled to the ceiling with champagne, whisky and beer. (A large number of road-houses, including those in Port Credit and in West Hill, east of Toronto, offered gambling and girls, as well as drinks.)

Raney's first targets, however, were not the roadhouses. They were the province's doctors, who were allowed to prescribe alcohol under the OTA. He had the licence board suspend 311 of the province's doctors from the practice of medicine for overprescribing liquor but, after an outcry from the Ontario Medical Association, issued a clarification saying the doctors had only their right to issue liquor prescriptions suspended.

Raney next decided to make Hamilton an example and sent "spotters" into town. "Spotter" was the name given to anyone enforcing the Ontario Temperance Act. From 1916 to April 1921, the chief enforcement officers were the licence inspectors employed by the Board of Licence Commissioners. When the Ontario Provincial Police Act was passed in 1921, these inspectors were transferred to the OPP but became a separate division, with inspectors, OTA, and constables, OTA. Regular OPP officers were also expected to enforce the OTA. The term "spotters" also referred to the informants hired by OTA inspectors. Often they were small-time crooks and informants, and *agents provocateurs.*

Under the command of OTA Inspector Albert Service, the spotters spread out around Hamilton, forcing their way into grocery stores and the express office to search for liquor. On the morning of February 1st, 1922, Hamilton police court was full of BOTA defendants and their lawyers. There was little room for spectators.

There was another shock to come. On the evening of February 2nd, the federal excise officer, Maitland C. Beasley, found a still and bubbling kettle of mash in the basement of Hamilton Constable Thomas Gravelle, a fifteen-year veteran of the city force. Gravelle was arrested, fired and put in jail. Jelfs convicted Gravelle and ordered him held until sentence was passed.

Three days later, however, the day Gravelle appeared for sentence, the OTA had outworn its welcome. Jelfs, who did all he could to stop the transport to the border, threw out the OTA cases on the ground of entrapment. One accused, an Italian grocer, said that the two spotters had pretended to represent a grocery chain. They offered him wholesale groceries cheap and when he agreed, asked for a drink to seal the deal. Then they arrested him.

Jelfs roasted the OTA constables: "When these men go out and deliberately set a trap for others to break the law, I do not regard their word on oath." He then turned to Gravelle and without comment fined him $500 or six months.

At about the time that the OTA officers were swooping into Hamilton, Olive Routledge, driven from Musclow by village gossip, had come back to the city with her two children. Her naive parents ignored the gossip, still believing that Olive was married to "Rocco Ross." She was determined to force Rocco to marry her or to pay for the upbringing of the children. On December 21, 1921, Rocco Ross had written an "endearing" love letter to Olive, saying the he would live with her.

Olive registered at the Stroud Hotel in Hamilton on

Tuesday, February 7th. She had decided to hire a lawyer to force Rocco to pay child support and she approached Lieutenant Colonel Frank Morrison, K.C. With her two children in his office, Olive nervously told Morrison her story. The lawyer agreed to represent her and to either help reach agreement with Rocco or start proceedings against him for child support.

Harry Stroud, the hotel manager, would later say that Olive seemed very nervous, would use the phone nine or ten times a day and went up or down in the elevator every twenty minutes. During one of Olive's phone conversations, Stroud overheard her crying and saying, "God will strike you dead for saying that." Then she hung up and cried even more.

On Friday, Stroud overheard her say on the phone, "If you come in your car, I'll go with you."

Rocco visited the hotel that evening. Olive left the oldest child in the hotel and, taking the baby with her, left in a car. Harry Stroud, already suspicious, asked employee William Dixon to follow the car to get its licence number. Dixon wrote it down: 56-659. He said the man was medium short, stout, brown-featured, and was wearing a brown coat and a dark hat. Rocco and Olive apparently came to an agreement that he would pay her $500, followed by monthly payments, and that he would help her relocate in another city.

Another guest later remembered that car returning to the hotel and the three-year-old, Autumn, who came out of the lobby saying, "Goodbye, papa."

On Saturday, February 11th, Olive visited Morrison a second time, probably to tell him about the agreement. The same day a car came to pick up Olive and a Ford truck arrived to move her trunks to the Hanrahan Hotel. She registered there under the name of Mrs Olive Routledge.

But that weekend, something went wrong. It may be that Bessie, who would later cancel other deals Rocco had made to support people in trouble, had stopped it. Or perhaps Olive's feelings of betrayal finally broke her mind. In the early hours of Monday morning, Olive climbed out the window of her room shrieking for help. Joseph Hanrahan, the owner, clambered out over a doorway and brought her back in. Once inside her room, Olive was quiet, and promised to leave in the morning. But a couple of hours later, she climbed down a fire escape rope from the bathroom window. Hanrahan spotted her and went out into the dark to find her wandering along Cannon Street. Once more, he brought her back to her room.

That morning she checked out of the Hanrahan and registered at the Wentworth Arms, again as Mrs Olive Routledge. That evening, Olive told clerk James Allen that her oldest child was sick. Allen summoned the hotel doctor, who recommended that the child be taken to St Joseph's Hospital. At first Olive refused, but then she agreed. After the child was taken to hospital, Olive returned to the Wentworth Arms, took her baby and checked out.

At 1:00 A.M. she entered Noble's Lunch on King Street East and went over to two men, Harry Basula and Alf Kelderoni, and asked one of them to hold the baby while she made a phone call. Basula did not listen to the beginning of the call, but George Carroll, another diner, heard her ask for Regent 8267w.* As the conversation became louder, Basula overheard Olive, whom he did not know, talking to someone called "Bessie." He heard Olive mention the "Wentworth Arms." Finally she said, "I forgive you all," dropped the phone and a piece of paper, and ran from the restaurant. The astonished Basula was left holding the baby. Carroll picked up the piece of paper and gave it to the restaurant cashier, who passed it on to Basula.

Basula and Kelderoni, both recent immigrants, decided to take the baby to the Wentworth Arms, where Allen, the desk clerk, told them that the older child had been taken to St Joseph's Hospital. Basula took the baby to the hospital, but spoke only broken English and the staff kept him there until the police, always suspicious of foreigners, arrived. They questioned Basula until 5:00 A.M. and then went to the Wentworth Arms to find Olive Rougledge. She was not in

---

*The "w" means that it was a party line. The Perris would soon get a private line.

her room, but early in the morning she was picked up by detectives Chamberlain and Thompson and taken to police headquarters.

Asked why she had abandoned her children, Olive told the two detectives she thought it would be better for them if they were left in an institution. They asked her why. When she began to tell the story and told the name of the father, the detectives sent for their boss, Inspector of Detectives Donald Campbell and for Detective Ernest Goodman. The three would later describe Olive as being "quite normal but rather excited."

She told them that she had found out that Rocco Ross was Rocco Perri, that she had come to Hamilton to make an agreement regarding the support of the children. Rocco had promised the $500 payment and a certain amount every month, Olive told the four policemen.

Olive was quite calm when she left the office and Campbell then walked with her to Morrison's office so she could consult her lawyer. She met Morrison for a few moments, then left with two detectives for another law office, that of Charles W. Bell. One of the detectives suggested that Bell's help would be appreciated. Although Rocco Perri had not appeared in a Hamilton court recently, it was apparently well known that Bell now represented Rocco.*

Bell was a prominent member of the local Conservative party; a man with ambitions to be elected to the House of

---

*Bell was born on April 24, 1876, the son of William Bell, a prominent civil lawyer in Hamilton. Educated at Hamilton Collegiate, the University of Toronto's Trinity College and Osgoode Hall, Bell disappointed his father by choosing criminal over civil law. He made his name in his first murder trial, successfully defending a man mistakenly accused of poisoning his wife. Bell was also a playwright. (He wrote each morning before going to work.) He had had three plays on Broadway, beginning with *Her First Divorce* at the Comedy in May 1913. His third attempt, a farce called *Parlour, Bedroom and Bath,* was a hit when it opened on Christmas Eve, 1917. He had also written the book for a musical, *A Dangerous Maid,* with music by George Gershwin and lyrics by Ira Gershwin. It had opened poorly in April 1921 in Atlantic City and closed in Pittsburgh in May. In the winter of 1922, he was working on the book for a new musical called *Elsie.*

Commons. Rocco Perri now had two lawyers, one from each of the two main political parties.

Apparently Bell had already met with Morrison to draw up the child-support agreement, but now Olive asked Bell to take steps to force Rocco to marry her.

It was now up to Bell to give Olive the bad news that marriage with Rocco Perri was impossible, that he already had a wife. Rocco had obviously not told his counsel that this marriage was not a legal one.

Shortly after noon, Olive returned to the offices of Frank Morrison on the seventh floor of the Bank of Hamilton building. The office was closed and the elevator boy, Tommy Armour, noticing Olive waiting, offered to take her to a place where she could sit down. Olive told him that she was all right and stayed. When Morrison's secretary, a Miss Stevenson, returned from lunch, she let Olive into the office.

They would later remember that Olive was not dressed warmly enough for a February day in Hamilton. She was wearing a fur-collared jacket, a black hat, light blue stockings and light summer shoes.

To Stevenson, it seemed that Olive was acting strangely. She went to the office of C. E. Bull & Co. next door to ask Owen Dunn, a tall, dark, well-dressed young man for help. Stevenson told him she was afraid "the woman might jump out of the window." Dunn went into the office, thinking it was all a joke. At first they could not see Olive. Then Dunn heard a window go up and saw the young woman climbing out onto the sill.

"Come here!" Dunn yelled and jumped toward the window. Olive stood for a moment on the sloping masonry coping, her hand on a ledge. Dunn grabbed for the wrist and at that moment, Olive jumped sideways and down. "She never uttered a sound," Dunn would later recall.

She fell seven stories in front of hundreds of lunchtime passersby. A *Spectator* employee who witnessed the plunge said he heard the screams of witnesses and turned to see Olive hit the pavement, narrowly missing an ice-cream driver.

There was no blood on her body and none on the sidewalk. She had died from internal injuries. Once police knew who the suicide victim was, Detective Ernest Goodman was assigned to investigate the case. Coroner Dr George Rennie called an inquest. Even in those years, when suicides were reported, it was unusual to call an inquest on such an obvious suicide.

But if the police thought that they could haul Rocco Perri into a coroner's court, where he could be forced to testify under the protection of the Canada Evidence Act, they were wrong. As he was to do time and time again in years ahead, Rocco skipped town and left Canada before Goodman could serve a subpoena.

The local press coverage was sensational. The *Herald* had a huge front-page banner: "AWFUL LEAP TO DEATH." Two days later, the *Spectator,* reined in by the possibility of libel, told how Olive had met a man "she believed to be of honourable intentions." They identified Rocco by saying, "He was arrested on a charge of selling whisky but got off with a fine. A subsequent arrest found him sent to jail without option of fine and she was thrown on the world with her two babies."

Rocco's first arrest was the January 1919 bootlegging bust. He may have lied to Olive about the second arrest. The Hamilton police record shows no further arrests of Rocco Perri in that city, but a covering letter from the Chief of Police, William R. Whatley, attached to Perri's record, notes that: "information was received that he had been in some trouble at Guelph under some other name and that he had a criminal record prior to that."

On Thursday, Olive's father, George, arrived in Hamilton. He had read of his daughter's death in the newspapers. Routledge spoke to the police, visited his grandchildren, who were in the care of the hospital and then told reporters what he knew of his daughter's story. Routledge was described as "nervous and distraught." By Saturday, February 18th, the press learned that the father and chief witness had left town. Rocco, still unnamed, had left instructions with Bell that the unsigned child-support agreement was still to be carried out. Bell also made arrangements for Olive's funeral. The more sensational *Herald* tried an old trick to get around the libel laws. In its lead it reported that the unnamed father had fled the country but in the last paragraph mentioned that among the witnesses to be subpoenaed was Rocco Perri, listed in the city directory as a "macaroni manufacturer's representative." The *Herald* also hinted at blackmail, saying that friends of G. W. Routledge had said that when Olive had discovered Rocco was married she had threatened to expose him to his wife. By this time, Bessie did know about the affair, and while she probably tolerated Rocco's affairs — he had at least two more while Bessie was alive — her tight control of Rocco's purse strings would soon be notorious and she certainly wasn't going to pay for the support of Olive's children.

On Monday, February 20th, police denied allegations that they had been lax in subpoenaing Rocco. They pointed out that he had committed no crime and that they had to wait until Dr Rennie had formally called the inquest.

That afternoon, the inquest into the death of Sarah Olive Routledge opened in a Hamilton court packed with morbidly curious onlookers. The first witness was Frank Morrison, who told only the date and time of each of Olive's visits. He refused to give any details about what Olive had told him. An ordinary citizen could have been forced to testify about his role in the death, but Morrison successfully cited lawyer-client privilege. Then witnesses described Olive's movements in the days before her death.

The final witness was the doctor who had performed the autopsy. He told the inquest that Olive Routledge had literally died of a broken heart. Death had been caused by a broken rib puncturing the heart at the moment of impact. The inquest was then adjourned for a week.

On Tuesday, the funeral arrangements were complete. Olive was buried in secret, attended by her father, two relatives from Grimsby and a local Methodist minister. Her invalid mother had still not been informed of her death.

The following Monday, February 27th, the inquest resumed. George Routledge now told his daughter's story, how she had met and fallen in love with Rocco and had borne him two children. He told of his surprise at finding her registered under the name Perry in the St Catharines hospital. When his daughter had left Musclow three weeks before, her father had believed Olive was going to get money from her husband so she could buy a farm for her parents.

The four detectives testified about questioning Olive that morning at headquarters. After her death they had searched her room and had found two trunks, a suitcase and two club bags. She had a large amount of money and furniture stored in St Catharines. They found two letters in the room, the one from Rocco dated December 21, 1921, in which he had offered to live with her, and a second from her mother in Musclow.

Morrison was recalled to answer one question: whether he had drawn up an agreement between Rocco and Olive for child support. An unnamed witness testified that he had glanced at the paper Olive had dropped in Noble's Lunch and it was a support agreement between people named Routledge and Perry. The agreement, however, had disappeared.

Testimony showed that the car in which Olive had left the hotel, licence plate number 56-659, was registered in the name of Bessie Perri. Similarly, the phone number, Regent 8267w, was in the name of Bessie Perri.

Bell testified that he had paid the funeral expenses out of his own pocket. "I was not authorized to do so by my client," he said. "I took this on myself, as I felt sure my client would agree to it." Bell said that after he had met with Olive he had spoken to Morrison because he believed the children should be taken care of. Bell said that he was prepared to pressure his client into providing maintenance payments, but negotiations had been progressing satisfactorily until the suicide.

Bell said Olive's death was such a sensation that a settlement had become impossible. He went on to state that the fuss and the "phantom punishment" threatened to his client stopped all negotiations and caused him to leave town.

He refused to give the name of his client, citing lawyer-client privilege.

The coroner's jury believed the cops. Their verdict: "We the jury find that Olive Routledge met her death on February 15, by throwing herself from the seventh storey of the Bank of Hamilton while suffering severe mental strain. We recommend that Rocco Perry [sic] or Ross be apprehended and forced to provide for the children. We regret that the law does not provide for a more severe punishment for the man in such a sad case."

On Wednesday, March 1st, the grief-stricken George Routledge left Hamilton with his daughter's effects. Detectives Goodman, Chamberlain and Thompson had helped him pack the goods and paid for his ticket home. Later, the authorities would release the two young children into his custody.

CHAPTER 4

THE BRIDGEBURG CONNECTION

Spring came early for Rocco Perri in 1922. Following Magistrate Gundy's decision the previous summer, the term "bootlegger" applied only to those who were illegally selling liquor in Ontario. Since export was recognized to be legal, the exporters were technically not bootleggers, no matter what the U.S. Bureau of Prohibition thought.

In 1915, a year before the passage of the Ontario Temperance Act, there had been fifty-six breweries and twelve distilleries in the province. By 1922, there remained twenty-two breweries and five distilleries. Most were ready to serve the export market. However, to export legally the booze had to be shipped through a port where a customs officer checked that the excise tax had been paid and the proper clearances issued. Then all they had to do was get into the United States while avoiding American authorities. There were two easy places to do it, along the St Clair and Detroit rivers near Windsor and along the Niagara River between Fort Erie and Niagara-on-the-Lake.

The main crossing point on the Niagara River was above the Falls at Bridgeburg, a village on the outskirts of Fort Erie, Ontario. It had been built to handle the rail traffic that crossed into Canada from the United States. The American counterpart of Bridgeburg was the village of Black Rock, New York, on the opposite side of the Niagara

River. In 1922, Rocco was one of several bootleggers using the Bridgeburg crossing, but by now he was taking steps to control most of the export trade.

Hamilton was in the centre of what became known as the "Bootleg Triangle." To the north was the apex, the twin cities of Kitchener and Waterloo, where Rocco Perri bought whiskey from the J. E. Seagram and Son's distillery, which would remain in the control of the family until the company was sold to Samuel Bronfman in 1928. Next door to Seagram's, in Kitchener, was the Kuntz Brewery, then one of North America's largest, and the largest supplier of beer to Rocco Perri over the next ten years. Kuntz had started a line of soft drinks during the war years, including Sasparilla, Stone Ginger Beer, Strawberry Soda and McLeann's Dry Diet Gingerale, but their biggest business was already in exported beer. Seagram's and Kuntz were strategically close to both the Windsor and Bridgeburg border crossings.

In the eastern end of the Bootleg Triangle, Rocco bought liquor from both the Gooderham & Worts distillery in Toronto and the smaller Corby distillery at Corbyville just outside Belleville.

Gooderham's, which was still in the control of its founding family, was a logical supplier of liquor for the Toronto market. Not only was the distillery conveniently located on Trinity Street in the city's east end, but the Gooderhams had connections with the Italians and Jews in the Ward. In 1907, George Gooderham had approached Ward businessman Serafino Castrucci with the idea of starting an Italian-language newspaper in Toronto. Gooderham bankrolled *La Tribuna Canadese*. The next year Gooderham was elected from Toronto South, Seat B — the Ward — to the Ontario Legislature.

Corby's was then part of the giant Canadian Industrial Alcohol group, which controlled Consolidated Distilleries of Montreal and ran five distilleries across the country. Corby's was the largest in the group. A later investigation by the Internal Revenue Service in the United States would reveal that Consolidated was one of the first Canadian distillers to be contacted by New York bootleggers in the early days of Prohibition. One of the largest customers was associated closely with Johnny Torrio, Al Capone's mentor in Chicago. The deals were bankrolled by New York gambler Arnold Rothstein, the man who became famous for fixing the 1919 World Series.

The general manager of Corby's was Harry Clifford Hatch, who held a number of Corby's shares and who was an assistant to the president of Canadian Industrial Alcohol. When Hatch took over at Corby's in 1919, the distillery was producing 500 gallons of alcohol a month. In the spring of 1922, Hatch was completing a program to build Corby's capacity to 50,000 gallons a month. Hatch would later comment, "I built the Corby firm and they built me up."

Like Rocco Perri, Hatch had been in the mail order booze business, but he came from far different roots. He was born in 1884 in Robins Mills, east of Belleville. In what would later be described as a Canadian Horatio Alger story, Hatch began working for his father in the hotel business and, in 1911, bought a liquor store in Whitby for $2,500, earned $8.40 on the first day of business and sold the store two years later for $18,000. Together with his brother, Herbert, Harry later operated a liquor store on Toronto's Yonge Street until the Ontario Temperance Act was proclaimed in 1916. The brothers then moved their operations to Montreal, where they conducted a mail order business, buying their supplies from Consolidated Distilleries, until they were put out of business by the War Measures Act decree. It was later reported that during the short time the Hatchs were in the mail order business they had made a fortune.

The western end of the triangle was, of course, Windsor, the location of the Hiram Walker distillery and the Walkerville and British American breweries. Rocco Perri certainly had contacts in Windsor: his main business with the city was exporting beer from the local Hamilton brewery, Grant's Spring, and the Taylor and Bate brewery in St Catharines via the Windsor-Detroit pipeline.

It appears that there were no "deals" as such made between Rocco and other Canadian bootleg-exporters and their Ontario-based suppliers at this time. The extended "mail order" business with the United States still took place on an ad hoc, order-by-order basis.

It was during this time that Bessie Perri came into her own and proved herself to be the financial brains of the Perri operation. She was the one who placed the orders with the three distilleries — Gooderham & Worts, Corby's and Seagram's — and at least three breweries — Kuntz, Grant's Spring and Taylor and Bate. The standard procedure was to have a contact in the United States telegraph the supplier with an order, but Bessie would often phone in orders from the Bay Street mansion herself, requesting that the liquor be shipped to New York state. Bessie Perri handled the cash, and the money went into various accounts in Bessie's name.

She also handled the day-to-day tasks. The Olive Routledge investigation revealed that Bessie registered three Perri vehicles on the same day, the big Marmon that Rocco drove, in her name, a luxury McLaughlin in the name of a gang member and the bootlegger's basic transportation, a Reo speedwagon (capable of outrunning police cars) in the name of yet another gang member.

Rocco had gathered around him a core of gangsters who did the day-to-day bootlegging operations, whether for export or in Hamilton. His allies, the Scaroni family, still controlled bootlegging in Guelph and Brantford and the rural areas north and west of Hamilton, and they had a bit of the export trade.

Rocco's gang included his close cousin, Mike Serge; Frank DiPietro (a.k.a. Frank Lapietro); the Romeos, including Frank, a senior Hamilton Calabrian gangster, his brother Joe and his cousins, James and Mike Romeo; Calogero ("Charlie") Bordonaro (who in the 1950s and 60s would be a senior mob don in Hamilton); and Rosario Carboni, a young Perri cousin who had come to Hamilton from Gary, Indiana. Antonio ("Tony") Papalia, who had emigrated from Calabria in 1900, was another Perri driver and bootlegger, as were the Brassi, Moranda and Italiano families and the Rossi brothers, Frank and Tony. The Rossis shortened their name to Ross, but "Ross" also seems to have been a common alias for all gang members, including Rocco, who, of course, used the name in his relationship with Olive Routledge. Out-of-town gang members included James and Domenic D'Agostino in St Catharines and the Sylvesters in Guelph and Niagara-on-the-Lake. In Fort Erie, Jim Sullivan was Perri's front man and partner in the export trade. Perri also employed many young Canadians as drivers and boatmen, including the "Gogo gang" of St Catharines. Many gang members were involved in Rocco's other criminal activities as well.

Almost every afternoon, one of Rocco's big Reo trucks would pull up at Gooderham's or Seagram's distillery to load up for the trip to Bridgeburg. There were usually three young men on the truck: the boss, a close associate of Perri's such as Frank DiPietro, and two helpers. In the loading yard, Rocco's men and others in the employ of the distillery would load the truck with about twenty ten-gallon kegs or the equivalent, eight hundred quart bottles in about eighty cases. Once the truck was loaded, a customs officer would arrive with two forms. The first was the B-52, which showed that the excise tax on the shipment had been paid. The second was the driver's ticket to the border, the B-13, the Canadian government's export permit.

The situation was freer at the Kuntz Brewery and other breweries in Ontario. Excise tax was paid on hops, not beer, and therefore no customs officers checked on outgoing shipments. Kuntz was shipping about 630 cases of beer for export each day.

Once the order was filled, Rocco Perri faced the problem of how to get to Bridgeburg. Although on January 9, 1922, Chief Justice Meredith of the Ontario Supreme Court had ruled that transportation of liquor was legal as long as the trucker had bills of lading and B-13s made out to customers in the United States, Ontario Attorney General W. E. Raney was determined to stop the transport. He ordered that all shipments of liquor or beer by truck in the province of Ontario be seized until it was proved the consignment was legal.

Once the liquor-laden truck left the distillery or brewery, it would head to a point somewhere on the road to Bridgeburg where Rocco would be waiting. He never carried a load of liquor himself, but would always be nearby when a shipment was going through, watching from his expensive Marmon coupe.

If the liquor-laden truck managed to escape the notice of police departments along the route from Toronto to Niagara — and Rocco's payments ensured that some of the officers looked the other way — it was clear sailing once the truck reached the export dock at Bridgeburg.

There it would be checked by Canadian Customs officials to make sure the paperwork was in order. The name of the ship's captain was filled in on the B-13, even if that ship's master was the captain of a rowboat. Customs officials were supposed to make sure that the bills of lading were for genuine customers and that those transporting the liquor knew the consignee. After that check, everything was considered legal and the liquor was loaded into the boats for the dash across the Niagara River. It was always at dusk that the boats headed for the U.S. shore. Canadian regulations required that the export boats leave in daylight, but the shipments had to be unloaded in darkness on the other side.

One evening in late February 1922, the river was clear but ice still covered the shore. Rocco, his men and the smugglers had gathered at a hotel at the end of Bridgeburg's main street, where a lot more than the legal 2.2 percent beer was being served up. Then, late in the afternoon, the drivers moved their trucks two hundred yards from the hotel to a small dock. The liquor was carried down rickety stairs and loaded into rowboats and launches. The customs officer or the Mountie made a quick check and determined that all was satisfactory. The launches could tow the rowboats downstream a mile to a sheltered cove called Cory Dell to await dusk and the race across the river.

Around a bend in the road, a quarter mile from the railway bridge, about twenty feet from shore, large rowboats, most with three-man crews, were beginning to gather. It was twenty minutes to six.

Rocco, was standing aloof on the shore in a fur coat, the "uncrowned king of legal shippers," that February evening when Roy Greenaway of the Toronto *Star* approached, escorted by an RCMP constable. Rocco declined to have his men photographed by the press. In this case, there was no fear of arrest, just publicity.

"Not a chance, not on your life, no pictures of us," Rocco told Greenaway. "This outfit has enough notoriety already. It would be conspiracy against the United States authorities."

At ten minutes past seven, a car on the American shore shone its headlights through the twilight, and the boats headed across the river. Rocco, Greenaway and the Mountie stood side by side watching as the boats disappeared into the gathering darkness. Somewhere on the other side, American authorities likely had their telescopes trained on the Canadian shore trying to calculate where the loads would land.

On Bird Island, opposite Fort Erie, there were about forty boathouses, homes and shacks that provided excellent hidden landing spots. The U.S. government had ordered that they be demolished, but there were more old buildings on Squaw Island and squatters' dwellings on the Erie Canal bank facing Bridgeburg and running north for over a mile. Further to the north was Grand Island and the main shore of Tonawanda, New York, each with hundreds of hiding places. The American officials had no small task to carry out.

Whenever they failed to spot one of the speeding boats, a Bridgeburg smuggler made $1,200. A case of Seagram's cost $35 in Waterloo, and that included the $14 excise tax. Wholesale at the Buffalo border a case went for $50. The average wholesale price in New York City of a case of whisky smuggled in from Canada was $140.

If a case was seized, it was often discovered that much of the pure whisky had been topped up with moonshine grain whisky, water, artificial colouring and flavouring, if any of the original whisky was left at all. Of the "real" scotch that also crossed the border, Johnny Walker went for $50 a case, Gordon's Gin for $42 and Haig & Haig for $53.

Not all the whisky and scotch reached the American

shores, however. M. H. Stapleton, the U.S. Prohibition Director declared that most of the whisky exported at Bridgeburg actually found its way back into Canada. It was just what Attorney General Raney and the Ontario Temperance authorities feared the most: reimportation.

The export of bootleg booze was covered in the newspapers on a daily basis, and continued to provoke heated debate. The Dominion Alliance demanded that the federal government bring in nationwide prohibition. When the new prime minister, Mackenzie King, met the temperance delegation on March 28, 1922 in Ottawa, he thanked them for their petition, but took a typically middle-of-the-road stance, declaring that his government would not introduce any measures that would "harm rather than assist the Dominion Alliance." "Reform must come slowly," he told the temperance delegation, "line upon line, and precept upon precept." The federal government would learn from the various provincial approaches, he said, and then act on that experience.

While the discussion continued, Rocco Perri came to the attention of the federal government for the first time. On March 13, 1922, he made a routine appearance before Judge C. G. Snider at the Hamilton General Sessions for naturalization as a British subject in Canada. Rocco told Judge Snider that he was a traveller. Asked if he had been in any trouble, Rocco replied that he had been fined a few times for driving too fast. Judge Snider apparently approved the application. The record is unfortunately damaged and Snider added his own handwritten comments to the printed form. *Subject as follows* I find the Applicant qualified and fit to be Naturalized as a British subject. *This man has the reputation of being [involved] in illegal liquor traffic quite extensively out of...* [remainder of form damaged].

It was Rocco's misfortune that his name was included in the Hamilton *Herald* that day in a routine list of those applying for naturalization. Two protest letters were sent to the secretary of state's office in Ottawa. The first, from Mrs Thora D. McIlroy, governor of the Citizenship Committee of the Local Council of Women, outlined briefly the Olive Routledge case and pointed out that Rocco had been convicted under the Ontario Temperance Act.

The second letter was from Lieutenant Colonel Charles R. McCullough, Honourary President of the Association of Canadian Clubs. McCullough wrote directly but "unofficially" to Thomas Mulvey, undersecretary of state, suggesting that Rocco be "debarred from citizenship" and noting that Mulvey could get more information from William R. Whatley, Hamilton's chief of police. Mulvey took McCullough's advice, writing to Whatley on March 21, 1922, requesting "a report as to the character of one Rocco Perry."*

William Whatley was forty-four years old, six feet six inches tall, with a big moustache — an authoritative man who was often seen walking along Hamilton's King Street in a uniform splendid with campaign ribbons, and sporting a silver-handled ebony cane. He came from an old Somerset farming family and had gone to South Africa, in 1897, at the age of nineteen, where he volunteered for the Coast Mounted Police, serving in the Boer War and afterward until 1906 when he came to Canada. After three years as a Lieutenant in the Twenty-third Northern Pioneers, Whatley had heard of a vacancy for a deputy chief of police in Hamilton. He appeared before the police commission and talked himself into the job, the first outsider to be appointed to that command rank. Magistrate Jelfs would later remember that Whatley "had to put up with considerable inconvenience caused by local jealousy over the appointment of an outside man, but I never knew a man who possessed more tact." When Chief Alexander Smith died in June 1915, Whatley was named chief of police. Whatley was later president of the Chief Constables Association of the Dominion of Canada and chairman of the Ontario Provincial Enforcement Committee on Combatting Venereal Disease.

Authorities in Hamilton had already taken their own steps to make sure that Rocco was not naturalized. Whatley had ordered a raid on his house at 166 Bay Street South on

---

*Rocco signed his citizenship form "Perry" and used both spellings at this time.

March 16th to try to find something incriminating on the premises. Rocco wasn't at home, but the raiding party, under the command of Detective Ernest Goodman and including Detective Joe Crocker, did grab two men as they tried to flee the house. They were Rosario Carboni, who was staying at the Perri mansion, and Luigi Coruzzio, who lived in the boarding house at 104 Caroline Street, where Alberto Naticchio had been staying at the time of the Martino killing in 1919. In his report on the incident Detective Goodman described Coruzzio as "employed by Perri as a chauffeur" — most likely driving bootleg trucks. Coruzzio still worked for Rocco Perri in 1926 when his name was spelled Luigi Corruzi in an RCMP intelligence report.

The detectives found that Carboni had a fully loaded automatic revolver in his suitcase and Coruzzio had an automatic in his hip pocket. Both men were charged with possession of illegal weapons.

At that moment Rocco, accompanied by several men, returned home. He submitted to a search which found no illegal weapons. The police then searched the mansion for contraband and found nothing. Obviously, they missed the hidden cellar.

A couple of weeks later, Rocco would describe the raid in an affidavit. He stated that Carboni was visiting from Indiana and that he had no knowledge of the revolver in the man's suitcase. He maintained that Carboni had acquired the gun while in the U.S. Army and thought that he had the right to carry it in Canada. As for Coruzzio, he came to the house while the Perris were out. Rocco claimed he did not know the man and therefore had no way of knowing that he was carrying a gun.

Carboni and Coruzzio appeared before Magistrate Jelfs, who convicted them, gave them a severe lecture and fined them both $100 and three months, with an additional month for nonpayment. Rocco's lawyer, Michael J. O'Reilly, who appeared for the two men, complained that the punishment was too severe. Jelfs replied that it was time to stop foreigners from carrying illegal weapons.

Whatley had Goodman and three other detectives write

reports on their dealings with Rocco Perri and sent them with a covering letter to Thomas Mulvey, saying that Rocco Perri "is not, in my opinion, a fit and proper person to be granted Canadian citizenship."

As well as the four negative reports from the detectives, Whatley also included one from a Constable Sayer:

> Re: Rocco Perry
> I have known above named man for several years and have heard many things concerning his way of making a living etc. but I never had any dealings with him other than to seek information which I received from time to time.

This leaves the question of how and when and why was Rocco Perri acting as an informant for Constable Sayer? Perhaps he was informing on his rivals.

On April 12th, Thomas Mulvey wrote to Rocco: "I regret to inform you that the Secretary of State in his discretion has decided not to grant your application."

On April 27th, O'Reilly appealed the case of Carboni and Coruzzio in Judge John G. Gauld's Wentworth County court in Hamilton. The judge reduced the sentence imposed by Jelfs to a $100 fine. In his judgment he held that the fact the men were on private property when the weapons were found had considerable bearing and that it would have been a more serious matter if they had been found carrying revolvers on the highway.

In May, Charles Bell appealed the decision rejecting Rocco Perri's application for Canadian citizenship. In a letter to his Conservative ally and member of parliament for Hamilton West, Thomas J. Stewart, a former mayor of Hamilton, Bell included the affidavits that Rocco had written giving his side of the story in the disorderly house and OTA incidents. To that Bell added:

> In connection with the disorderly house charge and the OTA charge, Perry might well have been given the benefit of the doubt. Unhappily we know all too well the bent of Magistrate

Jelf's mind — the doubt is always given *against* the person charged. Jelfs cannot help that — it's the way he's built — but I think the minister may fairly be acquainted with the fact, so that he can judge these very debatable convictions in their true light.

With regard to the two men with revolvers, that surely might happen to any Italian who had another visiting him — if it were taken into account, there would be few Italians ever naturalized.

I feel that if this is all that has come up about Rocco Perry in 15 years residence in this country, he is better than the average foreign resident and may fairly be granted naturalization.

Then he added the key paragraph:

Don't you feel I am *right?* If his naturalization application is granted, I am sure we can count on him in times to come.

Bell and Stewart, after all, were Conservatives, while the Mackenzie King government was Liberal. Perhaps they were hoping for future favours from Perri. In any case, Mulvey replied to Stewart on May 15th, rejecting the appeal. Mulvey noted that "Perry admits the convictions and tries to explain them away.... The magistrate is in a better position to judge credibility and Perry should not ask the Department to accept his unsupported statements in view of the whole circumstances which his affidavit discloses."

Meanwhile, the guerilla legal war against bootleg exporters continued.

Frustrated by the court, Raney announced that he would amend the Highway Traffic Act to outlaw the transport of liquor by truck.

CHAPTER 5

BLOODBATH:
THE FALL OF THE HOUSE OF SCARONI

The few Calabrians who immigrated to North America intending to continue a criminal tradition brought with them the cell system of their homeland. Each family or cell was connected to others by a web of relationships, kinship and personal friendships from the old country, some forged in North America. One of the major means of communications was a round of social visits where, at the appropriate moment, the business of the day would be discussed.

By the end of the First World War, the mob had established itself in southern Ontario and western New York. There were already key crime families:

THE SCARONI FAMILY

The Calabrian cell in southern Ontario was led by Domenic Scaroni* who settled in Guelph in 1912, when Rocco was still a construction labourer in Toronto. Scaroni was known in Guelph as a well-to-do baker, but police and news reports make clear he was Ontario's first godfather. He also used the name "Joe Verona." Domenic's brother, Joe Scaroni, and

---

*The name was also spelt Sciaroni, Sciaronnie, Sciarannie, Scaranie, Saranie, Scoronie, Schroni and Shoroni in police and newspaper reports.

their sister settled in Brantford, where Joe ran a fruit business. Their sister was married to a man with the same last name, probably a cousin, Sam Scaroni.

The Scaroni family had lived in the United States after leaving Calabria and had kin ties with Buffalo, where Domenic's wife, Mary, came from. Domenic Scaroni may have lived in Toronto before moving to Guelph as he was naturalized as a Canadian in York County in 1912. Joe Scaroni was the family hitman and enforcer, often travelling across the United States using an assumed name at his brother's bidding. He was almost certainly involved in a shooting in upstate New York late in the decade.

THE SERIANNI FAMILY

The Seriannis were a Niagara Falls, N.Y., Calabrian crime family closely allied first with the Scaronis and later with Rocco Perri. Joseph Serianni of Niagara Falls was named in OPP and newspaper reports as the boss, involved in bootlegging, drug smuggling and mail robberies. Joseph's brother, Samuel, was killed in a gun battle with hijackers in Buffalo in 1922. Charles Serianni was tied to Niagara Falls and Buffalo bootleggers throughout the 1920s.

THE GALLIARDO FAMILY

Only the name survives in OPP intelligence reports. "Don" Totto Galliardo was described as "one of the many Italians who never work, living on the proceeds of bootlegging and criminal activities." Galliardo and his brother Joe, the family enforcer, were Sicilian gangsters based in the Toronto Ward and rivals of the Calabrian mobs.

The Galliardo's allies included a powerful Niagara Falls Sicilian crime figure named in police reports throughout the 1920s as Don Simone. In Buffalo, a shadowy godfather headed a group calling themselves the "Good Killers," from Castellamare in Sicily, that was also active in New York City, Detroit and Chicago.

It began as a vendetta.

It was 1918, and the Taglerino family was lying low after John Taglerino's conviction for Black Hand extortion. A key mob figure in the city was Joseph Celoni, a crude extortionist who used the traditional terror methods of criminals from southern Italy to get money from the Italian community in the city. His front was a candy store and restaurant he had opened at 72 York Street sometime in 1917. Rocco Perri had known Celoni since 1914, at least a year before he and Bessie settled in Hamilton, so Rocco obviously had key connections even at the time he was working in the mud of the Welland Canal.

On Tuesday, April 16, 1918, Joe Celoni was shot and killed outside his Hamilton candy store. Rocco was in the store at the time. Two young men, Domenic Speranza, sixteen, a young relative of Black Hander Ernesto Speranza, and Domenic Paproni, twenty-one, were charged with murder. According to witnesses, Celoni had left his store, crossed York Street and grabbed at Speranza, shouting at him. Speranza drew a gun, fired at Celoni and broke away. Then he returned and fired two more shots. Speranza and Paproni both fled, but they were quickly picked up by police.*

The trial of Speranza and Paproni began on November 14, 1918, three days after the end of the First World War and six weeks before Tony Martino was shot at Rocco Perri's Hess Street grocery store. Michael O'Reilly defended Speranza, W. T. German of Welland defended Paproni and W. C. Mikel appeared for the Crown.

In their cross-examination of Crown witnesses, the defence lawyers began to establish that Celoni had an

---

*Speranza's brother hired defence lawyer Michael J O'Reilly, who then asked the police to check their records on Celoni. The search revealed that there had been numerous complaints that Celoni had terrorized the "Italian colony" as it was called then and extorted money but that there had never been enough evidence to bring a case to court.

unsavoury reputation. York Street merchants told how Celoni was "supposed to be in the candy business or something," and at times there were as many as twenty-five men in the store.

Rocco Perri was called as a Crown witness. He explained that he had known Celoni for four years, Speranza for a year and Paproni for a couple of months. Rocco said he was a frequent visitor to the store and often saw both young men, although he claimed he did not know why they were there. On the afternoon of April 16th, Rocco was in the store. After a couple of minutes, Rocco said, Celoni left, telling Rocco to wait, as he wanted to talk to him. Rocco said that he then heard a shot, which he thought was a tireburst, and that when he heard a second shot, he left the store to see the crowd gathering around Celoni's body.

"Was he expecting trouble?" asked Crown Attorney Mikel. No, replied Rocco, explaining that Celoni had been sitting in the store playing cards just before he had left.

O'Reilly cross-examined Rocco on behalf of Speranza.

"During the time you knew Speranza and Celoni were they friendly?"

"They called each other by their first names."

"What kind of boy was he?"

"A good boy, not quarrelsome," Rocco replied.

"What kind was Celoni?"

"Quick-tempered," Rocco said. "I've seen him slap fellows when he didn't like what they said."

"Did you see him take any fellows down the cellar?" O'Reilly questioned.

"Yes," Rocco answered. "In March, I saw him take Speranza and draw a razor. I stepped between them and took it away. I've seen him hit and kick Italians three or four times since he was in Hamilton."

"Was he doing it to get money?" asked O'Reilly.

"I think so, because that is the way he lived," was Rocco's answer.

"Do you know that for a fact?"

"I don't know," Rocco hedged, "but he didn't seem to be getting a living any other way."

Rocco then told how he had been in the candy store

about two months before the shooting. He had heard a cry from the basement and had gone down the stairs to find Celoni standing over Speranza, who was on his knees. Celoni had a razor in his hand. Rocco said he told Speranza to go upstairs and then persuaded Celoni to drop the quarrel. How did he do that, O'Reilly wanted to know.

"I take him nice and easy, I take him good," Rocco answered.

The Crown called more witnesses to tell what they saw of the shooting and of the capture of the two young Italians.

Paproni was called to testify in his own defence. He had come from Welland at Celoni's invitation and worked unpaid at the candy store until he found a job as a shoemaker. He had been walking along the street and met Speranza at the store. Celoni came out, caught Speranza by the neck and hit him in the face, demanding $50 for "a baptism." Celoni then drew a knife and Speranza shot him.

When Speranza was called, he told O'Reilly that on Saturday, April 13th, Celoni was going to a baptism in Guelph and had demanded the money from Speranza as a gift for the child. Speranza had refused either to go with Celoni or to pay any money.

"Celoni came out and said, 'Listen, I want to speak to you,' and grabbed me by the throat," Speranza testified. "He said, 'I want $50 because you didn't come to the baptism.' He tried to grab me and take me into the store to beat me up and kill me. I said, 'Forgive me, I haven't $50.' He answered and said, 'This is the last day you live.' Then Celoni pulled a knife from his waistcoat pocket. I didn't know what he was going to do. I was afraid and pulled my gun and fired. I was like a drunken man from the blow I received. I don't know how I shot."

Paproni was acquitted but Speranza was convicted of manslaughter and sentenced to life imprisonment.

Paproni himself was dead within months, shot and killed in Welland as he walked to work. It was well known that Celoni's friends were determined to avenge his death. Later, during other investigations, OPP Senior Inspector

John Miller* would report that it was Joe Scaroni who had killed Paproni on orders from his brother Domenic.

The death of Joe Celoni represented the passing of an era in the Hamilton underworld. As in Chicago, where Big Jim Colossimo was murdered in 1920, and in New York, where New York Mafia boss Ignazio "Lupo the Wolf" Saietta had been imprisoned, the old-fashioned crime bosses were giving way to a new, more business-like generation.

The Scaroni family controlled a good deal of the bootlegging area around Guelph and Brantford and, at least in the early days of 1920, were more powerful than Rocco Perri.

In 1920 the Scaronis were supplying a bootlegger in the village of Carlisle, halfway between Hamilton and Guelph, later part of Rocco Perri's territory. Just two years later, Rocco would be regarded as one of three equally powerful Calabrian bosses: Perri, Domenic Scaroni and, in Buffalo, Joe Serianni.

With the thirsty United States demanding liquor, old vendettas were fuelled by new business rivalries. Details on the Niagara bootleg war are sparse, and reports on some of the events have disappeared long ago. The events of the war can be reconstructed to some extent, however, from summaries contained in two OPP murder investigations and a third report, obtained by the Toronto *Star*, from unnamed "insiders" at the time of the Bessie Perri murder.

Some of the murders give an idea of the bloodbath which took place.

• Thomas Mathews, a farmer who had dealings with bootleggers, was the first victim. His body was washed up on a beach near his Stoney Creek farm in September 1920. He had been killed by the thrust of a long knife under his left arm.

---

*Miller had joined the OPP in 1907 and was the most experienced working detective in the OPP's new Criminal Investigation Division, formed in 1921. Miller was a tenacious investigator and a stubborn man. In September 1921, he stood up to senior officers on an isssue of principle. Whatever the issue was, Miller won and an inspector resigned.

- Ralph Mandrolo, forty-one, of Niagara Falls, Ontario, was walking along a street when a shotgun was thrust from a window. The blast blew his head off.
- Fred Tedesca was shot in Guelph in late 1920. OPP Inspector John Miller later reported that Tedesca was murdered in a vendetta by Joe Scaroni and a Toronto mobster, who were acting on the orders of Domenic Scaroni.
- Angelo Salvatore was stabbed on the Bay Street bridge in Hamilton on November 29, 1920. In hospital, Salvatore said that he had been stabbed by "Jimmy." OPP Inspector William Stringer later identified the assailant as Hamilton gangster Vincenzo ("Jimmy") Loria.
- Angelo Fuca was shot on a Hamilton street on Christmas morning, 1920, after an all-night party. At first police believed that the party had been at the home of John Marenga, and he was charged with murder. At the trial, however, it was revealed that the party had actually been at the home of Napoleon Campanelli, who had threatened the Marenga family. At the trial in April 1921, it was revealed that Hamilton police were searching for Napoleon's brother, Luigi Campanelli. Nick Marenga, the twelve-year-old son of the defendant, testified that Fuca, dying on the sidewalk, had said, "Oh, Luigi, you have killed me." John Marenga was acquitted. Two years later Luigi Campanelli was charged in Italy with the attempted murder of another member of the Fuca family.
- The body of Frank Pizzuto of New York City was discovered on May 18th on the outskirts of Buffalo. He was one of the bootleggers who ran Canadian whisky from Buffalo into New York. His body was hacked almost beyond recognition. Police attributed the murder to a bootleggers' vendetta.

On June 18, 1921, two little girls searching for berries outside Crowland, near Welland, found the badly decomposed body of a man in a field half a mile from the nearest house. It had been there about a week. Not until the body was taken to a local funeral parlour was it discovered that the man had been stabbed in the chest with a long dagger, which had pierced through his back. Death had been instantaneous.

Hamilton Detective Ernest Goodman, who assisted the Crowland police in the investigation, reported that a wallet was found on the body containing a 1920 chauffeur's licence in the name of James Saunders. The address on the licence was 166 Bay Street South. Saunders was also wanted by Hamilton police for a series of cellar-stock whisky thefts that had occurred in the city in May.

Rocco told the police that Saunders had worked for him as a chauffeur and had lived in the Bay Street mansion for a while, but had later moved out. The investigation turned up the fact that Saunders was also a driver for Domenic Scaroni.

Despite his English-sounding name, the twenty-seven-year-old Saunders was identified as an Italian. He had been last seen alive a week before the discovery of the body when he had told friends he was leaving Hamilton to go to Welland. A report in the *Herald* said Saunder's real name may have been "Nunzio Corazzo."

On June 25th, the inquest into Saunder's death came to the verdict, "murder by person or persons unknown." Testimony revealed that Saunders had been killed by a man strong enough to drive the knife or stilletto through him in a single blow. The body had then been taken to Crowland and dumped. Although Saunders had been in an argument over a woman, the murder was likely part of a growing feud between the Calabrians on the Canadian side and the Sicilians on the American side for control of the bootleg trade.

Reports a year later would identify Rocco Perri's cross-border rivals as an obscure Sicilian group known as the "Good Killers." The boss of the Good Killers in New York City was none other than Stefano Magaddino, who would later rise to be the crime overlord of the Niagara region, first in the United States and later in Canada.

Stefano Magaddino was born in the Mafia stronghold of

Castellamare in northern Sicily in October 1891, and had come to the United States in 1902. In later years, Don Stefano ("The Undertaker") Magaddino would become a member of the ruling Mafia "commission" from his powerbase in Buffalo. He lived in Lewiston, on the American side of the Niagara River, and his legitimate front was a family-run funeral parlour.

On August 15, 1921, New York Police acting Captain Michael Fiaschetti received a phone call from an Italian barber named Bartolomere ("Bartolo") Fontano, who was wanted for the murder of a Camillo Calazzo. Calazzo's bound body had been found near Asbury Park, New Jersey. He had been killed by a blast from a shotgun.

The barber's confession surprised even the experienced Italian squad members. Fontano said that a group called the "Good Killers" was responsible for the murders of at least seventeen people that had taken place in New York and Detroit during the previous seven years. The killings began, Fontano said, when a group of Sicilians attempted to take over the numbers racket then based on the Italian State lottery.

Fontano and another hitman, who was picked up later, told the police that the core of the gang had come from the area around Castellamare twelve years before. They began to victimize Italians in New York through holdups and Black Hand extortions. After the numbers, their next targets were Italian card games and related gambling. The gang gradually expanded their operations across the United States. Business was so good that new recruits were brought over from Sicily. The gang's reputation grew in the underworld and its members began to be known as the "Good Killers" for the professional way in which they carried out hits, first of men who informed against them and later for hire.

Fontano said that Magaddino, then living in Brooklyn, had threatened him into murdering Calazzo, who had killed Magaddino's brother in Castellamare. Fontano, who had been

Calazzo's friend in Sicily, tricked him into going to a farm near Averne, New Jersey. Fontano took Calazzo for a walk in the woods and at the moment he least suspected, pressed a shotgun against Calazzo's side and pulled the trigger.

Fontano was afraid of being killed himself: the Good Killers had threatened to "bake him" in the oven of a Brooklyn bakery. He had also begun to dream about Calazzo's ghost.

Fontano phoned Magaddino from police headquarters and told him he needed help in getting out of town. He asked Magaddino to meet him at Grand Central Station.

While detectives loitered nearby, Fontano waited. Magaddino arrived, talked briefly to Fontano, gave him some money and told him to go to Buffalo, where the "chief" would take care of him. Even in those days, Magaddino must have had close connections with Buffalo. At that moment, the police moved in and arrested Magaddino. Soon afterwards, six more members of the Good Killers were taken in.

Two days later, police were saying that the Good Killers were responsible for 125 murders in New York, Pittsburgh, Detroit and Chicago. In Buffalo, police were searching for the man said to be the chief of the Good Killers across the United States, who controlled a $200,000 defence fund to be used on the behalf of any member of the group who was arrested. It was the practice of the group, followed to this day by the mob, to import out-of-town hitmen to do the job, with Detroit gangsters going to New York to murder at the command of the shadowy godfather in Buffalo.

Since the headquarters of the Good Killers was in Buffalo, it is clear that that gang had a major stake in the Niagara bootleg trade and were both chief customers and adversaries of the Canadian-based Calabrian bootleggers led by Rocco Perri and the Scaroni Family.

The months between August and November of 1921 were quiet and profitable as more liquor was shipped south to the United States. But Magistrate Gundy's August decision to legalize the export of liquor raised the stakes. Old vendettas and the rivalry between the Sicilians and Calabrians escalated into open gang warfare.

These were the casualties of the fall of 1921 and winter of 1922, as listed by the OPP:

• On Novembr 10, 1921, George ("Toni") Timpani was shot four times in the head as he climbed Clifton Hill in Niagara Falls, Ontario. Timpani had told police that he had left a Black Hand organization and that its members were out to get him.

• Vincenzo Castiglione's body was found on Ridge Road in Saltfleet on the outskirts of Hamilton on November 30, 1921. He had been shot behind the left ear, in the heart and in the ankle. The body had then been soaked in coal oil and set alight. Wentworth County Police Chief James Clark and Stoney Creek Coroner Dr Green ruled it a suicide, despite demands from the Castiglione family for a murder investigation. In the summer of 1922, the case would be declared murder and reopened.

• On Sunday, February 12, 1922, Pasquale ("Patsy") Villella and Domenic Predota, accused each other of squealing to the police about bootlegging activities. A couple of hours later, they killed each other in a pistol duel during a howling blizzard in the alley that separated their two houses. The first reports of the shooting indicated that both men may have been victims of the Black Hand. OPP headquarters in Toronto assigned Senior Inspector John Miller to investigate.

The press began speculating on the role of the Black Hand in the deaths of Predota and Villella. The Hamilton *Spectator* said the Black Hand "is a powerful organization even in Canada, and is believed to have directed its attention to bootlegging and rum running since the Prohibition Act."

Edward Taylor, the Italian court interpreter in Hamilton, said that he had been in contact with the organization in the city. "I have come in contact with people who have been threatened by them, but as a rule, they confine their attentions to Italians, who, in the majority, fear to inform the police, and therefore their activities are rarely known. The murders in Welland are typical of their methods. They are daring and cunning and will not let anything stand in their way."

Hamilton Police Chief William Whatley laughed at the whole idea: "There may be such a society in Italy, but I do not believe that their activities extend to Canada. The trouble is that whenever an Italian commits a crime, everyone say it's the Black Hand."

Whatley was right about one thing. The press was too eager to blame Italian murders on the Black Hand, and Black Hand extortion imitators were common both in Canada and the United States. But in denying the existence of Italian organized crime, Whatley was typical of senior North American law officers from the 1920s right up to the 1970s (when Allan Lawrence, then Ontario's attorney general, stated the Mafia did not exist in Toronto).

Inspector Miller quickly found out that the Predota-Villella case had been a deadly duel and not a mob hit. But there were more killings.

• The body of farmer John McNichol was found suspended from the limb of a maple tree on the shore of Lake Erie near Bridgeburg on February 27, 1922. McNichol had likely interrupted the activities of a bootleg gang.

• Mike Lobosco of Welland was shot outside his South Main Street barber shop and pool room on March 16, 1922. Although Lobosco lived for twenty hours after the shooting, he refused to tell police anything about his assailant. Informants told Welland Police Chief W. C. Crabbe that Salvatore ("Sam") Licato had left Welland that night and crossed into the United States by bootlegger's launch. A wanted poster was issued for Licato.

• The body of Maurrizzio Bocchimuzzo, twenty-six, was found by hunters on the outskirts of Niagara Falls, New York, on April 2nd. There was a handwritten sign nearby saying, "Death! Here! Look!" Police concluded that Bocchimuzzo, who was known to be running booze across the border, had been killed by a rival gang.

On the evening of May 10, 1922, a mob banquet was being held at Louis Divitis' saloon in Niagara Falls, New York. One of the guests was Domenic Scaroni, who had left Guelph that afternoon and met Rocco Perri at Freelton, halfway between Guelph and Hamilton, and probably on the border of their territories.

Scaroni left the banquet early — or was forced out — with four men. At 11:30 P.M. a driver for the Niagara Falls Grey Bus line found Scaroni's body on Lewiston Hill, part of the Niagara escarpment. Scaroni, forty-five, had been shot three times in the head and once in the shoulder, at close range. His body had been tossed from a speeding automobile.

The murder of the Guelph mob boss received scant attention in the press. Only the Hamilton *Herald* hinted at Scaroni's position, noting that he was "thought to be the leader of one faction of two bands of feudists. He was well known in the Italian colonies of several Canadian and American cities." It is clear that the press did not realize the significance of the Scaroni murder to the Ontario and western New York underworld. His importance emerges only from the reports on other murders by OPP Inspectors John Miller and William Stringer.*

On Saturday, May 13, 1922, Domenic Scaroni was buried at Guelph. The routine funeral report in the *Mercury*, a common society news item in the newspapers of the day, gives a hint of what was a major gangland funeral. Rocco Perri was part of the funeral procession, which moved from the "Verona" home to the Catholic cemetery. "Many visitors from Welland, Kitchener, Hamilton, St Catharines and Toronto were in attendance to pay their last respects to the deceased, who was popularly known among the Italian population through the province."

Rocco's friend, A. R. Deconza, of St Catharines, delivered "a touching oration on the life of the deceased." Among the pallbearers were men who were prominent in the Rocco Perri organization. They included Rocco himself; Deconza; Frank Longo of Welland; Frank Romeo of Hamilton,

---

*Stringer was a twelve-year veteran who left the Toronto police force in 1910 to join the OPP and was posted for five years in north-western Ontario. He was often the only cop in the area between Fort William, Fort Francis and Kenora. He travelled by freight train, hand-car and snowshoe and became a crack investigator because he so often had to work alone.

also a pallbearer at the funeral of Joseph Celoni; and James and Domenic D'Agostino, both of St Catharines.

The murder of Domenic Scaroni meant that Rocco was now the senior Calabrian gang boss in Canada.

Like Scaroni's murder, the Niagara gang war as a whole got little press coverage, even in the Canadian newspapers. One reason is that the major bootlegging wars in Chicago and New York were yet to erupt. The Niagara war was a rural one, which was taking place away from the competing big-city dailies of Toronto and Buffalo. And unlike the feuds in New York and Chicago, the Niagara border war was being fought in different police jurisdictions: two nations, several New York and Ontario counties and a number of cities. Any communication between the various police forces seems to have occurred only on an ad hoc basis. No one gave a much needed overview. Bigotry also contributed to the reactions of the press and police. As long as it was an "Italian feud" and no innocent bystanders were hurt, the war was considered to be little more than a violent curiosity.

Five days after the funeral of Domenic Scaroni, farmers found a man's body in a lonely, overgrown swamp in Beverley Township, Wentworth County. A trail of dried blood and footprints knee-deep in the muck led from the side of the road into the swamp. Wentworth County Police Chief James Clark found a cryptic note, a love letter and two locker keys on the body. He requested assistance from the OPP, who dispatched Inspector William Stringer to take charge.

Stringer arrived in Hamilton on May 19th, and began going over the evidence collected the previous day. The autopsy showed that the man had been shot by an automatic pistol. The bullet had entered the base of the back of the skull, severed the spinal cord and lodged in the upper mouth.

Stringer reported:

> Apparently the deceased got out of the car to urinate as his private was out of his trousers when his body was found, and while in that favourable position for killing, the fatal shot was

fired from behind. Death, no doubt, was instantaneous and the deceased fell on the road, which accounts for his face being bruised and scratched. His body was then dragged into the position where it was found.

The man had identification cards in the names of "Vincenzo Lauria," 349 MacNab Street and "Jimmy Lorreo." In his hat was a slip of notepaper with large orders for seven brands of liquor. There was also the mysterious note, written in Italian, speaking of robbery, weapons and a secret society.*

The next day, Stringer entered the maze of the city's underworld as the *Spectator* and *Herald* both reported that the Good Killers of Buffalo were behind the death. The man who had run Loria's boarding house on MacNab Street was Sam Fuca, brother of Angelo Fuca, who had been murdered in 1920. Fuca sent Stringer to Sam Taglerino, who identified the body as a man known as "Jimmy Loria." Taglerino also told Stringer that Loria had been living at 32 Railway Street with two men named Charles Restivo and Joe Scime.

Stringer spent the next few days tracking down leads on the Loria murder. Whatley passed on to Stringer an anonymous letter he had received. Addressed to the "most illustrious Mr Magistrate," it said that the men who had killed Loria lived at the residence of Napoleon Campanelli, the man who had threatened the Marenga family. The letter said that two days before the body was found, Loria had gone for an automobile ride with Calogero Barter (Bordonaro?), Charles Restivo and Michele Florida. A check by Stringer determined that farmers had heard shots at about 5:00 P.M. on Tuesday, May 16th, two days before the body was found; the time of death was thus established.

The picture that emerged was that of a Mafia soldier.

---

*It mentioned a robbery, a carbine, a dagger, two revolvers and a bottle of poison. It spoke of two brothers, one in the hospital in Palermo, "who is curing himself of a quarrel" and the other, who has become a monk. It asked, "Who was the one who brought this brotherhood — Count Tosca Garibialdi and Mazzini. Who was the head of all this?"
The brotherhood referred to in the letter is the Mafia.

Loria had come from Agirogenti in southern Sicily. He was the one who had stabbed Angelo Salvatore on Bay Street in Hamilton two years before, although Salvatore still denied it. Stringer reported his frustration with Salvatore, who "didn't know the deceased, although the deceased lived and worked in his section for several years!...Italians not giving information."

Taking a trip to Niagara Falls, New York, Stringer unearthed more details about the Calabrian-Sicilian war. Rocco Perri was named as the surviving Calabrian boss in Canada. Stringer and Niagara Falls detectives began working on the theory that Loria had been one of the hitmen who killed Domenic Scaroni, even though he had been a friend of Scaroni's brother Joe and had worked for Domenic in the bootleg trade.

The inquest into Loria's death concluded on June 10th, with the usual verdict: "murder by persons unknown."

On June 4th another murder took place. This time the victim was Toronto mobster Tony Leale, (a.k.a. Frank Cici and Antonio Barboni) originally from Alcamo, Sicily, near Castellamare. Leale was later reported to be a "blood relative" of the Scaroni family and it was known that he had worked for the Scaronis under the name of "Cici."

Oakville farmer Gordon Joyce was out for an evening walk when he came upon a man attempting to pull himself out of a roadside ditch, bleeding from a head wound and babbling in Italian. The man died an hour later. Oakville Police Chief David Kerr ruled out robbery as a motive; he found $60 in counterfeit American bills on the body. Inspectors Stringer and Miller were assigned to the case and a Secret Service agent was summoned from Buffalo.

A Toronto plainclothesman, Samuel Boyd, recalled how "Frank Cici" had pulled a gun on him during an August 1921 OTA raid on a whisky-filled house on St Patrick Street in the Ward. Boyd had knocked him cold with his billyclub. The gun got Leale three months in jail and led to a break with the Scaronis, since the family had promised to support him in jail but then failed to make good on the promise.

The "death car," damaged by a fight that had taken

place in the back, was found on Bloor Street on June 9th. At the inquest on June 20th, witnesses could not positively identify a man seen near the golf club soon after the murder. The familiar verdict was again returned: "murder by person or persons unknown."

On June 15th, Salvatore ("Sam") Scaroni of Brantford (brother-in-law of the murdered Domenic) and Jim Forti, his partner in a fruit business, were shot at after they closed their store late in the evening. A Ford, its lights off, had drawn up and three shots had been fired from it. All missed. Scaroni and Forti refused to identify the people in the car, but OPP intelligence reports identified them as Patsy and Nunziana Nardo of Welland. The Ford was registered in the name of Hamilton bootlegger Calogero ("Charlie") Bordonaro, who worked for Rocco Perri.

A web of circumstances ties Rocco Perri to all four shootings. He met Domenic Scaroni before his death and was his pallbearer. Loria was probably taken for a ride by his Railway Street friends, including the Restivos, who worked for Perri. If Loria had been one of the hit men who killed Domenic Scaroni, revenge by Perri would be the logical motive. Leale had a grudge against the Scaronis, so he could have been in on the hit and also killed in revenge.

If the police intelligence report was correct in saying that Bordonaro's car was used in the Scaroni hit, then a different explanation is possible — that Perri was setting about to eliminate the Scaroni family. In that case, Loria and Leale could both have been still working for the Scaronis. That leaves an intriguing question. Why did the surviving Scaronis still continue to trust Rocco Perri with their lives? Did they believe that their enemies were the western New York Sicilians and not their Calabrian "allies"?

The summer that followed was a quiet one — with one exception. Early on the morning of July 4th, neighbours reported that a house was on fire at 85 Simcoe Street in Hamilton. The building was burning "like a furnace" when firefighters arrived and it took an hour to put it out, as liquor had soaked through the wood of the house.

Three stills were hidden in a false ceiling in the attic. Ten forty-gallon kegs were found, partly or fully filled, containing a total of three hundred gallons of alcohol. The house was owned by John and Sam Taglerino, but the tenant in the house, a Mrs Poleto or Polegla, was charged with excise violations. She had not called the fire department. It was not until neighbours saw flames breaking through the roof that the blaze was reported.

On Sunday, September 3rd, Joe and Sam Scaroni took the 9:00 A.M. train from Brantford to Hamilton, and then went to 166 Bay Street South, where they had lunch with Rocco and Bessie Perri. In the afternoon, the Perris, the Scaronis, a man named Mike Romano and an eighteen-year-old identified only as Frank drove in the Perri car from Hamilton to Guelph, where they visited Mary, Domenic Scaroni's widow, paid their respects at the dead man's grave, and then had dinner before the Perris, Romano and Frank returned to Hamilton.

On Monday, Joe Scaroni told Mary he was going out to "get" the men who had killed Domenic and asked her if he could borrow a shotgun. Apparently she refused. Scaroni then took the train from Guelph to Hamilton, carrying the automatic he always had with him. He was met at the train station by Charlie Bordonaro, apparently driving the same Ford used in the shooting attempt on Sam Scaroni. Bordonaro then drove both Rocco Perri and Joe Scaroni to meet with A. R. Deconza in St Catharines. There Scaroni met a man named John Trott, whom Rocco would later publicly claim to be a close friend, and who was the last man to see Scaroni alive. Trott drove him to nearby Merritton and then to the bake shop owned by James D'Agostino, another close Perri associate.

On September 5th, the body of a man was spotted at the bottom of the Welland Canal by the skipper of the boat *Joyland*, who informed three men who were working on the bank. The body had been bound and was face down in the mud, weighed down by four large stones. It was Joe Scaroni.

On September 9th, William Connelly, chief constable at Brantford reported that Scaroni had been killed in Hamilton at the headquarters of a local Black Hand gang. Other members of the gang, Connelly said, were Frank Longo; Domenic Corde, an associate of Perri; and Joseph D'Agostino.

On September 11th, the OPP put Inspector Miller in charge of the case. The inquest was held the next evening in Welland City Hall in a room crowded with Italians from Welland, Brantford, Hamilton and Guelph.

Anna Scaroni, wife of the deceased, was the first witness. She was dressed in deep mourning but appeared to want to tell little to Crown Attorney H. D. Cowper.

"Had your husband any enemies?" Cowper asked.

"I didn't think he had any."

"Had he no bad friends?"

"I don't know."

She explained she had been afraid to let her husband go away ever since his brother Domenic had been murdered.

"Can you tell me anybody you are afraid of?" asked Cowper.

"My head thinks, but I can say no name," Anna Scaroni answered.

Rocco Perri was called and briefly explained that he had known Joe Scaroni for quite a few years and he did not know of any enemies he might have had. The verdict was the usual: "murder by person or persons unknown."

Inspector Miller continued to look for the killer until the end of October.*

Miller repeated the same frustration that had been voiced by Inspector Stringer on the Loria case: "The more we get into this case, the more proof we get of the great fear in the hearts of the Italians if they do any talking. Joe Scaroni ... was suspected of being one of a gang of thugs who

---

*An informant named Peter Orquin reported to Miller the case of a man named Frank Cici who worked for the Scaronis as a bootlegger and had been promised by the family that they would look after him if charged or jailed. Orquin said Cici was jailed for four months but "the Scaronis left him cold." "Frank Cici," of course, was an alias used by Tony Leale, and, according to the newspapers, Miller was one of the officers on that case. But there is no indication anywhere in Miller's reports on the Scaroni murder that he made any connection between the Leale and Scaroni killings. Miller reported on September 30th, almost four months after the murder of Leale, that he was trying to locate Cici in Toronto.

has been committing crimes all over the United States and Canada. There has not been a murder committed in Ontario in the last ten years among the Italians but that the name of Scaroni has been connected with it."

Miller discovered that Anna Scaroni had lived with Domenic Paproni before he was murdered and that it was Joe Scaroni who had killed him. Miller's report adds, "This woman, we are informed, has been living with six different men who have been murdered. She has been living in Guelph, Brantford, Welland, Montreal and different points in the United States. What connection, if any, this woman has had with the different crimes, we are at present unable to say."

The next day, in Guelph, the name of Don Simone of Niagara Falls surfaced. Miller did not give the source, but he reported that many people "strongly suspected" that Don Simone of Niagara Falls, New York, had ordered the killing of both Domenic and Sam Scaroni and that a man named Frank Cordino (Perri's man Corde) was also involved. Mike Romano, who had driven with Joe and Sam Scaroni and the Perris to Guelph "is also mentioned," Miller reported. In Guelph, they were also told that Mrs Sam Scaroni, the sister of both dead men, had said that she would tell all if she was given the chance.

Miller reported: "We frequently get the opinion that the Scaroni family are all doomed to be killed because of something they did years ago."

Two detectives questioned Mary Scaroni, Domenic's widow, and she told him that Joe had intended to meet with three men, "Deconza, John Trott and Simone." Mary told Miller that the Scaronis had had regular meetings with Don Simone in Welland.

On Monday, September 18th, Sam Scaroni and his wife, who had been winding up their affairs when Miller questioned them, fled from Brantford to California.

On October 5th, in Toronto, Miller was told that the man who killed Joe Scaroni may have been Joe Galliardo, the brother of Don Totto Galliardo, the bootlegger from Toronto's Ward. Joe Galliardo had left for New York the day after Scaroni's body was discovered. Miller also reported that Frank Molinaro, while he had received threatening letters from Black Hand extortionists, also used the name Delaurenza and was an associate of the Galliardo mob.

In October, Miller tried to locate the three Perri men who might have tied up the case. The first was Frank Cici, probably the dead Tony Leale, who had lived in the Ward at 18 Walton Street. The second was Charlie Bordonaro, who had driven Scaroni from Hamilton to St Catharines and who had left town soon afterwards. "This man has switched from bootlegging to selling narcotic drugs," Miller noted. The third man was John Trott, who was not at his Merritton farm. Miller reported that he was told the rugs found around Scaroni's body belonged to Trott, although the inspector was unable to obtain any evidence either that Trott had driven Scaroni or that the rugs belonged to him.

Even though there were good indications that Don Simone of Niagara Falls had ordered the murder of the Scaroni brothers, it seems that neither the police in Ontario nor the police in New York made any effort at conducting a joint investigation or setting up any system of intelligence sharing beyond Inspector William Stringer's flying visit to the American side in May. It is probable that Joe Scaroni was such a liability that Rocco and his men set him up and left him where the Sicilian American hit men could get him.

It is strange that neither Miller nor Stringer made an effort to question Rocco Perri about the murders, although it was clear that Perri had met with each of the Scaroni brothers shortly before their separate murders.

Miller concluded his file on the case with what could well have been Joe Scaroni's epitaph: "There is one thing evident — that Scaroni has been such a bad man himself, many think what happened was coming to him and there was little sympathy."

There is one footnote to the war, a series of bombings on Simcoe Street in Hamilton: one at the home of Vincenzo Napoli at 32 Simcoe in September and the second at the home of a poor Sicilian widow named Lombardo in October. The latter was probably aimed at Angelo Salvatore, the man stabbed by Jimmy Loria, who lived next door at 34 Simcoe.

After a third bombing at 33 Simcoe in March 1923, Hamilton police picked up four men for vagrancy in connection with the bombings. They were Charlie Bordonaro, described as a labourer; Joseph Restivo, a shoemaker and possibly the man named in the anonymous note addressed to the "most illustrious Mr Magistrate" as one of the last to have seen Jimmy Loria alive; Joe Scibetta of Buffalo; and William Pasquale of James Street North.* Bordonaro and Restivo both worked for Perri.

The bombings mark the end of the Niagara bootleg war, which appears to have been aimed mostly at the elimination of the Scaroni family and its allies. It was time for a new generation. Rocco Perri was thirty-five in 1922; the Scaroni brothers were in their late forties. The old feuds of the Scaronis had to end. They were bad for the lucrative business of running liquor across to the United States.

Rocco Perri's role in the deaths is shrouded in the secrecy that always surrounds mob bosses. He had met Joseph Celoni just before he was killed. He had met Domenic Scaroni on the afternoon of his death. Joe Scaroni had met with Rocco before setting out to avenge his brother. Rocco was always just around the corner when there was action, but never directly involved.

Rocco took over the Scaroni family business, and later he was able to say publicly that he controlled the bootlegging in Hamilton, Guelph and Brantford. He continued his business relationship with Joe Scrianni in Niagara Falls and by October 1923, Rocco Perri was doing a profitable business with Joe Sottile, who worked for Don Simone. Rocco may have switched sides at one point and set up the Scaronis for the Sicilians — but whatever role Rocco Perri played, he emerged from the war the winner.

---

*The Scibettas became one of the leading mob families in the Hamilton-Niagara region. Joseph's brother Santo was a "respected" mob figure in Hamilton from the 1950s to his death in 1985.

CHAPTER 6

SHOOTOUT AT ASHBRIDGE'S BAY

With the elimination of the Scaroni family, a measure of peace returned to Hamilton and the Niagara border region. Rocco and a few others were supplying the American side with quality Canadian liquor. Their methods were different now, though. Attorney General W. E. Raney had succeeded in getting the Liquor Transportation Act passed — in June 1922 — thus restricting export liquor cargos to one common carrier, the railways, and this had effectively deterred the transport of liquor by truck. Rocco and his competitors simply switched from trucks to boats and took longer trips, from Toronto or Hamilton to the American shore. Although both the Canadian Pacific and Grand Trunk railways officially refused cargos of booze for the United States, whole box-carsful were getting across the border disguised as hay and other products.

In January 1923 at Windsor County Court, Judge J. J. Coughlin declared the Liquor Transportation Act unconstitutional. In May the Court of Appeal upheld the ruling and Ontario's highways were once more open for the transportation of legal export liquor to the United States. Raney had lost.

Later, in May, the *Chicago Daily News* ran an investigative series on cross-border smuggling, claiming that one hundred thousand gallons of liquor were brought into the United States from Canada each day. Smugglers numbered in the "thousands," the *News* reported. Most of the booze came through Windsor-Detroit but it was reaching Chicago by other means as well.

Rocco Perri had connections with Chicago by 1923. In April, the Chicago Crime Commission had invented the term "Public Enemy" by issuing a list of "persons who are constantly in conflict with the law." Public Enemy no. 1 was Alphonse Capone, alias Scarface Al, alias Al Brown. Public Enemy no. 2 was Capone's aide and bodyguard, Tony ("Mops") Volpe. At the same time that he was working for Capone, U.S. Justice Department records show that Volpe was running a racket of his own, counterfeiting two-cent American postage stamps. The gang also ran off at least 94,000 bogus 1919 United States War Savings Certificate Stamps.

One of the men mixed up with Volpe in the counterfeit racket was Domenic Sacco, described as a "west-side saloon keeper."*

Rocco would later say that Domenic Sacco was his Chicago contact for booze and other matters — and Sacco's brother Nino was one of Rocco's bootlegging customers in Buffalo. Those Saccos were cousins of a young bootlegger in Niagara Falls, Ontario, Jimmy Sacco, then twenty-one, who worked for his father at the Fifth Street grocery and bakery. The father was an "export representative" for an Ontario brewery. The Niagara Falls Sacco family were closely allied to Rocco Perri. A younger brother, later called "Black Pete" Sacco, would also join the family business.

On June 23, 1923, Manitoba voted for the establishment of government liquor stores, ending prohibition on Ontario's western boundary — and two days later, an Ontario provincial election was held. Drury and Raney and the United Farmers of Ontario were swept from office by the Conservatives led

---

*Evidence at the counterfeiting trial in 1925 showed that the plot was hatched at Sacco's place at 841 South Halsted Street in Chicago during the spring of 1922 and put into operation in 1923 and 1924. Sacco had already served a year in Leavenworth in 1921 for an undisclosed offence. He was fighting deportation to Italy while counterfeiting the stamps. In the counterfeiting case, Sacco pleaded guilty and was sentenced to four months in the DeKalb County Jail.

by G. Howard Ferguson. The Tory leader's position on prohibition was so ambiguous that Raney called him "Mr. Facing-both-ways." In May, Ferguson had said that he would not compel anyone to "any particular line of thought." He promised that the OTA would be enforced in the spirit of its author, the late premier Sir James Whitney, "not in the spirit of fanaticism."

Soon after the election, information came to OPP headquarters in Toronto that one of the OTA officers in Hamilton was on the take. A "special operator" was transferred from Brockville to take over the Hamilton post. But it was soon apparent that the new man had also been corrupted. He was transferred to Stratford, where he would be under the watchful eye of Inspector Frank E. Elliot, one of two OTA inspectors in charge of liquor investigations in Ontario. One day the "special" confessed to Elliot that he had taken bribes from Rocco Perri and had deposited the money in a bank in Buffalo. Inspectors Elliot and Airey then took the man to Niagara Falls to close the account and get the cash. Back in Toronto, the two inspectors brought the man before Alfred Cuddy, who had become OPP deputy commissioner in May 1922, and the new attorney general, William Nickle, Conservative MPP for Kingston. Perri was not prosecuted. The unnamed "special" never formally gave the OPP the name of the man who paid the bribes.

Meanwhile, the United States was becoming determined to close its borders to booze. It began worldwide diplomatic pressure to stop the smuggling of liquor, approaching Great Britain, France and other European nations. But the biggest push was aimed at Canada. A special United States commission was formed to carry out the negotiations. The meeting would take place in Ottawa in November 1923.

As part of its preparation, the State Department requested confidential reports from the U.S. Customs Service on the state of smuggling along the Canadian border. James L. Gordon, special agent in charge at Buffalo, described the situation: "Row-boats, launches, scows, tugs and other vessels ...have been loaded with beers and liquors under Canadian

Customs supervision." Most clearances, he reported, were for the United States, but many of the small boats were cleared for Cuba. (In one famous case, a boat was recorded as having left for Cuba four times in one day.) Since Magistrate Gundy's decision had come down in August 1921, Gordon told Washington, smuggling "from the breweries and distilleries in Canada has reached *enormous proportions....*"

Three to five carloads of beer and ale a day were loaded into boats at Cobourg and Port Colborne. Vessels were clearing daily from Belleville, Port Stanley and Port Dover. Gordon also reported:

> It is also the practice of the Canadian Collectors of Customs at Port Stanley and Belleville (from which ports great quantities of beer, ale and whisky have been exported to the United States this summer) *to issue false clearance* papers under Government seal to such vessels as are required by law to make entry at United States ports. These clearances state that the vessels carry "No Cargo," whereas they are loaded with 600 to 1100 cases of intoxicating beverages, under the supervision of the very officials who issue, sign and seal the false documents....

It was Rocco Perri who was running much of this liquor from Belleville to Buffalo. On the evening of October 1, 1923, the *Hattie C.*, a gasoline launch with a small cabin, was loaded with Corby's whisky from a railroad boxcar at the Belleville cement dock. Along the shore of Lake Ontario the men spent time breaking open the crates of whisky and putting the bottles into sacks, two dozen bottles wrapped in straw in a total of 56 sacks. It was common, on longer bootleg journeys, whether in Ontario or the Maritime provinces, to load the contraband liquor into sacks. They took up half the space of crates, were easier to handle, and, if necessary, could be dumped overboard and later retrieved with a minimum of loss.

The *Hattie C.* showed up late on Friday, October 5th, at a marshy landfill site at the foot of Leslie Street in Toronto, near Ashbridge's Bay. Leslie Street ended in a series of tracks leading down to a jagged waterline with small inlets.

The *Hattie C.* had put her nose into one of the inlets and the crew were unloading the sacks of whisky and taking them to two Reo trucks, a Marmon and a Cadillac car.

At 12:30 A.M. on the morning of October 6th, the Toronto City Police Station on Pape Avenue received a call saying that two trucks and two cars had gone down to the foot of Leslie Street and "something was going on."

The desk sergeant dispatched a car with uniformed Patrol Sergeant William Kerr, uniformed Constable James A. Rooney and plainclothes constables William H. Mitchell and George Fraser. They were expecting rum runners, for the Ashbridge's Bay area was a prime unloading spot for those who illegally "reimported" booze that was then sold in the city.

Warned by the approaching lights of the police car, the rum runners scrambled for the bushes while the *Hattie C.* began to back into the dark waters of Lake Ontario. Constables Mitchell and Rooney jumped from the car to head the men off. Sergeant Kerr grabbed a man who was standing beside one of the trucks and handed him over to Constable Fraser. Kerr was running towards the other two constables when Fraser yelled, "Watch out for the boat."

Kerr turned and ran toward the water's edge, whistled at the boat through his fingertips and yelled to the crew to stop their engines. "Come in, we have you cornered." The boat was still pulling away towards the south shore of the narrow channel.

"Stop your engines or I will sink you!" yelled Kerr.

He drew his pistol, fired one shot in the air, then three rounds at the boat.

"Sink it," Kerr yelled.

The other policemen drew their guns and fired at the boat. A man ran out of the darkness, first shouting something in Italian and then in English, "Don't shoot — there are people on that boat."

The boat, its engine cut, drifted against the south shore of the bay and Mitchell leapt aboard, drawn gun in one hand and flashlight in the other. Entering the cabin, he saw two men supporting a third, who was wounded, while a fourth lay groaning on the deck. The wounded man was gasping for breath as he bled from a wound to the right side of the chest. Mitchell yelled to Fraser to call an ambulance. By the time Sergeant Kerr entered the cabin, the wounded man was on a bunk and an older man was looking after the man on the deck who had been hit in the jaw.

The ambulance had trouble reaching the *Hattie C.* and by the time it arrived, it was too late. The seriously wounded man, later identified as John Gogo, aged twenty-four, of Port Dalhousie, Ontario was officially listed as dying on the way to hospital — a single .32 calibre slug had pierced his heart and left lung. The other wounded man, shot in the jaw, was Gogo's uncle, James Gogo, thirty-four, of Toronto. He was taken to St Michael's hospital. The other two in the cabin were Sidney Gogo, fifty-four, of St Catharines, father of the dead man and Fred Van Winkle of Toronto, who said he was the cook on the boat.

Arrested on shore were men who gave their names as James and Michael (Mike) Romeo, Francesco (Frank) DiPietro, Frank Book and Francesco Serge, all of Hamilton, and Louie Corron of Toronto. They were taken to the Pape Avenue police station while some officers loaded their trucks with the whisky before driving them to the station.

Seven of the men appeared in police court on Saturday morning, charged with illegal transportation of liquor. All pleaded not guilty. Bail was set at $3,000 each except for Sidney Gogo. Defence lawyer W. B. Horkins pleaded with the magistrate E. C. Jones:

"Last night this man was locked up by the police and not even allowed to be with his son during his last moments. The boy was left to die alone. The mother and sister do not yet know of his untimely end; the uncle is wounded. Who is to tell them but the father?" asked defence lawyer W. B. Horkins.

"I shall allow him to go," said Jones. "He owns the boat. I will accept that as bail. Gogo you may go to St Catharines." The others were remanded in custody. Sidney Gogo, who seemed stunned, mumbled his thanks to Jones and left the court.

Horkins went on to say that the operation of the *Hattie C.* was within the law. He produced waybills showing that the whisky was meant for customers in Lewiston and Lockport, New York. The boat had had engine trouble, Horkins explained, and so arrangements had been made to transfer the whisky to rail for shipment to New York. The Crown didn't believe a word of it.

By Saturday afternoon, Bessie Perri had arrived to bail out Rocco, who had maintained from the moment of his arrest that his name was Francesco Serge (Mike Serge was one of Rocco's cousins). Bessie also claimed both the Marmon and the Cadillac that had been discovered at the water's edge, saying that both cars belonged to her. Meanwhile, Chief Coroner George W. Graham and Chief Crown Attorney, Eric Armour were examining the *Hattie C.* Of the eleven bullet holes that they found in the boat, eight had penetrated the hull and cabin. The question the newspapers were already asking was this: Are the police justified in using firearms in enforcing the Ontario Temperance Act? Graham and Armour decided that an inquest was needed.

On Monday, Toronto Police Chief S. J. Dickson issued a statement defending his men and saying that Sergeant Kerr had instructed his men to shoot to sink the boat. "There was no thought of injuring anyone," Dickson said. The police chief added that he had had the boat examined and tested on a trial run and that there was nothing wrong with the boat.

W. B. Horkins replied, "I have examined the boat, too. There is not a bullet hole in the thwart or stern. They are all in the hood of the cabin. The four men were fired upon like rats in the trap. They did not have a chance."

Eric Armour was now promising a "wide-open" inquiry, not only of police use of firearms but of the operations of bootleggers as well. He said that "Rocco Perri of Hamilton, the well-known Italian, whose two automobiles were found near the ship, will be summoned to tell why his cars were at the foot of Leslie Street."

At the inquest Armour put Sergeant Kerr, a sixteen-year veteran of the Toronto force, through a gruelling examination.

The Crown attorney read police regulations stating that revolvers were provided for police on night duty and were not to be used unless in defence of life or other emergency. Kerr admitted that his life was not in danger and that there had been no firing from the boat.

"Do you think this was an emergency that justified them being used?"

"For the purpose we used them for, I do — to prevent escape," Kerr replied.

Asked if he had considered whether he was firing high or if there was a possibility of a shot ricocheting, Kerr replied, "There was not much time to consider anything."

"Would you expect to sink a boat of that size with .32 calibre shots?"

"I think I would," was Kerr's response.

Coroner Graham drew from Kerr the admission that if men with liquor had been fleeing in a truck, he would not have used his gun except in defence of a life or to prevent a prisoner from escaping. Kerr said he had no instructions from senior officers in the· use of a firearm in case of a breach of the Ontario Temperance Act.

Armour concluded the questioning by saying that the *Hattie C.* could not have escaped from the narrow lagoon. Kerr replied that if the boat kept turning, because of the irregularity of the bank, it might have escaped.

Constable Mitchell followed Kerr and testified that he had fired on Fraser's orders, that he had heard the words, "Fire low and sink her." Mitchell said he fired three shots, Fraser four and Rooney five. Mitchell said he felt he was justified in using his firearms to prevent the rum runners from "going to beat it." He told Graham he felt justified in using his revolver to prevent an escape — "no matter what the charge."

Sidney Gogo testified that he owned the *Hattie C.* but had leased it to his son John for the summer to haul liquor. They had loaded whisky ordered from Consolidated Distilleries in Corbyville by A. Guyon of Lockport, New York: 100 cases were going to Lewiston and 110 cases were going to Lockport.

Gogo said that the *Hattie C.* had run into rough weather and had sprung a leak. (His story, of course, was aimed at proving there was no intentional reimportation of the whisky.) At Leslie Street, Gogo said, they were shifting the cargo so they could unload better. "The engine was at neutral — it was not in gear. We were just moving with the wind and we were about to move her around. Then the shots came."

"Why didn't you holler?" Armour asked.

"I did. I shouted we were all there, we were not trying to get away." Gogo said no one went to shut off the engine because bullets were flying all around. He also said that when the police came aboard, they paid no attention to his pleas for a doctor.

Horkins asked his client, "You were not trying to escape?"

"No, I knew we couldn't," Gogo replied.

H. Hartley Dewart, K.C., a shrewd lawyer and the former provincial Liberal leader, was representing the police. He tried to make Gogo admit that he had landed cargos of liquor at Whitby or Frenchman's Bay. Gogo emphatically denied it.

"I don't know that I've got to tell you," Gogo replied.

"And you were to take this load up the Niagara River? How were you to get it to Lewiston?"

"That's our lookout," Gogo said.

The next witness was Rocco Perri. It was the first time he had appeared as a witness in Toronto. Reporters and police had come to know that he controlled most of the bootlegging in southern Ontario, and the man who gave a phoney name on the night of John Gogo's death was news. Rocco told the inquest that he was a traveller for the Superior Macaroni Company.

"Do you know Mr Gogo?" Armour asked.

"No, never heard of him."

"What was your car doing there?"

Rocco said he had "accidently" run into his friend Frank DiPietro in downtown Toronto. DiPietro had asked him the way to the Woodbine race track. Perri said he then led DiPietro, who was driving a car, and two trucks to the foot of Leslie Street.

"When I seen that they were going to unload whisky, I wanted to go home," Rocco said. "Then the police came and started to shoot...I told them not to shoot — that there were people in the boat, and one policeman, he say, 'I don't care.' Then I hollered to the people in the boat to shut the engine off and come in or they would be killed. I don't know whether they could hear."

Rocco said the Cadillac was his and one truck belonged to the Romeos and the second to DiPietro.

"You drive trucks in your business," asked Dewart.

"Yes."

"Do you ever carry anything other than macaroni?"

Rocco grinned.

"A little liquor?" prompted Dewart.

"Can you prove it?" Rocco asked.

"No, I am expecting you to admit it."

A marine engineer testified that the engine of the *Hattie C.* was in good working order except for slight flooding. There was a possibility, he said, that the boat, with a four-and-a-half-foot draught, could strike the bottom of a shallow lagoon when loaded with more than two thousand bottles of whisky.

"Would a .32 calibre revolver sink it?" Armour asked.

"No."

Constables Fraser and Rooney both testified that they felt justified in firing at an escaping prisoner.

Outside the courtroom that day, Rocco met Sidney Gogo and promised that he would pay him compensation both for the loss of his son and for the loss of the *Hattie C.*

When the inquest resumed on October 23rd, Mike Romeo said he had received a call from Frank DiPietro, asking him to drive his Marmon* car to Toronto to take a

---

*Mike Romeo had driven the Marmon that was registered in Bessie Perri's name. Romeo considered it his car, however, and Bessie sold it to him for $1,400 in early 1926.

load of liquor to the Queenston, Ontario, border crossing. DiPietro assured him that the shipment would have the proper papers. Mike Romeo said that his cousin, James Romeo, who lived with him, and DiPietro had each driven trucks to Toronto where they had first met Tony Larro on Elm Street, then had gone to the landing site.

James Romeo gave much the same testimony. He drove his truck for the Levi Mattress Co., and DiPietro had asked him to come to Toronto to pick up a load. DiPietro had said the boss would pay them.

"Who's the boss?" Armour asked.

"I don't know," Romeo replied.

"Did DiPietro tell you who the boss was?"

"No."

Frank DiPietro testified that he also used his truck in deliveries for the Levi Mattress Co. The man who hired him was an Italian from Buffalo and Niagara Falls named Guyon. Guyon had come to DiPietro's house on Caroline Street in Hamilton at about 7:30 P.M. on the night of the shooting to take a couple of trucks and pick up some liquor in Toronto. DiPietro said that Guyon was a friend he had known for four or five years but this was the first time Guyon had asked him for such a favour.

"How did you find your way down there?"

"I met Rocco Perri and asked him to take me down."

"What was Perri doing in Toronto at that time?"

"I don't know."

"Can you give me any reason why he should be there?"

"No."

Fred Van Winkle testified that it was common for the *Hattie C.* to unload either just east of the Niagara River or further along the American shore of Lake Ontario. All the loads were dropped at night. Van Winkle repeated the story that the *Hattie C.* had been driven into a wharf in heavy weather and had sprung a leak, making it necessary to offload the whisky.

The final session came three days later on October 26th. Charles Tweedie, a meteorologist, was called to rebut the testimony about the storm. He said that there had been moderate winds along Lake Ontario that week. The final witness was Inspector Nat Guthrie, who commanded the number 3 station at Pape Avenue. He testified that he had carried out a test run of the *Hattie C.* loaded with the equivalent of the whisky cargo and had had no difficulty operating the boat. There were no leaks, apart from some dampness near the bullet holes, and no engine trouble.

Coroner Graham summed up by explaining the constitutional difference between federal criminal law and provincial law, the powers of police to arrest without a warrant on "reasonable and probable grounds" and the justified use of firearms under the Criminal Code. He also called for the jury to decide whether Toronto police were properly instructed in the use of firearms. Graham called Rocco's testimony "weird and wonderful." "He happened to be present at the opportune time to assist DiPietro and show him the way to the dump. I don't for a moment believe Perri is telling the truth. In fact, I think he is telling only a short portion of it."

The jury came back with the verdict that John Gogo had died from a shot fired by a police officer on duty apprehending men in breach of the OTA. The jury then added, "The OTA being a provincial law and its breach not a criminal offence, the jury find that the police officers, possibly not fully understanding their instructions in firearms, made use of them without justification."

Three days later, the attorney general, William Nickle, ordered Eric Armour to take the finding of the coroner's jury before the grand jury sitting for the fall assizes. On November 2nd, the grand jury returned a true bill charging Sergeant William Kerr and constables William Henry Mitchell, George Fraser and James Anthony Rooney with manslaughter. Bail was set at $3,000 each, in what the *Star* called a "spectacle unprecedented in the annals of criminal procedure." A private citizen, Robert J. Fleming, former mayor of Toronto and an ardent prohibitionist, put up the $12,000.

On November 3rd, Rocco Perri and the other men involved in the incident were arraigned on charges of unlawfully having liquor in a place other than a private dwelling house. This charge was added to the original count of illegal transport of liquor.

The trial of the bootleggers opened in November 14th before Magistrate E. C. Jones. The prosecutor was a young, up-and-coming lawyer, then assistant Crown attorney and later chief justice of the High Court of Ontario, J. C. McRuer. W. B. Horkins, who had represented the gang at the inquest, defended.

Evidence introduced at the trial showed that twenty-one out of twenty-four sample bottles from one sack contained nothing but dirty water. Although the bottles looked as if they had not been tampered with, a careful examination revealed that the seals had been carefully removed, the whisky had been taken out and replaced with water and the seals had then been replaced.

"The evidence shows that 210 dozen bottles left Corby's and 212 dozen bottles arrived," McRuer told the court.

After his case was closed, McRuer was permitted to introduce new evidence over strong objections from the defence. Hamilton OTA Inspector William McCready was called to describe a raid at Frank DiPietro's place at 12 Bay Street North. McCready said that he found 75 to 100 broken whisky cases under the verandah of DiPietro's home at 12 Bay Street North. He said the crates were all relatively new and all came from Corby's.

William Turnbull, secretary for Consolidated Distilleries in Montreal, was called, and he explained that the Montreal office had received two orders for whisky from "D. A. Goyon," which were then phoned to Corbyville. The books of the company indicated that while the shipping records showed that a boxcar of liquor was shipped by the Grand Trunk Railway to Belleville for shipment to Havana, Cuba, the $3,000 excise tax on the whisky had been paid and it was entered as for "home consumption."

"Why was that done?" McRuer asked.

Turnbull replied, "After that the *Hattie C.* could go anywhere." Which is, of course, what the documents carried by the *Hattie C.* showed. Lewiston is a long way from Havana. If anything it proved Gordon's report that most of the boats shipping from Belleville carried false papers.

Magistrate Jones delivered his verdict on November 21st. He found Sidney Gogo, owner of the boat, and Frank DiPietro, whose truck was half full of liquor, guilty of breaching the OTA and fined each $1,000 or three months. He dismissed the charges against Rocco Perri and the rest. Jones called the evidence of the witnesses "incredible." He found that there was no damage to the *Hattie C.*, calling the story of the leak "the merest pretence."

Jones went on to remark, "A search of the pockets, etc., of the prisoners and a careful search of the boat revealed no papers which indicate any lawful act of the defendants... and although substantial sums of money were found upon some defendants, there were no guns found; one of the defendants remarking, 'No we don't need guns in this business — all we need is lots of money.'"

Horkins immediately filed notice of appeal. In the meantime, Bessie Perri and a man named Charles Glasco acted as sureties for the men. The bail was now $1,000, equal to their fines.

The manslaughter trial of the four policemen began on November 5th. This time Sergeant Kerr denied that he had sworn he believed the men were bootleggers. "The men were acting in a suspicious manner in the dead of night. They might have been handling stolen goods." In his summation on November 23rd, Harley Dewart told the jury, "you have been called upon to try one of the most remarkable criminal cases that have been heard in this court. Never before have the lowest criminal elements in the community been raised to the dignity of Crown witnesses — men who are fattening upon the appetites of others whose sordid minds are bent on the acquisition of gain at the expense of the degradation of the body and soul and mind of the youth of our province."

Turning to the charge of manslaughter, Dewart said, "If they took reasonable precaution they are excused under the common law of England...

"Don't give comfort to the rum runners of this province with your verdict. The men of the Toronto force are known for uprightness, honesty and straightforward manliness and are a credit to the community."

The trial judge, Justice John Orde, said that a constable had no right to use firearms as a means of preventing escape from arrest merely for breach of a provincial act such as OTA.

Although the Saturday papers expected a quick verdict, they were wrong. By late afternoon, the jury was deadlocked. Asked by Justice Orde if further instructions were wanted the foreman replied no. Orde ordered a new trial at the January assizes.

The second trial went before a jury on February 9th, 1924. Again the jury disagreed. The next day Attorney General Nickle dropped the charges, preventing a third trial. Crown Attorney Armour said that the point had been made that police in Ontario were not justified in using firearms to enforce the OTA.

The question remains as to whether Rocco Perri had intended to land the liquor at Ashbridge's Bay, "reimporting" the whisky into Ontario. The truth is most likely somewhere in between the Crown's contention that the liquor was deliberately landed at Toronto, which was never really Rocco's bootlegging territory, and the defence's claim that the load was intended for Lewiston. The *Hattie C.* had dropped fifteen loads on the shores of New York state. It is likely that the boat did run into trouble and that Rocco, always an opportunist, made the best of the situation by unloading where he could, intending to sell the whisky where he could, either in Toronto or Hamilton.

There is one postscript to the death of John Gogo, contained in a later OPP report by Inspector John Miller. When Sidney Gogo arrived at 166 Bay Street South to claim the compensation that Rocco had promised, Bessie, the bookkeeper and keeper of the purse for Rocco Perri, told him to "go to hell."

CHAPTER 7

A SPRING FOR SCANDAL

On February 13, 1924, Hamilton licence inspectors William McCready, John Williamson and Milligan raided the Perri mansion at 166 Bay Street South. McCready had made sure that no one could tip off the Perris. He told no one, not even his men, where they were going. Rocco had a large, legal cellar supply of liquor. (When the appeal court had released the liquor seized from the Hess Street grocery in 1919, it was returned to Rocco's new mansion under the requirements of the OTA. But Licence Inspector Sturdy had marked each bottle so that Rocco could not resell it.) McCready and his men missed the booze in the hidden cellar. They left empty-handed. Of course, no charges were laid.

Bessie was at a doctor's appointment when the maid phoned and told her that four men were in the house, "breaking open the cupboards." Bessie returned home and called the cops, asking for Detective Joe Crocker. She then told Crocker, who had the reputation of being an honest cop, that the licence inspectors had stolen a roll of $2,000 from a bureau drawer. A few minutes after detectives Crocker and Chamberlain arrived at the mansion, Rocco showed up. He said he was the one who had taken the roll to "go shopping."

On March 13th, a month after the raid, the headlines reported accusations of major misconduct in the Hamilton police force. A lawyer named Charles Morgan filed a

$25,000 suit in the Supreme Court of Ontario against Chief William Whatley alleging "conspiracy and malicious procedure." Morgan filed a second suit against Whatley's brother-in-law Norman Nicholson and the firm of Nicholson Sales and Service, also for $25,000, on the grounds of "conspiracy, malicious procedure and slander."

Rumours swept Hamilton that Morgan was accusing Whatley of being on Rocco's payroll. Whatley had no comment. Morgan said he was taken against his will to the Hamilton insane asylum on January 25, 1923, because, according to the commitment papers, he was addicted to drugs. After several weeks he escaped. Morgan had arranged to take the place of a trusty who was being taken to a curling rink.

At the rink, Morgan threw the stone the length of the ice, then leapt through an open window and into the darkness. He hid at a friend's house while being examined by doctors and getting certificates of sanity, which he sent along with an affidavit to Attorney General Nickle.

After hiding for two weeks, Morgan went to the police. His father-in-law and wife were waiting in Jelfs' court to present evidence on his behalf. But Morgan was taken straight to the asylum in handcuffs and placed in the homicidal ward. He was accused by the doctor of not being able to control himself and showing it by running away. He was kept in solitary confinement for ten days before an order for his release came from Toronto.

By the following Wednesday, March 19th, more rumours were sweeping the city because of news dispatches from Toronto that Attorney General William Nickle had ordered Chief Provincial Inspector John A. Ayearst to investigate "certain information that has reached his department" from Hamilton.*

---

*Ayearst was himself a controversial figure. A Methodist minister who had volunteered to become a provincial licence inspector in 1916, he was cleared after the 1919 election of taking kickbacks. Then, in 1921, he was accused of using crooks to enforce the OTA and again cleared, this time by the Public Accounts Committee. But in June 1922, the new OPP deputy commissioner, Alfred Cuddy, was named to head the OTA, while Ayearst, who retained the title of chief provincial inspector, was assigned to special duty.

The Toronto *Globe* reported the next morning that the investigation had to do with the flotation of a company and the methods used to get purchasers of the stock. Ayearst "is endeavouring to determine if in return for purchases of stock, protection was promised the bootleggers," it added. That afternoon Cuddy visited Hamilton for a secret meeting with Magistrate Jelfs and the members of the Police Commission. The Hamilton police were indeed being investigated for lax enforcement of the OTA and "charges of an even graver kind."

On Friday, March 22nd, rumours of major corruption in the city police department were circulating. Two controllers called for an inquiry to clear the air. Jelfs, who was also chairman of the Police Commission, replied that unless formal charges were laid, there could not be an investigation. Hamilton Mayor Thomas W. Jutten issued a similar statement the next day.

Five days later, after Ayearst had made his report to Nickle, the attorney general sent a copy of it to the Hamilton Police Commission and virtually ordered the commission to investigate OTA enforcement by the Hamilton police. Jelfs, as chairman, announced that there would be a public meeting of the commission to investigate the charges. Then the magistrate stated emphatically that the commission would hear evidence — hearsay would not be accepted. Jelfs had seen Ayearst's report. "He came up here and reported on the rumours and on what he had heard. His report deals with nothing definite." But he admitted that a "local lawyer had specific charges."

At the Police Commission meeting on the evening of March 28th, Whatley said, "I would appreciate it greatly if this inquiry is held so that things may be brought to a head at once. A thorough investigation will put an end to these ugly rumours." Mayor Jutten said the witnesses would be Charles Nicholson; Sinclair Richardson, trustee of Nicholson Sales and Service; and G. Brown, the company secretary.

"We should have a man from the attorney general's department," Jutten said.

"They won't send one," Jelfs replied.

Nickle was perhaps passing the buck in a delicate situation.

It is also possible that he considered other cases more important. At the time numerous other investigations were going on: an inquiry into the collapse of the Home Bank and the related shady dealing by the former provincial treasurer, Peter Smith; a probe into the affairs of Ontario Hydro; and an investigation of lax law enforcement by the Kitchener police. All in all, it was a spring for scandal.

However, in the wake of calls for an independent inquiry by a judge, Jelfs thought it necessary to issue a statement. "The public seems to be of the opinion that I am taking the part of the chief in the affair. I have always found Chief Whatley upright in all his doings. He is the best chief of police Hamilton has ever had. I would be a coward if I did not stand by him when there is nothing to guarantee that I should not. I would be first to demand a show if there was sufficient reason."

What was going on? What were the rumours? The laws of libel prevented the newspapers from even hinting at them, which means that the papers themselves were having difficulty following them up. What can be said is that rumours alleged that there was a close relationship between Chief Whatley and Rocco Perri — just how close was not revealed at the time. It is difficult to substantiate these rumours. All records for the year 1924 from the attorney general's office, with the exception of the Home Bank collapse, disappeared a long time ago. It is interesting that that scandal-plagued year is the only year for which records are missing.

On Saturday, March 31st, Hamilton police raided six hotels, where the proprietors were asked to supply the police with bottles of their stock to ensure it was legally under the 2.2 percent limit. A police source told the *Spectator* that Whatley ordered the raids because the OTA officer had been lax in enforcing the act. "They could have acted months ago, no doubt, had they chosen," the source revealed. "Whenever Chief Whatley is given definite information he acts on it and not before." It was to be the chief's last official act.

By Monday morning, April 2nd, Whatley was reported to be sick. Dr James Simpson, Whatley's physician, said the chief was suffering from a bad attack of lumbago, which made it impossible for him to leave his home.

The commission investigation proceeded on the evening of April 3rd. The scheduled witnesses included Rocco Perri, Charles Morgan, Norman Nicholson, G. Brown, Sinclair Richardson, William Carroll (described as "a well-known tobacconist and sporting man") and James Lindsay.

"It is scarcely necessary to state the reason for the commissioners' meeting here tonight," Jelfs began. "It is common knowledge that there are certain hints and rumours about — well, I'll put it plainly — the chief of police. There are insinuations. I heard no definite charges and nothing to justify the step we are taking until I met the attorney general in Toronto. There I saw what we thought was a colored excuse and after seeing it, I quite agree with the attorney general that an investigation must be made. We are here to listen to any charges that anyone would like to make…. It is up to some person connected with the Nicholson firm to explain why certain others were in association with the firm. It didn't look good to me."

S. F. Washington, the former Crown attorney, rose to say that he was representing the Hamilton Police Department. "I understand it is that the police are charged with being lax in the OTA enforcement. Chief Whatley, I understand, is charged with some offence, but so far, I have been unenlightened. The chief is ill at present. He is so ill that I couldn't get an appointment with him, and hence, I have no instructions. I most decidedly object to the taking of evidence till the chief is able to be here. Let those brave men come forward and put their charges, if any, in writing, above their own names, with particulars and dates. All of these old women's fish tales are not right."

Charles Morgan flushed hotly and stepped towards the bench to tell Jelfs he had filed a statement with the commission on the advice of his solicitors. Beyond that, Morgan said, he had nothing to say.

"I've read over that statement and I have seen nothing

against the chief," said Jelfs. Commission member Judge Walter Evans said that no evidence could be taken in Whatley's absence but any charges should be recorded so the commission would know what it was investigating and so Whatley could respond.

"It seems to me the chief should be here," said Mayor Jutten. "British fair play demands nothing less."

Jelfs called again for anyone with information to come forward. No one did. Washington turned to Morgan. "We might get Morgan to act as an accuser. You've made no accusation against the chief of the force. There is nothing but idle gossip."

"My statement is filed in writing," Morgan said, then turned on his heel and left.

After he adjourned the hearing until April 17th, Jelfs told reporters that Morgan's statement accused members of Nicholson Sales and Service of selling shares to bootleggers or inducing others to part with shares to bootleggers. The allegation that Whatley was connected with the company through his brother-in-law, Norman Nicholson, was sufficient to warrant the probe. There are no indications from the newspapers that Rocco, summoned to attend, was actually present.

Nine days later, on Saturday, April 12th, Whatley was reported to be in critical condition with pneumonia. Mrs Whatley told a detective to get the chief's papers and documents from the vault and bring them to her. He died at his home, officially of pleuro-pneumonia, at 4:15 that afternoon. He was forty-six. His physician had apparently given up all hope and summoned Detective Joe Cocker. Both men were at Whatley's side when he died. Mrs Whatley was not present.

There was nothing in Whatley's character to find fault with, Jelfs said. Only Dr Simpson mentioned the rumours, saying, "All through the last days he kept reiterating the determination to get better to be able to attend the investigation. It was his one thought."

Whatley was buried with full police honours on Tuesday,

April 15, 1924. All available members of the local police marched at the head of the funeral procession. Behind the casket marched a platoon of firefighters. Honourary pall-bearers included Judges J.G. Gauld, Walter T. Evans., C.G. Snider, Magistrate Jelfs and his deputy. Police chiefs and officials attended from as far away as Montreal. Police forces from across Canada sent their condolences.

On April 16th, the Police Commission met and resolved: "It would be inexpedient to continue the investigation, until some formal charges against the police department or some present member is laid before it."

On April 30th, David Coulter, the deputy chief of police, who had joined the force in 1878 and had been a Hamilton policeman for forty-six years, was named to succeed Whatley.

On May 25th, Whatley's will was made public. He had left two pieces of land, his house and his personal property to his wife, Annie. The properties, worth $18,000, were mortgaged to $15,501.34. But the remaining $2,498.66 was wiped out because Whatley had given an $8,000 to $10,000 guarantee "to a relative in a business deal." The family had to ask for help from the Police Benevolent Fund and the city.

The rumours continued long after Whatley's death. In August 1926, the OPP used a Pinkerton detective of Italian descent to penetrate the Perri gang. He filed a report based on a conversation with a female bootlegger, Mildred Cooney Sterling:

> Not so long ago we had here in Hamilton a Chief of Police named Whatley who died of a broken heart because he was continually being criticized by the press for being entirely too friendly with the bootleggers. Why it was not anything to see Chief Whatley and his wife in Rocco Perri's car with his wife going through the main drives. I remember very well on one occasion when Perri stopped at a gas station with his car and Perri made an effort to pay for the gas and Chief Whatley interfered and said to the man at the station, "Never mind, just charge that to me." That expense was put on the books and paid by the people of Hamilton instead of Whatley. Why it is a joke for the authorities to try and ride

Perri. He really can tie up every business man in Hamilton. He has it on all the big guys in this town. No one would ever dare to go against Rocco Perri. He is entirely too powerful. He could break the biggest majority of these fellows in Hamilton....However, Perri is not the mastermind; it is his wife Bessie. She is the brains of the whole works, and she is Jewish. If it was not for Bessie he would be done long ago and wouldn't have anything, because Perri loses his big times. If the big fellows wanted to ruin Perri they could do it very quickly but they are afraid to open up because Perri has too much on them. Chief Whatley was presented with a new Studebaker car and it was only one of the many gifts that Perri gave away, not counting the shut-up-money.

In late 1930, the Toronto scandal sheet, *Hush,* alleged that Bessie was paying off Whatley. Although *Hush* was not exactly a reliable journal, its report at least seems to fit the events:

A reformed member of the Hamilton underworld told Hush part of the ugly story not long ago....Whatley had a terrible greed for gain, he got a young lawyer [i.e., Morgan] to sell some bonds for him in an auto accessory sales and service company on a 20% commission. The young lawyer sold $25,000 worth of bond to bootleggers and handbook men [bookies] who wanted protection, at the chief's suggestion! When it came to settling with the lawyer-salesman, Whatley balked badly. The lawyer threatened to sue the big thief but the chief had him arrested and put in the asylum. The lawyer broke away from custody and hastened to Attorney General Nickle who had asked the Hamilton police commission to look into it.

Magistrate Jelfs, who it is said had the wool pulled over his eyes by Whatley, asked for anyone to come forward who had a complaint to make. Not one of the bond holders in the auto sales company, now defunct, would come forward for obvious reaons, so the matter dropped. But the young lawyer was not satisfied. A provincial officer set a trap for Whatley. He rented a room overlooking the back of the Perri residence and then called up Whatley and arranged to raid the Rocco residence in the afternoon. Whatley, fearful that Bessie would get into a jam, raced up to the Rocco residence in the morning in the police car. A load of liquor had just been delivered and the report is the provincial officer photographed Whatley helping to remove some of the contraband into the police car.

Armed with this picture, they returned to Attorney General Nickle, who immediately ordered a royal commission or judicial inquiry. With this last picture (which he may have known nothing about) facing him and the Bessie photograph of him sitting drinking between two convicts in her house, Whatley was tipped off, the game was up. It is said he shot himself and the person who was called to the house to take the gun away was given $50 by some of the late chief's kind friends to keep his mouth shut. The whole tragedy was hushed up. The newspapers which suggested he died from pneumonia and his old friend, S. F. Washington who worked with him in the courts as Crown Attorney made a touching beautiful allusion to his career and sterling qualities of character! The Attorney General's department was satisfied and the affair ended, much to the relief of those high placed blackguards who brought Whatley to Hamilton and who were so anxious to hide the terrible end of a cowardly villain whom they had used for their own dirty schemes in Hamilton's subterranean life.

It is likely that Mildred Sterling's account comes closer to the truth than the article from *Hush.*

The *Hush* story is sensational and the time sequence it is based on is clearly incorrect. Perhaps Rocco and Bessie did have something on Whatley and tried to take advantage of a situation they thought would increase their influence over the police. Whether they actually succeeded or not is an open question.

In late May Rocco went to New York City and Newark on business. By 1924, the bootlegging business in New York had been consolidated under Rocco's fellow Calabrian, Frank Costello, and Costello's ally, rum runner Big Bill Dwyer. The man behind Costello was gambler Arnold Rothstein, who bankrolled "Rum Row," where ship's cargos of liquor were transferred to small boats off Long Island and New Jersey. Rothstein was also using the rumboats to smuggle diamonds and drugs into New York. It was Dwyer and Costello who had discovered the potential of the islands of St Pierre and Miquelon off Newfoundland in 1921 and turned them into a warehouse for illicit liquor to be imported into the United States. The main supplier to St Pierre in those early days was Canadian Industrial Alcohol of Montreal.

Rocco Perri, of course, had a piece of that business. He had been sending booze to New York via the Niagara back door for almost four years. He probably had a lot of business to discuss with men like Costello and Rothstein.

On the evening of May 28th, Bessie was at home waiting for a phone call from Rocco. The call came at about 1:00 A.M. on the 29th. As Rocco and Bessie discussed their New York business, shooting began outside the mansion. Rocco told Bessie to make sure all the jewels and valuables were in the safe and hung up.

Outside, the police were hunting a desperate gunman who had apparently been bent on breaking into the Perri mansion in Rocco's absence. He was thirty-five-year-old Jack Larenchuk, a Ukrainian bootlegger, gambler, safecracker and strong-arm robber.

The chase had begun at about 1:15 A.M. when off-duty motorcycle constable Joe Rolfe stopped to talk to Constable Ernest Barrett. They spotted a McLaughlin car coming down Hess Street. Rolfe thought it was a car he had been suspicious of earlier in the evening. They watched as it paused for a minute at the corner of Bay Street and then turned north. The two constables jumped into Rolfe's 1913 Ford and went around the block, hoping to intercept the suspicious vehicle. They arrived in time to see two men get out at a vacant lot behind the Perri mansion and vanish into the darkness. The McLaughlin then drove off. The officers sped to the lot where Barrett spotted not two but three men with guns emerging from an alley. Barrett drew his gun and yelled at the men to stop. The three gunmen increased their speed and Barrett fired. Two doubled back the way they had come, while a third seemed to stumble before disappearing into the darkness. Reinforcements arrived, but a search for the three proved fruitless. Barrett had been so excited he had forgotten to note the licence plate number of the McLaughlin. At 2:00 A.M., the search was called off.

Shortly afterwards, the police got a call from a widow, Mrs McCallum, who lived at 156 Robinson Street with her two young daughters. A man was crouching under her back verandah. Constable Barrett arrived on the scene and walked into the back yard. He shone his flashlight at the verandah to reveal a dark figure who was pointing a gun right at Barrett's head. Barrett left in a hurry, yelling out the suspect's location.

Another motorcycle officer, Constable Douglas McGregor, was waiting in the next yard. Upon hearing Barrett's cry, he climbed to the top of the fence, separating the two yards, perched on a vine and leaned over. "Stick 'em up," he yelled, shining his flashlight on the man under the porch.

At that moment, the vine broke. As he fell, McGregor fired three shots in the direction of the porch. Flat on the ground, he was about to boost himself back up when the man fired three shots through the fence.

Meanwhile, Barrett, who had reloaded, and Constable Herb Whittun were behind the fence in the opposite yard. Other officers had made their way around the yard and a fusillade of shots answered the man's firing. Then all was quiet. Duty Detective Joe Chamberlain told his men to sit back and wait until daylight.

As dawn broke, Sergeant Bert Thompson entered the yard and found that the man was dead, his head lying across a box. A bullet had entered his left cheek and exited at the right temple. None of the cops knew the man, although he looked familiar — he was "a foreigner" of dark complexion with a small moustache. He matched the description of one of three men wanted in connection with a series of recent armed muggings. There was no identification on the body and all labels had been cut off his clothing. Joe Crocker was put in charge of the investigation.

The next afternoon, William Pinch, the local finger-print expert, made a positive identification of the body. It was Jack Larenchuk, who had been active in bootlegging but not very successful, probably because of the competition from the larger Italian and Jewish mobs. His Ukrainian gang had then turned to robbery and mugging, and Larenchuk was suspected of being the cracksman in the $1,000 robbery of a Hamilton bakery.

Bessie Perri told reporters, and police had reason to agree with her, that Larenchuk knew from underworld sources that Rocco was out of town and was taking a chance to get 2,000 bottles of legal cellar stock that Rocco had stored in the basement of the Bay Street mansion. Larenchuk, it turned out, was also suspected of several other cellar-stock robberies.

The inquest into the death of Louis ("Jack") Larenchuk on June 3rd showed that he was already dying from loss of blood from Barrett's first shot when he had fired at the cops in the backyard of the McCallum home. The jury congratulated the police on their handling of the case. The *Spectator* gleefully headlined the story: "DEAD FOREIGNER GOT HIS DESERT."

On June 6, 1924, Canada and the United States signed the "Convention to Suppress Smuggling." It was one of the first treaties that Canada had signed independently of Great Britain. In the negotiations, Canada had stood up to American demands that bootlegging and narcotics trafficking be made extraditable offences. International law was on Canada's side: to be extraditable a crime has to be an offence in both countries, and exporting liquor to the United States was perfectly legal in Canada. However, Canada's treaty negotiations were not likely based only on principle. Prime Minister Mackenzie King was reluctant to see some of Canada's leading citizens hauled into American courts.

The negotiations had dragged on from November 1923 until April 1924, when farsighted bureaucrats made a deal. State Department files reveal that Canada proposed to go along with an extradition agreement on drug trafficking if the United States would drop the demand for extradition of bootleggers. The State Department agreed.

The Hughes-Lapointe treaty, named after Secretary of State Charles Evans Hughes and Mackenzie King's Quebec lieutenant, Justice Minister Ernest Lapointe, called on Canada to inform the United States of all vessels going south of the border and carrying clearances for dutiable goods (including liquor) and in cases of suspected smuggling. Canada also agreed to deny clearance to any vessel too small for the length of the proposed voyage. Violations of narcotics laws became extraditable offences for the first time.

Equally important for the mob, regulations under the treaty called for the exchange of intelligence information on anyone suspected of smuggling or trafficking in narcotics. The treaty would come into effect ten days after instruments of ratification were exchanged.

The smugglers soon found a way around the treaty. They would simply sail to a port other than the one listed on the B-13, thus negating the value of Canadian customs officers informing their American counterparts of the impending arrival of a load of liquor.

During that summer of 1924, it was common knowledge that the Conservative government of G. Howard Ferguson was contemplating a third referendum on the Ontario Temperance Act. But "Foxie Fergie," as the premier was called, was biding his time, well aware that a wrong move could wreck the Tories' chances of staying in office. At the mere rumour, however, A. H. Lyle, secretary of the Hamilton Temperance Federation, promised vigorous opposition to any vote.

KING OF THE BOOTLEGGERS

In late July 1924, more rumours of corruption began to circulate in Hamilton. The *Spectator* ran a strange front page item, headlined "CONSPIRACY LINKED UP WITH BLACKMAIL":

> For some time stories have been in circulation reflecting in a serious manner on certain officials of the provincial government and also on others prominently connected with the present administration. These stories are not unknown to the attorney-general's department. It is believed they are part of a deep-laid and cunning conspiracy to aid the bootleggers' cause.
>
> "The bootlegger must live!" That is the slogan that has been sent forth and any influence that falls foul of it must be killed. It is a notorious fact, and admitted by the authorities, that Hamilton is the center of the cleverest bootlegging organization that can be found in the province. Desperate, unprincipled men with plenty of means and who will stop at nothing are at the head of it....

There was no further reporting on this subject in the paper. Rocco would certainly have been flattered to be told he was running the "cleverest bootlegging organization" in the province. Of course, the story may also have contained veiled references to the rumours surrounding the Whatley case. It is all the more intriguing because Attorney General

William Nickle's missing records from 1924 might have revealed just what the *Spectator* was hinting at.

It was at about this time that Hamilton's new police chief, David Coulter, appointed Ernest K. Goodman, the first Hamilton detective to investigate the Perris back in 1917, Inspector and Chief of Detectives. One of Goodman's first acts was to modernize and improve the previously rather ad hoc record keeping in the Hamilton detective department.

On September 6th, Rocco's men were unloading a shipment of Gooderham's whisky on Burlington Street on the Hamilton waterfront while Rocco watched nearby, his standard operating procedure. The unloading was interrupted by the beat cop, Constable James Pickup, who noticed two Ford trucks backed up to a boathouse. He saw three men loitering nearby, watched for a moment and then followed them into the boathouse. There he saw two trucks being loaded with whisky. Pickup left the scene to turn in the alarm.

But Rocco Perri beat Pickup to the punch. As Chief Coulter would later relate, Rocco called the police to report that whisky was being unloaded at the boathouse. The patrol wagon was already setting out by the time the constable got through to headquarters.

On their arrival, the police found the boathouse was piled to the ceiling with cases of whisky and gin. They estimated the total haul at $5,000. The owner of the truck and the boathouse, Edward Fowell, was uncommunicative before Magistrate Jelfs. He refused to say whether the liquor belonged to him or where it came from. Jelfs gave him the maximum fine, $1,000. Coulter could give no reason why Rocco called the station to report the whisky, but Rocco sometimes took a childish pleasure in playing such tricks. He knew the booze was lost anyway and probably got a kick out of calling in the tip.

On September 10th, OTA Inspector McCready stopped a Chambers touring car in Hamilton. In its trunk were found five one-gallon cans of alcohol. The occupants, John Rosse of St Catharines and Andreas Cantanzaret were charged with illegal possession and transportation of liquor. Cantanzaret secured $1,000 bail within an hour or so, but Rosse remained in the cells until he appeared in police court the next morning. Charles W. Bell appeared to represent him, bail was set at $1,000 and Bessie Perri was on hand to sign the bond. Rocco, also in court that morning, watched.

"Foxie Fergie's" OTA referendum of October 23rd drew a heavy turnout throughout the province. There were two innovations: the appointment of the first women returning officers and women scrutineers in the province and, in Hamilton, the live broadcast of returns after the polls closed on the new medium of radio on station CHCS. That morning, A. H. Lyle, secretary of the Hamilton Temperance Federation, was claiming that the opposition was attempting to stuff the ballot boxes. The Moderation League denied the charges, noting that they expected to win in downtown Hamilton but lose the suburbs.

The drys won, but by the narrowest margin yet across the province, 36,682 votes. In Hamilton the wets won by 13,773 votes: 283 out of 343 polls were wet. Premier Ferguson accepted the vote and announced that from then on, the Temperance Act would be strictly enforced. Ferguson told reporters that if necessary, the OTA would be amended to ensure that bootleggers had no option of a fine but went directly to jail. Those statements, it was reported, brought rumblings of revolt from within the Conservative party.

In early September, Inspector Goodman's new record system had revealed that thirty-five people had been reported missing in Hamilton during August. Of that number, twelve were still missing. One of them was Joe Boitowicz, who was reported to have left his home on August 7th to go to the races. His worried wife had spent days at the police station, claiming that her husband had met with foul play and that he had been threatened by bootleggers.

On Monday, October 27th, Fred Genesee, a Hamilton taxi driver, disappeared. On the afternoon of Saturday, November 6th, a group of Boy Scouts decided to search the

Hamilton mountain for the missing man. Instead they found a group from a Sunday school class and decided to play war. During the game, an eleven-year-old boy spotted a man's arm under a bush. The Sunday school teacher called the police. The body was badly decomposed, but was identified as that of Joe Boitowicz. The police found a racing form on the body and decided that it had been the July 31st race that Boitowicz attended before he died.

A grief-stricken Mrs Boitowicz told the *Spectator* that "a local foreigner, well known to police," was behind her husband's death. She said the gang had sent a man to the house to tell her husband that he would be "got" for squealing. Her husband "never told on anyone," the widow said. She said she had insisted to the police that the man was behind the murder, but they didn't believe her.

Inspector Edward Hammond of the OPP's Criminal Investigation Branch came from Toronto to take charge of the investigation. At noon on November 15th, he received a phone call from Crown Attorney George Ballard. Another body had been found on the Hamilton mountain, this time near Stoney Creek. It was the body of the missing taxi driver, Fred Genesee.

Hammond arrived at the scene, accompanied by Wentworth County Police Chief James Clark. Genesee was lying on his back with rope wound tightly around his neck. The autopsy showed that he had been hit on the right side of the head with a hard instrument, and then strangled. The body was later dragged to where it had been found.

Genesee, Hammond wrote in his report, "is an Italian well known in Hamilton and considered by the police one of the best in that community that they know of and the last one to think of being murdered by his compatriots." Hammond ruled out robbery; Genesee's change box was found intact with $12.30 in change. The inspector noted the similarities between the Boitiwicz and Genesee cases — both bodies dumped on the mountain — and the unusual way in which Genesee had been killed: most mob murders were stabbings or shootings.

The next day inspectors Hammond and Goodman learned from Genesee's wife that he had been carrying $200 in cash for a mortgage payment when he disappeared.

Unlike the gang war in 1922, these two murders got the attention and captured the imagination of editors at both the Toronto *Star* and the *Globe*. Gang murders were hot news. Dion O'Banion had just been murdered in Chicago. The *Globe* had its own theory. While not ruling out "vindictive bootleggers," it pointed to an "analogy between these two crimes and the three or four flaming crosses which burned along the edge of the escarpment." The *Globe* had been investigating the infiltration of the Ku Klux Klan into Canada and it knew that in Hamilton, two men were vying for the leadership of the Klan. The newspaper speculated that the Klan's anti-foreign sentiment could be behind the murders. (But in Toronto, the new commissioner of the OPP, General Victor Williams, would later say that the Ku Klux Klan had nothing to do with the murders.)

While all this was going on, Rocco Perri was in Welland attending the murder trial of John Trott, the last man to have seen Joe Scaroni alive in 1922. Trott was charged with the murder of Police Chief Joseph Truman of Merritton on the evening of December 17, 1922. While Trott was in the prisoner's box, Rocco Perri sat behind defence counsel W. M. German of Welland (the lawyer who had defended Domenic Paproni in 1918) and consulted with him frequently.

Truman had been zealous in his enforcement of the OTA and had received calls threatening his life. Early on the morning of December 17th, in a blizzard, he was at the railway station in Merritton. A figure had come out of the snow and Truman left the station to ask the man what he was doing. There were three shots, one from Truman's .38. Truman was killed by two shots from a .32. It was impossible to trace the killer's tracks in the blowing snow.

OPP Inspector William Stringer had spent eighteen months tracing the murder weapon to South Porcupine in northern Ontario. Trott was arrested soon afterwards in Niagara Falls, New York. Ballistic evidence confirmed that the .32 was the murder weapon, but the rest of the evidence was circumstantial. On November 14th the case ended with a hung jury.

For the *Star* the Hamilton murders called for implementation of the platoon system, invented by publisher Joe Atkinson and executed by city editor Harry Hindmarsh. A flying squad of reporters and photographers was on call twenty-four hours. Every available reporter was sent in to get every possible angle on the story. The flurry resulted in two stories in the Monday, November 17th edition of the paper. The first, "Mountain of Murders," made the connection between three bodies found recently on the mountain: a missing child discovered in August and the two more recent killings:

> Hamilton mountain has become a place of skulls, a mountain of human sacrifice. It is like one of the stone pyramids on which the blood thirsty Aztec priests cut the throats of innumerable victims....

The second piece in the *Star* was less florid and put the blame on one man in a story that today would not pass the eagle eye of a libel lawyer. It was reported that the police now believed that both Genesee and Boitowicz were killed by the same gang of bootleggers. The story was based on the statements of Mrs Boitowicz and interviews with police sources:

> The opinion is shared here that the gang responsible for the death of Baytoizae [Boitowicz] and Genesee also murdered Joe Basile,* a former Hamiltonian, who was shot on the streets of Buffalo some months ago.
> Basile, who was alleged to have been at enmity with a well-known Hamilton ring of bootleggers and highgraders was a friend of Genesee and Baytoizae. From another source it was

---

*Joe Basile, a Hamilton and Timmins bootlegger, was shot on a Buffalo street corner in May 1924. The murder was connected with a fued which had begun in 1914 in Lockport, New York.

learned that the police have a very good idea as to the identity of the men who committed the crimes but are unable at present to fasten the evidence on the trio....

Not alone are foreigners loath to discuss the case, but Hamiltonians in general have no desire to say anything that might result in the wrath of the gang falling on them....

There is no doubt that there is a powerfully organized gang of bootleggers operating from Hamilton. One of the outstanding temperance officials who took a promient part in the recent plebiscite campaign told *The Star:* "It is no exaggeration to say that the king of the bootleggers in the province lives in Hamilton...."

"He is an Italian," said this official. "A few years ago he was only an ordinary fruit seller, pushing a cart of vegetables and fruit through the streets; now he has his motor cars and lives in luxury.

In most of the big mix-ups where the provincial police have confiscated liquor or where there have been shooting affrays, this Hamilton man has been close at hand. At the time of the Gogo shooting incident in the Toronto Bay, when the younger Gogo was killed, this Italian was waiting on shore in his high-powered car, but, unfortunately there was no evidence to connect him beyond doubt with the whole incident. The police were balked again and again and it came from very good authority that high police officials would give a thousand dollars to obtain tips to the bootlegger king's arrest on an adequate charge...."

During the Hamilton plebiscite campaign a clever rumor was circulated that the King of the Bootleggers had contributed $40,000 towards the temperance cause. This helped to disarm some of his enemies and help the dry cause, which, he naturally wished to see win. "As a matter of fact," said this temperance worker, "he didn't contribute a cent, for we knew where every dollar came from.

But the police know their man too well to be misled. Every time a specially good tip comes of some big bootlegging activity, the police, when they arrive, almost invariably find the King of the Bootleggers at the threatened spot in time to prevent arrests and confiscations."

The story had no byline but it was written by a young *Star* reproter by the name of David Rogers. His source was A. H. Lyle, the Hamilton Temperance Federation secretary. Rogers spoke to Inspector Goodman, who said that there

was no evidence that Genesee was connected to bootlegging, though Boitowicz had some connection. Goodman
found no significance in the fact that the bodies were found
close together. Goodman also said there was no evidence
that Hamilton had been used as a headquarters for
bootleggers.

Dave Rogers was twenty-three years old, from Amherst,
Nova Scotia, a graduate of Acadia University and the
Columbia University School of Journalism in New York. The
Toronto *Star* had offered him a job upon graduation and he
worked the court and legislature beats but was at his best, at
this time, in crime writing.

Rogers told city editor Harry Hindmarsh that he was
trying to get an interview with Rocco Perri. He phoned
Rocco and told him that A. H. Lyle said he was the biggest
bootlegger in Ontario — and could he have an interview? To
his surprise, Rocco agreed and Rogers called at 166 Bay
Street South in the early evening of November 18th.

Rogers began the interview with the sharp question,
"Who killed Joe Baytoizae [Boitowicz] and Fred Genesee?"

Rocco Perri, self-styled "king of the bootleggers," suave,
immaculate and unperturbed leaned far back into the luxurious
cushions of the chesterfield. There was a quick flash of sparkling,
white teeth; black eyes shone with sudden amusement; a
carefully groomed pair of shoulders rose slowly in a gesture of
perfect Italian indifference and then he spoke: "Who knows?"
he said with apparent puzzlement and then looked smilingly
across at his charming Italian wife. "Rocco Perri did it, I
suppose. Everything that happens they blame on Rocco Perri.
Why is it? Maybe because my name is so easy to say; I don't
know, it is amusing." His wife joined him in the soft laugh which
succeeded.

"It has been said that those two men met death at the hands
of an Italian bootlegging ring," The Star persisted. "You are the
recognized leader of the Italian population of Hamilton. Have
you not some theory to advance in respect to such an extraordinary sequence of murders?"

Signor Perri's face took on a more serious expression. "How
came these two men to be killed?" He repeated. "I know not,
but from what I have heard and from what I have read, I would

say that Joe Baytoizae was put out of the way because he was a squealer. He was a Polack. I have been told that he was a stool pigeon. There was a case some time ago in which he helped the police. There may have been others. He has paid the price. That's what I think, but I don't know."

"And Fred Genesee?"

"Fred Genesee, yes, but I do not known him. Maybe I have seen him. I don't remember. But he was not a bootlegger, I don't think. I have not heard that he was. Why was he killed? I don't know, but I think there was a woman in the case. I think it was spite."

The voice of Mrs Perri slipped naturally into the conversation. "Ah, yes, a woman, there must have been a woman. It would not be the first time that a man went to his death because of a woman, nor will it be the last."

"There is a report that Baytoizae and Genesee were killed in connection with a bootleg war," The Star suggested.

Mrs Perri was again the interlocutor. "Bootleg war, that is funny." She reached toward her silent husband and patted him easily on the back. "You tell them, Rocco, that there is no war. You are the king of the bootleggers. That is what they say. You should know."

Mr Perri was quick to respond. "There is no bootleg war," he declared with abrupt emphasis. "Next they will be saying it is the Blackhand or the Vendetta."

He was asked to differentiate between the latter two terms. "The Blackhand — that is to put away man if demands for money are not met. The Vendetta — that is to kill a man for revenge."

From across the richly furnished parlor of the Perri home at 166 Bay Street South, one of Hamilton's finest residential sections, came the soothing symphony orchestra. "It is New York," Mrs Perri explained stepping lightly toward an elaborate radio cabinet. "You would like something else, perhaps? But no, you are here to talk, and you must not be interrupted."

The conversation turned naturally toward the general subject of bootlegging. "Yes, they call me the King of the Bootleggers," Mr Perri admitted with absolute candor. "The uncrowned king," he added with a laugh.

"Now the OTA has been defeated [sic — probably misprint in original], you are doubtless greatly pleased?"

"No, no. I am just the opposite from pleased," he replied. "I am sorry that the OTA was not put away. With government control in it would be far better."

"Then it is not true that you contributed $30,000 to the cause of the drys?"

"Oh, it is a laugh," Mrs Perri put in. "Rocco helping them with the OTA. No, no, he was sick in bed all day when they voted and when I told him that it was to remain dry, he was sorry."

"You mean that you could do as well under government control as you do now?"

Signor Perri placed the palms of his painstakingly manicured hands together as if to lend weight to what he was about to say. "Better," he ruled without hesitation. "I say that my business would not be harmed. Look at Quebec, look at the other provinces. It would be better all around. There would be less crime."

"Why?"

"Because there would be no moonshine, because there would be no stools. Now what have you? Many hundreds of cheap bootleggers selling poison liquor. That is bad. It drives men crazy. They commit crimes. It kills them. And besides there is so much cut-throat competition. The little bootleggers, they try to get protection by telling on each other. You have them in your Ward, hundreds of them, Jews. They have no principles, they will sell anything, they will do anything to get the business of their competitor. That makes more crime.

"There are the boys and girls to be considered. Under the OTA they visit the dives because they think it is clever and smart. But how many of them would enter the authorized stores under a system of government control?"

Mrs Perri was playing idly with the glistening black knobs of the radio. She turned quickly when she heard the word "principles."

"You have heard that there is honour among thieves," she said soberly, "but maybe you do not know that there is such a thing as principle among bootleggers. Yes, we admit we are bootleggers, but we do our business on the level."

As if to drive home the point, Mr Perri began to tell something of his own business.

"My men," he said, "do not carry guns. If I find that they do, I get rid of them. It is not necessary. I provide them with high-powered cars. That is enough. If they cannot run away from the police it is their own fault. But guns make trouble. My men do not use them."

There came the sound of a telephone bell tinkling and Mrs Perri tripped noiselessly from the room to answer it.

"There is no business — I don't care what you name — in which honesty is a more important factor than the bootlegging business." It was the King of all the bootleggers speaking. One found it difficult not to imagine listening to a college lecture on business administration.

"I mean accredited bootlegging," went on Mr Perri. "The man who does not play the game as it should be played will not get far. Pure liquor, fair prices and square dealing. Those are the requisites of the trade. I have played the game and — "

He did not finish the sentence verbally, but the indulgent survey which his eyes made of all the attributes and rewards of wealth which surrounded him in the form of fine furnishings and costly clothes spoke volumes.

"You think you have a right to carry on the illicit traffic in liquor?"

Rocco Perri paused a moment and then pointed toward the open paper which told of the transfer of Peter Smith [the former provincial treasurer] to the penitentiary.

"Am I doing more wrong than men like Peter Smith...I at least play square with my customers."

"There is a law against selling liquor," The Star reminded him.

"The law, what is the law?" he asked scornfully. "they don't want it in the cities. They voted against it. It is forced upon them. It is an unjust law. I have a right to violate it if I can get away with it. Men do it in what you call legitimate business until they get caught. I shall do it in my business until I get caught. Am I a criminal because I violate a law which the people do not want?"

"And if you get caught?"

Rocco Perri laughed. "We will not cross that bridge just yet," he said laconically, "but one can fight the law and win sometimes."

He referred to the Truman murder trial in Welland last week. "They tried to put the blame on a poor innocent boy," he said. "He did not kill Constable Truman. We fought them with the instruments of the law. I was at the trial myself. The jury disagreed — nine were for acquittal. Next time he will go free. The boy is innocent; he did not do the killing."

"If you knew who killed Truman, do you not think it would be your duty to notify the authorities?"

Mr Perri considered for a moment. "No, I do not think so," he said. "If I knew and someone else was to suffer the penalty I might tell, but it is up to the police to find the guilty man."

He went on to say that if a man "squealed" on him he would find a way to punish him.

"I would not kill him, I would punish him. That is the law of the Italians. We do not go to the police and complain. That is useless. We take the law into our own hands. I would kill a man on question of honour, but not if he merely informed on me. We believe we have the right to inflict our own penalties. Sometimes it is necessary to kill a man. But I have never done it, and I don't want to."

The discussion drifted to the Ontario Temperance Act. "Do you find it difficult to evade it?" The Star inquired.

Again the King of the Bootleggers laughed. "They are like a lot of schoolboys learning to play ball, those who are trying to enforce the OTA," he said. "Now, everything happens which they cannot solve they place at the doors of the bootlegger. If there is a crime that they cannot explain, then it is the bootlegger's fault — and usually they find Rocco Perri to blame. Murders, bank robberies, burglaries — they say that Rocco Perri is at the bottom of it all. I laugh at them.

"What would they do if they did not have the bootlegger to blame, I wonder? I suppose they would say that it is the Blackhand. But now they declare that we are to blame for all of these different offences. It is ridiculous. But they must find someone to blame — and so we suffer."

"Have you found it any more difficult to operate since the tightening of enforcement since the plebiscite?"

"I have not noticed it yet. I have heard that they are imposing $1,000 fines in Toronto. That is no good. What is a thousand dollars? They can never enforce the act by increasing the fines."

But if jail sentences were added?

"That would help. That would do a lot, but always there will be bootleggers. If I am put out of business tomorrow, there will be others to take my place. They must stop the manufacture and exportation. That is what they must do if they want to enforce prohibition. And even then there will be leaks from other sources which they will have trouble in plugging."

A deep-toned clock struck ten. "And you have no objection to our publishing your views?" The Star inquired, rising to go.

"You may say to the people what I have told you," Rocco Perri declared, holding out his hand politely. "They blame everything on me now anyway. I have no good name to lose. My reputation is long since blackened. I am a bootlegger. I am not ashamed to admit it. And a bootlegger I shall remain."

Mrs Perri, petite, prettily gowned and smiling gaily, crossed the room to join in the farewells.

"Good evening. Come again when I can help you."
These were the parting words of Rocco Perri, debonaire, polished and confident, he remained bowing in the doorway as The Star passed out into the night.

Dave Rogers returned to the *Star* newsroom and wrote his story. When the story was set in type, city editor Harry Hindmarsh looked it over. He demanded that Rogers go back to Perri and get him to sign the galleys. Rogers returned to Hamilton, and as he explained years later, "that vain little man signed my proofs."

The story ran on the *Star's* front page on November 19th, with the head: "KING OF THE BOOTLEGGERS WON'T STAND FOR GUNS."

An introduction noted that Perri "hitherto had been a mystery man," and noted, "A proof of the interview, substantially as published below was submitted to Signor Perri and received his O.K. and signature. In giving his approval he indicated a desire to make two or three additions and these have been incorporated in the article."

It was a classic scoop. Newsboys in Toronto and Hamilton were mobbed. In Hamilton, the *Star* was sold out in minutes. Those who couldn't get a paper looked over shoulders or paid scalpers' prices. The Hamilton police, when they found out about it, had to pay two dollars for a paper. According to the next day's Toronto *Telegram*, which in those days was not known for its crime reporting, Rocco was in the hospital, visiting one of his men badly injured in an accident caused by a sabotaged booze truck, when he was handed a copy of the *Star*.

Anonymous reporters from the *Spectator* and *Herald*, beaten on their own turf, called at the door of 166 Bay Street South and requested an interview. It was granted, and the reporters, Rocco and Bessie chatted in the same living room where they had greeted Dave Rogers the day before.

"I am giving this story out," Perri said, "because some friends of mine called me on the phone a few days ago and told me that those killings that were going on have been blamed on the Gogo gang. Seven of my men were in that gang and authorities did not find a weapon of any kind on them. I give my boys fast cars, but I tell them they must not be armed. The police have caught my boys lots of times, but not once did they find firearms. If they are caught, then the law does the rest.

"I am kind of sore the way they blame everything that happens on Rocco Perri. If a boat goes astray, if a shipment of liquor is seized, if anything happens — it is Rocco Perri, always."

"I wonder why?" murmured Bessie with a nod.

"They went even further," Perri continued. "During the last election they spread around the report that I gave $40,000 to help the drys."

"If I had $40,000 to give away, I'd build a store and let the poor people run it," Bessie said.

Rocco agreed. "I was disappointed when my wife told me that it had gone dry again. The OTA, What harm it does! The very ones it is supposed to protect are the ones who now spend all their money buying poisonous moonshine and such stuff and this awful canned heat. I would like to see the days before 1916 back so the poor man might buy a glass of beer or one of whisky for a reasonable price. Now the rich have all they want and the poor have to do without or buy poison. They haven't the money to buy real whisky.

"We have broken the OTA all right, but in no other affairs have we interfered. Most of my business is in the United States. I have a large trade there. I suppose we should be sent to jail if we are caught, but we are not caught," he smiled.

Although Rocco had told the *Star* that jail would stop bootlegging, he now contemplated the personnel problems when his men were caught. "If one of my boys is arrested and fined $1,000, I go down the next morning and pay it for him. A jail sentence is different. If one of my boys is sent to jail for six months, then I have a harder time. I can't get him out and then it's hard to find another one to take his place.

"It cost me $80,000 in one year for liquor and cars

which were seized by the authorities and for wages and other expenses," he said.

"Is it true that you are known as the King of the Bootleggers?" the *Spectator* reporter asked.

"When I started a long time ago," Rocco replied, "I was the only one in the business; in fact I was the only one in this district. Now there are thousands behind me. Yes, I admit I am a bootlegger. Why deny it? Instead of sneaking around at night, why not come out and be honest about it?

"We're not crooks. We do not peddle from door to door, and we don't have to go up and down the street selling. If we get a chance to earn a dollar, we'll do it. If we're caught, then it's another matter. It's eight years now since I became known, and because I have not been convicted, everything has been put down to me."

"Is it true that you are known to the Italians living in Hamilton as their leader and head?"

"No," replied the godfather of Hamilton, "if an Italian comes to my home and wants help I give it to him."

"If anybody comes we give them help," Bessie added. "Not only Italians, but all poor people we help. Churches, bazaars, anything."

Perri then returned to his business south of the border. "I suppose the liquor you sell is the very best," the reporter asked.

"Nothing but the best," nodded Rocco. "In the States I sell hundreds of cases." He said that he sold as many as 1,000 cases a day, but his profits came from the U.S. business, not the Hamilton bootlegging. Operations have been carried out in a large way across the border, Perri said. The chief centers of distribution were Rochester, Detroit, Syracuse and other large cities. Perri said that an occasional boat load was brought into Hamilton but the "great bulk of wet goods is unloaded at other points."

"Who is there here that wants 300 cases at a time?" Rocco chuckled there were few such orders in the district.

Bessie, who knew because she did the ordering and

kept the books, explained that they never dealt in lots of less than hundreds of cases. "We'd never handle it in single cases, like lots of smaller bootleggers do here. We have never sold single bottles."

"We have been in business for eight years," Bessie said, "and during that time there has been no room for complaint. Only once was Rocco near trouble, and that time he was held by police for a few hours, and then released. That was when he was on Hess Street. He has never been convicted." This was true, since he won the appeal on his OTA case in 1919.

"I know that selling liquor is against the law, but it's like a game of wits. If they ever catch me, I'll be a good sport and admit that I'm beaten at the game. I want to be caught fairly, though, and not framed," Rocco said. "I've heard of cases where officers 'plant' bottles of liquor in the house and cars. I don't want that to happen to me.

"Still, I'm getting tired of being accused of everything that happens and I'm going to quit," he said.

Prominent Hamilton citizens were among his best customers, Rocco told the reporter. "Many of the prominent people of the town drink, and they buy from us because they are sure that what they are getting will be good. I never broke my word with them or broke faith. They want the best and are willing to pay for it. They never grumble about the prices."

Perri said he picked his customers carefully: "We do not sell to every man who wants it, no matter how much money he might be prepared to spend."

The reporter asked Rocco why he was being singled out for publicity when there were so many bootleggers in Ontario.

"The people would be surprised if they really knew how many are engaged in the business. Many Canadian born are bootlegging on a large scale, but their names are never mentioned."

Rocco rose to see the reporters to the door, "No one can

come here and pay for liquor. I have heard it said that people had been to Rocco Perri's home and got a drink. That's not so."

At the door he shook their hands warmly and bade them a courteous goodbye.

Meanwhile, Attorney General William Nickle and OPP Commissioner Victor Williams were at an emergency meeting at Queen's Park. Officials said they were surprised by Perri's statements and promised action. Nickle phoned Harry Hindmarsh at the *Star* and demanded the signed galleys of Rocco Perri's interview. Hindmarsh told the attorney general he was sorry, but somehow, the galleys had been lost.

Rogers would later say, "If Harry had turned those proofs over to the A-G, my life wouldn't have been worth a nickel."

A. H. Lyle, the man who had told Rogers about Rocco, said the interview was a challenge to those in charge of the OTA.

"One or two statements made by Mr Perri are worthy of consideration by our law makers. He says that a jail sentence would help curtail bootlegging and also that the only effectual way to prevent illicit sale is to stop the manufacture. In these opinions the temperance people of the city heartily concur." Lyle didn't mind publicity, as long as he got it.

In the afternoon, Attorney General Nickle met with the press. Nickle was lucky that the legislature was not in session that month or he would have faced a gruelling Question Period.

"A man may say anything he likes about himself," Nickle said. "Even if he says he is a criminal, the Crown would have to secure proof that he was, before it could put on his defense. If this man were a bootlegger we would require proof that he had violated the OTA before we would charge him with such an offense. A boast is not proof of guilt."

That statement only further infuriated the temperance and religious community. A. T. Enlow, who had been chairman of the East Hamilton Prohibition Committee during the plebiscite, apparently had a sneaking admiration for the opposition. "If this man Perri is really going to get out of the bootlegging business, it might be wise to fix up some deal where he looks after the enforcement of the OTA for a while."

There were murmurings that Rocco should be deported to Italy, so the *Herald* checked with Bessie, who told them that Rocco had been denied naturalization. She then added that the late police chief, William Whatley, had reported to Ottawa that Rocco Perri was not a fit subject for naturalization. The *Herald* reported that statement without comment, but it raises some questions. The information sent to Ottawa was confidential. Had Whatley boasted of ordering the raid on 166 Bay Street South and the reports he sent to Ottawa, or did Bessie have sources of information within the Hamilton police? Or, perhaps, was there truth in the rumours that Bessie had become close to Whatley?

Hamilton Inspector John Cruickshank took issue with Rocco's statement that he sold pure booze: "I caught Perri myself when I raided his former home at 105 Hess Street North and seized a quantity of raw alcohol and several bundles of spurious labels of well-known brands of liquor ...Perri used to be down in this district quite often but we see little of him now."

"I was aware that Perri was a bootlegger," said Detective James Bleakley, a former Hamilton licence inspector, "but I don't think he ever kept illegal liquor on his premises. Scores of times my men stopped his cars and trucks. I must say his drivers were polite on all occasions. I am convinced that none of Perri's men carried revolvers and foreigners who were in touch with his movements assured me of this."

At the end of the week, sources in the attorney general's office said, "We're doing nothing." Jelfs confirmed that nothing could be done on the strength of Perri's remarks: "The only thing I can see is to deport Perri and that would be up to the Dominion government. The strength of his confession that he is breaking Ontario laws would permit such action but I am doubtful if it will be carried out.

Perri has admitted that he is going back to Italy and it is hardly likely that he would object to being deported. Think of the expenses he would not have to pay." That was wishful thinking on his worship's part. When Rocco had claimed that he was going to retire, he had made no mention of Italy.

One man who was watching all of this with great interest was the young American consul stationed in Hamilton, Richard Fyfe Boyce. (In the 1920s and 30s, an era of slower communications, the United States maintained consulates in Ottawa, Toronto, Kingston, Hamilton, London, Niagara Falls and Windsor. Their original function was to handle commercial traffic and normal consular affairs, but during Prohibition they became intelligence posts watching the activities of rum runners.)

After the signing of the Hughes-Lapointe treaty, the State Department had instructed the various consuls in Canada to contact local authorities to request co-operation in suppressing smuggling. For Boyce in Hamilton, the immediate problem was to find a way to stop the shipment of beer in boxcars from the two local breweries to the border points. He began by contacting Police Chief David Coulter, who assured him of co-operation but then directed him to the liquor licence bureaucracy that dealt with OTA enforcement and federal export regulations.

On November 21, 1924, two days after the interview with Rocco appeared in the *Star*, Boyce sent a confidential report to the State Department with copies for the Treasury and Justice departments:

It is common rumor in Hamilton that...whisky is not only sold to private persons for home consumption but it is sold in public places....I personally believe the police give protection....The American government cannot expect cooperation with dishonest officials. So far as the city of Hamilton is concerned I am personally of the belief little can be done.

In this connection I have to enclose herewith the newspaper account of an interview (and photograph of) with Rocco Perri, self-styled "king of the bootleggers." Perusal of this interview will show how secure he believes himself to be, which indicates that rumors of dishonest officials must be at least partially true.

While public attention focused on the Rocco Perri interviews, the investigations into the deaths of Fred Genesee and Joe Boitowicz continued. The early sessions of the inquests reached no conclusion. At the Boitowicz inquest on December 3rd, Amelia Boitowicz testified for two hours, repeating that her husband had been threatened. Both inquests were then adjourned.

The same day, the *Herald* published the comment of a competing bootlegger: "Rocco Perri, he talk too much, he busta da biz." Indeed, the police were cracking down as a result of the interview — but not too successfully. The only way to stop bootlegging, one cop told the paper, was if officers could "stop and search every car, wagon and truck entering the city." The same story revealed another interesting fact: one group of Italian bootleggers was now working together with a Ukrainian gang that had once been a deadly rival. The allusion was to the fact that Rocco Perri now commanded the late Jack Larenchuk's former colleagues. An OPP report filed two years later would note that "Russians" were active members of Perri's largely Calabrian organization.

The Boitowicz inquest resumed on December 8th in a crowded courtroom. This time, there was sensational evidence. On December 3rd, Inspectors Hammond and Albert Boyd had arrested Mrs Amelia Boitowicz and a man called "Yakman Zebo." They were held on nominal charges of vagrancy. At the inquest, Crown Attorney George Ballard asked that the court be cleared of the public. Then he called as his first witness seven-year-old Tony Boitowicz, son of the murdered man. The boy told how he had watched from the dining-room table as his father came home from the races. He had lost all his money. Then, the boy testified, his mother, Amelia, had picked up a poker and hit her husband over the head. He dropped to the dining-room floor. She hit him again as he lay on the floor. But Joe Boitowicz managed to get up and stagger to his bedroom in the basement.

The child became tired under the questioning and so he completed his testimony on Coroner George Rennie's knee. He said his mother said that men, friends of hers, came and took away his father. Then Tony's brother, Walter, who was nine years old, told how he saw men cleaning up a red stain in the basement the next day and then, when his mother sent him to the store for sugar, he saw them take a bundle out of the cellar window and put it in a car. The nine-year-old saw his father's shoes sticking out of the bundle.

The jury decided that Joe Boitowicz had been murdered by Amelia Boitowicz, brothers Panko and Yakim Stabo, Bill Shermett and Mike Radich. So the woman who had told the newspapers that Rocco Perri had ordered the death of her husband was now facing a charge of murder herself. She was later acquitted due to insufficient evidence and contradictory testimony.

The day after the inquest a group of local clergy appeared at the regular meeting of the Police Commission to ask that something be done about Rocco Perri. "The way I see this is that Perri has been swelled up with his own success, and then wanted to boast about it. He wanted the publicity." Magistrate Jelfs chuckled and then added, "If he were put in the witness box he would probably deny everything."

Jelfs suggested that the reverend gentlemen circulate a petition demanding Perri's deportation. Apparently this suggestion was turned down by the clergy, who said they were too busy.

"The proof of good intentions is the manner in which you work for them," Jelfs said drily and turned to routine business.

The Genesee inquest resumed on December 14th. Police were now saying there was no connection between the two murder cases. Inspector Hammond had no additional evidence to offer and the verdict was "murder by person or persons unknown."

On December 15th, another development rocked the city. Attorney General Nickle ordered Magistrate Jelfs to submit his resignation. The official reason was Jelfs' advanced age: seventy-two. Although the attorney general truly did want to pension off magistrates at age seventy, sources at Queen's Park disclosed that the real reason was Jelfs' attitude towards the Ontario Temperance Act and the fact that he often imposed only minimum fines. Jelfs, now a thirty-one-year veteran of the bench refused to quit. He wrote to Nickle asking him to reconsider and the Hamilton establishment came to his defence. Jelfs went to Toronto for a face-to-face meeting with Nickle and the Premier, G. Howard Ferguson.

The attorney general backed down, allowing Jelfs to stay on for a few more months. In fact, Jelfs served for five more years.

And Fred Genesee? In January 1925, Inspector Hammond was still working on the case. According to his reports, in late December he had questioned Mrs Genesee again. Until then, she had maintained that her husband did not drink. But on December 21st, six days after the inquest into her husband's death, she admitted that her husband did drink, and that he went to "parties" at the blind pig of Italian bootlegger Pete Brassi, two miles east of Stoney Creek.

Hammond zeroed in on two men who frequented Brassi's blind pig. It was known that Genesee would occasionally lend his car to the two men whom Hammond described as "bad, good-for-nothing fellows." Hammond discovered that Genesee had met with the two toughs at Brassi's place the night he disappeared and that he still had the $200 mortgage money with him at that point. After the murder, the two men disappeared. One suspect returned to Hamilton in January with a brand-new $50 overcoat. Hammond asked him how he'd got it. The man said someone gave him $74 at the Royal Connaught Hotel. That was all. He wouldn't say anything more. No one was ever charged with the murder.

Ironically, Rocco and Bessie Perri had no connection with the two murders that set in motion the events that brought them to national attention. Rocco was justifiably annoyed at the press for blaming him for murders with which he had nothing to do. But he obviously liked to give the impression that he knew about everything that was going on in the Hamilton underworld. Joe Boitowicz may have been an informant, but it is likely that Rocco had culled that information from the newspapers. As for Fred Genesee's mystery woman, she is never mentioned in the reports on the case. Rocco must have made it up.

CHAPTER 9

POISON BREW

On Sunday, March 1, 1925, Orville A. Preuster, a special agent with the U.S. Customs service in Niagara Falls, New York, was blown to bits by a bomb when he pressed the starter of his car.

Preuster was the man charged with stopping cross-border liquor smuggling in the Niagara region. In December 1924, he had been offered a bribe by a man named Pasquale Curione (a.k.a. Patsy Corona) after Preuster had intercepted a car filled with $12,000 worth of Canadian ale. Preuster accepted the bribe and arranged to meet Curione at the Niagara Falls post office. When Curione delivered the money, both he and Preuster were arrested. It was only at the police station that Curione found out that he had been set up by the customs agent. It was a sting.

The bombing death of Orville Preuster was connected with previous bomb attempts on two local ministers who were his allies: Rev. Littleton Smith of the United Presbyterian Church in Buffalo had escaped a bombing attempt in April 1924. In August, Rev. Arthur Mercer's Baptist Church had been wrecked by a bomb. Both Smith and Mercer were leaders of the anti-vice crusade in western New York. Smith, who had gone on raids on Grand Island with Preuster, said his sources had told him that two hitmen from Rochester had set the bomb in Preuster's car.

A probe by the U.S. Bureau of Investigation (later to be called the FBI) found that two men ordered Preuster's death. They were Joe Serianni, Perri's Calabrian ally in Niagara Falls, New York, and Joe Sottile, who ran the giant distilling plant in the city. Inspector William Stringer of the OPP would also report that Sottile was responsible for Preuster's murder. Joe Sottile was born in Philadelphia on May 28, 1891, of Sicilian parents. In June 1916, he was convicted of armed robbery in New York City. In 1919 he showed up in Niagara Falls and was refused entry when he tried to enter Canada at Queenston, although he later crossed the border with ease. Sottile dealt not only in raw alcohol, but also in good Canadian whisky and in sacramental wine that was diverted by a Lockport priest — and he took part in counterfeiting and in running aliens into the United States across the Niagara River.

In partnership with his brother-in-law Joseph Spallino, Sottile operated out of the Third Ward Political Club on 13th Street in Niagara Falls, New York. Next door, in the abandoned National Theater, the gang built a plant with one 500-gallon still, two 250-gallon stills, two 5,000-gallon vats, two 500-gallon vats and one 100-gallon galvanized tank, along with two boilers and the equipment needed for distilling and redistilling alcohol. They began operations in November 1923 when they took over the Falls Tonic Company and obtained a permit from the U.S. Internal Revenue Service to use denatured alcohol, officially for the manufacture of perfume.

There were two ways to make illegal alcohol during Prohibition in the United States. One was old-fashioned moonshining, which wasn't really so old-fashioned, for the high-volume "alky-cookers" had little of the quality control that some of the best mountain moonshiners used. The stuff was produced in filthy conditions, with everything from good grain mash to rotten fruit and scraps from garbage cans. The rot gut was contaminated with byproducts the old-time moonshiners knew how to avoid and with metallic poisons from the distilling equipment.

Redistilled alcohol could be even more deadly. The

idea was to distill out the poisons that had been added to denature the alcohol. The most common denaturant was methanol, poisonous wood alcohol, which has a boiling point just below that of ethyl, or grain, alcohol. It was almost impossible to separate the two.

Sottile's redistilling operation was better than most: he had chemists on retainer to analyze the product. Allied to Sottile was the Jopp Drug Company, a mob front, set up in 1922 ostensibly to manufacture toilet water but which in reality was buying vast amounts of denatured alcohol to supply to Sottile. By the spring of 1924, Sottile's business was booming. He was supplying not only Buffalo but New York City and, across the border, Niagara Falls, St Catharines, Hamilton and Toronto.

Rocco Perri was one of Sottile's customers. His books showed that Rocco bought large amounts of redistilled alcohol that found its way back to Hamilton either hidden under coal in trains or by boats on their return trips. The arrangement was that Rocco would supply Canadian liquor and beer to Sottile in return for redistilled alcohol. On at least two occasions Rocco attempted to supply Sottile with a load of denatured alcohol from Canadian Industrial Alcohol in Montreal. The first load, consigned to the ubiquitous Joe Penna, was cleared by customs on behalf of Rocco's close ally in Port Credit, Joe Burke. After the load sailed, the local customs officer queried Ottawa and was told to stop the second load of denatured alcohol leaving Canada.

Sottile also supplied Max Wortzman, the Toronto bootlegger, with huge amounts of redistilled alcohol (4,004 gallons for the Christmas trade in December 1925) and Jimmy Sacco, the head of the Niagara Falls, Ontario, bootlegging ring.

In the summer of 1925, Sottile made a trip to the French island of St Pierre. There he met a man from Saint John, New Brunswick, one James Lavallée, who was running liquor to the United States and the Maritime provinces. Between them they came up with a brilliant money-making scheme.

Liquor from St Pierre offloaded at Rum Row near New York City commanded a premium price. It was thought to be legitimate and safe, called the "real McCoy" after one of the first bootleggers on Rum Row, Captain Bill McCoy.

Anyone who bought liquor in St Pierre, cut it with alcohol, and then sold it as the real thing in New York could make a fortune. It is likely that once the liquor reached the New York speakeasies, that city's unsuspecting bootleggers would cut it again with more redistilled alcohol.

Lavallée and Sottile went ahead with their plan. The redistilled alcohol from Niagara Falls, New York, was shipped in the empty boats that were returning after having carried real scotch, French brandy and wines down the St Lawrence from St Pierre and Miquelon. Rocco Perri, one of Sottile's big customers, provided assistance to those boats and it is likely he was aware of and took his cut in that racket. Somewhere off New Brunswick or Nova Scotia the good European liquor was cut, put in bottles with counterfeit labels and sent on to New York.

In October 1925, while he was staying in Toronto with bootleggers Max and Harry Wortzman, Sottile made an application for Canadian citizenship, claiming falsely that he had been in Canada five years. In November he was in Saint John, and there he hired a lawyer in an attempt to hurry up the application so he could take a business trip to Europe. The Secretary of State's department ruled that Sottile had to wait the statutory ninety days, but External Affairs provided him with a special travel permit, which he didn't really need: he had been issued an American passport on March 24, 1925.

In Saint John, RCMP Sergeant Frederick Lucas checked out Sottile and reported that he suspected Sottile intended to go into the rum-running business. Unable to get a hearing on his citizenship in Saint John, Sottile approached a Montreal Liberal Member of Parliament named Samuel Jacobs and asked him to intervene on his behalf. In the meantime, Sottile returned to Niagara Falls to oversee his redistilling operation.

In May 1926, Buffalo Prohibition agents began a crackdown

with a May 8th raid on a brewing plant and restaurant. Agents seized fermenting tanks, kegs of beer, pumps, fifteen stills, sacks of unlabelled beer and five hundred quarts of imported wine. On May 14th, Mark Crehan, who was in charge of the special alcohol squad, led ten other Prohibition agents in a raid on the Third Ward Political Club, interrupting the stills that were cooking away there. They seized the equipment, 12,000 gallons of alcohol and 5,000 gallons of whisky. Joe Spallino was arrested in an ice-cream plant that was connected by a passageway to the offices of the illegal operation.

Two days later Crehan and another agent returned to the now-wrecked premises and drilled the safe in Spallino's office. Inside they found five ledgers, along with cheque books, bank passbooks and cancelled cheques, which served as an invaluable guide as to who was involved in organized crime on both sides of the border.

The immediate result of the destruction of Sottile's distilling operation was a shortage of raw alcohol in Buffalo. The OPP's William Stringer reported: "There are so many rings within rings it is much easier for traffickers in this 'slow poison' to form new combinations than it is for the authorities to break up existing ones."

One of those rings was headed by a man named James Voelker, a bootlegger connected with Sottile and Don Simone. Voelker sent word to "Davey" Burden in New York that they needed raw alcohol fast.

Meanwhile, Sottile was fleeing to avoid arrest. His friend, the Lockport priest who had been diverting sacramental wine, smuggled him across the border. Then Rocco took over, and brought Sottile to Max Wortzman in Toronto. On June 8th, Sottile walked into Judge Emerson Coatsworth's court in Toronto, and requested a special hearing on his citizenship application. The hearing was granted. For one reason or another, the reports from the RCMP in Toronto and Saint John were ignored, and eight days later Sottile received confirmation that he was a Canadian citizen. He made his way to Saint John.

Between May and July, James Voelker made numerous phone calls to Canada, including nine calls to Louis Sylvester, a Perri bootlegger in Thorold, setting up the new business. In the meantime Burden had delivered, shipping twenty 60-gallon drums of alcohol from New York City. Eight drums were sent to James Voelker, who had them routinely analyzed. It was deadly poison: 93.9% wood alcohol, 0.49% acetone, 1.13% acetic acid with traces of ethyl alcohol, formaldehyde and formic acid. By then it was too late. Alcohol from eighteen of the drums was already in Buffalo. On Monday, July 19th, the liquor from the remaining two had been sent across to Canada in cans of one and five U.S. gallons. Whether or not Voelker knew about the results of the analysis before he shipped out the alcohol, he made no effort to let the recipients of the shipments know.

It took just two days for death to strike. On Wednesday three men died after a drinking party in Allanberg, near Welland. That afternoon Bert D'Angelo, a Hamilton fruit peddlar, sold a gallon tin to William Maybee, who ran a gas station and refreshment stand on Dundas Street, five miles from Oakville. Maybee and his son, Walter, sixteen, cut the gallon can with water and colouring to produce twelve bottles of alcohol. The first to die were James Lyons, a neighbour with a heart condition, and James Johnston, Maybee's father-in-law.

The death toll kept climbing. Weekend parties killed thirteen in Buffalo, where police raided and closed the "soft drink" establishments that had served the lethal potion. On Monday, July 26th, the toll was thirty-one, on Tuesday it was thirty-seven and by Thursday forty-one people had died. In the end there were forty-five confirmed deaths: fifteen in Buffalo, four in Lockport, six in Hamilton, five in Oakville, four in Toronto, three in Allanberg, three in Sudbury, two in Bridgeburg and one each in Brantford, Parry Sound and Niagara Falls.

The *Star* sent its flying squad into action, and detailed accounts of each of the deaths covered the front page, the second front and three inside pages on Monday, July 26th. Bert D'Angelo, jailed in Milton on manslaughter charges, told the *Star* that he was just a subagent for others. He broke down in tears, saying the deaths would never have happened if there were government liquor stores in Ontario.

James Voelker surrendered in Buffalo on Tuesday. Two days later, July 29th, the U.S. Attorney in Buffalo, Richard Templeton, announced ninety-one indictments as a result of the May raids on the Third Ward Political Club. Rocco Perri topped the list of Canadians, followed by Max Wortzman, James Sacco and others. The Americans included Sottile, Spallino and Pasquale Curione, who, reports said, were also under investigation for smuggling drugs into the United States at Niagara Falls.

Templeton said the investigation had traced the redistilled alcohol as far as Saint John and Halifax. The phoney drug companies had paid $1.10 a gallon for the denatured alcohol. At rebottling, if it was done in Toronto, the price jumped to $14 a gallon. Templeton did not venture a guess at the profits that were made when the alcohol was mixed with Canadian and European liquor in the Maritimes and sold in New York City.

At Queen's Park, acting Attorney General W. H. Price (Nickle was on holiday) and OPP Commissioner Victor Williams laid charges of manslaughter against all the Canadians indicted at Buffalo. However, Buffalo news reports noted that only a few of those indicted in the Third Ward Political Club were involved in the poison cases.

Max Wortzman and Harry Goldstein surrendered in Toronto on July 30th. In Hamilton, police picked up Joe Romeo, John B. ("Ben") Kerr and two small-time operators. Jimmy Sacco and two others were arrested in Niagara Falls, Ontario. Rocco Perri, as usual, was nowhere to be found. An OPP team was dispatched to Musclow to see if he was there visiting his children, but by the time they arrived on July 31st, Rocco had showed up at Hamilton police headquarters, accompanied by both his lawyers, Charles W. Bell and Michael J. O'Reilly. (The case came up in the middle of a federal election. Bell was a Conservative candidate in Hamilton West, O'Reilly a Liberal candidate in Hamilton East.)

Rocco was neatly dressed in a grey suit and straw hat. He smiled as if he didn't have a care in the world. Detective Joe Crocker gave him a seat in the detective office beside a cool fan — it was a hot, humid July day — until it was time for his appearance in court. In the corridor, Rocco nervously puffed on a cigarette before being called, but once he was in the prisoner's box, he was once again cool and confident. Crown Attorney Ballard requested an adjournment for one week, no bail, and then it was back to the detective office where Rocco greeted the police officers he had known for years. After a brief interrogation by Crocker and the OPP, reporters tried a few questions.

"You better talk to my lawyer," Rocco said. "He'll do my talking for me."

Just a couple of questions, the reporters asked.

"I don't feel much like talking this morning," Rocco said. "I've got a headache."

"How did you know you were wanted?" a reporter asked.

Rocco shrugged his shoulders. "I knew," he smiled.

"Have you been out of the city for the past forty-eight hours?" one asked. "That's my business," Rocco replied. He refused to discuss the U.S. indictments. Then the police took him down to the detention cells.

A *Herald* reporter called at 166 Bay Street South to ask Bessie why Rocco had surrendered. "Why not?" she replied. "When the papers came out with the pictures and all that, it was the thing to do at once. And why not? There is nothing in it."

Hamilton police were also doubtful the charge would stick. They told reporters that they had received orders from Queen's Park to pick up Perri after the U.S. indictments. They knew of no evidence against Rocco. In fact, one source said, when the deaths first occurred, Rocco had walked into Hamilton police headquarters, asking for Inspector Stringer of the OPP. When he was told Stringer wasn't there at the moment, Perri had walked out unhindered. A glance at the warrant showed that Rocco was charged with the manslaughter of John Lyons of Oakville.

On August 1st, the Conservative prime minister, Arthur Meighen appointed Peter White as a special Crown counsel in the smuggling cases. On August 4th, White laid additional charges against all suspects, including Rocco Perri, for customs violations. Not to be outdone, acting Attorney General Price appointed McGregor Young, who had represented the provincial government in civil cases, as a special prosecutor for the manslaughter cases.

In Buffalo, the case was already coming apart, charges of murder and manslaughter against the "soft-drink dealers" were dropped because the police, alarmed at the deaths, had not waited for proper warrants when they began their raids.

In Toronto, the Stock Exchange was adding its own footnote to the poison alcohol cases. The most active issue in the first week of August 1926, was Gooderham & Worts, up fifteen points. Far-sighted investors were gambling that Prohibition would soon end in Ontario.

On August 6th, a coroner's jury in Oakville found that John Lyons and James Johnston had died from poisoning by wood alcohol supplied by Bert D'Angelo. On August 11th, a Toronto inquest found Bert D'Angelo responsible for two of the deaths. On August 13th, the jury in Hamilton considering the deaths of five people in that city simply found that they had died from drinking wood alcohol received from a mystery woman named Margaret.

The next day Rocco appeared in court along with Joe Romeo, John B. ("Ben") Kerr and the two small-time bootleggers, Edward Miller and Harry Sullivan. Ballard opposed bail, but he was unable to tell Jelfs when he would be able to proceed with the charges of manslaughter and administering poison. Peter White opposed bail because of the international aspects of the case. O'Reilly headed the defence team and told Jelfs there was little evidence against the five and none had been named at the inquests. For the legal arguments, O'Reilly deferred to R. H. Greer of Toronto, who was representing Ben Kerr. Greer jumped to his feet and addressed Jelfs, using numerous quotations from the Magna Carta. After an hour-long discussion, Jelfs released the men on $20,000 bail.

By this time Nickle was back from vacation and it was clear from the memos he read that the only evidence was against Bert D'Angelo. Nickle decided to hire an undercover operative from the Pinkerton Detective Agency, and an Italian-speaking agent using the initials J.C.S. was dispatched from Philadelphia to penetrate Hamilton's gangland.

On his first day, J.C.S. visited a pool room where he made an acquaintance who took him to the Gobia's blind pig on Mulberry Street. There he met Mildred Sterling, who told him, "I have driven many a load myself in my Marmon car....I have been across the river many times and I have smuggled thousands of dollars of chinaware into Canada without any trouble...."

J.C.S. would spend a month listening to underworld gossip in Hamilton and Niagara Falls, most of it about Rocco Perri. An Italian pastry chef told him, "The authorities have nothing on Rocco Perri and it doesn't seem as if they care to get anything on him as it would implicate too many higher-ups. Perri is not handling anything right now; he is releasing plenty and making money just the same." Mrs. Gobia offered the Pinkerton man a job, driving a truck for Frank Romeo, paying $100 a week. A man named Dan told J.C.S. that Rocco immediately fired anyone, except the most senior members of his gang, who were caught. "He only handles people with clear standing in Canada."

The gossip in the barbershops, pool halls and blind pigs of Niagara Falls named Don Simone as the top man, but his connections with Buffalo and Niagara politicians were so strong that he couldn't be touched. Sottile was the number two man. It was James Voelker who hadn't waited for the analysis of the liquor and who, on learning it was poisonous, had made no attempt to recall it and had shipped the rest out anyway.

Partly as a result of J.C.S.'s daily reports and the information the provincial government received from the U.S. authorities, on August 27th, Ontario offered a $2,000 reward for the arrest of Joseph Sottile.

On August 28th, Rocco Perri and the Hamilton accused appeared in court as they had the previous Saturday. Before they could line up at the bench, Ballard told Jelfs he was not ready to proceed and asked for another week.

"Make it longer if you want to," said lawyer Michael J. O'Reilly.

Jelfs asked when Ballard would be ready.

"I'm not in a position to do that," Ballard replied.

"Who is then?" Jelfs asked.

"No one here," Ballard said.

Jelfs suggested the case be adjourned indefinitely, but Ballard objected. He asked that the case be adjourned week to week until the Crown was ready. It was agreed that the defendants' names would be called, but that they would not appear until the Crown notified them it was ready to proceed or the case had been dropped.

The dapper Mr Perri (as the papers called him) was met at the court-room door with a hug from Bessie.

"I guess they don't want us anymore," Rocco said.

"Looks like it," a friend replied.

On September 20th, the U.S. attorney in Buffalo, Richard Templeton, left with Nickle for Washington to consult with the U.S. Justice Department. Nickle had a case summary written by Stringer, showing that the poison alcohol was indirectly tied to Rocco Perri. Bert D'Angelo's statement provided a chain. Joe Romeo was the wholesaler of the poison liquor. Romeo sold it to distributor Harry Sullivan. Sullivan's delivery man, Edward Miller, had gone to Romeo's place at 25 Railway Street, picked up the liquor and paid Romeo's wife. Miller then delivered a can of alcohol and a case of Grant's Spring beer to Bert D'Angelo. Although it was known since the Gogo case that Joe Romeo worked for Rocco Perri, there was no mention of Rocco in the case summary. In Washington, Templeton and Nickle met with the attorney general, John G. Sargent and with President Calvin Coolidge, who had taken a personal interest in the case. At a news conference later that day, Coolidge told reporters that efforts to stop the smuggling of alcohol from Canada were meeting with increasing success.

On October 5th the OPP raided Joe and Frank Romeo's house at Railway Street and seized a number of cheques that had passed through a bank in Niagara Falls, New York. The next day, OPP Inspector Albert Ward was back, and this time he searched the empty house at 27 Railway Street. He seized 130 U.S.-gallon cans of alcohol, sending some to Toronto for analysis to see if they contained poison alcohol.

On October 7th, an unnamed OPP informant reported a conversation with bootlegger Edward Miller, who had appeared in court with Rocci Perri in August. Miller told how the Romeo brothers got large amounts of alcohol from Perri, but he avoided any questions about the poison shipment, saying Perri's men had told him to keep his mouth shut. But an eleven-year-old girl in the house told the informant that her older brother said Miller had got the poison alcohol from Perri. That statement, the hearsay of an eleven-year-old, is the only document in the files on the case that ties the deaths directly to Rocco Perri.

On October 19th, Premier G. Howard Ferguson called a provincial election for December 1, 1926. The Tory machine was oiled and experienced, having backed Arthur Meighen's federal Conservatives in the elections of 1925 and 1926. There was one issue: abolition of the Ontario Temperance Act and the introduction of government-controlled liquor sales in the province. The sentiment in small-town and rural Ontario was still dry, but the cities were wet, and the deaths of twenty-one Ontario citizens from poison alcohol probably contributed to Ferguson's decision to go to the polls.

But within hours of the election call, W. F. Nickle, who as attorney general had guided the 4.4 percent beer amendment through the legislature, resigned and announced that he would stand in favour of the OTA as an Independent Conservative. Ferguson immediately named W. H. Price to the attorney general's post.

Nickle's resignation had one effect that he probably had not expected. At the time, the two Canadian special prosecutors, Peter White and McGregor Young were pressing Templeton, the U.S. Attorney, for photographic copies of the books seized from the Third Ward Political Club. It was the evidence that they needed in order to secure convictions in Canada. But on hearing of Nickle's resignation, Templeton cut off the exchange of information with Ontario. Templeton didn't trust Price — he was a wet. Templeton stalled on sending copies of the evidence to Canada and ordered Bureau of Investigation agents not to confer with any officials in Ontario without permission.

Templeton soon had his own problems to deal with. The lawyers for Joe Spallino filed a motion asking the court to return the books on the grounds that his safe had been opened illegally by the raiding officers. The court ordered Templeton to hand the books over to the U.S. Marshals, who put them in a safety deposit box. Templeton's delays now meant that Canadians would not get the evidence they needed to convict Perri and other senior gang members.

However, bootlegger Edward Miller decided, despite threats against him, to turn King's evidence. He testified before Jelfs on October 30th that he had supplied Bert D'Angelo with cans of alcohol and a load of beer from Grant's Spring. Jelfs committed Harry Sullivan and Joe Romeo for trial. Rocco Perri's case was adjourned.

On November 18th, a jury convicted Bert D'Angelo of manslaughter, and he was sentenced to four years. The next day charges against the Niagara Falls bootleggers, including Jimmy Sacco, were dropped.

On December 1st, Ferguson was swept back into power. Nickle lost badly in Kingston, and W. H. Price was now attorney general for the new administration. His first job would be to end Prohibition in Ontario by repealing the Ontario Temperance Act and writing a new Liquor Control Act.

On December 4th, the provincial prosecutor, McGregor Young, appeared before Jelfs, told him that American witnesses for the manslaughter case were unavailable and asked for more adjournments. But Jelfs' patience was at an end. He dismissed the manslaughter cases against Rocco Perri and Ben Kerr, who, as part of the agreement, were not in court to hear the news.

During the weeks that followed, most of the other charges against Perri and Kerr were dropped or dismissed. At the end of Kerr's hearings, Rocco came over to shake Kerr's hand. "I'm going home and eat three or four plates of spaghetti," he announced to the court and then sauntered out.

Meanwhile, in Buffalo, James Voelker went on trial for murder. The jury found him guilty of manslaughter and in January 1927 he was sentenced to fifteen years in Auburn Penitentiary.

Of the 123 originally charged in the incident, just two, D'Angelo and Voelker, were convicted. All the other manslaughter cases in Ontario ended in dismissal or acquittal, and by the end of January the Canadian Federal government had dropped all remaining smuggling charges. If Templeton had not cut off the evidence during the provincial election the story might have ended differently.

And Joe Sottile? After the May raids he hid out in Saint John, New Brunswick, for a while with James Lavallée, but when things got too hot Lavallée hid him with two Greek bootleggers, George and Jim Monolopolis, who ran the Sea Grill on Hollis Street near the Halifax waterfront. The Monolopolis brothers were connected with Mike Morro, a Halifax bootlegging cargo master; a Montreal bootlegger named Sam Stamas; and one Peter Costas of St Pierre, who supplied liquor from the island.

The RCMP began intercepting Lavallée's mail and soon learned that Sottile was hiding in Halifax. Surveillance proved fruitless, however, because Morro had rented a large house on posh South Park Street for Sottile, while the Mounties were concentrating on cheap downtown boarding houses.

One of Sottile's letters to Lavallée proved to be an eyeopener for the Mounties. In it he said that he had paid $3,200 to Montreal MP Samuel Jacobs and an unspecified amount to the "Hon. McDonald" to obtain Canadian citizenship. The latter was likely Edward Mortimer Macdonald, a lightweight MP from Antigonish-Guysborough, who got the post of Minister of National Defence because King needed a Maritimer in his Cabinet. The resulting RCMP investigation revealed that the minister's son, Welsford Macdonald, had ties to Sottile.

Sottile was waiting in Halifax for the Mafia alien smuggling network, which was most often used to get mob members out of Mussolini-ruled Sicily to North America. In the meantime, he was receiving letters from the United States addressed "Dear Godfather" and "Don Peppe," telling him of the progress of the operation. Eventually, a man arrived from Italy with papers in the name of Giuseppe Faillia. Sottile left for Montreal hours before the RCMP raided the South Park Street house. There he obtained an Italian passport in the name of Faillia, boarded the White Star liner *S.S. Regina* and sailed for Liverpool, where he convinced Liverpool police he was Faillia and made it safely to Palermo.

In 1930, after the Buffalo charges were dropped, Sottile returned via the same smuggling network to Niagara Falls, New York, where he was honoured with a mob banquet.

CHAPTER 10

MOST FLAGRANT PERJURY

In the early months of 1926, a bootlegging scandal erupted that eventually brought down the Liberal government of William Lyon Mackenzie King and sparked the constitutional crisis known as the "King-Byng Affair."

In the October 1925 federal election, 116 Conservative members had been elected, one of them Charles W. Bell, Rocco's lawyer. The Liberals had 101 seats, and the Progressives held the balance of power with 24. King, who lost his own seat, formed an alliance with the Progressives and retained power while campaigning for a new seat in Prince Albert, Saskatchewan. The Tories, feeling they had been cheated, sought ways to bring down the government.

The Tory ammunition came from a group of businessmen who had announced in late August, 1924, in Ottawa the formation of the Dominion Smuggler's Protective Association. The group said that thousands of dollars' worth of silk and other merchandise was being smuggled into Canada by bootleggers who had, in the early days, been returning with empty boats after runs into the United States. The businessmen said that the smuggling not only represented unfair competition for legitimate merchants but also lost the government thousands of dollars in revenue.

On February 2, 1926, Vancouver Conservative Harry H. Stevens rose in the House of Commons to expose massive corruption in the Quebec division of the customs department, including the activities of Joseph E. A. Bisaillon, the chief preventive officer in Montreal. Among other exploits, he had allowed a trunk of $35,000-worth of opium into Canada in 1919, stopped Quebec Liquor Commission officers from seizing 16,000 gallons of alcohol being smuggled from St Pierre and siphoned $69,000 of taxpayers' money into his personal bank account. Stevens accused the Liberals of trying to cover up the affair by kicking the Customs Minister Jacques Bureau upstairs to the Senate and allowing him to take nine filing cabinets of documents home that were then destroyed.

King was not in the House — he was still campaigning — and ironically it was the aging Edward Macdonald, the man who had apparently helped Joe Sottile become a Canadian citizen, who led the Liberal defence. On February 5th the Liberals countered by appointing a special Commons committee to investigate the charges. The Tories on the committee included Stevens, R. B. Bennett and Charles W. Bell.*

The committee report was ready on June 18th, and included the recommendation, six weeks before the poisoning incident, that all denatured alcohol be declared non-potable. The committee criticized both Bureau and the new minister of customs, George Boivin, who had used his influence to spring a New Brunswick bootlegger from jail.

After the committee report, the Tories introduced a motion of censure. The motion passed as amended by an Independent MP — it not only condemned the King govern-

---

*One of the things Bell could now do as a Member of Parliament was to see Rocco Perri's naturalization file. On May 17, 1926, he requested a copy of the file from Thomas Mulvey, the Under Secretary of State, putting the emphasis on "a memorandum from you listing the convictions or other black marks against Perri, also a copy of the affidavit by him which we sent in." On May 26th, Mulvey sent Bell copies of the reports by Chief Whatley and Detectives Goodman and Thompson. On June 4, Bell acknowledged receipt of the material sent to him by Mulvey, noting "This letter, with enclosures, contains the information I was anxious to have, and I am indebted to you for it."

It was unclear whether Bell was considering reopening Perri's application for citizenship or whether he was worried that as an MP and a member of the committee he might have to explain his representation of Perri in court in the past. Whatever his motives, Bell dropped the matter.

ment but set up a royal commission to investigate smuggling and bootlegging. By June 28 the King government had effectively lost the confidence of the House, but the governor general, Lord Byng, refused King's request for dissolution and handed power to Conservative Arthur Meighen. His government fell three days later, and a general election was called.

King campaigned against Lord Byng and claimed the scandal was a Tory vendetta against Quebec. Meighen was confident of victory and campaigned on regional issues and against Liberal corruption. On election day, September 14, 1926, King was returned with an effective majority of 130 seats. The Tories were reduced to 91 members, including Bell, who was re-elected in Hamilton West by a huge majority. In Hamilton East, the former coroner, Colonel George Rennie, a Conservative, defeated Rocco Perri's other lawyer, Liberal Michael J. O'Reilly, by 8,970 votes.*

The Royal Commission on Customs and Excise, which had been held up during the election campaign, began hearings in Ottawa on November 17, 1926. James Thomas Brown, Chief Justice of the Court of King's Bench, Saskatchewan, was chairman. William Henry Wright, a justice of the Supreme Court of Ontario and Ernest Roy, Puisine Judge of the Superior Court of Quebec were the commissioners. Commission counsel was Newton Wesley Rowell, K.C., former Liberal leader in Ontario who led his party to defeat in 1914 on a prohibition platform. He was a Methodist and, at least in the early days, had a sincere belief that prohibition would bring a better world. He was assisted by R. L. Calder, K.C. and two junior lawyers. Major A. E. Nash of the firm Clarkson, Gordon and Dilworth was the auditor. The RCMP investigative team consisted largely of officers stationed near the border.

On Monday, March 28, 1927, Harry Hatch, president of

---

*One result of the election was a Conservative leadership convention in Winnipeg in October 1927. Some members of the party wanted to nominate Bell, but he declined. The winner was R. B. Bennett. If Bell had been ambitious, Perri's lawyer might have been Canada's prime minister when the Tories won in 1930.

Gooderham & Worts, appeared before the commission in Toronto. It was to Hatch the first questions about Rocco Perri were put. Under questioning by R. L. Calder, K.C., Hatch explained that Gooderham & Worts manufactured all types of alcohol, potable and non-potable, including rye and Scotch whiskies. Since it was illegal to call the Canadian manufactured product "scotch," Gooderham & Worts called it "argyle." They sold liquor to the United States, China, Japan, Cuba, Bahamas, Uruguay, Great Britain, Panama, Jamaica and Trinidad.

Trying to determine whether Hatch's exporting activities led to breaches of the American Volstead Act, Calder asked, "It is not likely that you would export to the United States through any of your agents. I think we can take that for granted?"

Hatch laughed. "I suppose you could say that. We are not strictly interested in the Volstead. I never saw it. Don't know anything about it." Hatch was still laughing. "I know there is such an animal over there."

"You also know that the animal prevents your exporting without considerable danger?" probed Calder.

"No it does not," Hatch chuckled. "It does not prevent us from exporting at all. It prevents somebody there from importing." He paused. "There is a distinction."

Hatch said they had no U.S. salesmen or agents but that they did have people south of the border to whom they paid commissions. Orders came in by letter, telegraph and telephone anyway.

"Let me make myself clear," said Hatch. "We accept orders by telephone, by telegraph and by letter. We do not care where they come from so long as the goods are for shipment to a legal point, the United States or anywhere else."

Hatch then asked to make a statement. "I just want to point out two things. Mr Calder has gone to great trouble to try and establish that there is a very grave possibility of these goods coming back to Canada or remaining in Canada. I wanted to say that so far as I know we have shipped many, many thousands of cases of whisky to the United States, and

as far as I know we have never had one of our customers successfully prosecuted for breach of the OTA. There have been
one or two prosecutions, but I do not know of any convictions."

The next witness was Lionel L. Sinclair, manager of the
Gooderham & Worts shipping department.

"Do you know a person called Rocco Perri in Hamilton?"
Calder asked.

"I do not know him. I have heard of him," Sinclair said.

"Have you ever spoken to Mrs Rocco Perri or some
person holding herself out as Mrs Rocco Perri on the
telephone?"

"Not that I know of."

"Did you ever meet Rocco Perri or Mrs Rocco Perri?"

"No, sir. I have no knowledge of them."

Sinclair said that Joe Penna was a frequent consignee of
liquor from Gooderham & Worts. Many of the orders came
from a woman. Sinclair said he would then phone Niagara Falls,
New York, for the covering telegram.

The next witness that afternoon was Joseph Burke, the
manager of the Lakeview Inn in Port Credit. He owned two
motorboats, the *Patricia* and the *Meredith*. He rented them
to "fellows from the American side." One of them was Joe
Penna. Burke said he ordered from Gooderham & Worts
"informally" on behalf of his friends.

"Do you know Penna personally?" Calder inquired.

"No, I only met him once," Burke responded. He
described Penna as an American, not an Italian American,
who had come from the United States to see him once in
Port Credit.

"Did he come from Hamilton?" Calder asked.

"No. He certainly did not."

"Is not his real name Rocco Perri?" Calder was sharp.

"No."

"You sure of that?"

"Positive."

"If you do not know him, why are you so positive that
'Rocco Perri' is not his real name?" asked Mr Justice Wright.

"Because I know Perri, and I only met Penna once."

"You know Rocco Perri?"

"You bet."

"Where does Rocco Perri live?" Calder asked.

"I do not want to answer anything about Rocco Perri. I want to answer only about my own personal affairs," Burke objected.

Burke denied taking liquor in boats to either his hotel or the abandoned brickyard next door. The commission adjourned. The stage was set for the appearance of the feature witness the next day.

Bessie Perri arrived at the commission hearings dressed in a fashionable, fur-trimmed brown coat, brown suit and a dull orange, wide-brimmed hat. She posed for press photographers and then went inside to wait until she was called. She faced Calder, cool and composed. He asked where Rocco was. He had gone to Ottawa about ten days or two weeks ago, Bessie said. She had not heard from him since and she could not indicate where he was.

"What is Mr Perri's business?" Calder inquired.

"He used to have a store," was Bessie's answer.

"What is his business now?"

"At present, nothing."

"When did he give up the store?"

"He gave up the store on account of my health; I have been sick."

"He gave up the store on account of your being sick?"

"Yes," said Bessie.

"As a matter of fact, Mrs Perri, does not Perri go about the United States and Ontario taking orders of liquor?"

"I could not say that."

"Will you state positively on your oath that he does not?"

"I could not tell you because he never tells me his business."

She denied making long-distance calls to Gooderham & Worts. Lots of people, though, came into her house to use the telephone, including many friends from the United States.

"Are these friends rum runners?" asked Calder.

"I could not say that."

"You do not know what their business is?"

"No."

"Mrs Perri," said Calder, emphasizing each word, "you will not mind if I say you are the most incurious woman I have ever met."

Calder asked Bessie if she knew a Mr Penna in Hamilton. "No," she replied. She confirmed that her husband was Italian but said she didn't know much about the Italian colony in Hamilton. She also said she had a savings account at the Bank of Commerce in Hamilton.

"Has your husband got a bank account?"

"I could not tell you about my husband; if he had got it, he would not tell me."

"Do you mean you do not want to tell me, or that you do not know?"

"I do not know; if I knew I would tell you."

Bessie said that she did not have her bank book with her when Calder asked her to produce it. The account was in her name and no one else could draw on it. She couldn't remember how much she had in the bank at the beginning of the year — about $800, she thought. She had never made payments to Gooderham & Worts, never handed money to her husband to be handled in the business. She denied ever sending drafts to Niagara Falls. She did not know either Herbert Hatch or Larry McGuinness.

"We have got this much," the frustrated counsel summed up. "A number of people from the United States used to come into your house and telephone Toronto from time to time?"

"They might telephone to Toronto; they might telephone any place if they want to do so," she replied.

Asked why there were so many long-distance calls to Toronto, Bessie replied that she called her two daughters in Toronto every day. She couldn't tell if the visitors called Gooderham & Worts; she didn't listen in on other people's conversations. She only knew some of the people who came to the house.

"Do some people come in who you do not know?" asked Mr Justice Brown.

"Well, I do not interfere with my husband's friends, you know," she said. "They are his friends; he is an Italian and so are they; they are his friends."

"Mrs Penna, will you —"

"Not Mrs Penna," snapped Bessie.

"I beg your pardon," said Calder.

Calder asked if it was only men who made phone calls from the house. Bessie replied a lot of her women friends came to make calls.

"Then you know who they were?" asked Calder.

"Sure, I knew who they were," replied Bessie.

"Why would they come into your house to call up Toronto?"

"I did not know where they called, I did not watch them."

"Then in that case, why" — Calder's question was pointed — "did you insist on being given the telephone company's call records? When you paid your telephone bills why did you ask the company for its telephone records, telling them that they were no use to them and that you wanted them? [There were two records, the bill sent to the customer and the call record.] I suggest to you that you wanted the company's call record in order to destroy all traces of your calls?"

"No."

"You swear that?"

"I swear that."

The next morning, Calder called John A. Gorrie, district manager of the Bell Telephone Company in Hamilton. He produced two large bundles of call records, which showed calls almost every day from Hamilton Regent 8267 to Toronto Main 0427, the number of Gooderham & Worts.

Calder thumbed through the first bundle. "In this one parcel alone," he said, "there are — I've lost count of this number — you'd require a bank teller."

Bessie was then recalled to the witness box.

Calder showed her the bundle of phone slips. "What do you have to say about these?" he asked.

"I couldn't tell you anything about them," Bessie replied.

She explained she was away in June, July and August 1926, going to Buffalo or Crystal Beach and then returning home for a day or so.

"Why not tell the truth?" asked Mr Justice Ernest Roy, one of the commissioners.

"I am telling the truth," Bessie told His Lordship. "I didn't telephone those places. I'm only a woman, I'm not concerned who telephones to distilleries."

"Being a woman, you might stay at home," commented Chief Justice Brown, the commission chairman.

"When I was at home, I was usually in the kitchen downstairs...."

"We'll leave you in the kitchen," suggested Chief Justice Brown. "Weren't you struck by the fact that someone unknown to you was using your telephone practically every day for three or four months and running up heavy bills?" he asked. "Did you inquire who it was?"

"I did and Perri said it was a friend of mine, they'll pay for it."

"I think," said Calder, "that overnight, you determined to have Mr Perri responsible for everything."

"No."

Bessie was excused.

The next day, Friday, April 1st, commission counsel N. W. Rowell called Herbert F. ("Pat") Kuntz, grandson of the founder of the Kuntz Brewery, who had taken over the firm in 1925. Rowell got right to the point.

"Did you have any conversations, Mr Kuntz, with Mrs Perri at Hamilton?"

"No, never," he replied.

Rowell had a phone slip.

"There has been produced here some telephone conversations. Here is one with Herb Kuntz, Kuntz Brewery, from Mrs Perri's telephone in Hamilton. Do you remember any conversation with —"

"Mr or Mrs Perri?" Kuntz inquired.

"Yes?" said Rowell.

"Never."

Rowell pointed to the slip. "You don't remember that conversation?"

"No, sir," Kuntz answered, asking to see the slip and then telling Rowell the call had gone to the company switchboard. Rowell then showed there were several phone calls from the Perri house to the Kuntz Brewery.

Meanwhile, the RCMP were still looking for Rocco Perri so they could order him to appear before the commission. Finally the Mounties turned to the Hamilton police for help. On the evening of April 1st, two Hamilton cops sneaked into the garage behind Perri's house and made a lot of noise. Perri came out of the kitchen, which was attached to the garage, to investigate. There he was served a subpoena and was handed five dollars "conduct money." He was ordered to appear on the afternoon of Monday, April 4th.

Hamilton Crown attorney George Ballard was pleased. "I wonder what Perri will do when he is faced with some interviews that he gave to the newspapers a while ago? He came out rather strongly then and made a few admissions. It will be interesting when he goes on the stand, for the court has the power to make a witness talk."

It was a smiling, debonair Rocco Perri who entered the witness box on Monday afternoon. Although this time Michael J. O'Reilly was in court with Rocco and Bessie, they did not request protection under the Canada Evidence Act.

"What is your business?" Rowell asked.

"Nothing at present," Rocco replied, explaining he had a fruit business until 1919, then travelled for a while in olive oil and Italian groceries.

"Then you have been living on your means since 1920?" inquired Rowell.

"Well, we have a little rent coming to us," Rocco said.

"You do not do anything to supplement that income?"

"No."

"And never have?"

Rocco couldn't remember.

"How did you get the reputation of being a bootlegger?"

Rocco laughed. "The *Star* reporter came up here and wanted me to give them a little news, they bothered me everyday, so I had to give them a little news."

"So you admitted you were a bootlegger?"

"No, I was doing a little export and mail order business." Rocco claimed he couldn't remember when exactly the *Star* interview was, but he claimed he had given up the business sometime before the interview.

"And you remember signing the interview? They asked you to sign it before they published it?"

"Yes, I think they did."

"And I suppose you told the truth?"

"I was not telling them the truth, but was telling them a little story to get them away from my door."

"Did you sign a statement that you were engaged in the bootlegging business?"

"Not at present, not when I signed the paper."

"What did you say in the statement?"

"I said I was in the bootlegging business before that."

"You called it the 'bootlegging business' yourself. Did you call yourself the 'King of the Bootleggers?'"

"We had done a pretty good business in mail order," Rocco answered. He said he had started the mail order business in 1918 or 1919, but had stopped it a long time before the *Star* interview, just when he couldn't remember. Rocco claimed he never said, "There is no business — I don't care what you name — in which honesty is a more important factor than the bootlegging business."

"I never said that; I could not explain that if I wanted to," Rocco said.

"You signed the statement?" Rowell asked again.

"I may have signed it, but I could not read very good English."

"What is that?" Chief Justice Brown asked.

"I do not read English very good."

"Now you say you did not understand what you were signing?" the judge asked.

"Well," said Rocco, "I remember that he bring the

advertisement over there once and he read it to me. Of course, the piano was going —"

"Who was playing the piano?"

"The wife was playing the piano."

"And you could not hear?"

"I could hear but I could not understand exactly every word, what was explained."

The questioning turned to Rocco's whereabouts during the previous two weeks. He had been in Welland, St Catharines, Port Weller. He hadn't seen Bessie until last Thursday. He insisted it was hard to remember details. Mr Justice William Henry Wright, another commissioner, threatened Rocco with punishment for perjury. Rocco still had difficulty remembering exactly when he was where.

"That is ridiculous; a child would remember that," said Chief Justice Brown.

"I know it is ridiculous, but I cannot remember," Rocco replied.

And the game went on. Rocco said that he did not even know Bessie had been subpoenaed. He must have been out of the house when the subpoena was served.

"She did not tell you that; it is a funny kind of woman to be living with that would not tell you she had been subpoenaed to come down to Customs?" Rowell commented.

"I don't think I seen her; if I did see her she don't tell me, I don't know why," Rocco responded.

At that moment something must have dawned on Mr Justice Ernest Roy. "Is it Mrs Perri?" he interrupted.

"Yes," replied Rocco.

"Is she your wife?" asked Mr Justice Roy.

"Yes."

"When did you get married?"

"I live with her about fifteen years," Rocco said.

"When were you married?" Roy asked.

"We are not married." There was an audible gasp in the courtroom.

"I think Mrs Perri had better be excluded while we are continuing the examination," Rowell told the three commissioners, and Bessie was ushered out. Then Rowell turned to Rocco's bootlegging activities. Rocco told the same story as Bessie: friends come to the house to use the phone.

"I want the names of the people and where they live." said Rowell.

Rocco named Joe Penna, State Street, Buffalo; Nino Sacco, Jersey Street, Buffalo; Domenic Sacco, South Halstead, Chicago; Rocco Pitsimenti, Mulberry Street, New York. Penna used the phone most often and placed most of the orders, with both Gooderham & Worts and Seagram's. Rowell mispronounced Penna "Penn" and Rocco played with that name.

"How much did you get a case?" Rowell demanded.

"A case for what?" Rocco responded.

"For the goods ordered over the phone?"

"I never ordered no stuff over the phone."

"How much were you paid?" Rowell repeated.

"All I pay or they pay me?" was Rocco's question.

"They pay you?" Rowell wasn't sure if it was a question.

"Who?" asked Rocco.

"Penn."

"Penn pay me?"

"Yes."

"What for?" asked Rocco.

"I told you what for," Rowell echoed. "Answer my question."

"Penn came down here like a friend and he use my phone whatever he pleased and he called up distillery. He never pay me a case of whisky or anything at all. He pay me for my call, that is all he pay me for."

"What were you calling Joe Burke for at Port Credit?"

"I think it was Joe Penn calling Joe Burke," Rocco answered.

"What would he want Joe Burke for?"

"I don't know what he want him."

"Do you want us to believe that?" Rowell asked.

"Well, they had a business between the two."

Rocco Perri's police mug shot, 1926.

Bessie Starkman Perri, c 1925.

Magistrate George Frederick Jelfs, who presided over many cases involving Rocco.

Charles Bell, Rocco's lawyer.

OPP Inspectors William Stringer and Edward Hammond, two veteran Perri investigators.

OPP Inspector John Miller, who investigated both the 1920s gang war and the murder of Bessie Perri.

Hamilton Police Chief William R. Whatley, who was accused of corruption and a relationship with Bessie Perri.

Wounded Rocco Perri accompanied by Hamilton Police Chief Joe Crocker minutes after Rocco's car exploded into pieces.

Olive Routledge, Rocco's mistress from 1917 to 1922.

DEPUTY TREASON

ERS" GUNS

"KING OF ONTARIO BOOTLEGGERS"

REFUSE LEAVE FRON

Exclusive interview with the King of the Bootleggers on the front page of the *Toronto Star*, 1924.

Perri's rum boat, *The Hattie C,* and his high-speed Reo truck under police guard after the shootout at Ashbridge's Bay in 1923.

The Flow of the
Famous Poison Brew

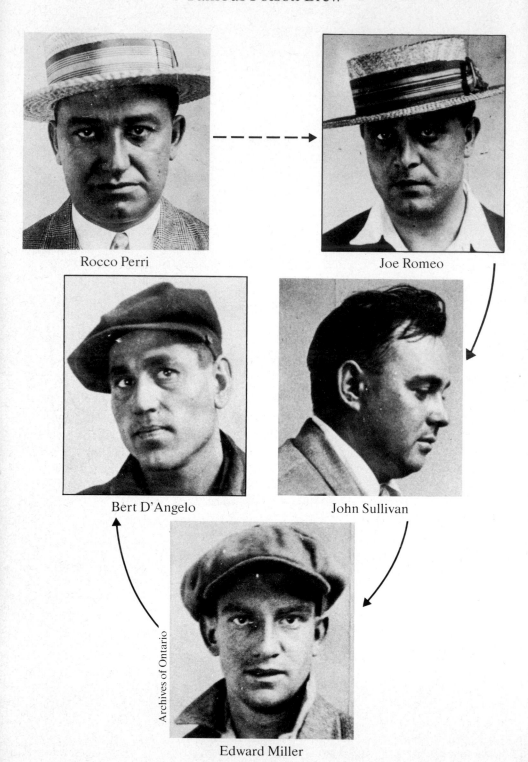

Rocco Perri

Joe Romeo

Bert D'Angelo

John Sullivan

Edward Miller

RCMP Inspector Frank Zaneth, who risked his life to infiltrate the Perri mob.

Rocco Perri on the stand at the 1927 Royal Commission, with Newton Rowell, Commission Counsel, conducting the cross-examination.

Rocco and Bessie with Crown Attorney Eddie Murphy.

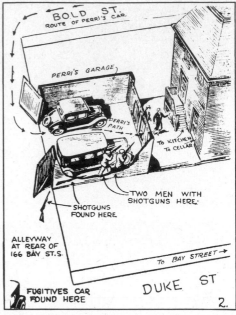

Toronto Star feature on Bessie's murder, showing the Perris' mansion, the garage and the shotguns used to kill Bessie.

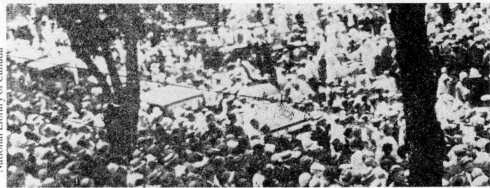

Thousands line the streets outside Rocco Perri's home on the day of Bessie's funeral.

Rocco Perri in tears at the graveside of Bessie. He collapsed at the site and was almost pushed into the open grave by the crowd.

The bombed-out remains of Rocco's car. Rocco escaped with minor injuries, though two of his underlings were seriously injured.

Annie Newman in her mink coat, captured by a *Windsor Star* photographer as she enters the Windsor courthouse during the 1940 customs case.

Rocco Perri calmly smokes a cigarette as he awaits trial in 1940.

Annie Newman in her later years.

Rocco Perri laughs as RCMP Constable George Ashley escorts him to court in Windsor.

"What was the business — shipping liquor?"

"Shipping liquor, I suppose," Rocco answered.

"You know. What is the use of talking that way? You know it was shipping liquor."

"I don't know whether they were shipping liquor or what they were doing." Rowell asked about Port Colborne. Rocco said he called a friend named Frank Ross, who had a cigar and candy store.

Rowell asked Rocco why he made so many phone calls to a man named Secorza in St Catharines.

"Oh, he is my godfather," Rocco explained blandly.

"Your grandfather?" asked Mr Justice Roy.

Rocco just smiled and nodded. "Joe Penn" had made sixty-four calls to a club in Waterloo and calls to Thorold. The forty-eight calls to Frank Longo in Welland came after Longo's wife had had an operation in Hamilton.

"Do you know Mike Bernardo?" Rowell asked.

"No."

"Now, steady..." Rowel cautioned. There was a long pause. "Do you know Mike Bernardo?"

"I do not think so."

"Mike Bernardo, please stand up," Rowell called. A man stood up among the spectators.

"I know him now," Rocco said, but in answer to the next question said he had never called him; a fellow from Rochester had called him.

Rowell turned to bank accounts. Rocco replied that he had had no bank account for seven or eight years, ever since he had one at a branch of the Imperial Bank in Hamilton.

"Do you put all your money into her (Bessie's) bank account?"

"When I have money, I give it to her."

"All your money?"

"No, I keep some for myself."

"Where do you keep your money?"

"In my pocket."

"Only in your pocket."

"Yes."

"Mrs Perri promised to bring her bank books, but we have not yet got them," Rowell commented.

"If she promised, she must bring them," Rocco assured him.

Rowell changed the subject, telling Rocco that Lionel Sinclair had said that most of the calls from his house in Hamilton were made by a woman. Rowell wanted to know who she was.

"Maybe the operator call," answered Rocco.

"No; the woman who was speaking from your house."

"From my house?" queried Rocco.

"Yes," answered Rowell.

"Unless it was Mr Penn's wife."

"Mr Penn is not a woman," Rowell stated.

"No, but he had his wife with him," Rocco answered.

"Are Penna and Penn the same man?" inquired Mr Justice Wright.

"Oh, no," Rocco assured him.

"Are you sure?" asked His Lordship.

"I am sure," Rocco said.

"Will you produce him for us?" Rowell asked.

"If I had the power to do it I would do it," Rocco told him. "Why don't you send a couple of people over there to investigate? I will give you the name and address and telephone number if you want it."

"Who was telephoning in a woman's voice from your home?" Rowell asked again. Rocco claimed it was Mrs Joe Penna, not Bessie using that name.

"If Mrs Perri knew I touched any liquor, she would leave me tomorrow," Rocco said.

"Who remits the cash?"

'What do you mean?" asked Rocco.

"For these shipments that are ordered in the name of J. Penna?"

"I do not know; it is between the distillery and Mr Penn," answered Rocco, sticking to his original story.

Rowell asked a series of questions about the Third Ward

Political Club. Rocco said that he had never heard of it. Someone else was using his name to order the alcohol.

"If I knew who was using my name, I would have him arrested," Rocco said.

"You would have him arrested?" It was probably more than Rowell, the former leader of the Prohibition movement in Ontario and a veteran of inquiries into political shenanigans, could believe. "Back as far as 1924, your name appears in the books of the company as a large buyer of alcohol," he said.

"Which company?" Rocco asked.

"This company over at Niagara Falls," Rowell replied.

"Anybody could go over there and give my name."

"Why would they charge it to your name?"

"They know if they mention my name, they would get it," Rocco explained.

"You are known as a man who handles liquor?" Mr Justice Roy interrupted.

"It is not that," Rocco commented. "They know I was well-known at the time, and if they go over there and say, 'Perri sent me here to get some liquor,' they would treat them good."

"You think somebody went over there?"

"Yes, but you can be sure I did not get alcohol."

"Somebody went over there and Mr Perri's name was so high in the fraternity that all they had to do was to mention it and they could get alcohol?" Rowell inquired.

"They would have to pay for it, I suppose," Rocco offered.

Rowell had had enough. He told Rocco to stand aside and let R. L. Calder take over the proceedings. Calder had Bessie step into the witness box and asked for her bank book. She handed him a bank book from the Canadian Bank of Commerce, at King and James streets in Hamilton. It showed a balance of $98.78.

"Where is the bank book before that?" Calder demanded.

"I do not know," Bessie said, "I may have left it at home."

"You did leave it at home, as a matter of fact," said Calder.

"No," said Bessie.

"And you brought only this book with one entry in it?" Calder asked.

"That's all I have got," she said.

"What is the date of the entry?" asked chairman Chief Justice Brown.

"March 9, 1927, my Lord," replied Calder. "It appears to be very, very recently written in."

Calder asked for Bessie's authorization to have the accounting firm Clarkson, Gordon and Dilworth examine her account. Michael J. O'Reilly handed her the prepared paper and she signed. Then the Perris were excused.

Over the next few days, witnesses were called to tell what they knew about the Perris. On Thursday, April 7th Mike Bernardo, a Toronto garage man and boat charterer, took the stand first. He said he acted for a man named Sullivan in New York City and loaded whisky for him at Gooderham & Worts in Toronto and from Corbyville near Belleville. The large steam yacht *Allen* also brought liquor back into Canada from St Pierre, but Bernardo didn't know much about it. At one point Bernardo said he couldn't remember the name of the captain.

"You have not the failing memory of Mr Rocco Perri?" Rowell asked.

"Don't put me in the class of Rocco Perri," Bernardo retorted.

"You object to that?" asked Chief Justice Brown.

"Why certainly," replied Bernardo, who still couldn't remember the name of the captain. Rowell was trying to find out whether tax-free Canadian alcohol was being smuggled back into Canada by the boat that plied between St Pierre and the Great Lakes.

Rowell asked Bernardo why he had had a large number of calls from Rocco Perri. He admitted that the Perris sometimes called him, but often it was Joe Penna or some other person from the United States. Under questioning from Chief Justice Brown, Bernardo admitted that he had met both Rocco and Bessie Perri. Under questioning from Rowell, Bernardo then admitted that the Perris called him at least once a week, perhaps several times a week. Bernardo denied ever having paid money to the Perris. He did say he had received one cheque from them when they wanted to buy a carload of beer to ship to Port Dalhousie. Bernardo thought that Mrs Perri had signed the cheque, but he hadn't paid much attention.

The commission moved from Toronto to Windsor, where Herbert E. Hatch testified that Hatch & McGuiness was a sales agency for Gooderham & Worts, with a considerable share interest in the company itself. It sold liquor anywhere it could outside of Ontario. He admitted that the books of Hatch & McGuinness held orders from a "J. Penna."

"Have you ever taken orders from the Perris?" asked Calder. Hatch said he wasn't sure; he took phone and direct orders from people "he took to be Penna." It wasn't Rocco Perri. Penna lived in Niagara Falls, but he had met Penna at Rocco Perri's house, where Penna gave him orders for liquor.

On May 9th, the royal commission began its hearings in Hamilton. Rocco and Bessie Perri were called again. They did not answer. Rowell explained to the commission that he had given notice to their lawyer Michael J. O'Reilly that the Perris would be required at the Hamilton hearings, but O'Reilly had been unable to locate them. Richard Boyce, the American consul, was in the audience, taking notes for his intelligence reports to Washington. The rest of the day was spent in routine questions about how customs worked in the Niagara region.

Meanwhile, the Toronto *Star* had tracked down a real Joe Penna in Buffalo. On the phone he claimed he had never been to Wilson, New York. Yes, he knew Rocco Perri, but had never used his phone. He had been in Ontario only once — in St Catharines. Did he ever buy liquor? "No, it's against the law here," Penna said just before hanging up. Obviously, Penna was not integrally involved in Perri's operation but was being paid for the use of his name.

Nash, the auditor, was called on May 12th. He said he had found eight of Bessie's bank accounts, which showed that from the beginning Rocco and Bessie had been making money. In Bessie's Hamilton accounts, as of March 1927, there was $25,000 in the Standard Bank, $200,000 in the Bank of Commerce and $40,000 in another Commerce account.

Mike Romeo was called on May 13th. He claimed to have had no dealings with Rocco Perri. Nor had he had any business dealings with Bessie Perri, although he had gone to the bank for her as a favour to deposit cheques.

"She could not hop into her Marmon car and go up to the bank herself, so she gave you various amounts of money...for the purpose of carrying the money to the bank for her? She didn't give you the money to buy beer and you did not put the profits in the bank for her?" asked Calder.

"No."

The next witness was Rosario Carboni, who claimed that he used to run beer but didn't do it anymore. He told the same story of taking money to the Bank of Commerce in the old Bank of Hamilton building (where Olive Routledge had jumped to her death) as a favour to Bessie.

"For a period of time you took money nearly every day to the bank for Mrs Rocco Perri?"

Carboni could not remember.

"Very often?" Roy asked.

"Yes," Carboni replied.

"Every day except Sundays and legal holidays," chuckled the chief justice of Saskatchewan. Carboni did not answer. Calder then showed him a whole series of cheques, all with his endorsement. Carboni repeated that Bessie had called him on the phone and asked him to make the deposits. Carboni had to admit that while he lived half an hour away from the bank, the Perris lived just ten minutes away. The three justices laughed at that one.

Carboni told the commissioners that he did not know what the Perris' business was.

"You draw money for his wife and put money in the bank for his wife and yet you do not know their business?" asked Calder.

"I do not know their business," replied Carboni.

The last witness was Charlie Bordonaro. He said that he obtained alcohol from "a Jew fellow" in Toronto called Tommy. He paid $10 a gallon — in cash, never by cheque — for the alcohol, which was delivered in one- and five-gallon tins.

"I test it myself," Bordonaro said.

"You drank it?" Roy asked.

"I test it, it was good before giving the money. I tested it. I test three or four gallons and took it up a bunch," was Bordonaro's answer.

"Do you know Rocco Perri?" asked Calder.

"Yes."

"Did you ever have business dealings with him?"

"No, sir."

"Ever have any dealings with his wife?"

"No, sir."

"During the past five or six years, you have not bought any liquor of any kind whatever from Rocco Perri?" asked Calder.

"No, sir," Bordonaro replied. "Because he never been doing business in alcohol. *I* am in the alcohol business."

"You are in the alcohol business exclusively, as a specialty?"

"Yes."

Bordonaro was excused.

The testimony of Romeo, Carboni and Bordonaro shows the insulation that mob members usually give to their boss. Also, it proves that rumours about Bessie Perri were true, that it was Bessie who handled the money, amounting to thousands of dollars each week, that was paid in and out in the bootlegging racket. And it was often to Bessie that men like Romeo and Carboni reported.

With the conclusion of Bordonaro's testimony, Calder

addressed the three justices on the commission — Brown, Wright and Roy — asking that perjury charges be laid against Rocco and Bessie Perri.

"The main allegation," said Calder, "would be that Rocco Perri swore he was not in the liquor business, and I think it is abundantly proved, not only by direct confirmation, but by the clearly evasive answers of certain witnesses called, that Rocco Perri was in the liquor business and was in the business exclusively.... Perjury charged against Mrs Perri would be the assertion that she had at all times only one bank account, that she produced a bank book showing a balance of some ninety-odd dollars and swore that that was the only bank book she had.... And we now know that she has a large amount of bank accounts in the name of Bessie Perri and Bessie Perri in trust.... The whole tenor of their testimony is perjury."

"We quite agree with the suggestion that a charge should be made forthwith against Rocco Perri and Mrs Perri," said Chief Justic Brown. "What we have learned since they gave their evidence at Toronto has satisfied us that they are guilty of the most flagrant perjury and we think that action should be taken without delay." Brown ordered that the officers of the commission go before a magistrate in Toronto, where the offence occurred, and request warrants for the arrest of Rocco and Bessie Perri.

"If these people are still in the jurisdiction, then they should be prosecuted at once. If they are outside the jurisdiction of Canada, in the United States or elsewhere, then the issue of the warrant may have the effect of keeping them there," said Chief Justice Brown. The Hamilton session was over.

Rocco and Bessie had indeed skipped town after their testimony. Or had they? In May it was reported that they had crossed the border to the United States and maybe even sailed to Italy. Police, however, believed they were hiding somewhere near Hamilton. Rocco was reported seen in the city. A cross-Canada alert was issued.

On June 4th, Mike Romeo, Louis Sylvester, Jimmy

D'Agostino and Frank Vale were arrested leaving the Thorncliffe races. They were driving one of the Perri Marmons. They told police that Bessie Perri had lent them the car the night before. But now they had no idea of where she and Rocco were.

It would be late that fall before it became safe for the Perris to return to their home on Bay Street in Hamilton.

CHAPTER 11

FAMILY
FORTUNES

Business problems were looming for Rocco and Bessie. On March 8, 1927, shortly before the royal commission hearings opened in Toronto, G. Howard Ferguson's Conservative government introduced the Liquor Control Act. Ferguson was able to restrict debate on the merits of the liquor bill, so the legislature didn't fall into the old battles over prohibition. Government-controlled liquor stores — six in Toronto and twelve more across the province — would open June 1st.

The new Liquor Control Act was more restrictive than similar acts in some other provinces. Parts of it are still on the books to this day. The government required that anyone over twenty-one who had been in the province for at least a month had to acquire a liquor permit and pay a fee. (Sir Alec Guinness, a stranger in a strange land at Stratford in the 1950s, perhaps best called the system "registering as alcoholics.") Non-residents were allowed to obtain thirty-day permits. But the local option factor remained in the legislation: in any given area, liquor stores could not be set up and liquor licences could not be obtained unless three-fifths of the population voted wet. One neighbourhood in the west end of Toronto remains dry to this day under this law.

Beer, liquor and wine were sold only in sealed containers to individuals who held permits. Beer parlours still would not exist and hotels and restaurants could not sell beer or wine with meals: sale by the glass was forbidden. Nevertheless, a visitor could get a permit, buy a bottle at a Liquor Control Board store and get pie-eyed plastered in his hotel room.

On June 1st, there were long lineups at the liquor stores across the province. Customers would continue to crowd into the new outlets for the next week, as parched citizens presented their permits, got their rations of liquor and made their exits, bottles carefully concealed in brown paper bags.

For Rocco and Bessie Perri it meant that the bootlegging business would dwindle, but not die. There were still customers in local option dry areas. Bootleggers would supply liquor after hours, and the blind pigs, clandestine beer parlours and social clubs would continue operations as they had until after the Second World War.

There was another obstacle, however. All the distillers and brewers were now selling their product in Ontario through the provincial liquor commission. And although bootleggers could resort to the old standby of reimporting exported goods, demand was dropping because customers knew that if they bought from a government liquor store they would be getting the genuine article. With bootleggers' goods there was always the possibility of the old three-to-four dilution with redistilled alcohol.

During the Ontario provincial election in the fall of 1926, the Conservatives campaigned for repeal of the Ontario Temperance Act and against Rocco Perri in full-page newspaper ads.

Hamilton Herald/National Library of Canada

Meanwhile, the Royal Commission on Customs and Excise was winding up its hearings in Ottawa. (It had been unable to locate Max Wortzman, the only major bootlegger to escape testifying before the commission.) Nash testified what he had learned about the connections between Joe Sottile, Rocco Perri, Max Wortzman and the Maritimes, and how Canadian beer was exchanged for redistilled alcohol. Max Wortzman was the man who purchased and imported the largest amount, 80,000 of the 150,000 gallons of alcohol into Canada, Nash said. In 1926, the Wortzman brothers' operation was worth $1,400,000.

The conclusions contained in the commission's report were to bring the Perris back into the spotlight, along with some of the big-name booze manufacturers in Ontario. The report contained the following note:

ROCCO PERRI, BESSIE PERRI, OR SPARKMAN [sic]

Rocco Perri and Bessie Perri, his alleged wife, have been living in Hamilton, Ont. for many years. They have been engaged in the liquor traffic on a very large scale, purchasing their stock from different breweries and distilleries. The sales were made in Canada, partly for consumption therein and partly to be smuggled into the United States.

The two parties gave evidence which was proved to be false, especially in connection with their bank accounts.

The commission noted that action had already been taken on the recommendation that they be prosecuted for perjury. It further recommended that since the Perris had filed no income tax returns on their large profits, they be investigated for income tax evasion, although there is no indication that this was ever done.

The Kuntz Brewery, the commission concluded, was a major exporter of beer to the United States. Whole boxcarload lots were commonly sold right at the brewery siding, as cash sales to anyone, no questions asked. No records of purchaser were kept on the company books. During the period of the commission's investigation, the company had brewed 3,812,236 gallons of beer. Its books showed 2,866,336 sold, leaving 945,000 gallons, or 24.8 percent of production, unaccounted for.

As for Gooderham & Worts, the commission reported that the company had always had customers in the United States. It paid little tax on the goods it exported to them, and the commission noted that action was already being taken against the company for evasion of sales tax.

In fact, ten days after the royal commission had left Hamilton, the federal government filed suit against Gooderham & Worts for $439,744.05 for sales tax evasion and accumulated interest at five per cent.

Overall, the pattern the commission reported was one of mass corruption across Canada. Bessie wasn't the only one who misplaced books. Old established firms seemed to lose a lot of them, and the ones they did have were often sloppy or tended to disappear upon the issuance of subpoenas. There was widespread bribery of U.S. officials, and Canadian customs officials seemed to think it was their job simply to accept payment of duties from those willing to pay, letting the unwilling ones slip goods across the border at no extra cost. The high profits in the liquor trade were responsible for widespread fraud, smuggling and corruption. Finally, the commission recommended that the government stop the system of permitting liquor clearances to the United States.

In Hamilton, yet another investigation was taking place. It was Richard Boyce, the American consul, who had initiated it. On May 10th, he had sat in on the royal commission hearings that were focusing on the Kuntz Brewery. Calder called Victor L. Armitage, a U.S. Treasury agent on special assignment, who had been sent into Canada to spy on bootlegging activities. Armitage told how he had staked out the Kuntz Brewery in Kitchener and watched the loading of a boxcar at a siding alongside the brewery. The boxcar was moved to London, Ontario, where it obtained a waybill stating that the shipment was being sent to the American Tanners' Product Corp., Pittsburgh, Pennsylvania, from the

Kitchener Rag & Metal Company. The contents were scrap leather, the waybill said.

In Pittsburgh, where there was no such company as American Tanners', Armitage led a raid as the barrels were being unloaded from the car. Inside were a total of 278 barrels, each containing 30 bottles of Ye Olde Inn Ale, manufactured by the Kuntz Brewery. There was also a large quantity of scrap leather that had been cleverly packed around each door in the boxcar. Armitage, who earlier apparently had had no permission to spy in Canada, afterward returned to the brewery accompanied by an RCMP officer and found labels for 9 percent beer identical to those seized in Pittsburgh.

After hearing Armitage's testimony, Boyce went back to the filing cabinets in the consulate. His secret dispatches to the State Department reveal how beer was shipped from Hamilton to the United States. In those days, anyone shipping legitimate goods to the U.S. filed a copy of the invoice with the nearest consulate. Normally these just gathered dust. On May 12th, Boyce began the tedious job of checking every invoice, first pulling the invoices for shipments that had been intercepted.

He then wrote to the destinations of various cargos requesting confirmation of arrival. If the cargos were consigned to individuals, he wrote to the postmaster in each city, asking for confirmation that the individual existed.

He had known since he arrived in 1924 that boxcars full of beer had been intercepted in the United States, disguised as hay, turnips, scrap leather, rags, paper and rubber. He was seeking a pattern and soon found one. The same man who shipped the load of scrap leather intercepted by Armitage had been shipping turnips to the United States the previous year. But there were also legitimate shipments of turnips, some to the Campbell Soup Co.

By late June, Boyce had received enough replies to establish what was going on. Most of the invoices were sent to the consulate in batches, *after* the boxcar had left. The brokers and custom officers at the border at Niagara Falls, New York, or Port Huron, Michigan, simply ignored the delayed paperwork. To help business, the State Department had ordered consuls to certify invoices even if they were delayed. In this case, the smugglers took advantage of a bureaucratic bottleneck.

Boyce requested an experienced investigator, and Treasury Agent Clarence Rhodes was assigned from Cleveland. Boyce asked for an RCMP officer to accompany Rhodes "to insure truthful answers." The Mounties assigned Sergeant George Fish, and the two visited Hamilton, Galt, Preston and Kitchener-Waterloo. The investigation revealed "flagrant violations of laws and corruption of railroad authorities," Boyce reported.

Together Boyce, Rhodes and Fish discovered how Rocco Perri's men sent beer from the Grant's Spring, Kuntz and Taylor and Bate breweries south to the United States. The contraband was shipped in random lots, part of legitimate shipments to legitimate companies — a better idea than the common method of simply using phoney invoices and camouflaged loads.

From April 1 to June 23, 1927, six shipments of hay were sent from George Bowman of Hagersville to Dwyer Reed Inc. of Newark. One boxcar was sent to the real Dwyer Inc. in Newark. The other eleven boxcars went to phoney Dwyer addresses in Montclair, Englewood, Garfield, Manuet and Raritan, New Jersey.

Boyce got little satisfaction from his investigation. The State Department sat on his recommendations and the Customs Department ignored his findings. He then attempted to bypass the bureaucracy by including a sealed letter in his dispatch addressed to the assistant attorney general in charge of prohibition enforcement. The State Department refused to pass the letter on to the Justice Department because it was "inadvisable." Boyce tried proposing a card index file and systematic certification of invoices. The State Department balked, noting that "the system...would cause irritation among innocent shippers out of all proportion to its probable value in preventing the shipment of liquor." He was told to stick to his defined duties and to inform U.S. Customs of suspect shipments, a system that had already failed. Boyce finally had to settle on using his own money to pay for a rubber stamp to flag suspect invoices.

The investigation revealed that in just over 12 weeks in 1927, 60 boxcars of beer left Hamilton, Kitchener or St Catharines for the United States via Niagara Falls. Rocco's profits must have been enormous. The Royal Commission reported the border price of a dozen pints of Canadian beer in 1927 was $3.25. If the boxcar Armitage seized was an indication of an average load, there were 278 barrels each with 30 bottles. That load would have been worth $2,258.75. Sixty boxcars of beer in 12 weeks means a gross take of at least $135,525.

Gooderham & Worts had been targeted by the government as the test case to get back the unpaid taxes. To collect those taxes, the Crown had to prove that the liquor was not exported as the company claimed, but that it had been sold in Canada for Canadian consumption. To do that, the best witnesses were, of course, Rocco and Bessie Perri. A deal was made for their testimony, and Rocco and Bessie returned to Canada, back to the comfort of their Hamilton home, ready to testify on the behalf of His Majesty the King against the firm of Gooderham & Worts.

It had been a busy year for Harry Hatch. He had taken over the firm of Hiram Walker, strategically placed in Walkerville, Ontario, across the river from Detroit, and now headed a new company, Hiram Walker Gooderham & Worts, whose Canadian Club whisky would remain popular in the United States long after prohibition. He had lost out to the Bronfman family in an attempt to buy the British giant, Distillers Corporation Limited, for $200 million.

The trial of Gooderham & Worts opened in Toronto on December 5, 1927 before Mr Justice Grant. N. W. Rowell appeared for the Crown, and W. N. Tilley for the company. The government was asking for repayment of $490,191.39 in taxes and interest from September 1921 to February 1927.

The subject of the Perris came up on the second day when Lionel Sinclair, the shipping department manager, again told how he received orders by long distance telephone from Hamilton, from either a man or a woman.

Harry's brother Herbert Hatch was called the next day and explained that he was a commission sales agent for Gooderham & Worts in partnership with Larry McGuinness.

"Who approached you or whom did you approach with regard to the account of J. Penna?"

"The Perris."

"Did you solicit orders from Joe Penna?" asked Rowell.

"I don't know that I did," Hatch said.

"The Perris ordered a great deal of liquor?" Rowell asked.

"I don't wish to say that," Hatch answered.

"They paid for a great deal?"

"Yes."

"To whom did you go in connection with Penna's accounts?"

"To Rocco Perri or Mrs Perri."

Hatch told the court that he had first started dealing with Rocco and Bessie Perri in 1925. He also had an account in the name of J. Johnson, which as far as he was concerned meant the Perris, because the Perris paid the account if the boatman didn't. Hatch said that he had never met Johnson.

On the morning of December 8th, Herbert Hatch was recalled. He testified about the system of telegraphing orders from New York, but insisted that most of the orders loaded into boats did go to New York state. Rowell then asked that Bessie Perri be called. Her name echoed three times through the court corridors, but no one came forward. Rowell then asked that a bench warrant be issued for Bessie's arrest. Mr. Justice Grant, noting that the Perris' Toronto lawyer, A. G. Slaght, had been in the court room earlier, put off issuing the warrant until late in the afternoon.

The next morning Rocco and Bessie Perri appeared in court. Bessie was in an expensive mink coat, a black satin dress and a wide-brimmed black hat. Rocco went into the witness box first. This time he requested and was granted the protection of the Canada Evidence Act, which meant he could not be prosecuted for anything he said as long as he did not commit perjury. Slaght was standing by as Rocco testified.

Rowell asked Rocco why he used the name J. Penna to order his shipments. Rocco replied that Larry McGuinness had told him that he had to have a name on the other side to protect the shipments, so he had arranged with his friend Joe Penna to use his name. In 1926, again at the suggestion of Larry McGuinness, he began using the name Johnson for orders because there were too many orders going to Penna.

"Where were they sold??" asked Rowell

"In Canada," replied Rocco. He wasn't cheeky this time. His answers were direct, his English improved.

Perri said he had telephoned Niagara Falls, New York, to telegraph orders to Toronto on instructions from McGuinness. Sometimes it was Bessie who would make the call; sometime it was Rocco's partner Jim Sullivan.

"When were payments made in Penna's case?" asked Rowell.

"First it was at the distillery for two or three loads when we started on April or May of 1925," said Rocco. "Then Mr Hatch or Mr McGuinness would come to the house once every two weeks and get the money."

"Where was your money?" Rowell asked.

"In the bank."

"Under whose name?"

"Mrs Bessie Perri or Bessie Stark."

Defence lawyer W. N. Tilley asked Rocco how he and his partner, James Sullivan, divided the business. Rocco explained that Sullivan had taken the boat and then profits on each load were shared half and half.

"You speak of McGuinness and Hatch," said Tilley. "Did you ever see anything of the other Mr Hatch, the one in Gooderham & Worts?"

"I don't remember," answered Rocco.

"Have you ever been in the liquor business in the United States?"

"Not myself," Rocco lied.

"I'm not asking about yourself," snapped Tilley. "Have

you ever been connected with the liquor business in the United States?"

"Not me."

Rocco hastened to assure Tilley, "I sell lots, too, in Hamilton and Guelph and Brantford and other places."

"You are still under another charge at present?" Tilley asked

"Yes. Perjury."

"Why?"

"For evidence before the royal commission. I refused to tell the truth."

"Were you under oath?"

"I don't know."

"Who looked after the banking?" Tilley changed the subject.

"Mrs Perri."

"How about Mr Sullivan's share?"

"Well, we both paid it to her."

Rocco was excused and Bessie called.

She admitted that it was her role to phone orders and she did so under the names of Perri and Starkman, although sometimes Mrs Sullivan phoned in orders.

"Why the second name?" Rowell asked

"No reason," Bessie replied.

"Who drew the cheques and paid out money?"

"I did."

"You were the cashier?"

Bessie chuckled softly. "I suppose so."

Sometimes she paid Hatch or McGuinness and sometimes she and Rocco would go down to the distillery and pay them or Mr Sinclair, Bessie explained.

In his cross-examination, Tilley asked Bessie if she had received many cheques.

"I used to get a lot of cheques until I quit it," Bessie replied. "Then, after I quit taking cheques, I made people give me cash money." That was after Herb Hatch had refused to take cheques. She kept taking cheques from a few.

"From the better class of people," suggested Tilley.

"Yes," Bessie agreed.

That was the end of their testimony.

That same afternoon, in another court room, the sessions grand jury returned indictments on seven counts of perjury against Rocco Perri and nine counts against Bessie Perri. But like the Hatch family, Rocco and Bessie would now have to wait until the outcome of the Gooderham & Worts trial.

On December 22nd, summing up for the Crown, Rowell said Gooderham & Worts had "a well conceived and efficiently operated plan to sell liquor under circumstances which would in all probability prevent detection by the officers charged with enforcement of law..." in both Canada and the United States.

Tilley's summation was largely an attack on Rocco Perri, pointing out to Mr Justice Grant the two main witnesses, the Perris, were at the mercy of the Crown. Tilley then told Grant that Rocco and Bessie should be indicted anew for perjury for their testimony in the Gooderham and Worts case. He said Rocco had been explicit when talking about selling liquor in Ontario but "his mind was a blank" when testifying about selling to the United States.

Tilley's legal argument was that the government couldn't establish that Gooderham & Worts was involved in criminal activity and then ask them to pay taxes on that criminal activity. "It would be taxing the commission of a crime."

On March 18th, Mr Justice Grant found the distillery had to pay $439,744. In an 118-page judgment, he said that the aim of Gooderham & Worts "and others in a like position, was to escape the penalties of the Ontario statutes and liability for Dominion sales tax by making export sales (or what might pass inspectors and serve that purpose) and at the same time avoid personal conflict with the laws of the United States by having the exportation (if any) handled by others."

—— He congratulated the defendants on their "marked ingenuity in some of the plans and means adopted" but added that "sending whisky to Mexico City was barefaced subterfuge."

His Lordship then turned to the issue of the testimony of Rocco and Bessie Perri. He found it to be credible, as it has been supported by documentary evidence and could not be shaken by a skillful cross-examination.

The government had won its test case. Now it could proceed against all the other breweries and distilleries that had been part of the booming bootleg business. The back tax and interest totalled $5,000,000: including $26,645 from Grant's Spring Brewery; $124,227 from the Kuntz Brewery; $100,000 from John Labatt Ltd.; $973,677 from Consolidated Distilleries; $79,918 from Joseph E. Seagram and Sons; and $25,751 from the Taylor and Bate brewery in St Catharines.

On April 23rd, Rocco and Bessie Perri appeared in Toronto magistrate's court to answer the charge of perjury. Rocco pleaded guilty to a single count.

Their lawyer A.G. Slaght, then addressed Judge Emerson Coatsworth, asking that Perri's apparent truthfulness at the Gooderham & Worts trial be considered. Crown Attorney Murphy said he had nothing to say beyond the fact that Perri had certainly gone over to the other side and told the truth. "This and in view of the assistance he has been to the government in its inquiry since impresses one that he should have only a nominal sentence."

"Six months at the jail farm or six months definite and one month indeterminate if he be sent to the Ontario Reformatory, which would your client prefer?" asked Coatsworth.

"Does the Ontario Reformatory mean that he would be sent to Guelph?" asked Slaght.

"Either Guelph or Burwash."

"Very well, he would rather be sent to the Ontario Reformatory in Guelph."

Perri smiled throughout the proceedings, although there was a nervous twitch in his fingers. His smile was wider and he was more relaxed once sentence was passed.

Bessie was next called into the prisoner's box. She was very nervous. Mr Slaght elected trial by Judge Coatsworth and pleaded not guilty. Crown Attorney Murphy accepted the plea and the charges against Bessie Perri were dismissed.

No doubt a deal had been made; Bessie would not serve

any time and Rocco went to jail in Guelph — his own territory.

After a night in the Don Jail, Rocco arrived at Guelph and was booked as prisoner #40075. This was his profile:

Age: 39
Born: Italy
Residence: Hamilton
Occupation: Storekeeper
Religion: Roman Catholic
Married
Elementary education
Moderate drinker
dark complexion
black hair
brown eyes
5'4"
166 pounds
scar on left cheek.

The sentence expired on November 22nd, the remission date was October 23rd, but the jail records show that Rocco was released on September 27th.

There are two footnotes to the royal commission investigation. In December, 1928, the U.S. attorney in Buffalo, Richard Templeton, announced a major indictment against thirty people: Canadian distillers, brewers and bootleggers and their American allies. Harry Hatch was at the top of the list. His brother Herbert Hatch and Herbert's partner Larry McGuinness were also indicted. Others included Joe Penna and James Johnson, Rocco's friends and "namesakes"; Rocco's customer in Port Credit, Joe Burke; Gooderham & Worts' Lionel Sinclair, and Dominick Mosier, the man who, the grand jury alleged, had sent all those telegrams from Niagara Falls, New York, back to Gooderham & Worts.

Neither Rocco nor Bessie Perri was indicted, despite the fact that the indictment seemed to be based on the evidence they had given before the royal commission and at the Gooderham & Worts tax trial. Hatch and the rest were now facing the mirror image of the charge they had faced in Toronto.

Where the Canadian government had claimed they had been responsible for reimporting the liquor into Canada, Templeton was claiming the liquor *had* gone to the United States.

The Canadians had nothing to worry about though, for they couldn't be extradited. (The *Star* was most concerned that Harry Hatch might not be able to follow his race horses to Saratoga for the season.) The next day Hatch issued a statement saying he was "not interested" in the Buffalo findings. The American case had come to nothing.

Almost a year later, on September 13, 1929, the Kuntz Brewery settled with the federal government, agreeing to pay $200,000 out of the $336,863 the government had demanded. After the Wall Street crash, a few weeks later, the beer business was in trouble. The good times were over.

The Kuntz Brewery was the target of a young up and coming businessman from an Ottawa brewing family, Edward Plunket Taylor, who was building a brewing empire. Kuntz, with its three million gallon capacity, was to be the cornerstone. Taylor intended to take on the giants, Labatt's and Molsons. After Kuntz, E.P. Taylor had his sights on the O'Keefe brewery, the Carling, and two of Rocco's suppliers, Taylor & Bate in St Catharines and the Grant's Spring in Hamilton. He acquired a controlling interest in Kuntz in November 1929. The company had a cash problem after it paid the fine. Then, despite or because of the crash, Taylor put together the Brewing Corporation of Ontario in March, 1930 by getting options on brewery shares.*

---

*The young E.P. Taylor had had little interest in the family brewery in the early 1920s, but he was on the board of the Brading Brewery during the OTA years.

The report of the Royal Commission says Brading "sold large quantities of beer to customers residing in the province of Ontario...the company also made some export shipments to the United States." After the commission's report, the federal government sued Brading for $5,732.04.

Two giant Canadian corporations who owe part of their start to Rocco Perri recently became part of international conglomerates. What was Harry Hatch's Hiram Walker Gooderham and Worts became the distillery division of Hiram Walker. It is now owned 51 % by Allied Lyons PLC and 49 % by the Reichman brothers' Gulf Canada after a 1986 takeover battle.

The Kuntz brewery became Carling-Kuntz and then just Carling. Carling O'Keefe, successor to Canadian Breweries, sold the old Kuntz Brewery to Labatts in 1977. Carling's is now owned by the Australian brewing giant Elder IXL, makers of Foster's.

In 1929, Rocco had his own problems to face. Prohibition was over in Ontario and the end was in sight in the United States. Of course, there were always other ways to make a fast buck.

CHAPTER 12

THE PERRI CONNECTION:
PENNSYLVANIA, WINDSOR, TORONTO, HAMILTON

In the early twenties there was as epidemic of drug use and narcotics trafficking in southern Ontario, which sparked a police crusade against the abuse of cocaine, morphine, heroin and opium by the general public. As early as 1921, Hamilton newspapers were full of stories of widespread drug abuse and the resulting social, pyschological and enforcement problems. This followed a period during which drug use in Canada had declined after the new toughened Narcotics Act, which became law on September 1, 1920. The law seriously limited legal access to imported drugs by licensed druggists and dealers who had to file written declarations and keep careful records of the drug flow. Still, in February 1921, the Hamilton *Spectator* ran articles about a major dope ring operating in Hamilton and articles about the rising number of victims of the "dope habit."

In sentencing dealers, Magistrate Jelfs was severe: "It's worse for a man to be selling drugs than taking them himself. I want to give it out right straight now that every man found guilty of having drugs illegally in his possession is going to get the utmost penalty of the law."

In February 1921, the *Spectator* featured several more narcotics stories under the police court headline, "ARE BREAKING UP 'DOPE RING' IN THIS CITY." It turned out that the supply centre for the two convicted dealers was one Si Ming, described as "a dapper young Chinaman," who had been arrested for selling dope. One dealer, Charles Thomas, testified that he had paid Ming $3 for a deck of "snow" (morphine) so often that he couldn't remember the number of times. An addict named Lloyd Alger from Kalamazoo, Michigan, described by the police as "a likely-looking young man...a fine fellow but for the dope," appeared in court as a witness against Ming, confessing his guilt to illegally purchasing drugs to support his drug habit. "I spent all the money I had to get the stuff," he plaintively told the court. The lawyer for Ming, Norman McKay, argued that evidence from these two "dope fiends" (Thomas and Alger) could not be accepted. However, Magistrate Jelfs found that because they were dope fiends "that makes the testimony all the stronger, because it usually is so difficult to get people to reveal their source of supply." Ming was convicted and sentenced to a six-month prison term.

Three days later another victim of the city's dope ring was before Magistrate Jelfs. Under the headline, "MOTHER WANTS GIRL CURED OF DRUG HABIT," the *Spectator* gave the following succinct account of the story in its sub-headlines: "Mrs Levines, Aged 22, Admitted She Was Victim of Narcotic Drugs and Stated She Had Been Vainly Trying to Break Herself of the Habit For Last Two Weeks/ WILL BE PLACED IN ONTARIO HOSPITAL/ Mother Pleaded with Magistrate to Send Her There Instead of the Mercer Reformatory, and Girl Gave Cry of Rage as She Was led out of Court." Jelfs certainly had his hands full with drug cases in 1921.

At one point there was reportedly enough dope brought into Hamilton from Toronto "to supply all the local addicts for a year." The Spectator's informant relates that the drug peddlars were caught by police but not charged because of lack of evidence, and that they were allowed to return to Toronto after "disposing of their quantity of drugs" in Hamilton.

In a feature article in the *Spectator* on the drug problem in Hamilton just days after the March 1922 arrest of Rocco Perri associate Bruno Atillo (and a week before his conviction and sentencing), Hamilton police declared once more that things were now under control:

> The police are waging a constant struggle against the drug and illicit dope peddling that goes on in the city. The other day, Tony Bruno (i.e., Bruno Atillo) an Italian residing on Bay Street North, was arrested, and a quantity of cocaine, heroin, and morphine was seized. A further and more thorough search of his premises revealed a large quanitity of cocaine, and the police believe that Bruno was retailing the stuff to addicts in Hamilton....
>
> When retailing the dope, it is usually done on the street and passed over quite openly in small packages. In the stock recently seized, there were at least ten packages of folded paper, containing a small quantity. These packages would last a drug user for perhaps a day or two at the most, and, the police say, then a fresh supply would be obtained.
>
> For some time, cocaine and heroin were the most popular drugs, but now police officials have learned morphine is becoming very popular. This is sold in tablets, which are afterward heated and rendered into fluid, later being made to the required strength and injected into the arm. From time to time police have seized primitive "needles." Sometimes the needle is one used by doctors, and is a hypodermic, and often, very expensive. The usual kind, however, is an ordinary fountain pen filler, with a small metal attachment that goes over the glass. There is a small instrument, hollow, that punctures the skin and permits the dope to enter the vein. The police have seized a surprising amount of the "filler needles," as they are called.

While this article puts the Atillo arrest in perspective, it fails to identify the source of the drugs or explain the international gang needed to supply a city like Hamilton. Local cops apparently believed that the dope was not being dispensed on an organized scale and that many of the dope pedlars were users themselves. There was no attempt in 1922 to try to get at the bosses in the upper echelons of the drug business. It is more than likely that Rocco Perri and his gang were organizing some of the rampant dope-trafficking activity.

It was a letter from William T. Duffy, the head of the United

States Bureau of Narcotics office in Pittsburgh, Pennsylvania, that prompted the first formal RCMP investigation of Rocco Perri and his gang for drug trafficking. "Secret and Confidential" files of the RCMP on Rocco Perri's drug activities contain hundreds of pages of letters, memos, intelligence and field reports detailing over ten years of RCMP undercover operations. The letter refers back to his earlier (now lost) correspondence with the RCMP in 1924 regarding one "Joe Perri in Pennsylvania whom the Narcotics Bureau suspected of being a major player in the international narcotics game. And on June 10, 1924, Duffy sent another letter to Staff Sergeant M. A. Joyce, the RCMP officer in charge of Niagara Falls, Ontario, requesting help in his drug investigation of Joe Perri.*

Sergeant Joyce dutifully replied later in June that there was a "Rocco Perry alias 'Rocco Perri' Alias 'Rocco Sussino' " in Canada whom the RCMP "suspected of dealing in narcotics on a large scale." Joyce's analysis was based on Ontario intelligence information on Rocco and his gang, and the successful prosecution of at least two senior Perri gang members, Bruno Atillo and Guisto Tobaccharo, for drug trafficking in 1922 and 1923, respectively. At the time of this early exchange of letters between Duffy and Joyce, Perri was at the height of his notoriety, with the publication of the Toronto *Star* interviews about his bootlegging activities.

Another letter from William Duffy in March 1926, requesting more information on a "R. Perry," reactivated RCMP interest in Rocco's possible involvement in the international drug trade. This time Duffy had found a definite connection between his Pennsylvania drug investigation and Rocco. A known dope pedlar named Joe Pandillo (alias Joe Pandaglio) of Webster Avenue, Pittsburgh, had received a letter from R. Perry which the Narcotics Bureau had intercepted as part of their surveillance of Pandillo. Duffy states in his letter that "we have information that

---

*No connection was ever established between the two Perris. Joe Perri was later arrested with three other Pennsylvania mafiosi for robbing a Philadelphia savings society.

would warrant us in taking Pandagilo (as I know him) into custody right now, but want to bag as many possibilities, as this outfit also connects to Fayette and Westmoreland counties, Penn., which is close to Pittsburgh. They are receiving letters [including the one from Rocco Perri] at 1311 Webster Avenue, which is a small confectionery store and the hangout for Italian gunmen and dope handlers." Duffy signed off his request to Sergeant Joyce by recalling their previous exchange and asking if this R. Perry is the same man who lives at "106 [*sic*] Bay Street, South Hamilton, Ontario Canada." As a result Corporal Webster, the officer in charge of the RCMP in Hamilton was ordered to launch an investigation into Rocco Perri's alleged drug activities. Webster's subsequent undercover work resulted in a revealing rundown of Perri's activities, including the first major indication in the RCMP files that Rocco was a major international drug trafficker. Corporal Webster's memo of March 23, 1926, outlined all RCMP street intelligence data on Rocco Perri that had been obtained up to that time:

> This man (Rocco Perri) is the biggest liquor smuggler in this district and at the same time is believed to be concerned in the smuggling of narcotic drugs, though there is no direct evidence of this.
>
> Rocco Perry [sic] is stated to have connections over a wide area, including the border points of Ontario, and employs a large gang of Italians, many of them with police records; but the members of his gang are frequently charged, Perry using them as he sees fit, thereby keeping them all under his thumb. There is not an Italian in Hamilton who will give this man away. The majority of his men are employed in the liquor smuggling, but there is some evidence that narcotic drugs are also handled.
>
> Perry is a clever and dangerous crook exercising an extraordinary influence over the men in his employ, and any who are not in his employ are afraid of him. He is the "King-pin" directing all operations, but the members of his gang when caught shoulder the responsibility and pay the penalty.

Webster went on to link Rocco directly to the most savage of the criminal acts in the Hamilton area:

In Hamilton during the last few years there have been several bombing outrages and murders among the Italians, and it is freely stated that these have all been in connection with the members of Perry's gang of smugglers, who are desperate men and will stop at nothing. Again the directing hand is stated to be Perry.

Perhaps the most important part of Webster's memo was the last section, in which he listed the most prominent members of the 1926 Perri gang and provided a brief annotation on some of them:

Among the local Italians who are suspected of being in Perry's gang are the following:

Guisto Tobaccharo, Italian, lives with Charles Austin & wife three miles from Hamilton on Caledonia Highway. Was convicted August 1923 of having narcotic drugs illegally in possession. This man is known to be in the employ of Perry.

Mrs Charles Austin, Englishwoman, very much interested in Tobaccharo and travels around with him in car.

Luigi Coruzzi, said to be a cousin of R. Perry, lives at 102 Caroline Street North, Hamilton. Was convicted of unlawful possession of loaded revolver 16th March 1922.

Nick Curto, Bay Street North, Hamilton. [He was one of the Black Hand bombers convicted in 1922 after bombings on Simcoe Street.]

P. Zanglino, 259 Bay Street North, Hamilton.

M. Romeo, 263 McNab Street North, Hamilton.

Albert Naticchio, G. Pasquale, John de Greno

Bruno Atillo, convicted 1922 for breach of Opium and Narcotic Drug Act.

Harry Barresse, 131 Caroline Street North, Hamilton, arrested for shop-breaking and theft. Is a chauffeur by trade.

Mike Curmo — *Bordanaro* [Charles Bordonaro, a Black Hand bomber and later Mafia leader]; *Restivo* [a Black Hand colleague of Curto's and Bordonaro's and involved in the murder of Loria]; and a man named *Joe Napolitano*, grocer of Hagersville.

Most of these men have large and powerful Touring cars registered in their name, or did have last year, but in reality these cars are said to belong to Rocco Perry.

This highly detailed memo (for which Webster was later paid $1 over his regular wages because of the extra undercover duties it entailed) was forwarded to Duffy in Pittsburgh by Superintendent H. M. Newson, the commanding officer of the Western Ontario District in Toronto, with the following defensive explanation of why the RCMP had yet to get their man: "I attach a report for your information giving you some idea of this party [Perri], from which you will notice that he is a man who is extremely hard to catch, generally employing others and keeping in the background although the directing hand."

It is true that these Perri associates were actively involved in the then thriving Hamilton drug trade as early as 1922. Bruno Atillo of 242 Bay Street North *was* convicted of breaching the Narcotics Act on March 15, 1922. He had been arrested while selling drugs on the street outside a boarding house on Bay Street. Using a warrant police searched his room and discovered a tin containing thirty decks of morphine and a box containing a large package of cocaine. They also discovered a concealed revolver. Atillo admitted to three Hamilton police officers that he "made his living by selling dope." Surprisingly, at his trial, Atillo was defended by Rocco's lawyer Michael O'Reilly, K.C. The only excuse Atillo could come up with in court for being in possession of so many drugs was that the previous occupant must have left them in his room. On March 22, 1922, he received a six-month sentence plus a $500 fine for possession of drugs, as well as a three-month concurrent sentence for illegal possession of a revolver. Another Perri associate and small-time drug pusher, Guisto Tobaccharo, was also convicted, in August 1923, of pushing drugs. Rocco Perri's associates in Hamilton obviously had more than a passing interest in the smuggling and selling of narcotics as well as booze as early as 1922 and 1923. These arrests and convictions however did not lead to any major investigation of Rocco Perri's involvement in the drug trade at that time; the authorities had their hands full investigating his bootlegging activities.

Webster's memo did not mark the end of the Duffy

connection to the Canadian side of the Perri drug investigations. In April 1928, Zeno Fritz, Assistant U.S. Attorney in the Western District of Pennsylvania, came back to the RCMP for assistance in the Pandillo/Pandaglio case that he was prosecuting. Fritz stated that he was "in possession of evidence showing that Pandaglio has been in connection with and has received narcotics from Rocco Perry." He wondered whether the RCMP had uncovered "any evidence concerning Rocco's dope smuggling activities" in the course of their investigations. The Pandaglio case was scheduled for May 8, 1928, and Fritz requested that an RCMP witness be available to come down to Pittsburgh to testify to Rocco Perri's "activities in your country."

No witness was supplied for the Pandaglio trial. But the Pennsylvania officials managed to take care of the Pandaglio ring on their own. Nineteen defendants in the drug ring were charged on November 18, 1927. The name of Rocco Perri did not appear in any of the indictments, and it is unlikely that his name came up at the trial, as the source of the drugs was not in question in the case.

After a lengthy trial, Joe Pandaglio was convicted on May 15, 1928, and was sentenced to two years in the Federal Penitentiary in Atlanta. Most of the other defendants received simliar sentences. Neither Fritz nor Duffy formally requested any further assistance from the RCMP after the convictions. It appears that both the RCMP and the Pennsylvania authorities dropped the matter after the 1928 convictions. And none of the defendants, including the Pandaglios, come up again in any of the numerous RCMP investigations of the drug activities of the Perris. If Rocco was supplying the Pandaglio mob, as suggested by Fritz and Duffy, then he seems to have severed the connection after the arrests of Joe Pandaglio and his gang in November 1927.

The RCMP began an undercover operation in Windsor in late May 1929 when two drug addicts in Toronto were arrested with decks of dope that had been mailed to them from Windsor. The RCMP moved in to locate the drug source.

Archie McFarlane, on the face of it, certainly didn't appear to be a run-of-the-mill dope pedlar. His background was impeccable. He was "an officer and a gentleman" who had won the prestigious Medal of Valour for his bravery in France during the First World War. However, when he came back from the war he couldn't find employment, as times were lean in Windsor, so he joined with Rocco Perri's gang of rum runners. Later he was recruited into the dope-trafficking business, running cocaine and morphine across the Detroit River back and forth from Detroit to Canada.

It was during the preliminary hearing of McFarlane and an associate, "Ginger" Pentland, on July 4, 1929, that the name of Rocco Perri first surfaced publicly in relation to the cases. Sergeant George Fish and his colleagues in the RCMP, Detective Paul Miller and Constables Irwin and Nelson, testified before Magistrate W. A. Smith that they had arranged to make an undercover buy of dope from McFarlane and Pentland by using Rocco's name as a reference and pretending that they were big cocaine and morphine dealers in Hamilton. They testified that on the street, everyone knew that the Perris were into drug trafficking and the drug dealers didn't try to check their credentials.

Detective Paul Miller was the chief Crown witness. He stated that when trying to buy "mud" (opium) from McFarlane and Pentland he mentioned the name of Rocco Perri, which struck paydirt immediately with the pair. They were very impressed ("Do you know *him*?" McFarlane gushed).

A few days before the Wall Street crash, on October 18, 1929, Archie McFarlane, the officer and the gentleman, pleaded guilty to both possession of narcotics and attempted sale of narcotics. He was sentenced to three years in Kingston Penitentiary and fined $500 by Mr Justice Jeffrey of the Ontario Supreme Court after he had tried to get Pentland off the hook by taking all the blame. The next day, however, "Ginger" Pentland was found guilty after two hours of jury deliberation. He was sentenced to four years in jail and fined $1,000.

While the information concerning Rocco Perri in the

McFarlane-Pentland trial was merely hearsay, it fitted neatly into the pattern that the RCMP had already begun to discern.

In addition to their Windsor operation, the RCMP were working closely with U.S. federal narcotic officers on a massive international dope smuggling ring which extended from Germany to Canada and the United States.

As part of this all-out, worldwide offensive against drug trafficking and as a result of developments in an ongoing Toronto operation, Superintendent Jennings (the officer in charge of the RCMP "O" division in Toronto) decided to assign Sergeant Frank Zaneth to full-time undercover work on the Perri drug mob in Hamilton. "Rocco Perri is now in the drug gang," Jennings reported to the Commissioner on June 15, 1929. "At the moment we are engaged in a drug deal in Toronto but it would seem that important as the case is in Toronto, the Hamilton end of it would appear to be more so...."

The Toronto operation under Zaneth started out modestly enough in May 1929, with the objective of getting at the source of the dope that was flooding southern Ontario. Rocco and Bessie Perri themselves were not targeted specifically at first, though word on the street quickly established that they were the leaders of the largest dope-trafficking ring in Ontario. The Toronto undercover operation, featuring Frank Zaneth as intrepid master of disguises, originated with the same May arrests that stimulated the Windsor infiltration. Zaneth, a legend within the RCMP, has been variously described by RCMP veterans as "a cross between Little Caesar and Columbo" and as "a mixture of Sherlock Holmes and Sydney Reilly," "a master of disguises," and a "man of a thousand faces." Frank Henry William Zaneth, born Franco Zanetti in Gambolo, Italy in 1890, had emigrated to Regina, Saskatchewan, where he joined the North West Mounted Police in 1917. He had been promoted to detective corporal in 1919 and to detective sergeant in 1920, and had later spent several months working in the Drumheller Coal Mines posing as a union organizer in order to infiltrate suspected subversive groups. Zaneth, assigned to infiltrate the Perri group in Hamilton, could speak fluent Italian as well as Ukrainian and French. He was a match for Bessie and Rocco Perri.

Zaneth and his colleague Detective Constable Hugh Mathewson had developed an undercover agent in Toronto's underworld who was never named in the newspapers or in RCMP files. He was Ernest Tomlinson, a "reformed" criminal who had five convictions from 1919 to 1922 for everything from breaking and entering to being a pimp, for which he had served over two years in Kingston Penitentiary. He was hired at a monthly salary by the RCMP to be their eyes and ears in the Toronto underworld. With his criminal background and known propensity for both using and selling narcotics, he was perfectly situated to penetrate the Toronto drug scene with a view to entrapping the top Toronto dope suppliers.

Throughout May and early June of 1929, Tomlinson was working under the supervision of Mathewson and Zaneth. At the time, Sergeant Zaneth was infiltrating the Toronto underworld himself, posing as a major Quebec-based drug dealer and arranging buys of morphine and cocaine through several intermediaries in Toronto, including Tomlinson. Among informer Tomlinson's drug contacts who were later charged with narcotics trafficking were: 1) Antonio Brassi, 51 years old, of 587 Dundas Street West, Toronto, 2) Tony Defalco, 23, a bootlegger from Toronto, 3) Ned Italiano, of Dundas Street West, Toronto, whose relations in Hamilton had long criminal records and were close associates of Rocco Perri, and 4) Tony Roma, 40, the owner/manager of a Toronto underworld gambling joint, the Marathon and Enosis Club on Dundas Street East near Yonge Street near "the Ward." Roma was an American citizen from the New York City/New Jersey areas, residing and operating in Toronto with Rocco Perri's consent.

During the course of the undercover operation, Tony Defalco sold Tomlinson more than a hundred cubes of morphine (there were 110 cubes per ounce) on May 8, 1929. Defalco took Tomlinson to the Madison Taxi Company, where he phoned Tony Roma for the order. Defalco then took Tomlinson to a pool hall at Yonge and Dundas and then to Roma's nearby club, the Enosis. Roma met them there and drove them to Elm and University, where he produced a hundred cubes of morphine in a small tin — about a two-week supply for a heavy user. Tomlinson looked over the white cubes and paid Roma for the deck.

Tomlinson bought more drugs from Defalco on May 23rd for $1 per cube. This occurred at the corner of Yonge and Terauley Street, where Defalco first phoned his colleagues for the order. Tony Brassi, a member of the family that ran the blind pig in Stoney Creek where Fred Genesee had last been seen alive in 1924, returned shortly thereafter with the drugs. Detective Constable Mathewson was discreetly watching the transaction from across the street.

On the second buy made by Tomlinson, Tony Roma himself took part in the selling, but, again, Brassi actually delivered the goods and Defalco collected the money. Clearly, Brassi was simply an errand boy for the gang. Tony Defalco was also in a junior role, mainly as Roma's driver, and Tony Roma was calling the shots. The gang dealt with Tomlinson only on a cash basis, collecting each time after the drugs were delivered. Zaneth and Mathewson had all the cash carefully marked so they could later use possession of the money as evidence against gang members. On June 11th, Tomlinson tried to buy more morphine from Roma, but Roma told him on the phone that he was out of morphine but could provide him with cocaine, if that would do. Tomlinson said that it would have to do, and met with Roma and Brassi five hours later to complete the transaction. Tomlinson had also earlier introduced Sergeant Zaneth as a buyer to Roma, and Zaneth testified that on June 13, 1929, he bought six ounces of cocaine and two ounces of morphine for $210 from Tony Roma. Zaneth was later able to buy more morphine from Roma at his Dundas Street Club on the afternoon of June 21, 1929. The money, of course, was marked, and $100 of it was later recovered by a police raid.

In the end, all three men were charged with narcotics trafficking.

One of the most dramatic events of the Toronto undercover operation was the raid on June 21st on the home of gang member Ned Italiano on Dundas Street. It appears from all the evidence that Ned Italiano was the key go-between for Roma with Rocco and Bessie Perri. Significantly, Defalco, Roma and Italiano had all come from the same area of Calabria as Rocco. Furthermore, Ned Italiano's close relatives lived in Hamilton, and several of them worked with Rocco in various criminal enterprises, including bootlegging. (Alex Italiano was convicted in 1924 under the OTA; Domenic Italiano, who was later convicted of a serious shooting on the streets of Hamilton, lived next door to and worked with Tony Papalia, a cousin of Ned Italiano and a driver for Rocco.) And it was at Ned Italiano's house that police discovered a huge cache of drugs worth over $3,500 on the street, along with most of the marked money that Tomlinson had given to the dope gang for his purchases.

Incredibly, two hours into the police raid, even as the police were interrogating Ned Italiano and searching his house, Bessie Perri walked in. The stunned investigators quickly searched her and discovered that she had hundreds of dollars in cash on her person. But investigators soon determined, much to their disappointment, that none of the considerable wad of cash was the marked money from the operation. Bessie said that she was just making a social call on Italiano and that she always carried money with her. While Mathewson knew Bessie's real reason for being there, he didn't have enough evidence to charge her with anything. According to Corporal Nelson who was with Mathewson on the raid and who later talked anonymously to the *Mail and Empire* about it, "as far as we were concerned she was on a collection trip."

Later, on September 24, 1929, when the fact of Bessie's untimely arrival at the Italiano house was made public during the testimony of Mathewson at the trial, her name hit the headlines of all the Hamilton and Toronto papers. Mathewson told the hushed court that Bessie Perri was said by his Toronto and Hamilton underworld sources to be "one of the biggest drug operators in the game." Mathewson then told the court that Mrs Perri had gone to Italiano's home to collect money for drugs delivered there. R. H. Greer, Italiano's lawyer, broke into the testimony with "what do you base that opinion on — idle rumour or the reports of others?" "No," answered Mathewson, "from shadowing the house" for weeks on end and observing first-hand the comings and goings of Mrs Perri and her husband. According to police testimony, Rocco and Bessie had visited the house on at least three occasions before Bessie's arrival during the raid. Questioned by his attorney, Ned Italiano testified that the Perris were at his house because he was seeking a loan from them "on some building property" and that Perri had come down "to look over the land."

The papers had a field day with Mathewson's dramatic testimony. The Toronto *Telegram* offered, "MRS ROCCO PERRI DESCRIBED AS NARCOTIC TRAFFIC LEADER," as its page one headline. Similar stories appeared in the *Globe,* the *Mail and Empire,* the Windsor *Star,* the Hamilton *Herald* and other papers across the province and country. The Italiano house was called "the headquarters of a large dope ring."

Greer unsuccessfully argued before the jury that his client was "the unfortunate victim of his environment." Crown Attorney Tom Phelan was able to convince the jury that Italiano's money — which was probably really Rocco and Bessie Perri's money — was used to buy the drugs. Phelan also argued that while one should have sympathy for the drug addicts, "they could have no sympathy with the people who made addicts possible." Italiano was sentenced on September 27, 1929, to six months in jail and fined $300 for possession of drugs. Defalco received a similar punishment. Ironically, the messenger, Tony Brassi, who had testified that the drugs found at Italiano's home belonged to Roma, received the stiffest sentence: three years in Kingston Penitentiary. Brassi was the only one who had pleaded guilty to selling and possessing narcotics (which Greer said meant that he "at least has the virtue of being honest") and Greer pleaded that Brassi was simply Tony Roma's "catspaw." It was Tony Roma whom Greer pointed the finger at as the major drug trafficker, not his client. "Roma was the man who took the orders for the drugs," he said.

In the underworld of the time it was considered that Ned Italiano had taken the "fall" for Bessie Perri. Indeed, it was later reported by gang members that Italiano's family became destitute once Ned Italiano went to jail. The Italianos had appealed to Bessie Perri for money to tide them over, but Bessie was said to have refused them. This caused much bitterness between the Perris and the Italianos and their relatives and allies.

In the meantime, Tony Roma had missed the entire trial, as he had jumped his $10,000 bail and skipped the country not long after his indictment in June. Roma was no fool. He knew he would go down on this case and wisely made his escape long before the trial. He realized, too, that in his absence the other defendants had a better chance. Roma also revealed to RCMP underworld informers that he had bought the drugs from Rocco Perri's people because it was "much cheaper" than buying from other mob groups in Ontario. Roma's common-law wife, Helen Groves, was said to have been bitter that Perri had not provided money for Roma's escape, but Roma is said to have laughed it off with, "Rocco has too much money [in drugs] and cannot take a chance to show his hand in this thing."

A warrant was issued for Roma's arrest and the bail was forfeited, but it later turned out, not entirely surprisingly, that the real estate used as surety for the bail was greatly overvalued. Roma's escape had positive consequences for others as well. Because of Roma's flight, the conspiracy charges against Ned Italiano were dropped, as the presence of Tony Roma was felt by the Crown to be essential for proving conspiracy.

One week before Bessie's arrival at Ned Italiano's house on

the very day of the RCMP raid in June, Superintendent Jennings took the fateful decision to assign Sergeant Frank Zaneth to conduct his own undercover operation inside the Perri gang in Hamilton itself. The decision was largely the result of Zaneth's own promptings. He had sent Jennings an urgent memo on June 15, 1929.

REF. No. "O" Div Ref. 21/1150   Toronto, June 15, 1929
The Officer Commanding,
Royal Canadian Mounted Police,
Toronto, Canada

      RE: Rocco Perri, 266 [sic] Bay Street South
      Hamilton, Ontario, Opium and Narcotic Drug Act

Sir,

I have the honour to report that on the 14th, whilst in Hamilton in connection with another investigation, an Italian whom I have known for some time and who was connected with the Mutual Steamship Agencies, approached me and informed me that Rocco Perri was the big gun in the smuggling and distribution of narcotic drugs in this province.

During the conversation he also mentioned one Frank Ross, residing at 255 Barton St. West as being the first lieutenant of Rocco Perri, and that the distribution of drugs rests with him. I was also advised that Rocco Perri conducts a garage at 108 Merrick Street, Hamilton, but the place is used as a blind [pig] more than anything else. I may also point out that Frank Ross drives very expensive cars, never works, and lives the life of a millionaire.

While on this subject, I may suggest that Tony Defalco, Tony Romo [sic], and Mr Italiano [vide report re] came from the same town as Rocco Perri. These Calabrians generally stick together and do not associate with anybody else. In view of the fact that on three different occasions, when drugs were purchased from Defalco's gang, a part of a Hamilton newspaper was used to wrap up the drugs in question which would indicate that the drugs originally came from Hamilton, Ontario, whether from Perri or Ross it is not yet known.

Your Obedient servant

(signed, in code)

Operative No. 1 [Zaneth]

GETTING THE DOPE ON ROCCO AND BESSIE:

OPERATIVE NO. 1 AND INFORMANT "Q"

Even as the Toronto operation continued, with the major raid on Italiano's headquarters just about to take place, Frank Zaneth began the formal assault on Rocco Perri in Hamilton. On June 17, 1929, with orders from the highest levels of the RCMP, Zaneth drove to Hamilton with his colleague Sergeant H. Darling and began a five hour surveillance of Rocco Perri's garage and Frank Ross's residence. According to Darling they decided to watch both Ross's house and Rocco's garage in the belief that the supply of drugs expected to arrive would be split there, some being sent to Defalco in Toronto. Zaneth and Darling were on a futile, last-minute mission to develop hard information that could be used to strike at the brains of the organization. Significantly, they were unable to cover Rocco's house at 166 Bay Street South, "as there were people on the verandah apparently acting as a lookout." Zaneth and Darling also spent some time trying to locate Overland car #28-339, the alleged transport vehicle for the drugs. But they had no luck, and Darling reports that "no trace of the Overland car could be found and after patrolling Hamilton until nearly one o'clock on the morning of the 18th, we returned to Toronto arriving back about 2:30 A.M."

After the raid on Italiano's house on June 21, the flat-out effort was to go after the Hamilton end of the drug empire. The RCMP now believed that Rocco and Bessie

Perri were "the controlling party of the drug ring handling morphine and cocaine" in Ontario, according to Sergeant Darling's report. With Detective Hugh Mathewson working directly under him, Frank Zaneth lost no time in getting things going for what was to be his major offensive against the Rocco Perri mob in Hamilton. An extraordinarily detailed, ten page memo from "Operative No. 1" to Jennings, dated July 8, 1929, outlines Zaneth's plan of action, explains the new developments and suggests a bold course for future action. Zaneth's reports from this period provide a unique and astonishingly vivid picture of the sordid reality of the Canadian underworld at the time and a rare, inside glimpse into the secret world of RCMP undercover operations of the period.

That fruitless evening was just the beginning of an investigation that would put to rest the myth that Rocco Perri was a benevolent bootlegger who would never touch drugs. It is impossible to analyse the files on this investigation and come to any conclusion other than that Rocco and Bessie Perri were up to their necks in the narcotics trade of the 1920s.

Very early on in the Hamilton end of the Perri drug investigation, Zaneth recruited an ex-con closely connected with the Hamilton drug scene to work with him and to set up Operative no. 1's criminal connections. He was James Curwood, codenamed Informant "Q". Zaneth also decided that Operative no. 1 would pose as Arthur Anderson, a visiting mobster from Chicago, who was working with the infamous "Bugs" Moran,* and that only the top brass would be briefed on this super-secret operation. Zaneth realized that the police had made serious mistakes on the earlier operations by giving the Perris too many indications that

---

*George ("Bugs") Moran was a key lieutenant of Dion O'Banion, the leader of the gang that ran Chicago's North Side in the early 1920's. Moran was listed as Public Enemy no. 12 by the Chicago Crime Commission in 1923, was a major rival to Al Capone, and in 1929 was Capone's target in the infamous St Valentine's Day massacre, which resulted in the deaths of seven of Moran's gang. Zaneth, in pretending to be a member of the notorious Chicago North Siders, was trying to establish impeccable mob credentials.

something was afoot. The deputy magistrate in Hamilton had even ordered Constable Mathewson to notify Hamilton police of their impending raids against Ned Italiano and Tony Roma. This was one of the things that alerted the senior members of the Perri drug ring and resulted in the extreme cautiousness which spared them discovery.

Zaneth's report of July 8, 1929 speaks for itself:

Re: R. Perry alias Rocco Perri, alias Rocco Susino,
Hamilton, Ontario, Opium and Narcotic Drug Act

With further reference to previous reports, in connection with the above-mentioned man, I have the honour to state, that on the morning of the 4th instant, accompanied by Det. Const. Mathewson, H.P. driving Police Car no. CA48651, I proceeded to Hamilton, Ontario, for the purpose of arranging with Informant "Q" to make a purchase of narcotic drugs.

On arrival in Hamilton, Informant "Q" communicated with me. Here I will mention, that on the previous day, Det. Cons. Mathewson had interviewed this informant and it was then arranged, whereby I would be introduced to the parties who had the drugs to sell.

During the conversation with Informant "Q" I gathered that he had told certain people that he had a friend coming from Chicago that night, who expected to examine the drug and make the buy immediately. This informant also advised me that he had told a certain Negro, by the name of Gordon Goins, that his friend would be carrying a large sum of money and consequently he would carry a "Rod."

It was then decided that I should go to Brantford, Ontario, and there take the 8:58 train for Hamilton. Informant ["Q"] would meet me at the station, introduce me to the Negro and from there I would be taken to the King George Hotel. In the meantime Det. Const. Mathewson would shadow our movements.

At 9:45 P.M. ST I arrived in Hamilton and at the station I met Informant "Q" and the Negro, Gordon Goins. [Goins was well-known by Hamilton police for being a nuisance. He had been convicted twice in 1926 for being a vagrant.]

Informant "Q" hired a taxi, and directed it to the King George Hotel. On the way I was introduced to the Negro as a Chicago gangster, and during the short conversation a number of gun-men were mentioned as our friends. When we arrived at the hotel, informant said, "I bet you have with you a good Rod," to which I replied, "Yes, my best one. Here it is." The Negro opened his eyes wide, and in order to justify myself I said, "Well, I am in a strange city; I am carrying about five grand and I am not taking any chances." I then produced a large roll of American bills, which by the way, I had obtained from a Hamilton bank, in lieu of Canadian currency, approximately $300.00 in all. This was arranged so that a fifty-dollar bill was on the outside, a twenty-dollar bill underneath, and a large number of one's and five's in the centre. [Some scams just don't change.]

Informant ["Q"] had procured a case of beer, and a bottle of liquor, and after a few drinks I entered into a conversation with the Negro as to whom I was going to deal with. He stated that they were Italian. He mentioned the names of Frank Ross, Tony Ross, Frank Romeo, and finally Rocco Perri. All these people are well-known characters around Hamilton, Romeo being the only relation of Rocco Perri's, while the Ross brothers, who are also Italians, their correct name being Rossi, used to be Perri's first-hand men while he was engaged in running liquor.

In due course, I was taken with the informant, by the Negro to 72 Sheaffe Street, a blind-pig run by an Italian but owned by Tony Ross. There I was requested by the Negro to remove my hat and allow the Italian to see my face. He then said to the Italian in the Italian language, "Here is the boss himself from Chicago. He wants to see stuff by tomorrow morning." The Italian, who looked somewhat frightened, said to the Negro, "I have not got it now. What I was talking to you about was shirts." The Negro laughed and said, "Never mind, we will be back in the morning."

Being convinced there and then, that this Negro was not in the confidence of these Italians as much as he had told the informant he was, I adopted a careless attitude, without conveying the impression to him that I had understood what had been said in the house, and told him that I had come a long way to meet a bunch of suckers; that they had never seen thirty ounces of drugs (this being the amount I was supposed to purchase), and that their limit was a two-dollar deck, otherwise they would have been present to make the deal, but that I was confident that the big man he told me about was still out in the corner trying to sell his last deck.

The Negro seemed to get excited and informed me that he would take me to the big boss. He then drove on Caroline St. and stopped in front of the residence of Frank Romeo. There he asked where Frank was, meaning Frank Ross, and he was told by

Frank Romeo that he did not know. When the Negro re-entered the taxi, he said, "Did you see that fellow? Well, he is worth three million dollars. Once upon a time he had Rocco Perri under his thumb...."

The Negro then visited a number of places for the purpose of locating either Tony Ross or his brother Frank, but all to no avail....

It was then decided to leave me at the Hotel and the Negro with the informant would go to locate them [the Italians]. I may say that informant met Frank Ross a few days ago, but the Negro never mentioned to him that Ross was the man with the drugs, and waited until my arrival before he did so.

About 3:30 A.M. the Negro and the informant returned to the hotel accompanied by a man named John Flynn, residing at 73 Sheaffe Street. This man I noticed sitting on the steps of this address during my first visit to 72 Sheaffe Street.

During the conversation, Flynn informed me that he was an addict. He also stated that he had been purchasing drugs from Tony Ross and Frank Ross since 1923, and that at times he acted as their runner. He further stated that during the afternoon of the previous day Frank Ross approached him and requested him to endeavour to sell six ounces of cocaine and ten ounces of morphine. This man promised to get in touch with the Ross brothers first thing in the morning and made an appointment to meet him at 73 Sheaffe St. at 9 o'clock and felt positive that by that time he would have a quantity of drugs in his house for examination.

After having purchased some lunch, I waited until the Negro and Flynn were out of sight and then proceeded to the Royal Connaught Hotel, where I instructed Det. Const. Mathewson to obtain a search warrant to cover the premises of 72 and 73 Sheaffe St.

This was done but Det. Const. Mathewson informed me that James Mackay who is assigned to take all complaints, advised him to see the City Police on the matter before he would issue him a search warrant.

No doubt the City Police can be trusted, yet, in view of the fact that it is common knowledge that Rocco is behind the drug traffic and drug ring and that Frank and Tony Ross are his right-hand men and have been operating for years without being caught, it would have been best if we could have kept the information to ourselves, however, there is nothing we can do on the subject but hope for the best. [Here Zaneth had diplomatically put his finger on a major problem, which, as we have seen before, worked to strengthen Rocco's hand. Perhaps Zaneth was also aware of the possible corruption of former Police Chief Whatley.]

At the appointed hour, accompanied by the informant, I proceeded to 73 Sheaffe St. to meet John Flynn. Det. Const. Mathewson shadowed us there, keeping a respectable distance away.

As soon as we arrived Flynn went across the street to no 72 and there spoke to the Italians employed by Tony Ross to run the blind-pig. He returned almost immediately and informed me that they directed him to speak to Tony Ross. He then telephoned to him and about 20 minutes after, he came up driving a Chevrolet Coupe, Ontario License no. 99-178.

There both the informant and Flynn spoke to him for a few minutes but I could perceive that something was wrong.

When the informant and Flynn returned to the House I was taken aside, and away from the Negro's hearing and was informed that the Ross brothers had shut down on everybody because they were scared of me.

Flynn went on to say that the Ross brothers do not suspect me of being a police officer, but owing to the fact that the Negro had told all and sundry that he had a friend coming from Chicago with five thousand dollars to invest in a drug deal, who would carry a gun, being a leader in gangland. Therefore these people were frightened and were afraid that they would be stuck up and lose their goods or have the Police jump on them.

He also stated that Tony Ross informed him that he could not understand and did not believe the Negro when he told him how a man like Gordon Goins would be able to introduce a man with so much cash to purchase a large amount of drugs, while he, the Negro was only a deck man.

As soon as I heard this, I was convinced that Goins was not enjoying the confidence of these Italians and that the informant had placed too much confidence in him.

I then, before the informant and John Flyyn, told the Negro that I was disgusted; that I had come a long way for nothing and asked him to get out of my sight, which he did in a hurry.

On talking the matter over with John Flynn, who seems to be under the impression that he stands in making a couple of hundred dollars if the deal comes through, I learned that Tony Ross and Frank Ross have two separate caches, but that Romeo and Perri are the real bosses.

Zaneth then went on to describe an elaborate game of

cat and mouse. Various street people were contacted by "Q" in attempts to reach the Rosses, but Rocco's people evidently sensed that there was somenting wrong. Perhaps Zaneth was trying too hard; perhaps Rocco had heard about the search warrant for 73 Sheaffe Street. After exhausting the possibilities, Zaneth decided to pretend that "Arthur Anderson," fed up with the delaying tactics, was returning to Chicago. A few days later he was back.

My reason for returning to Hamilton this day was for the purpose of convincing these people that I was on my way back to Chicago, having purchased about twenty-five ounces of drugs in Montreal, but in order to make up the load, I was quite willing to purchase another five ounces from them.

This purchase would have been made with marked money, but no action would have been taken. In so doing I would have been able to gain the confidence of these people in the hope that in the near future I would have been successful in connecting with Perri direct.

As they were under the impression that I was to leave Hamilton for Chicago that afternoon, I told Crawford that whenever he could secure a certain amount of Morphine and show it to Jimmy (Informant "Q"), he would notify me and would come down to make the deal but I would not do so unless I was certain to be able to purchase not less than thirty ounces.

I left Hamilton at 3:15 P.M. of the 9th instant, arriving in Toronto at 5:00 P.M. of the same day.

I may mention that Tony Ross, Frank Ross, Frank Romeo and Rocco Perri are not the usual type of men found engaged in the distribution of narcotic drugs. These people are always on the alert, and do not deal with anyone at all. These people also gather data from newspapers of any drug cases in the Province, and whatever they learnt from there, they use to the best of their advantage.

When the raid at 887 Dundas St. West was being conducted we came very close to Rocco Perri, and had we known what we do know now, our subsequent action would have been different. There are a number of incidents which may be attributed to our failure of making a purchase of drugs from the above mentioned men. First, that when 887 was raided Mrs Perri was present, and she knew then that the Police were looking for marked money. Second, that when an effort was made to obtain search warrants in Hamilton, the Deputy Magistrate requested Det. Const.

Mathewson to advise the City Police of his intention. Third, that during the preliminary hearing of the case of Fred Pentland and Archie McFarlane in Windsor, the name of Rocco Perri came out very prominently.

Any of the three above incidents were sufficient to have these traffickers cease their operations. Furthermore, I might have been over zealous in getting close to Rocco Perri, as when the Negro failed us I should have dropped the matter. But as the informant and John Flynn seemed to think that I would have been able to make a purchase, I ventured to go as far as I did.

However, as it stands now, I feel that no further action should be taken in this connection and that the matter should be allowed to stand for at least two months. However, should the informant advise that Crawford has produced to him five ounces of drugs for inspection, and ask that I go up to make the purchase, I believe that another effort should be made and allow the first purchase to go through without taking action.

Inspector C. D. LaNauze, the acting commander of "O" Division for the duration of Jennings' absence from Toronto for annual leave, adopted Zaneth's suggestion that the potential buy be allowed to go through.

...This man |Rocco Perri| is, as you know, exceedingly alert and with the publicity given to his name in Windsor, and having in mind our operations here, and their connection with Perri, coupled with the reluctance now shown to do business in Hamilton, I consider that for the time being we should refrain from attempting to make any buys. Of course, should the opportunity occur to make a "silent" buy and retain the evidence for a future occasion or buy without covering, to maintain contact or gain the confidence of Perri, I would recommend that this be done.

The next memo from Operative no. 1 is dated July 15. In it Zaneth reports that on July 1, Informant "Q" came into Toronto to tell him that Tony and Frank Ross were *not* suspicious that he was connected with the police. Zaneth goes on to report that "the reason why they refuse to do business at the present time is because the big boss (Perri) has instructed that no large sale is to be made until the Windsor and the Toronto cases, at present in Court, are terminated." Perri was shrewdly waiting until all the RCMP cards were out before exposing himself and his gang to further risks. This was Rocco's practice in bootlegging, and it is consistent with the caution he demonstrated over many years of controlling criminal activity.

But Inspector LaNauze* wrote a "Personal and Secret" memo to RCMP Commissioner Cortland Starnes in Ottawa a week later, on July 24, 1929, suggesting that the danger of exposure had passed and that the operation should now be re-started and dramatically expanded. He hoped to be able to catch Perri by taking fingerprints from drugs he had handled or by using marked money. He also requested permission to buy a gangster-style car to be used specifically for this undercover operation.

> This informant also advised that these people do not suspect Operative no. 1 of being a policeman, and seem satisfied he is from Chicago and in the drug game...
>
> I submit the following proposition for your consideration, knowing that by getting Perri we can safely say it will be the biggest scoop we ever had in this Division insofar as the illegal traffic in drugs is concerned:
> (1) In order to do business with these people, a motor car is required. Same does not necessarily require to be an expensive one, but must be decent enough to give colour to the suggestion that Operative no. 1 is a drug runner from Chicago.
> (2) An Illinois marker should be obtained in order to strengthen this supposition in case Perri decides to check-up.
> (3) Our police cars are known and we cannot afford to take a chance on using them other than for the purpose of taking police action when the case is being brought to a conclusion.
> (4) The purchased car must be used exclusively on this case and at its completion must be disposed or retained for other Police investigations of a secret nature.

---

*Charles Deering LaNauze, known by his friends as "Denny", joined the RNWMP in 1908. In a long and distinguished career in the RCMP, he rose to become Assistant Commissioner before his retirement in 1944. He was famous for his exploits in the North, for example solving the mystery of the murders of Fathers Le Roux and Rouviere by two Inuit (Eskimos) in the Great Bear Lake district in 1915.

(5) If it is possible to purchase the car in question in the State of Illinois and bring it into Canada under a six months' bond, this would afford excellent cover...

In order to be successful in this investigation, our plans must be laid out very carefully as we are dealing with a clever gang who do not seem to take chances and would rather close down temporarily than take any unnecessary risks....

Rocco Perri has been in the narcotic drug traffic for many years according to our present information, and I am strongly of the opinion that every possible advantage should be taken of the position we are now in. Operative no. 1 is able to connect with his chief runner and if this can be followed up by making purchases of say five to ten ounces on two or probably three occasions we may be able to bring Perri to justice [Starnes' emphasis].

On July 27th the RCMP commissioner authorized the purchase of a McLaughlin-Buick by "O" Division to be "placed at the disposal of Sergeant Zaneth for this case." In order to disguise the car further, Zaneth was to drive to Chicago and obtain Illinois markers and "make discreet inquiries as to how markers may be obtained in future years for similar purposes." The RCMP had decided to go for broke in their most ambitious operation to date against Rocco Perri. The successes of the Windsor and Toronto operations, and the apparent success to date of the Hamilton operation, had raised expectations to a fever pitch in Ottawa. Zaneth now thought that he could "clean up the Perri matter in about three weeks or a month."

Operative no 1's next major report to LaNauze is dated July 31st:

...On arrival in Hamilton I located the informant, and during a short conversation he apprised me that one Jim Harris, who has been in the bootlegging business since 1916, and closely connected with Perri, was awaiting me at the residence of a bootlegger.

We then proceeded there and informant "Q" introduced me to the above-mentioned bootlegger, who stated that he had the biggest connection in this country regarding narcotic drugs. He went on to say that before he could do business with me, he would have to satisfy himself that I was a bona fide drug runner, and asked me why I did not purchase drugs in Chicago or even Detroit. To this I replied that the drugs were badly cut, and even though the price was between $17 and $19 in Detroit, yet I preferred to go to Montreal and pay $25 or $28 and get pure goods, and that if there was any cutting to be done, I would do it myself. Mr Harris produced a book and asked me to give him the names of two or three men in Chicago or Detroit who would vouch for me. I was taken by surprise and for a second did not know just what to say, but finally told Mr Harris that I would not give him the names and addresses of my friends, as he was a stranger to me. He then asked the informant to vouch for him, which he did, but even after that I told Mr. Harris that I would have to obtain the consent of my friends before I could give their names out. This seemed to satisfy him, for he stated that he would wait until such time as I would be able to give him these names. When I left him he was under the impression that I was proceeding to Montreal, and that I would be in Hamilton on the 8 o'clock train on Thursday morning, August 1st, when I would further discuss the matter....

In conclusion I may say that after Mr Harris had a few drinks he talked considerably and made it quite clear that I would be dealing with Perri, probably not direct on the first purchase, but in the second purchase he may come into the open himself.

The method employed by these drug runners is a safe one. They will require that the man they are dealing with is in the drug game, and if they are satisfied there will be no more secrets between them, drugs will be taken to a room for examination, and if proved to be satisfactory, money will be passed over and the deal will be consummated right in the room....

At this point there were several internal RCMP memos about who should have access to the fancy new McLaughlin that they had purchased for the operation. The Commissioner was firm that only Zaneth have authorization to use the flashy vehicle and that it be kept in a "special garage" for Zaneth. But it seems that some mounties were jealous of Zaneth's new status. Zaneth even had to disobey the orders of a superior in order to preserve the integrity of the operation. It took several memos back and forth from Headquarters in Ottawa to ensure that the Commissioner's orders were strictly followed by Zaneth's colleagues.

For the next phase of the undercover operation, Zaneth proceeded to Chicago, fabricating his Chicago mob background. On August 9, 1929, he related the dramatic story of his one-week Chicago trip in a long, informative memo to Superintendent Jennings. First he had to meet up with Informant "Q" in Hamilton, where Zaneth found out that "Q" had been helping Perri's men run liquor for the previous few days.

Quite a development! Not only was Informant "Q" moonlighting on the RCMP, he was also involved in illegal operations with the very man they were targeting. And he was collecting two salaries: one from the RCMP and one from Rocco Perri. But Zaneth immediately seized on the positive side of this duplicity: it provided "Q" with a perfect position for introducing the RCMP into Perri's gang. Zaneth continued his narration without commenting on the ironies of the situation, though it was clear to him that "Q" was becoming more and more unreliable:

In my last report, under the same caption, I recommended that this Informant be allowed to accompany me to Detroit, in order that he might look up some one who would vouch for me in case the members of Perri's gang make inquiries regarding my connection with the underworld. But when I informed him that he would only receive his transportation back to Hamilton, and no other expenses, he advised me that all he had was one dollar and fifty cents and felt that he could not make the trip on that amount.

Before I reached a definite decision I asked him who he had in mind in Detroit who could be safe in exposing himself. His answer was vague, and he thought that some of his relatives in Chatham, Ontario, could vouch for me. This assertion was not satisfactory to me, as I had told Jim Harris, in the presence of this informant, that I had no friends or enemies in Canada.

I then decided to proceed on my way alone, as I did not want to take a chance in allowing this Informant to disclose my identity to anyone whom I did not know, and also that I did not feel like paying his expenses....

Finally, Zaneth went off to Chicago:

I left Hamilton at 9:20 A.M. [on August 1]...arriving in Chicago at 8 P.M. [August 2].

During the morning of the 3rd, I proceeded to the office of the "Intelligence Unit," U.S.A. Treasury Department, Room 587, Federal Building, where I made inquiries....

My Informant in this office was one C.L. Converse, attached to the "Intelligence Unit...[Clarence L. Converse, "famed for his fearlessness and clever disguises" was a member of the IRS Task Force targeting the Capone family]. This gentleman informed me that it would require at least five days before I could obtain the Illinois markers, as my application would have to be forwarded to Springfield, Illinois. To avoid the inevitable delay, he asked me to accompany him to the City Police Station, where he would introduce me to Deputy Commissioner John Stege, a man of good reputation and integrity....[John Stege was known as the only honest cop in Chicago. He was later demoted for being too efficient in getting at civic corruption and organized crime.]

...In a few words I explained to this Official that I was desirous of obtaining a set of Illinois markers to use on a secret investigation in Canada, and thought that he could help me in receiving them sooner than a private individual would.

Deputy Commissioner Stege called Lieutenant William Cox, in charge of the stolen cars Department, and introduced me to him. He also instructed him to furnish me with two Illinois markers, preferably belonging to a Buick car, and to make certain that such licences were untraceable. Lieutenant Cox informed me that he had none on hand, but that if I returned on Monday morning he would be able to comply with my request.

Still accompanied by Mr Converse, I proceeded to 60 East 30th Street, where I was introduced to one Patrick Horan, who is conducting a bootlegging joint and dancing hall at this address, known as the Garage Café, in partnership with one Sam Constantino*....

Mr Converse introduced me to Pat Horan and briefly explained to him what was required. This gentleman assured me that he would tell anyone who makes inquiries regarding Arthur Anderson that he has known him for years, and that he is running some sort of racket, the nature of which he does not know.

---

*It seems that Zaneth is referring to Chicago mobster Sam Cosentino alias Frank Galgano, who was sentenced to three months for fraud in 1931 and seven years in 1937 for running an interstate stolen goods ring with other mob members in the mid-thirties. He was quite a high-level mobster to be working as an informant for the Chicago police in 1929, but this probably made it possible for him to keep the Garage Café open.

However, as Sam Constantino was not present, Mr Horan requested me to return during the evening to meet his partner, who may probably be approached regarding my identity.

On the evening of the 3rd, I returned to this blind-pig and there met Sam Constantino. Mr Horan instructed him to tell anyone who might inquire about me, that he had known me for a number of years and that I was in a racket of some kind. While at this place, Mr Horan and Mr Constantino made a successful effort to convince all the racketeers visiting the place that they had known me for a number of years and that I had been absent from the city of Chicago for some time.

On Sunday evening, in order to establish my good standing in that place, I returned to the Garage Café, where I spent a few hours with Mr Horan and Mr Constantino and a number of friends. In this connection I feel confident that if anyone in the drug ring in Hamilton makes inquiries in Chicago, Mr Constantino and Mr Horan will vouch for me, as they seem to be in debt to Mr Converse over something.

On August 5th Zaneth went back to Lieutenant Cox and received the Illinois markers and a Chicago licence. He then drove to Windsor, where he put on his new plates and called "Q" in Hamilton to arrange a meeting for Wednesday, August 7th, in Hamilton.

In due course I met with Informant ["Q"] and Jim Harris, who asked me to drive out of the city in order that we might talk things over. This having been done, Mr Harris advised me that the people whom he had been acting as intermediaries for, were willing to do business with me providing they could satisfy themselves that I was a bona fide drug runner. I then supplied him with the names of Constantino and Horan, and their addresses. During the conversation Mr Harris informed me that the man who had the drugs was in Windsor to attend the race meet. This man being under the impression that I was on my way to Montreal for a load of drugs, informed me that he would phone to Windsor and ask this man to come to Hamilton to see him.

About 8:30 P.M. of the same day Jim Harris informed me that he had telephoned to Windsor and his "boss" had advised him that he was coming to Hamilton right away to see him. Jim Harris had a few drinks, and during the course of the conversation informed me that this man had been going to Switzerland and Germany for drugs and that same were coming up from New York City. I may say that the name of Rocco Perri had been mentioned by Jim Harris a number of times, but so far nothing definite has been ascertained.

...When I return to Hamilton on Monday the 12th, I will not close any deals with these people, but I will make every effort to ascertain who the people are that I am to deal with, and if I am satisfied that Perri is at the back of the ring and there is hope of reaching him, I would respectfully request the authority be granted to purchase thirty ounces of drugs, when marked money will be used, and in all probability a "knock-off" will be made.

But, on the other hand, should I find that Perri cannot be implicated or that I am dealing with another angle of the drug ring, my cards will be laid on the table, and a new line of action will be adopted.

Zaneth went back to Toronto on August 8th. His next memo, dated August 13th, reports on his August 12th visit to Hamilton with Constable Veitch, a man assigned to tail Zaneth's contacts to see who *their* contacts were. Because he was ill, Harris did not show up, but through Informant "Q" asked Zaneth to come to his house for a meeting. There he told Zaneth that he had been unable to contact the drug source in either Montreal or New York.

Zaneth's next meeting with Harris was in Hamilton on August 17th. Harris again asserted that he was serious about doing business with Zaneth, and Zaneth said he would be in touch when he came through Hamilton on August 21st on his way "back from Montreal."

Before leaving, Mr Harris asked me to supply him with my address in Chicago, which I will do on my next visit to Hamilton. The address I will supply him is the residence of Mr C.L. Converse....Converse should be advised of this and if any inquiries have been made at Pat Horan's place about Arthur Anderson.

It is interesting that at this stage in the operation, Zaneth felt that the Perri gang was stalling until the trial of Italiano, Defalco and Brassi came up in a month's time. But this only partially explained their reluctance to deal with him, as he was to find out at his next rendezvous with Harris on the 21st, which Zaneth attended, significantly, without Jim Curwood, Informant "Q."

> ...In due course I met Mr Harris, and during the conversation he informed me that he was very surprised that a man in the business that I was, should associate with a man of the type of Informant "Q." He also stated that his men expressed disappointment in "Q," as he is so constituted that he would only mix with the riff-raff of the town, and talk considerably after having consumed a few drinks. Mr Harris apologized for having been somewhat cool to me during my last visit to Hamilton, but assured me that his men were quite satisfied with my standing, but were afraid of Informant "Q," and warned me to be on the alert. Before leaving Hamilton it was arranged whereby I would stop and see Mr Harris every time I go through Hamilton between Chicago and Montreal. He promised to wire me should his men decide to do business. Mr Harris also requested that I supply him with my home address in Chicago, which I did. ...Mr Harris is expecting me in Hamilton some time next week.

After receiving this memo, Superintendent Jennings advised RCMP Commissioner Starnes, who had seen all Zaneth's reports, that he felt the time had come to remove Informant "Q" from the operation and send him north with Detective Constable Mathewson, who was conducting another narcotics investigation. From then on, Zaneth was on his own in the Hamilton undercover operation.

His next meeting with Harris was on August 26th, and the main subject, much to Zaneth's discomfiture, was the loyalty and character of Informant "Q" himself:

> ...In due course I met Jim Harris, who, during the conversation asked me again what became of Informant "Q," known to him as James Curwood. I advised Mr Harris that this man was not working for me, and that I had simply turned him loose in

Montreal to fare for himself; that I was through keeping him up as a go-between; and that I, too, was convinced that he was not to be trusted. Mr Harris stated that he felt almost certain that "Q" was a stool for someone, and asked me to keep away from him....

Before leaving, Mr Harris requested me, on the way back from Montreal (as he is under the impression that I was on my way back to Montreal) to stop in Hamilton as he is desirous of proceeding to Detroit, where he has an appointment with a friend of his on Saturday night. I informed Mr Harris that I might be back before Saturday night, but not knowing whether you would agree that I take this man to Detroit, I said I was not sure. However, I am convinced that it would be in the best interest of this investigation for me to oblige Mr Harris and take him to Detroit. Possibly it would be advisable for me to continue on to Chicago in case they have a shadow on me....In conclusion I may say that every endeavour is being made (without arousing suspicion) to bring this case to a head before the cases in Toronto come up for trial."

Zaneth and the RCMP as a whole were increasingly concerned about the upcoming trials in Toronto, for Zaneth, since he had run one of the undercover operations against Tony Roma and Ned Italiano, had to testify in the case against Italiano and his associates.

Superintendent Jennings agreed to Zaneth's request to go to Chicago with Harris because, as he wrote to Commissioner Starnes, "indications are that Jim Harris is checking up on him unobstrusively and were he to return to Toronto after dropping Harris at Windsor this would probably be spotted and Zaneth's Chicago story spoiled." Zaneth's next major report is dated September 9th, after he returned from his Chicago trip. As usual, there were several unexpected developments. Zaneth started the story when he picked up Harris in Hamilton on August 31st to take him to Detroit:

...During the drive as far as Woodstock, very little was said, but upon reaching the above-mentioned city he asked me to stop at a Gasoline Service Station, where he went to interview two men and a woman who were sitting in a Buick Sedan, N.Y. Licence No B 23-66.

Shortly after, he approached me and asked me to go and meet his friends, as he decided to return to Hamilton. He introduced me to them as Arthur Anderson of Chicago, while he introduced the driver of the car as Frank Poles. He also told me that they were the people who, when satisfied, would be doing business with me.

Soon after we parted, with the understanding that we would meet at the Ferry in Windsor.

On this trip I took two club bags with me, and upon reaching Windsor I checked one in the Crawford House and then met Mr Poles and his friends. While on the Ferry Mr Poles asked me how I was going to get the drugs across the border without being detected. I informed him that the bag containing the drugs was coming across by speed boat and that my man in Detroit was waiting to take it over and go on.

On the morning of the 1st I did not see Mr Poles and his party until about noon. They said that they were tired, having had some liquor during the night, and requested me to remain with them until later, in order to avoid the heavy traffic that we might encounter were we to start out during the day for Chicago. About 8:00 P.M. we left for Chicago, but upon reaching Coldwater, Michigan, we decided to remain for the night.

On the morning of the 2nd we left for Chicago, having gone first to Cicero to see some Italian friends of theirs, arriving in Chicago at 11:10 P.M. [Cicero, a suburb of Chicago, was in the heart of Al Capone's territory.]

Upon reaching Chicago I found it very difficult to break away from them, and before I could do so I was asked to take them to get a drink at my friend Patrick Horan's place, 66 30th Street East.

Owing to the fact that the traffic was very heavy, we were very tired, and I know perfectly well that the drinks were used as an excuse. What they wanted to know was if I knew Pat Horan and if I were allowed with strangers in such a place. Horan is a racketeer. He is running a rather tough place, and as soon as I reached the entrance, the negro who guarded it gave me the high sign and said, "Hello, Arthur. Pat wants to see you."

After having consumed a few drinks, Mr Poles, who acted as spokesman for the party, asked me to obtain a bottle of liquor and some beer. Pat Horan then gave me one pint of Bourbon whisky, and four bottles of draught beer. This liquor was given to the people when they reached their hotel, the Great Northern. I did not stop at the same house as they were under the impression that I was living at 5133 North Mason Blvd.

On the morning of the third I communicated with these

people by telephone and informed them that I would see them some time during the day. During the evening I went to the hotel and spent a few hours with them in the lobby, after which we parted.

On the 4th I only saw them during the evening for a few hours, having been busy with Captain Madden and Mr C. Converse, of the Intelligence Unit, U.S.A. Treasury Department. [Arthur Madden headed the IRS unit that finally nailed Al Capone. He was so successful that Capone later put a contract on Madden's life, but Madden was able to have the contract cancelled by putting pressure on Capone's hit men.]

On the morning of the 5th these people asked me when I intended to leave. I told them the sooner the better, as I was ready to go, and consequently we left Chicago at 9:30 A.M. arriving in Detroit at 6:30 P.M. We left Detroit at 10:00 A.M. on the 6th, arriving in Hamilton at 5:30 P.M., where we parted, but first we had another consultation with Mr Harris, who again requested me to see him on my way back some time on Wednesday, the 11th. I left Hamilton at 7:00 P.M., arriving in Toronto at 9:00 P.M. of the same day.

Regarding these people going to Chicago with me, I am positive that they were neither on vacation nor on any important business. The sole purpose in mind was to trail me, watch my actions, and see just whom I would get in touch with. I believe that I have played my part carefully, and that checking of the bag at the Crawford House tended to convince them that I was really in the drug traffic. This bag was picked up again by me on my way back, and they are under the impression that the drugs went over, not in a suitcase, but in a wooden box.

The only phase of the situation which I am afraid of is that they are very suspicious of Informant "Q" and that whilst in Chicago, and wherever we happened to stop, Mr Poles would broach this subject most carefully, asking questions such as how long I had known the man; whether he was ever in Windsor or not; and whether he ever worked for a man from Ottawa of the Mounted Police. I informed these people that I had no knowledge of Jim Curwood (Informant "Q") having ever worked for any Police Forces, and that as far as I knew he had never lived in Windsor, but that during my absence from Chicago he might have gone into Windsor at times on certain business....I informed Mr Poles that I had severed my connection with this man some time ago when I found he was not giving me any results....

These people, with the exception of Jim Harris, are all Italians, and the man Poles, as far as I could gather through their conversation, is a cousin of Rocco Perri, residing either in

Welland or Thorold, Ontario. These people are under the impression that I am Jewish, and do not understand the Italian language.

Before leaving Hamilton I informed these people that unless they show results I will not bother with them any more, and that on my way back to Chicago next Wednesday I shall expect a definite answer, as I am getting tired of driving such a long way and that I could easily have my stuff come to Windsor from Montreal, and from there have it transferred to Detroit, and get it from the latter-mentioned city. Mr Harris and Mr Poles were most emphatic in their remarks, saying that they would do all they could for me and the next Wednesday they would have good news.

At last Zaneth seemed to be on the verge of making the buy from the Perri mob. Jennings sent this report on to the commissioner with the note that "Q is at present in Toronto and is being kept under surveillance as much as possible by our Informer E.T. [Ernest Tomlinson], with a view to keeping him away from Hamilton." It seems that *everyone* was suspicious of Informant "Q" at this stage — the mob, the RCMP and even his handler, Sergeant Zaneth himself. Jennings had given "Q" a job in Toronto, "to work up a suppositions case here," to keep "Q" out of mischief. Ironically, at this point, the success of the whole undercover operation depended on keeping the RCMP's best informant *out* of action. He had now become a major liability.

...Jim Harris escorted me to the Market Hotel on York Street, where he introduced me to Jim Murphy. No mention of drugs was made, but Mr Murphy stated that he had heard of me and also had seen me a number of times in his hotel, accompanied by Mr Harris.

Later we proceeded to the corner of Barton and James St. North, where we met Pat Hays. I may mention that Mr Hays was one of the first men I met in Hamilton, on the occasion when I first met Jim Crawford through Informant "Q."

At 11:30 P.M. Pat Hays, Jim Murphy, and Jim Harris requested me to accompany them to Bessy's road house, just outside Hamilton, on the Lakeshore road. On arrival I was introduced to Teddy Bone, the proprietor of the place, and Jim Murphy told Mr Bone that any time I stopped at his place I should be given a room out of the way, as I would not like to be observed by anyone.

Twenty minutes or so after our arrival there Pat Hays proceeded to the telephone and called someone. Immediately after, Mrs Rocco Perri, driving a Marmon sport roadster, arrived at the place alone, and entered into a conversation with Mr Bone. She was then escorted to the private room where the four of us were, and there I was introduced to her as Arthur Anderson of Chicago, while she was introduced to me as Mrs Rocco Perri, [the wife of] the biggest man in Ontario. During the conversation Mrs Perri asked me if I were Jewish and I replied, "Yes." Fortunately she did not speak the Jewish language to me, and after having had a drink she left.

On the way home Jim Harris informed me that Mrs Rocco Perri was called to the road house in order that she might have a good look at me, and judging from what I could gather, this woman must have been satisfied, otherwise she would have shown it right there and then, as she is just the type that would not hesitate to say what she thought.

Before parting I informed Jim Harris and Jim Murphy that I thought they were putting me through a rather stiff process, and that I was taking a big chance in stopping there to have all these people giving me the "once-over," not knowing who they were. However, Mr Harris particularly informed me that these people were the biggest dealers in the country, and they did not take any chances until they were absolutely satisfied they were dealing with the right party.

On the morning of the 12th I proceeded to the Market Hotel, where I again had an interview with Jim Murphy. I may say that both these men are engaged in book-making and any other illegal transactions they may have the opportunity to handle. Jim Murphy is the proprietor of the Hotel, and judging from its appearance, it is a splendid rendezvous for underworld characters.

Before leaving, Mr Murphy and Mr Harris requested me to make another trip, and that they felt almost certain that by that time, say Wednesday the 18th, they would be in a better position to talk business with me, knowing that the boss had seen me.

In view of the above I would respectfully suggest that I be allowed to remain on this investigation until at least the week of the 23rd, when I must appear in court against Italiano et al. It may be possible that the Perri gang will not have a man in Toronto to see who makes the case against these people. However, after that date this investigation must be handled in a different way, and even though it may take a little time yet to make the case against him, yet once it is made it will be worth while, as they are for sure the biggest drug dealers in the Province.

Zaneth's last meeting with the gang before his scheduled testimony at the Italiano trial was on September 18th, and he reported on this productive meeting in his memo of September 20:

...Around noon I met Mr J. Harris and Jim Murphy in the Market Hotel. After having lunch Jim Murphy asked me to drive him to Toronto as he had to make delivery of a parcel in the Ward. At first I declined to comply with his request but after a while I decided that it would be best to do so in order to keep in good standing with them.

About 3:30 P.M. we left for Toronto arriving about 5:15 P.M. Mr J. Harris who was carrying a small club bag left me at the corner of University and Edward Streets and walked west to the corner of Centre Street, handed the bag over to a man who stood on the sidewalk and both entered the corner house which I later found to be an Italian restaurant.

We then returned to Hamilton and during the conversation I made an effort to force the issue and emphatically told them that if they could not produce the goods I was not going to bother with them anymore as I was under the impression that I was being strung along.

About 10:30 P.M. Mr Murphy and Mr Harris asked me to drive to Bessie's house. There the conversation was resumed and Mr Harris informed me that there was only one objection in the way, namely that they were afraid of Jim Curwood (Informant "Q") as this man had been in Windsor and had made an effort to make a case against an Italian there who was connected with the same gang. Again I informed Mr Harris that I had severed my connection with Jim Curwood and that I had nothing at all to do with him, furthermore the business was being done between him and myself, and Curwood did not enter in any way, shape or form. He then telephoned to someone and approximately twenty minutes after, he was called out of the private room where we were and returned immediately after with approximately half an ounce of morphine in cube form identical to the goods seized in Italiano's residence. He asked me to examine the drug and if I was satisfied he thought that on my way back from Montreal on this trip about Monday or Tuesday he would be able to make a deal at $25.00 an ounce. I informed Mr Harris that I might not be in a position to purchase next week, as I was on my way to Montreal for a load and could not very well disappoint my connection there, but if he were willing to sell me the next day I would stop in Hamilton and wire to Montreal that I had been detained elsewhere. Mr Harris promised that he would do all he could for me and requested me at parting to meet him at noon the next day.

About 12:30 noon of the 19th I again met Mr Harris and Mr Murphy at the Market Hotel and during a brief conversation Mr Harris informed me that he had not been able to see his connection as the big boss was out of town and that he would let me know on my way back to Chicago next week just what they have decided to do....

I am of the opinion that these people are just beating time for something, whatever it is I am not in a position to know but I am convinced now that they have the goods and that they have enough confidence in me to go so far as to produce the goods to convince me and to try and induce me to be one of their clients. However, they are sceptical about the man who introduced me to them, which would appear to be the main objection.

Unfortunately I have to appear in court against Italiano et al. on the week of the 23rd and this will put an end to my activities with these people. However, we know who is at the back of this ring and probably someone else might be able to pick up the threads of the investigation and follow it up in case I am disclosed as a witness in the case of Italiano. I would, however, respectfully suggest that if it is at all possible for me to return to Hamilton on Monday morning on a hurried trip, I would like to do so in order to either make a deal or satisfy myself that these people are not selling until the Windsor and Toronto cases are closed. By doing so I would be able to be back in Toronto on the afternoon of the same day and if my testimony is not required until the next day it would be in the interest of this investigation.

On Monday, September 23rd, the Italiano trial began. Zaneth testified briefly and then boldly proceeded to Hamilton for his final meeting with the Perri gang. He guessed that his identity had not been observed by anyone who would have had time to report back to Hamilton yet. This would be his last chance to make the buy as an active agent inside the

Perri gang, as his own and Detective Constable Mathewson's testimony on the next day would be getting national press coverage — as would the naming of Bessie Perri as a major drug dealer. Obviously, from then on, Bessie, Rocco and their chief drug lieutenants would be most careful. On Wednesday the 25th, a day after the headlines over the RCMP revelations about Bessie and a day and a half after his last meeting with Harris, Operative no. 1 reported to the brass on his last meeting with the gang:

> ...In due course I communicated with Mr James Harris, who requested me to meet him at Pat Hays' place around ten o'clock. At the appointed time I proceeded there and found Mr Harris, Mr Jim Murphy and Pat Hays in consultation. These men received me in a friendly way but did not act the same as they used to during my previous visits. They seemed cold and uninterested and it appeared that something was weighing heavily on their minds.
>
> During the conversation I made every effort to press the issue but Jim Murphy informed me that their connection had been lost; that their New York man had flown the coop and that they were not in a position to say when they could resume negotiations with me.
>
> Jim Harris also again mentioned [Informant "Q"] and stated that he had positive proof that the man was employed by the Mounted Police in Toronto. To this I replied, that ever since I commenced doing business with "Q" nothing had ever occurred to indicate that he was a stool; that he pulled a few deals for me and that all went off as nicely as could be expected but ever since he [Harris] had hinted that "Q" was not to be trusted I dropped him in Montreal, to shift for himself.
>
> Jim Murphy wanted to know when I saw "Q" last. I told him that I could not say for certain but it must have been over four weeks ago now. He also asked me if I knew where he was, and I replied to the best of my knowledge he was in Montreal yet.
>
> These men's attitudes clearly indicated that they were afraid to do business with me but I could not ascertain for a certainty whether they are simply scared of Informant "Q."
>
> This informant, while under the influence of liquor, would say most anything and I fear that it was during one of his drunken bouts that he let out who he was and also probably who I was.
>
> I am positive that if any of these alleged friends of mine are

certain that I am connected with the Mounted Police they would not hesitate in saying so. I am also convinced that my presence in court against Italiano was not the cause of these people changing their attitude, and I have no alternative but to attribute same to Informant "Q," who returned to Hamilton a number of times and was seen by these people while I was telling them that he was in Montreal.

There is no doubt this is the cleverest gang of drug runners in the country. Every one of these men used to be employed by Rocco Perri in rum running and when the liquor racket was exhausted they turned to narcotic drugs. I may also say that Mrs Perri is the brains of the whole gang and nothing is being done without her consent. The following are the men engaged in the narcotic racket:

Jim Harris   Hamilton
Jim Murphy   Hamilton
Pat Hays   Hamilton
Jim Crawford   Hamilton
Tony Ross   Hamilton
Frank Ross   Hamilton
Frank Romeo   Hamilton
Joseph Biamonte   Niagara Falls, Ont.
Frank D'Agostino   Merritton
Frank Poles   Thorold

There are others residing in St Catharines, Niagara Falls, Thorold, Merritton and Beaverboard, whose name I have not yet learned.

It would be advisable to drop the Hamilton end of the investigation for some time but if the services of a good informer would be obtained to work around the above-mentioned place, I feel that we may in time achieve the same result....

The names of the above drug runners were gathered by me from time to time while employed on this investigation. I may also say that the main distributing point is Beaverboard, Ontario [now part of Welland]. The name of the man at this point has not been learned yet but I was given to understand that he is one of Rocco Perri's first cousins.

Rocco and Bessie had won again. Zaneth was assigned to track down Tony Roma — the vital missing link in the Italiano case — whom he had heard from Perri associates was in the United States. The services of Informant "Q" were terminated by the RCMP commissioner and Rocco and Bessie went back to business.

In September 1929, the RCMP in Toronto had located a possible Italian recruit to replace the capricious Informant "Q." In a memo to RCMP Commissioner Cortland Starnes dated September 30, 1929, Superintendent Jennings advised that this possible agent, one P. Licastro, a Hamilton building contractor with financial problems, "believed he could furnish them with valuable information which [would] lead [them] to the source of supply of narcotic drugs." Licastro had already told the RCMP about Rocco Perri's old ally, Joseph Serriani, the Calabrian Mafia boss of Niagara Falls: "[He] is the man who takes care of the drugs on arrival from New York and Tony Roma was one of the chief agents on this side of the line but that Rocco Perri is the actual man behind the scenes." Licastro went on to state that Perri is a Calabrian like himself and from what he had heard "was the man who furnished Roma with sufficent funds to keep him going from time to time and also assisted on the providing of bail for the arrested parties."

This is very consistent with what we have seen of Rocco Perri's activities in the bootleg trade over the past 15 years and is consistent with his later activities as documented from those who worked for him. Rocco always arranged to pay the bail for those working for him, and in some cases is known to have arranged a means for certain underlings to escape to the United States or elsewhere if necessary before trial. It is very likely that it was Rocco who arranged the "disappearance" of Tony Roma.

Superintendent Jennings told Commissioner Starnes that Licastro would be valuable both in locating Tony Roma and in finding out more about Rocco Perri's connection with narcotics flow in Ontario. Jennings recommended that Licastro's services be engaged for one month at $4 per day plus board and lodging expenses for out-of-town trips. Liscastro had asked for $5 a day, but Jennings was not prepared to pay that much until he proved himself. P. Licastro was hired on October 5th for a trial period of one month.

On October 2, 1929, Inspector Phil Walter of the Ontario Provincial Police alerted Customs that a large trunk had arrived for Rocco Perri by truck from Thorold and that many of Perri's men were hanging around the place where it had been deposited. G. B. Fowler, Divisional Chief of the Customs Excise Preventive Service in Ontario soon suspected a drug delivery. E. B. Hyatt, District Chief of Customs at Bridgeburg, Ontario, had written him a memo on October 2nd saying: "We have had information that Rocco Perri was in the dope game and we have been trying to trace this matter for some time between the border here and Hamilton." Hyatt adds that "following this we made an early morning patrol along the Niagara River but found nothing of interest." Fowler notes on his copy of the memo sent on to Ottawa that "as you are aware the Rocco Perri referred to in this report is Rocco Perri (and Mrs Perri) who were before the Royal Commission in connection with liquor matters. At different times rumours have arisen that this man and his wife are connected in a large way with Narcotics matters." These memos are forwarded to Colonel C. H. L. Sharman, Chief, Narcotics Division of National Health in Ottawa.

Rocco and Bessie Perri had major international drug connections. The "International Trafficking" intelligence files of the Department of Pensions and National Health were maintained as part of Canada's obligations to the League of Nations to stop the worldwide drug trade. They contain information both on trafficking within Canada gathered by the RCMP and reports sent to Canada from the United States, Europe and the Far East.

A former RCMP drug investigator, Ken Hossick, then Assistant Chief of the Narcotics Division of Pensions and National Health, was responsible for the intelligence gathering. Hossick was no bureaucrat, but conducted his own investigations of drug dealers, including Rocco Perri.

The file on Rocco Perri is called "International Trafficking: Bridgeburg, Ont.," a hint of large-scale operations at the old bootlegger's crossing, but most of the material has been lost. Based on information from Canadian National Railways Police, Hossick reported how Rocco brought the drugs into Canada. Raw opium from the Far East was smuggled in at Vancouver, brought to Hamilton on CN freight cars and then taken across Lake Erie by motorboat from Bridgeburg. On return trips supplies of morphine and heroin were brought into Canada. A man named Sulvani (possibly Serianni?) was in charge of operations while "the controlling head of this gang" was Rocco Perri. Rocco and Bessie were the "Canadian connection" for Canadian and American traffickers.

The Perris' contact had likely been New York gambler and gangland banker, Arnold Rothstein, who was murdered in November, 1928. Rothstein had started importing drugs in 1923, paying $2,000 for a kilo of heroin and selling it on the street for $300,000. Buffalo was a major source of Rothstein's supply and several sources link Rothstein with Bessie Perri. In Bessie's obituary, the Windsor *Star* said she went to New York in 1928 with a huge portion of Rocco's money to invest in a major drug deal. We also know Bessie was purchasing drugs from the Rochester mob, possibly with Rothstein's help, and dealing with the Chicago mob as well.

A month after Rothstein was murdered, on December 8, 1928, U.S. narcotics agents in Buffalo seized the last load destined for Rothstein. Based on information found in Rothstein's papers, the agents then found two trunks full of dope in Buffalo, which they estimated was worth three million dollars. The gambler's "heirs," and probably the Perris' new connections were Charles "Lucky" Luciano and Louis "Lepke" Buchalter.

On October 31, 1929, Staff Sergeant Darling filed a report to Inspector LaNauze on the information from the new agent, P. Licastro. Licastro told him that it was understood among all Italians that "no mention [was] to be made of Tony Roma," and consequently he was having trouble getting any information. He informed LaNauze of a Niagara Falls businessman [name taken out by the RCMP] who was receiving the drugs, which were brought in by train.

He also referred to Stefano Magaddino as the "head of the Mafia" on the Buffalo side of the border. This is the first time that the term "Mafia" was used in the RCMP memos. Licastro intended to try to befriend the drug traffickers still in the "drug game" in southern Ontario. Sergeant Darling recommended to LaNauze that they continue Licastro as a paid informant for another month, writing that he "appears to be honest and anxious to do the best he can...and he appears to realize the seriousness and difficulty of the proposition and is working very cautiously." LaNauze agreed, stating that Liscastro's "services" should be continued for another month.

During the next month Zaneth travelled back and forth between Bridgeburg, Port Colborne and Thorold in his search for his elusive quarry. By November 25th, Zaneth had found a woman in Thorold, Mrs Domenic Frada, who knew Roma and his wife well and was also a close friend of the Perris. There is a great deal in the memos about a fur coat being delivered to her for Roma's common-law wife, Helen Groves. The lead is not too useful except that it introduces Mrs Frada as a possible source. At the same time, however, Zaneth had another lead — in Niagara Falls, New York. While in Niagara Falls, Ontario, Zaneth uncovered a drug courier, Mrs Antonetta "Steamshovel" White, a forty-year-old female with "large teeth." Mrs White's source of supply was none other than Perri's old friend, Joseph Serianni, the Mafia boss of the area. Zaneth had been alerted to this by Liscastro. He pondered allowing Liscastro to make a buy, but decided against it: Liscastro did not want to be revealed as an RCMP informer, and hence could not testify in court later. Zaneth said that Licastro appeared very much afraid of making a purchase or of giving evidence.

However, Licastro did have news. While in Hamilton he had recently had dinner with Rocco Perri. "During that conversation," Licastro reported to Zaneth, "Perri stated that had Tony Roma remained in Toronto to stand his trial, his confederates would have received a more severe sentence." So it was now clear that Rocco Perri co-ordinated Roma's escape and that he did so as part of a larger strategy to make sure that his other underlings and colleagues could not be convicted of conspiracy to traffick.

At this point, Zaneth told his superiors that while he felt that Licastro should not make any drug purchases, he believed that he was "the logical person to make connections with Rocco Perri and should also be able to get valuable information which should lead to the arrest of Tony Roma." However, since Licastro did not appear completely "to grasp what [was] required of him," Zaneth advised headquarters that Licastro had "outlived his usefulness." The experience with "Q" was making the RCMP very cautious with other informers.

After spending December 1929 travelling around Ontario and Quebec, looking for Roma and pursuing his ongoing investigation of Rocco Perri's drug empire, Zaneth sent out an excited memo on January 8, 1930. In it he reported that ex-Informant "Q" had just appeared in his Toronto RCMP office with one Riordan [who had] valuable information concerning the illegal traffic of narcotic drugs in Hamilton. Staff Sergeant Darling and Zaneth interrogated the walk-in informer, and while they were both skeptical of Riordan's abilities, they were impressed with his information. They ascertained that he knew "certain well-known pedlars who obtained their supply from Tony Ross and his brother Frank Ross, and from whom he said he could purchase as much as $20 worth of drugs at any time." Zaneth explained that "in view of the fact that we are in hopes that some day Tony Ross or Frank Ross will make a slip and sell at the wrong moment and enable us to bring them to justice, and futhermore, as these two men are known to us to be the Hamilton agents of Rocco Perri, we could not overlook this information." With this, the RCMP authorized Zaneth and Darling to give Riordan a trial run at being a paid RCMP informant.

On January 7th Zaneth went to Hamilton with Riordan and another informer. But again he was to have great difficulty connecting with the dealers — and no luck purchasing any dope. The Perri gang was lying low as usual when a new buyer appeared. The mission was a failure.

On February 12, 1930, new information cropped up right in Hamilton. A reporter from the Hamilton *Herald* approached Corporal Webster, the officer in charge of the Hamilton RCMP detachment. Webster later detailed their discussion in a memo to Superintendent Jennings:

I have the honour to report that a reporter on the staff of the Hamilton *Spectator* [sic], has informed me that he received information from a Hamilton man by the name of McGregor, who is said to be a bootlegger and smuggler, that Rocco Perri, 166 Bay Street South, Hamilton, or Mrs Bessie Perri, is engaged in smuggling narcotic drugs into Canada by means of aeroplanes.

This man McGregor apparently can be made to talk freely when under the influence of liquor and being an old school-mate of W. J. Nairn [the reporter-source later identified], he was induced to disclose this information regarding Rocco Perri. Nairn states that McGregor also professes to be against the smuggling of narcotics.

Rocco Perri, according to McGregor, has received narcotics from the United States by seaplanes which alighted on the lake near Burlington. Then the mode of delivery was changed to dropping the packages by silk parachute, Jack Elliott's old flying field near Hamilton being used. Then again delivery is said to have been made at a point further east in the Niagara Peninsula towards St Catharines.

McGregor is said to be now in Montreal but on his return Nairn will approach him again and endeavour to obtain further information regarding this matter. I have requested Nairn to endeavour to ascertain the source of the supply or who is at the American end of this aeroplane business and from what point they start.

McGregor cannot be approached by us, Nairn informs me, as he would not talk.

Two weeks later, on February 27, 1930. Zaneth dispatched two memos, one "Re: Rocco Perri" and one "Re: Tony Roma," each containing significant new information from Mrs Frada. It turned out that Tony Roma and his wife had had a major fight in Mrs Frada's kitchen on the day that Roma jumped bail and went to Buffalo. Here is Mrs Frada's account of their heated dialogue:

Miss Ethel [sic,Helen] Groves (Mrs Roma). What a fine friend Rocco Perri turned out to be. After he asked you to stop doing business with Jimmy (Frank D'Agostino, Merritton) and buy from him, in time of trouble he refuses to help you.

Tony Roma. The reason why I stopped buying from Jimmy is because Perri gave it to us much cheaper. Rocco has too much money and cannot take a chance to show his hand in this thing.

Mrs. Roma. At least he could have helped you financially to pull through your trial, whereas now you must leave the country.

Tony Roma. The reason why I am leaving is not the question of money but because I am wanted in Montreal on a murder charge and it will be better for the rest [meaning Italiano and Defalco] if I do go away.

Zaneth added in his memo that after this heated argument Helen Groves refused to go with Roma to Buffalo. "However, two months later she, too, left and it is almost certain that she went to join him," Mrs Frada added. In a significant aside, Mrs Frada confirmed that "Perri was the [drug] source of supply" to Roma and the others charged in Toronto.

Back in Hamilton, Corporal Webster was pursuing the lead from McGregor. On March 12, 1930, he reported that he had again interviewed Nairn, the Hamilton reporter "with regard to the operations of Rocco Perri" and that McGregor had now informed Nairn that Rocco Perri had been receiving narcotic drugs from Ohio," in tins which were hidden in the coal bunkers of a coal barge which comes to the dock of the Steel Co. of Canada or the dock of the United Fuel Investments Co., the Hamilton By-Products Coke company in other words." The barge's cook and his wife who ran a boarding house on Church Street in Toronto were put under RCMP surveillance, but the investigation was later dropped for lack of evidence.

Once again, Rocco and Bessie had won, and neither was ever charged with drug trafficking. The RCMP, however, eventually had better luck with Roma. But it wasn't until 1935, after Zaneth had chased him through the entire Eastern seaboard of the United States over a span of six years, that Zaneth finally ensnared him hiding in Los

Angeles. After a lengthy extradition hearing, for which Hugh Mathewson and others went to Los Angeles to testify, Roma was returned to Toronto in the summer of 1936.

The dealer's actual trial for drug trafficking was anti-climactic. It occurred at the height of the events leading to the abdication of Edward VIII, in December 1936, and in the press was completely overshadowed by the crisis, meriting only several short stories buried in the Toronto papers. Zaneth and Mathewson testified, recounting the events of 1929 that had been heard at the Italiano trial seven years earlier. Roma received a two-year term. Later Roma re-entered the United States, but was deported to Italy.

CHAPTER 14

MURDER ON BAY STREET

Bessie Perri was murdered on the evening of August 13, 1930. She was forty-one. Based on hitherto secret OPP and RCMP files as well as information provided by Rocco Perri himself in interviews with Athel Gow of the Toronto *Star* and OPP Inspector John Miller, the officer in charge of the murder investigation for the Province of Ontario, it is now possible, for the first time, to reconstruct most of the major events leading to the murder, including the activities and discussions of Rocco and Bessie on August 12 and 13. Inspector Miller's sources included the daughter of a Hamilton rabbi who was close to Bessie. In the weeks before her death, she had been having a dispute with the Chicago mob about the quality of the dope they were buying there, and she and Rocco had argued about whether to continue buying from them at all. In fact, several days before her murder, Bessie told the daughter that she might be killed because of the mob disputes that were wracking the underworld. Frank Zaneth's own sources later made even more sensational revelations about Bessie's problems with the American Mafia.

Bessie's murder was foreshadowed by a gangland killing in Port Credit on July 2, 1930. On the day of his murder, Philip Rumbold, a wealthy Tonawanda, New York, real estate salesman, had a dinner meeting with a friend in

Hamilton after which a Hamilton taxi driver took them to a Port Credit roadhouse. Rumbold's body was discovered by police in an abandoned automobile on a lonely road near Port Credit. He had been strangled, according to the inquest, by the usual "person or persons unknown." Police had found letters from a Buffalo area gangster at Rumbold's home. The Rumbold killing was one of over fifty such mob killings in the area over twenty years, a result of the ongoing mob rivalries in the liquor trade. Yet the timing of the murder, just three weeks before Bessie Perri's sensational murder, linked it in the minds of the press directly to Bessie's murder. Both were seen as a cause for growing concern over gangster violence in Canada.

On the morning of Tuesday, August 12th, the day before Bessie's murder, Rocco found himself in court over a bootlegging case against himself and Mike Serge, his cousin and sometime driver. The case was widely reported in the Hamilton newspapers: "ROCCO PERRI IS NOT GUILTY OF HAVING LIQUOR," screamed the front-page headline of the Hamilton *Spectator* on August 12th, "No Evidence to Convict Him, Court Rules/His Cousin Must Serve Three-Month term."

Mike Serge had been making a delivery of booze on the evening of August 2nd, to a grocery store on Beach Road, and Perri had been at the wheel of his car awaiting Serge's return when provincial police stopped the pair. Serge tried to run away, but Perri calmly stayed where he was, realizing that there was no evidence against him. Serge was captured and took the rap, stating that the alcohol was his own. Serge further claimed that Perri "was unaware of the nature of the stuff that was in the package." Perri was merely giving Serge a ride, as his own car wouldn't start. Serge said that he had received the booze "from a Toronto man."

"Do you know who you were going to deliver this alcohol to?" asked Crown Attorney Orville Walsh.

"No, I met him at the race track the night before, and I never saw him before," replied Serge.

"Then it might have been a provincial officer, for all you know," countered Walsh.

"It must have been," interrupted the irrepressible Perri, much to the amusement of those in the court.

Magistrate Burbidge, who replaced Jelfs when he retired, found that there was no evidence against Rocco and dismissed the charges against him. He found Serge guilty and sentenced him to six months in Barton Street jail. But Magistrate Burbidge was reminded by Rocco's lawyer, William Morrison, that "three months is the limit" for this type of offence, even though it was Serge's second conviction.

"Three months it is," Burbidge corrected himself.

Again, Rocco, protected by an underling, got away.

That evening all hell broke loose at the Perri household. In a memo stamped "Secret and Personal," Frank Zaneth explained what probably took place. (The memo, dated March 25, 1931, was part of Zaneth's ongoing investigation into Rocco Perri's role in drug trafficking.) It is almost certain that Zaneth's source was Mrs Domenic Frada, though since October 1930, he had been trying to recruit as an informer the long-time Perri maid, Mary Latika. At the very least Latika may have confirmed this important new information, which Zaneth dramatically reported in his memo. The report was later turned over to the Ontario Provincial Police for their "quiet but determined" investigation into Bessie's savage murder.

I...recently had the opportunity of interviewing a certain party who has known Mr and Mrs Perri for a number of years.

During the conversation I learned that some time previous to Mrs Perri being killed, she had purchased a large amount of narcotic drugs from a gang operating from Rochester, N.Y., U.S.A., with the understanding that she would pay immediately after delivery was made.

According to my informant, Mrs Perri refused to pay this debt and challenged the trafficker to go to the law if he wanted his money, fully realizing that he had no redress from this source. I was further informed that on the night before the tragedy took place, three men called on Mr and Mrs Perri at 166 Bay Street South, Hamilton, and demanded payment for the drugs. There a heated argument took place. Rocco Perri insisted that Bessie pay for the drugs but Mrs Perri refused to do so and ordered the men out of the house. The next evening Mrs Rocco Perri was shot to death while leaving her garage, which fact we all know.

My informant contended that although Rocco Perri had nothing to do with the murder of Bessie, yet he knows who did it, as he was well acqainted with the three men that called on him the previous night, and it is stated that it was the same men that killed her.

I also gathered that Rocco Perri does not dare report these men to the police as he fears that harm or possible death may come to him.

By 1930, of course, Rocco Perri had considerable power in both southern Ontario and northern New York state. He had gained strength and respect through his control of the bootlegging rackets and local gambling. But his entrance into the drug-trafficking field with Bessie changed the picture considerably. Other, more menacing groups were involved in the drug importation and distribution area in both Canada and the United States, and their code of honour, which obviously included paying for drugs bought through them, had always been enforced with ruthless efficiency. Bessie, in an attempt to make a quick buck, had clearly breached the rules of the game and ended up paying the penalty.

No doubt the threat of reprisal was on both Rocco's and Bessie's minds throughout the day after the showdown with the Rochester mob. It is safe to assume that a heated discussion ensued throughout the day about the wisdom of crossing the big boys in the American mob in major drug deals. Ironically, it may have weighed more heavily on Rocco's mind, as, according to underworld etiquette, it was up to him to discipline his erring business partner. He was most likely told that she would have to be taken care of, one way or another. And even now, more than eighteen years after they had met, Rocco was very much dependent on and in love with Bessie. Inspector Miller later concluded that Bessie's murder "almost certainly had to do with the drug trade."

On the afternoon of Wednesday, August 13th, Rocco and Bessie left home at 1:00 P.M. for an appointment downtown with William Morrison. They discussed Morrison's successful defence of Rocco and the possibility of Mike Serge's appealing his conviction and, according to the records of a later OPP interrogation of Rocco, arranged to get Mike Serge moved to a more "comfortable" jail, possibly a farm, to serve his time. After seeing Morrison for about an hour, Rocco and Bessie did some uptown shopping. She bought a beautiful new dress. Rocco then went downtown to conduct some mob business at an Italian bowling green. Since Mary Latika, the family maid, was cleaning the house, Bessie decided after lunch to visit Rocco's cousin's wife. Mary Serge, at 163 Bay Street North, for the afternoon. Rocco arrived for a short visit at about four in the afternoon, and Bessie modelled her new dress for him. According to Rocco, this tender scene took place in the Serges' living room: "I told her she looked beautiful. I took her in my arms and kissed her. I told her I loved her and she said, "Roc, do you mean it?" We were preparing to go away on a holiday somewhere. We had not planned to go anywhere in particular but just to drive away in the car and go where we liked."

Bessie stayed at the Serges' while Rocco went downtown to attend to some more business at the bowling green. He then returned to the Serge household for supper and spent the evening with Bessie and his cousin's family playing cards and chatting. It was a quiet family party, quite typical of a Perri evening in this period. As Rocco later testified, "We used to go there every night pretty near." Neither Rocco nor Bessie had been home since one o'clock that afternoon.

Bessie called home at five minutes to eleven to tell Mary Latika that she was on her way. Rocco's tall, slender twenty-eight-year-old half-brother, Mike Perri was staying with Rocco and Bessie at the time. When Bessie phoned, he was taking a bath. Mary Latika started to turn down the Perris' bed. She was about to supply Mike Perri with a fresh towel when she heard the dog, Rex, a handsome Alsatian police dog, bark. It was now five or ten minutes before the

Perris were to arrive back, about 11:15. But Mary thought nothing of it and simply told the dog to keep quiet.

Meanwhile, Rocco and Bessie were driving in their two-door Marmon coupe (what Rocco called his "little car") up nearby Bold Street and turned down an alleyway that led to the back of their house. They saw nothing unusual. They turned into their darkened garage, the doors of which had been left partially open, and moved into the spot next to their larger car, a seven-passenger, sixteeen-foot-long Marmon touring sedan, which was parked on the right side of the garage. It was a tight squeeze. Rocco and Bessie sat and talked for a few minutes about trading their heavy roadster in for a newer model. Bessie mentioned that they would probably lose some money in the deal on the Marmon, but said, "What the hell is a two or three hundred dollar loss on a car like that?" As was their routine, Bessie asked for the key to the back door and got out first in order to put the garage lights on so Rocco could close the garage doors. It was approximately 11:35 P.M.

Rocco got out and turned to close the garage doors — two heavy, wooden doors that opened onto a dark alley lined with backyard fences and other garages. He heard the first shotgun blast ring out. Bessie had got out of the car and was on her way to turn on the light switch. Rocco was only a few steps from Bessie, but he was heading away from the killers, towards the garage doors. Rocco turned around and screamed at the top of his lungs. Suddenly the garage was filled with smoke. He last saw Bessie alive standing in front of the Marmon touring car near the small door that opened onto the stairs leading to the kitchen door. He claimed that he unsuccessfully attempted to pull her out of harm's way.

Two seconds later another shotgun blast came from behind the Marmon sedan, between the garage wall and the car on the south side of the garage. The killers appeared to be standing on the running board of the Marmon touring car, where they had been crouching until Bessie alighted. After the second shot was fired, Rocco panicked and fled the garage in terror. According to Rocco himself, he "started to go out, and when the third shot was fired I was right in front of the garage door." In addition to the three shotgun blasts, Rocco also thought he "heard a revolver shot" as he was running up the alleyway.

He later claimed he couldn't see anything because "the garage was filled with smoke." He did not see Bessie fall or hear her scream. As far as he knew she was still standing. He then ran quickly up the alley towards Duke Street. As he passed Bay Street he ran into a man who stopped him and asked him if anything was the matter. It was David A. Robbins, a neighbour and son of a Hamilton school trustee, who was out walking his dog. Rocco hysterically told Robbins, "Somebody shot my girl," and dragged him back to the house to show him.

Having heard the shots, Mike Perri rushed out of the bathroom, half-dressed, to see what was going on. By the time he got downstairs Rocco had already returned with Robbins and had come in the front door of the house. Incredibly, Rocco testified that he asked Mary Latika, "Is Mrs Perri in?" to which she answered, "No." In an excited state Rocco proceeded down the stairs from the house to the garage with Robbins and the maid in tow and Mike Perri behind them. Rocco opened the door to the garage for Robbins, as if for a guest, who was the first to enter. There they found the bloodied body of Bessie Perri, face up, still draped with the expensive jewellery she always wore. The corpse was just where Rocco had last seen her standing — beside the light switch exactly nine feet from where she had left the car. It was still dark in the garage. The switch had never been turned on.*

Robbins phoned the police. They found that the murderers had used chiselled or "creased," shotgun shells and a double-barrelled shotgun to make sure the maximum damage would be done. Bessie had been killed by two shotgun

---

*Reporter Roy Greenaway, who had interviewed both Al Capone and Rocco Perri in his long career, later noted in "Big Shots," an essay on Perri, Capone and the mob, that "in a second or two more, she [Bessie] would have reached the electric switch beside the door opening towards the house...but she never touched it. Minion of the dark, she died in the dark."

wounds at close range. Over a hundred pellets had penetrated her body. The first shot had hit the north side of the garage door and had gone through a tin pan upon which Bessie fell. The second, more accurate shot, entered through her right ear, went through her head and through the jugular vein, exiting under the lobe of the left ear. The second wound, about two inches by an inch and a quarter in diameter, had been caused by the third shot. It had entered the lower part of the right shoulder, passed through the right lung, causing a good deal of bleeding, had torn away the ribs there, and left several pellets of shot between the right breastbone and breast. In her fall, she also injured her forehead and left knee slightly, though death had been instantaneous from the second shotgun blast. The gunmen had fled in a car that had been waiting near the back of the house.

Within minutes of Robbins' call, 166 Bay Street South was swarming with police and Rocco's friends and neighbours. The police contingent was under Rocco's old adversary, Inspector of Detectives Joseph Crocker. Rocco helped one of the policemen remove the jewellery from Bessie's body. It was given to Rocco and not kept by the police as evidence. The body was then removed to the morgue for further study.

Pandemonium ensued. People came to offer their condolences and police investigators attempted to take evidence. However, the police made little attempt to preserve the scene of the crime in its original state. Besides allowing Rocco to keep Bessie's jewels, they let him retain valuable papers and money, which OPP Inspector John Miller later thought might have contained evidence. Rocco was in an almost hysterical state — though eventually he collected himself and was able to answer most questions and talk to friends.

Not far from the scene, in the alleyway behind the house, police soon discovered the two twelve-gauge, breech-loading double-barrel shotguns used in the killing. Either they had been totally wiped of fingerprints or the killers had worn gloves. These were clearly professional hit men, who were not swayed by the excitement of the moment or any normal human emotions. "The killers," journalist Roy Greenaway later reported, were "apparently as unmoved as hunters shooting rabbits," as they went about their business. One gun had been found leaning against the wall in the corner, placed there cooly and carefully by one of the killers.

Later the police found two New York state licence plates that had been discarded a few blocks away from Bay Street. They had been stolen from an abandoned car belonging to a Niagara Falls, New York, resident named Isadore Ladictoiria who had moved to Hamilton. They became valuable clues in the police investigation.

The next day, police arrested and brought in for questioning Antonio ("Tony") Papalia* of 19 Railway Street, driver and friend of Rocco and cousin of Ned Italiano, who was known to have had sole access to the garage from which the getaway car's plates had been stolen. Papalia and Domenic Puglisse, also of Railway Street, had visited the garage on the previous Sunday, August 10th, on what police and garage personnel felt was a pretext. He had brought his Studebaker into the garage for some repair, but the mechanic, on looking it over, found only that some bolts fastened on by lock washers were missing and some were loose. The mechanic told police that it was his opinion that the bolts had been "purposely loosened by someone." Furthermore, Papalia was seen to pass near where the Ladictoiria car was being repaired. Inspector John Miller concluded that Papalia had been involved in the set-up of the murder. The report on the Tony Papalia interrogation was part of an all out police intelligence effort to find out what was known in the underworld about Bessie Perri's murder. "COMB SICILIAN HAUNTS FOR MRS PERRI SLAYERS" shouted a headline in the Toronto *Star* on August 16 in one of its four major front page stories on the murder. Papalia, called "Tony Popa," was portrayed as loyal to Rocco, and surrounded by his children

---

*He was the father and founder of the Papalia Crime Family of Hamilton of which Johnny ("Paps" or "Pops") Papalia is the most notorious living member.

he told the Toronto *Star* that "Rocco is my friend...even if I knew who did it, I would tell him first...not the police...."

When Miller later suggested to Rocco that his "friend" Papalia may have had a hand in arranging his wife's murder, Rocco at first balked at the suggestion, saying that Papalia "would not do anything against me," but after a while he granted that it could be a possibility. In his official report Miller reported that Rocco replied that though he "had never thought of it before in that light, he thought there might be something to it." Rocco went on to tell Miller that "it was too early to learn who committed the murder," but that he assured Miller he would find out if he wasn't himself "knocked off" first.

The murder was, of course, a very hot news item in the Hamilton and Toronto papers, and in other major papers across Canada. It was front page banner headlines in the Toronto *Star*, the *Globe,* the *Mail and Empire*, as well as the Hamilton *Herald* and *Border Cities* [Windsor] *Star*. Every angle of the case, every aspect of the investigation was covered in the minutest of detail. There was also a proliferation of lifestyle and analysis pieces on the Perri family and the Perri gang and numerous probing editorials and even editorial cartoons on the sensational, hitherto "American," gangland-style killing. Some of the reporters covering the case, such as the Toronto *Star*'s Athol Gow, were audacious, provocative and inventive in creating new angles as well as milking the obvious. Gow, for instance, goaded Perri into raising the reward money for information leading to the arrest of Bessie's killers from $2,000 to $5,000 just so he could later make a better front page story out of it.

The day after the murder, August 14, 1930, the Toronto *Star* took the lead with a "scoop" interview with Bessie's estranged husband, Harry Tobin. It is a good example of what Joe Atkinson later called the platoon system, when word of Bessie's murder reached Toronto, just about every reporter in the *Star* office was sent out to cover the story. The front-page right story was headlined, "'I CAN SAY THANK

GOD' SAYS LAWFUL HUSBAND OF BESSIE PERRI/ Murdered Woman Had Deserted Toronto Merchant and Two Daughters in 1913/Police Knew Facts/'She Died as She Deserved to Die,' Declares Man She Left." The story of Bessie's actual murder appeared front-page left under the headline, "Police Work on Theory Mrs Perri Was Victim of Bootlegging Racket/Say Revenge and Resentment Directed Bullets Which Riddled Woman Last Night/Search Road-houses/Alleged Renewed Activity in Liquor Traffic Suggested as Causing Gang Feud." In the middle of these two major stories on the front page of the August 14th paper were large pictures of Bessie and Rocco Perri under the banner "SELF-STYLED BOOTLEG KING'S WIFE SHOT BY GUNMEN."

In the "exclusive" Harry Tobin interview, Bessie's estranged husband was bitter and harsh in his condemnation:

"All I can say is 'thank God,'" said the legal husband of Bessie Perri to the *Star* to-day when apprised of the tragic death of the woman who left his home and children many years ago.[The *Star* did not name Harry Tobin, but the *Border Cities Star*, in picking up the Toronto *Star* story, did use the name, as did the Hamilton *Herald*.]

"She died as she deserved to die. Seventeen years ago she left me with two small children. She means nothing to me, and I have not seen her since she left me."

"I think it was over Rocco Perri that she left me," he said. "Anyway it was not for any good. Look what she has been into since. I was kind to her, and I had a good job. I was driving a wagon. She just vanished one day, stored the furniture, and left the two little children on the streets."

"As he talked, a door in the rear of the little shop opened, and a middle-aged woman looked in to call him to breakfast. He motioned her back. "Now I can marry her with a license," he said. "It's a long time to wait."

"Any children?" asked the reporter. "Four little ones. Hers. The other two are grown up now and married. I raised them till they were married. I have nothing to be ashamed of. Why must I come into all this? Seventeen years I have forgotten! People forgot. Only the police knew. I told them when she left me, I separated her, you see. Yes the police know all about it. There is nothing now to tell you. I was never mixed up in it. Never did I see her since she left me."

"And the two daughters. Did they ever see their mother after she left them with you?"

"Maybe yes. But they never say anything to me about it...."

A mysterious anonymous telephone call at 2:30 A.M. to-day broke the news that his wife had fallen victim to murderers' bullets a few hours before. He is mystified. He thinks the call was over long distance, but he cannot understand why anyone should have called him. Very few people knew that Mrs Perri had been married to him, he told the *Star,* and those who did, knew that he had put her out of his life the past seventeen years.

Mrs Rocco Perri, in the company of her husband, uncrowned bootlegger King of Hamilton, was a frequent visitor at the flat of her married daughter, Mrs Gertie Maidenberg, 489 Euclid Ave, the *Star* learned to-day in an interview with Mrs Yetta Greenwood, owner of the house and occupant of the lower floor.

"She tried to come here with Rocco, once a week, sometimes twice — sometimes only once in two weeks. She loved Mrs Maidenberg's baby, Stanley. A week ago to-day she was here the last time. Oh she never let Mrs Maidenberg buy anything for the baby. All the clothes, everything — she used to bring with her."

Mrs Greenwood said that the baby was 19 months old. Mrs Maidenberg, she added, had left for Hamilton about 12:30 this morning. She was apparently very much affected by the news of her mother's murder. "She was crying all the time," said Mrs Greenwood.

"Oh, but Mrs Perri used to come so often. She used to give Mrs Maidenberg money and she liked to play with the little fellow in the back-yard — yes, yes. Lots of times they'd come and stay for two, three, four hours, They loved each other.

Along with its massive front page news coverage, the August 14th issue of the Hamilton *Herald* ran the first of seven editorials on Bessie's murder and its implications for Hamilton and Ontario, which reflected part of a growing wave of repugnance sweeping the country. Entitled "THE PERRI MURDER," it was the first newspaper editorial on the killing (beating the *Spectator* by a day), and it began with a strong condemnation of the event, along with sensational speculation about possible links to American gang killings and the murder of Rumbold three weeks earlier. The third paragraph of this long and provocative editorial introduced a racist element that was to become more and more obvious in future editorials dealing with the mob:

> It is unfortunate for the reputation of the race over which Signor Mussolini presides that his people appear almost to have monopolized this traffic, and to be the leaders in the crimes that have been committed in conneciton with it. There are many of the finest of the Italian race, the Northern Italians especially, who deplore this fact as much as any Briton could do, but these vendetta-seeking and murderously inclined gangsters are a disgrace to any country and a plague in civilized communities.
>
> It is the duty and should be the active business of the Attorney-General to clean up this situation. Extreme measures are needed and the Attorney-General should not hesitate to take them. If it be found necessary to round up the whole Italian community, let that be done. There is no reason why a British city should be infested with banditti and the King's peace be broken in this tragical fashion merely to oblige the murderous instinct of these assassins. These men must be known to the Italian community. They must be suspected by the friends of the victims.
>
> ...Drastic measures are necessary. There is no doubt of that. A man with back-bone will not hesitate to adopt them. The boot-legging and other illicit operations carried on should not have the complacent apathy of the Attorney-General's department to sanction them. There should be the most vigorous policy adopted to end conditions which breed such dastardly and devilish crimes. Nothing else will satisfy the people, and nothing else will justify the Government.

In comparison to the extraordinary coverage in the Hamilton *Herald*, the *Border Cities Star*, and the Toronto *Star*, the Hamilton *Spectator* account of the murder was restrained and even dignified. Ironically, its front-page headline story was about the murder of Chicago gangster Danny Vallo, one of the suspects in the St Valentine's Day Massacre, who was gunned down in a Chicago surburb on the same day as Bessie.

On August 15th the Toronto *Star* ran no fewer than eight front-page stories as part of its sensational saturation coverage of the Perri murder. One story, headlined, "BESSIE PERRI 'DEAD' 17 YEARS TO OWN FAMILY," included interviews with Bessie's only sister, Mrs Bella Wexler, and Bessie's niece, a Mrs Kaplan who reluctantly admitted that they were Bessie's relatives after Mrs Wexler at first denied it, "Yes Mrs Perri is my mother's sister, but you see with all the disgrace she had brought, mother does not want to be called her sister." At this point Mrs Wexler opened up to the *Star's* reporter: "Well, I might as well confess Mrs Perri was my sister, but I haven't seen her for years." After leaving Bessie's only sister puzzling as to whether she, like Harry Tobin, should get a lawyer to stake a claim on Bessie's will, the intrepid *Star* reporters sought out Bessie's three long-lost brothers, Jacob, Ollie and Lewis Starkman, as well as one of the older Starkman brothers' sons-in-law, Charles Turk. As far as Jacob Starkman was concerned, "no relationship existed" between his late sister and himself. A devout Jew, he had never forgiven his sister for leaving her husband to live in sin with the Catholic Rocco Perri. Both Ollie and Lewis Starkman declined comment. It was Charles Turk who was the friendliest of the relatives interviewed. He called Rocco Perri, whom he claimed to know intimately, " a good fellow...he loved Bessie a whole lot...and gave her a lot of jewellery and placed a lot of property in her name ...nothing was too good for her."

Another story in the *Star* that day examined Bessie's wealth, including her Buffalo bank accounts, her "$15,000 trove of jewellery," which included some very expensive diamonds, her daily take from criminal activity ("single stops in her collection were worth a small ransom"), and the fact that the two Perri homes, the one in Hamilton and one in St Catharines, were in Bessie's name. Rocco officially owned nothing, earned nothing, and paid no taxes. The story also goes on to speculate as to the motives of the killers, including the alleged failure of the Perris to keep their promises to underlings to take care of them when caught. (This was confirmed in Miller's investigation, but it was always Rocco who made the promises and Bessie who broke them.) Rocco was quoted as saying that the motive for the shooting of his wife was robbery. Hundreds of mourners, relatives and close friends were reported to be stopping by to pay their respects to Rocco. But the most interesting aspect of this story was its glimpse into the Hamilton underworld of the day.

Whether from deference to the slain Bessie Perri or from the fear of stimulated activity in the forces of law and order, Hamilton's underworld was at a standstill to-night.

While squads of officers roamed the city and checked up on suspicious characters and hang-outs, known bootleggers ceased to function, and two known gambling joints did not operate. Habitués at these places put in appearances from time to time, but were advised by the men in charge that there would be no play.

The situation in regard to these alleged dens is peculiar. They are located near King and James Sts. which is in the heart of the retail business district.

One has been in operation, on and off for over two years. The other, alleged to be operated by a group of Perri's compatriots, has been running for two weeks.

Activities at these places is common knowledge but the police are almost powerless owing to the system of look-outs and elaborately guarded doors. Raids have been conducted, but by the time that the officers reach the inner rooms where the big crap tables are situated, there is no trace of the game or of the big sums that are wagered.

In the street opposite the Italian layout, the two proprietors sat last night in their car, for a full hour. No one ventured to enter. Outside the other place a man paced the brightly lighted street. Citizens walked past on the way home from the theatres or from social calls, oblivious of the situation.

But every now and then some individual who walked past would address quiet words to the young man who was keeping vigil.

Usually it would be "Anything tonight?" "Nothing doing," would come the terse answer....

In the industrial section of Sherman Ave. N., there is a Little Italy, very small, where every compatriot of Rocco Perri gives the impression that he knows who murdered Bessie Perri — but stoutly denies that he knows; where every Italian ridicules the idea of a vendetta or Black Hand organization, but declines to allow his name to be used in connection with an interview; where all declare there will be no reprisals for the murder, but leave the investigator with the impression that there are sure to be.

Last night a *Star* reporter wandered through this section of the city, along poorly lighted streets, sat in small Italian cafés, lingered among groups at the corner stores, visited the homes of influential members of the small colony. Everywhere talk was of the murder.

All the bootlegging and racketeering is confined to the Calabrese from southern Italy and to a few Sicilians, according to the Sherman Ave. N. Italians, most of whom are from central and northern Italy. The Calabrese and Sicilians, who are few in number, live in a different section of the city. Rocco is said to be a Calabresian. One man's estimate of the total Italian population here was 3,000.

There is a feeling throughout the colony that the next development will not be reprisal by Perri, but his own death.

The main story in the *Star* that day was based on an interview with Rocco himself by ace *Star* reporter Athel Gow and the huge front page banner headline read "'VENGEANCE IS MINE,' ATTITUDE OF PERRI." Gow had been admitted to the Perri mansion at midnight to view Bessie lying in state in her $3,000 coffin: "Like some queen of old in Egyptian days of pomp and splendor, Bessie Perri will be buried in a magnificent bronze and nickle casket, said to be worth $3,000," Gow wrote. "She looked peaceful — not a trace of any anguish...draped on the wall high above the mantle-piece, was an Egyptian goddess worked in tapestry, and a few chairs circled the bay window — but beyond the room was empty like some mausoleum." To Gow, Bessie in death looked "more like a bride" than a cadaver. When Gow had arrived at Rocco's mansion, his men at first tried to shield Rocco from the reporter by saying that he was asleep, but when Rocco heard who was there he ordered, "Come in — it is all right." Gow describes the scene:

There were words of sympathy as I shook hands...His happy, debonair manner, his flashing eyes and smile had vanished. He was dressed in black with a black bow tie. He hardly raised his eyes from the floor. From all appearances he looked like a worried man — one who seemed as if he feared he might yet meet death from a gangster's gun.

"They got my pal," Perri said in a low voice. "I wish it had been me." Standing in groups in the rear living room, hallway and dining room were fellow countrymen of Perri. They spoke in low voices. The Toronto *Star* is welcome in my home," said Perri. "They didn't do me any good back in 1927 but I trust you — I know you are on the level."

"What do you think of the killing?" I asked Perri.

"It is beyond me now. I can't think," he said.

Perri told the police, according to the *Star,* that if he knew who had killed his wife, he would not tell. Gow's own "authoritative" sources close to Perri told him that "someday — somewhere" the killers of Bessie would be paid in full: "They will be 'put on the spot' ["rubbed out" in twenties' gang slang] and killed just like they wiped out Perri's woman — then the account will be square." As Gow put it: "Perri's keen knowledge of the underworld gangsters both here and across the line brings him in close contact with hundreds of people. Some of these will tell him. Perri works in his own way. The Italian way. No one will talk to the police... That is the way — and he is the boss. The police say the same thing. So it is predicted here today — 'sometime — somewhere' gangland will get their revenge for the death of Bessie Starkman-Perri. It may not be in Hamilton. It may be many hundreds of miles away from here, but there will be an echo." Later Perri was to contradict this story by stating that he felt that the motive behind the killing had been robbery. This was a theory that he stuck to publicly for a long time, even though the killers had made no attempt to steal even one stone of the thousands of dollars worth of jewellery clearly visible on Bessie's person that evening.

In another feature story on August 15th, headlined "ITALIANS FEAR VENDETTA FOLLLOWING PERRI SLAYING/SUSPECT BLACK HAND" the *Star* broke the story that Bessie Perri was probably handling dope bought from the late American gangster Arnold Rothstein: "The entrance of the dope factor complicates the whole problem of who killed her, in the opinion of some of the Italian leaders who were interviewed. The possibility was given credence that Mrs Perri had been linked up with a great spider's web of the dope ring allegedly organized by Arnold Rothstein just before his sensational murder almost two years ago." It was thought that Bessie went down to New York City in 1928 with a great deal of Rocco's money to buy a large amount of dope from Rothstein, the American gangster. After Rothstein himself was gunned down in November 1928, it is documented that American Mafia czar "Lucky" Luciano took over Rothstein's narcotics business along with Louis "Lepke" Buchalter. It is conceivable that the payment that the Rochester gang was demanding on the evening before Bessie's death had already been made to Rothstein earlier. This would explain her apparently arrogant stance that evening. "Lucky" Luciano, a close friend of Stefano Magaddino, the Buffalo Mafia boss, might then have ordered the hit through the Rochester mobsters, who would not have accepted that the drugs might already have been paid for. Of course, the Toronto *Star* reporters did not have the information about the Rochester mob meeting with the Perris on August 12th; that surfaced only in Sergeant Zaneth's March 1931 memo, which remained classified until recently.

All this, for the *Star,* pointed to the assumption that "the dead woman was actively engaged in trying to get rid of this big shipment of dope [the late Arnold Rothstein's], a great deal of which is still believed to be in Hamilton."

In the same investigative story, the *Star* reporter brought in other intriguing developments, one being that Bessie might have been behind a recent flood of Black Hand letters to prominent Italians. "It is in connection with this dope and the desire to distribute it as soon as possible that Mrs Perri is accused of being behind the threatening epidemic of Black Hand letters and outrages in Niagara Falls, Ont., Welland, Port Colborne, Merritton, and other places. On more than one instance, Italians were killed." Hitherto secret OPP reports from Inspector William Stringer now confirm that the Black Hand was very active in southern Ontario extending into the late twenties.

There may also have been a division in the Perri mob about the handling of dope; the *Star* theorized:

> While Rocco's devotion to his wife constantly deepened, that of the gang did not follow suit. They themselves were all for the policy of alcohol and isolation. They scorned dope....Rocco and Bessie had become rich. She had determined that he would not return to the general racket of the old days. It is on this basis that many Italians build up an explanation for her death by the hands of men who wanted Rocco back in the game, and the only way to accomplish that was obviously to put her out of the way, since she would never consent to it and Rocco would do nothing against her wishes. It is most likely that hard times had come to the old rum-running crowd. The export trade had been banished. That used to bring easy money. They wanted him back again to organize...Bessie wouldn't let him come back, and she was knocked off to get him in with the gang again."

It is true that a number of Perri gang members had become jealous of Bessie's control over Rocco, as Inspector John Miller discovered in his investigation. Frank Ross, a key Perri lieutenant, was reported to have been angry with the way Bessie handled Ned Italiano's family after he went to jail for drug trafficking. According to Miller's sources, "Bessie had hurt the feelings of friends of this gang [Ned Italiano, Tony Papalia, Tony Roma, Tony Brassi, Domenic D'Agostino, Ross himself and others] and it is said that even friendly Italians to another can be bought off and can become willing participants in the crime of murder."

Miller adds that Perri gang member Frank Longo of Welland is a suspect "over a mortgage deal," and that Perri allies Mike and Tony Trotta of Niagara Falls, Ontario had reason to dislike Bessie.

Miller also found out that Bessie had promised Sidney Gogo that she would pay him for his boat, which was seized by police after a gunfight during which Gogo's son was killed in 1922. According to Miller's sources, when Sidney Gogo came to collect the money, Bessie coldly told him to "Go to Hell." However, after interviewing Gogo, Miller (and Inspector Stringer who himself interrogated Gogo for Miller) concluded that "Sidney Gogo had nothing to do with the killing of Bessie Perri. While it may be said that he has good reason to feel hard against them, the fact that he is married legally …and is working in a steady job and has forgotten the past" points the other way.

Also on August 15th, the Toronto *Star* and its affiliated papers, presented one of the more dramatic and alarming editorial statements on the murder in the form of a political cartoon. Under the headline, "IS GANSTER TERRORISM CROSSING THE BORDER," the cartoon showed a map of Ontario with the shadow of a black hand reaching over the Niagara Peninsula from northern New York State. In editorials in the *Herald*, the *Spectator* and now the Toronto *Star*, the focus began to shift to concern over Chicago-style gangland activities gaining a foothold in Canada, a civilized country where that sort of thing was simply unthinkable.

On Saturday August 16th, Athol Gow paid another visit to Rocco for yet another "exclusve" interview. This time he was determined to get a bigger story. Under the headline, "$5,000 OF PERRI GOLD TO BE OFFERED AS AID IN SEARCH FOR SLAYERS," Gow described how he and

Is Gangster Terrorism Crossing the Border?

Bessie's daughter, Mrs Gertrude Maidenberg, persuaded Rocco to offer the huge reward. Gow created the story he was covering.

> "Did you see where the city of Hamilton is offering $1,000 reward for the killers?" Mrs Maidenberg asked Rocco in the presence of the reporter.
> "Is that true?" [Rocco asked Gow].
> "Yes," [replied Gow], "and why don't you offer a reward?" I suggested.
> "If I do that, who do I see?" [Perri asks Gow].

The reporter then recommended that Perri see Chief Coulter or Inspector Joe Crocker of the Hamilton Police Department. Rocco decided to offer $2,000, but Gow upped the ante by suggesting that

> This is a serious crime... Why don't you make it worthwhile. If money can help to bring a tip from the underworld make the reward a big one," I urged.
> "What would you make it?" asked Rocco.
> "Five thousand dollars; it is worth it to solve this murder."
> "Then it will be $5,000," announced Rocco.

Rocco then started to get up to call Inspector Crocker, but Bessie's daughter stopped him with the suggestion that it should wait till after the funeral. Rocco then told Gow he would notify the police of the $5,000 reward on Monday after the funeral.

Perri told Gow he was "determined to plumb to the depths" the cause of the killing of his "business partner." Rocco, posturing even more for the credulous reporter looking for a scoop, then told Gow that he will help the police: "I will help every foot of the road. If it takes all my money, I will do it. I will never be able to pay back what Bessie has done for me. No one knows."

Having got his exclusive, Gow then proceeded to hit the

competition by "spiking" a story the *Telegram* ran saying that Rocco and the police had been warned two days in advance of the murder.

"That's all rubbish," thundered Rocco, "do you think we would have driven in alone into the garage or even in the back laneway if our lives had been threatened? We would have come in the front way, prepared for trouble. ...I have never been held up. Sometimes Bess and I have come into this house at midnight, two or four o'clock in the morning carrying $5,000, $10,000, and even $25,000 in cash on us. Never have we been interfered with. We had no enemies that I know of. She had none. She was well liked. The answer to that is the beautiful flowers in the parlour and the thousands who have called to see her. Bess and I have travelled everywhere together and this is the first attempt on our lives. We have never received even a threatening letter.

Thus Rocco glibly lies to Gow, who does not challenge any of these absurd assertions in the story even though he must know the truth about the Larenchuck incident and other attempts on the Perris known on the street and even published in the *Star* itself.

The interview in the Perri kitchen continued for over an hour. Rocco tells Gow that he thinks the killers were out to kill both Bessie and himself ("Why did they have two shotguns if they were only after her or after me?" Perri rhetorically asks Gow.)

"What could be the motive, if you believe your friends were loyal?" asks Gow.

"I still claim as before, that the motive was robbery. They were after her diamonds...she was crazy about diamonds," answered Rocco.

"But Rocco," countered Gow, "if these men who killed Bessie were out for robbery, why did they come to your back door with shotguns, hide in you garage and then shoot her down in cold blood. They never made any effort to get her diamonds or search her clothing. They ran away...If it was robbery they would have held you up somewhere on the road."

"I still figure the motive was robbery," Rocco lamely replied to Gow's interrogation. Gow next raises the question of Bessie's will. Through police sources, he knows that Rocco is the major beneficiary. But when he asks Rocco about the will, Rocco doesn't want to talk about it. Gow painted a sympathetic portrait of Rocco:

> Brooding, his nerves frayed to an edge, Perri has not slept since the murder...he continually spoke of his devotion to his Bessie, and repeated how he loved the woman who lay in the $3,000 silver steel casket..."You don't know what she meant to me," he said in a broken voice. "No one will ever know. She loved me. I loved her. My money, if I spent it all, would never pay back what she did for me...I wish I was going with her. Wish I was in that casket instead of her. Why did it have to be her?" asked a sobbing Rocco.
>
> "Don't say that," commented Mrs Maidenberg.
>
> "What will I do now that she is gone? She has left me forever," was the hopeless answer [from Rocco].

In yet another *Star* story, Mike Perri, in tears, gives the *Star* reporter a guided tour of the scene of the crime. Mike also states that Rex, their big police dog, did bark when the assassins entered: "He always barks when anyone comes except Rocco or Bessie. I say that he barked that night but stopped as soon as he heard the doors close...he thought then that whoever it was was one of us and stopped making a noise. That is why there was no alarm from him." The *Star* photographer then finds out firsthand that "the splendid animal is not passive when strangers were near." Rocco's cousin and bodyguard, Pat Moranda, had to "seize it by the collar just as it was about to leap, and hold it struggling while its picture was taken." So much for the previous day's story headlined, "THE DOG THAT FAILED TO BARK!"

Bessie's funeral, as we have seen, on Sunday August 17th, remains unrivalled in Hamilton. Thousands of curious on-lookers crowded the lawns and verandahs of Rocco Perri's neighbours. Many more lined the route of the procession to the cemetery to catch a glimpse of the fifteen flower cars and the $3,000 silver casket. The blinds on the bereaved's car were drawn tight. The noticeable presence of Mike Serge with his police escort at the funeral raised more than a few eyebrows in the Hamilton establishment. In an editorial in the Hamilton *Herald* on Tuesday, August 19, its third on the murder, it was stated what "while Serge was permitted the freedom to attend his cousin's wife's funeral…a young Canadian [in jail] was positively refused some months ago to visit his father who was dying and had expressed the keenest desire to see his son before he died." The *Herald* concluded its commentary on "potent gangster influence," with every sarcasm intended, by saying that "there must be some reason the Italian is treated differently than the Canadian."

Fred Griffin's description of the funeral in the Toronto *Star* of August 18 was reprinted in the *Herald* with predictable sensational banner headlines on the front page, "DISGRACEFUL SCENES MARKED FUNERAL CERE-MONIES/Mauling Mob at Burial of Bessie Perri/15,000 View Funeral of Gunmen's Victim/ROCCO FAINTS/Escapes Being Hurled Into Grave/Spectators Destroy Cemetery Fence."*

Various theories have been advanced to explain how Rocco Perri escaped the gunfire the night of August 13th. Frank Zaneth and the RCMP were aware of Bessie's apparent welching on a major drug debt to the Rochester mob. They were certainly suspects number one. Then there was the story about the alleged problems Bessie was having with the Chicago mob. Thirdly, there was the evidence, developed by Inspector Miller, that certain members of Rocco's gang were unhappy with Bessie for one reason or another (Ned Italiano, Sidney Gogo, Frank Ross and others), and there was the

---

*The pallbearers at Bessie's funeral were all young men, members of families closely associated with Rocco Perri. Three were cousins, Tony Moranda, Joe Romeo and Tony Serge. The others were Jules Speranza, Mathew Restivo and Sam Calubro.

The chief mourners were, as well as Bessie's daughters and Rocco, Joe Serge, Joe Romeo, Mike Romeo and Frank Catanzrite and their wives. Frank Romeo drove Rocco's car in the procession.

incriminating evidence of Tony Papalia's having unique access to the licence plates on the getaway car.

There is another possible explanation for Rocco's survival that night. Since Rocco was the main beneficiary of Bessie's estate, it was naturally suspected at the time of Bessie's death that he might even have had his wife murdered, just to loosen her grip on the purse strings. Beyond the money, Rocco's pride and reputation were at stake. Many in the underworld of the time believed that Rocco had had his wife killed, even though he was in love with her. A letter to the RCMP from the widow of a Rocco Perri lieutenant, states flatly, "Rocco Perri murdered his wife for her money and did a good job." And after all, the sensational murder of a high-profile wife in a garage is a recurring theme in Canadian crime. The conviction of Peter Demeter and the recent trial and conviction of Colin Thatcher spring to mind.

In a memo written more than a decade after the event, on November 18, 1942, OPP Inspector Phil Walter developed new important information on the murder. The source was a Windsor Italian racketeer and bootlegger using the name Donald ("Tony) Stevans. He told police that he had "been hooked up with Rocco Perri" and was with Rocco the night of the murder of Bessie. He also maintained that the murder was prearranged by Perri, and that he (Stevans) did the shooting.*

If Bessie broke mob rules, it is almost certain that Rocco had to accept the killing passively. It is the mob's way of dealing with those who refuse to accept its etiquette. As a mob boss dependent on the respect of his colleagues and allies — the Buffalo and Rochester mobs being consolidated by Stefano Magaddino, and his allies in Chicago, Pittsburgh and New York City — Rocco would have been forced to acquiesce. The OPP investigation did not come up with a more persuasive theory — only blind alleys. Perhaps Rocco himself had a hand in it after all, but the weight of evidence

---

*Since by this time Rocco was already in internment, the OPP did not follow up on this intelligence.

does not support any theory that Rocco actually arranged the murder of his common-law wife.

The death of Bessie Perri marked the end of an era in Canadian mob history. Never again would it be possible for Canadians to ignore the realities of organized crime influence in the country. One editorial stated, "roadhouses and gambling places flourished like so many green bay trees... [and] bootlegging was as common as January snows in Manitoba." Like it or not, gangsterism was not just an American phenomenon, it was now a fact of life in "staid old Ontario." Canada would never be quite so innocent again.

CHAPTER 15

ROCCO'S DEPRESSION

The inquest into Bessie's death was held at a Hamilton court house on Friday, September 5, 1930. Even though hundreds of people lined up to watch, only twenty members of the general public were let in as well as reporters and witnesses. The chief coroner was Dr George S. Rennie, and the jury consisted of ten Hamilton men, five of whom were listed as "merchants." George W. Ballard, K.C., acted for the Crown, and John P. O'Reilly, the son of Rocco's long-time lawyer, the recently deceased Michael J. O'Reilly,* acted for the witnesses. There were eighteen of them in all, including Mary Serge, Rocco Perri, Mike Perri, Mary Latika, several police officers and some neighbours and passersby.

The first witness, aptly named Dr Deadman, was the pathologist at Hamilton General Hospital who performed the post mortem on Bessie's body. He described the wounds in great detail, concluding that she had been killed by two massive wounds as already described.

The key witness at the inquest Friday morning was a subdued Rocco Perri, and his testimony, in at least one significant detail, is contradictory. To the edification of all present, he also answered questions about his criminal

---

*Michael O'Reilly had dropped dead in a Hamilton magistrate's court earlier in the year on the eve of being nominated the Liberal candidate to oppose Rocco's other lawyer, Charles Bell, in the upcoming Federal election.

activities and lifestyle. Here is an excerpt of the most revealing part of the examination of Perri by Crown Attorney George Ballard:

Ballard. Had you ever received any threats before that?
Rocco Perri. No sir.
Ballard. Do you know whether she had or not?
Perri. No sir, if she had she would tell me.
Ballard. And you used to be extensively engaged in what is called bootlegging?
Perri. Yes, sir.
Ballard. As a matter of fact I think you were considered one of the leaders here?
Perri. Yes, I was.
Ballard. You made a good deal of money out of it?
Perri. Maybe I did, maybe I lost.
Ballard. The deceased woman was a partner in your business enterprises, more or less, was she not?
Perri. Yes, sir.
Ballard. Prior to moving up to Bay Street you didn't have much money, you were not a wealthy man?
Perri. Had a little.
Ballard. Not wealthy, though?
Perri. No.
Ballard. You and Mrs Rocco Perri were fairly well-to-do at the time of the tragedy, were you not?
Perri. Yes.
Ballard. And I suppose most of that money you made out of the line of work we have been speaking of?
Perri. Whisky, yes, sir.
Ballard. Do you happen to know whether or not she had any dealings in drugs?
Perri. No, sir.
Ballard. You say you don't know or do you say she didn't?
Perri. She never had any dealings.
Ballard. You remember recently she happened to be in a house in Toronto where a raid took place and drugs were found. Do you know how she happened to be there?
Perri. A fellow wanted $5,000 and came to me.
Ballard. Did you have any disagreements or any disputes with anybody that you know of?
Perri. No, sir.
Ballard. You don't know of anybody who might have occasion to harbor a grudge?
Perri. No, sir.

Ballard. You and the deceased woman were on very good terms, I believe?
Perri. Oh yes, the very best.
....
Ballard. I suppose you had to pay a good deal of money out for some of the boys working for you?
Perri. Certainly I did. I make it and I pay it out.

Clearly, the Crown had not been briefed too thoroughly by the RCMP or the OPP on the details of Perri's criminal career or on Bessie's drug trafficking career. Of course, they didn't know yet about the Rochester mob, but they certainly knew about about the Perris' involvement with American mobs in the dope game. The OPP didn't have much confidence in Ballard as an interrogator. In arguing for a special prosecutor, OPP Inspector John Miller had stated in an August 15, 1930, memo to Assistant OPP Commissioner Alfred Cuddy that "it is felt here that some stronger man than the present Crown attorney should examine the witnesses to draw out the facts from the witnesses at the inquest."

Rocco Perri ended his testimony by stating that he used a shotgun only for hunting with friends and that yes, he knew what creased bullets were. One of his most perplexing responses came in answer to a question asked of him by one of the jurors. He was asked whether he knew that Bessie had been shot when he left the garage. Perri replied, "I didn't know whether she was shot or not." A strange answer, given the fact that his neighbour, David Robbins, testified that Rocco had babbled, "someone's shot my girl." However, no one thought to follow up this contradiction.

The next major witness at the inquest was Rocco's brother Mike Perri who used an Italian interpreter during his cross-examination because he could not explain himself in English. He testified that he was living with a cousin, Rozara Le Zario at 72 Sheaffe Street* but that on the night of

---

*This is the same house occupied in 1938 by Luigi Gasbarinni and his seventeen-year-old son Dante "Danny" Gasbarinni, convicted drug traffickers, and the very building that housed a blind pig Zaneth visited in 1929 to set up "Arthur Anderson."

Bessie's murder he had come over to his brother's house to take a bath as he did three times a week. He was in the bath when he heard the shots, but jumped up and threw on some pants and went right down. By the time he got to the back stairs, Rocco had come in and told him that "there had been some shooting in the garage." He then substantiated Rocco's story of accompanying Rocco, Mary Latika and Robbins to the garage.

David Robbins was the next witness. Describing himself as a "newspaper reporter" (he was, according to an Inspector Miller memo, "trying hard to become a newspaper reporter"). Robbins testified that he was at the northeast corner of Bay and Bold walking his dog when he heard the three shots. He also testified that he had seen one car, a small roadster, pass about a minute before the shots. Robbins stated that Perri was hysterical when he met him on the street: "He was talking and he was excited, kept saying a lot of different things.... He said something about 'somebody had shot' his girl. Kept saying "Mina" or something like that." Perri and he entered the house where Perri took him to the garage: "Mr Perri was in front and when we got to the door he made a step back to turn the light on, like you would for any guest in a house, and I went ahead of him downstairs. [He discovered] Mrs Perri crumpled up at the foot of the stairs."

Mary Latika, the maid, was the next witness. She testified that she had been with the Perris for nine months. Latika explained that Mrs Perri had phoned about five to eleven to ask her to "fix her room for her to go to sleep." At the time of the shooting she stated she was giving Mike Perri a clean towel in the bathroom. She couldn't remember whether he carried his bathrobe or had it on; quite a difference one would think! She told Mike that there was shooting downstairs. She also testified that Rex, the dog, barked ten to fifteen minutes before the shooting. She called to the dog from the kitchen to tell it to keep quiet. Why didn't she go out to check on why the dog was barking? "Because he barks lots of times." After the shooting she heard someone running in the alley and heard Perri scream.

She verified the rest of Robbins' and Perri's story as to the discovery of the body. When she saw Mrs Perri's body, she "started to cry."

Another witness, neighbour Morris Levy, testified that he saw two men get into a car after the shooting and proceed down Bold Street. It was a small sedan — four-seater. Another neighbour, George Thompson of 202 Bay Street south testified that he heard seven or eight shots. He also thought the screaming "sounded like a woman." Thompson also saw the getaway car on the other side of the alleyway — but he said it was a seven-passenger car with a driver sitting in it racing the engine. It drove by slowly after the shooting and at least one other man jumped into it. Another neighbour, William McCollen also thought the screams were those of a woman. McCollen saw two men emerge from the alley.

Constable Kingerly of the Hamilton Police Department testified that when he arrived Perri and his brother were in the garage. When he asked them what had happened, Rocco Perri stated that his wife had been shot and that "they had got away in a car." According to the policeman, he asked Perri to give him a hand in unfastening a watch on the corpse. Perri then pocketed the jewellery.

The final witness was Inspector of Detectives Joe Crocker, who outlined the trajectory of the shotgun pellets and testified that he took a "very excited and broken down" Rocco to his downtown office for questioning.

After only ten minutes of deliberation, the jury returned the following, altogether predictable verdict: "We, the jury, find that Bessie Perri came to her death from gunshot wounds inflicted by person or persons unknown." Dr Rennie, the coroner, then added that the inquest was over, and that he hoped "the Crown will proceed with the investigation of the case further, and I hope will meet with success." They tried, but they were never close to successful.

On Monday September 8th, the *Herald* published its sixth and most stridently racist editorial on the murder. This time it put all the blame, collectively, on the Italian community of Hamilton. Conveniently, the *Herald* had forgotten that organized crime was not new to Hamilton. In the nineteenth century, English, Scottish and Irish mobs had held sway over the underworld. The British establishment in Hamilton obviously felt seriously threatened by its new citizens.

CRIMINAL BARBARISM

We have had two notable examples of gangster methods recently in Hamilton, and the citizens feel that if there is nothing done by the Government to put an end to this sort of thing measures must be taken by the citizens themselves. There is no doubt of the origin of these crimes. They arise out of the character of our foreign-born residents. They do not begin to understand what civilization is, and they think that it is all right to take the law into their own hands and adjust their grievances for themselves. They must learn it will not do in Canada.

If those who came from foreign climes wish to remain here and do business the first thing they must get into their heads is that the customs and methods of this country must be adopted and the principles of our laws observed. First of these is that private revenge is not tolerated. If no assistance is given to the officers of the law, then steps will have to be taken to let the foreign-born community feel that their non-compliance with our regulations and support of law and order makes them unwelcome citizens.

The great mass of the citizens have no wish to discriminate between one race and another, but if any race sets itself deliberately to overturn the peace and order of the community, then the fellow-countrymen of such culprits must be held responsible. The need is acute enough for the declaration of martial law, and some such steps must be taken to impress the foreign-born population that they are not still living in Europe but in Canada, not in Chicago or Detroit, but in Hamilton, a city where law and order must be insisted upon.

Murder and arson and terrorism are the weapons of savages and uncivilized people, and such barbarous practices in Hamilton only shame the races who countenance them by their refusal to give information as to the real criminals. The situation is one that affects the national community to which the criminals belong, and if the community has any self-respect it will hasten to purge itself of its present silent complicity with these crimes.

When Bessie's will was read on October 13, it was revealed

that she had drawn it up on the eve of her testimony before the royal commission on Customs and Excise, on March 28, 1927. She left $3,000 apiece to her two daughters, Mrs Gertrude Maidenberg and Mrs Lillie Shime. Rocco was left the bulk of the estate, which consisted of $45,000 in cash; jewellery valued at $8,000; three properties, including 166 Bay Street South valued at $8,000; as well as a house in Thorold valued at $3,000 and a house at 56 North Street in St Catharines valued at $6,000. Of course the two cars had also been left to Rocco: the Marmon sedan from which her assassins fired the fatal shots and the smaller Marmon coupe from which she and Rocco had emerged seconds before her death. Other "vast sums of money" held by Bessie in other bank accounts under a variety of aliases, of course, were not reflected in the will. The Toronto *Star* suggested that Rocco might have trouble establishing title to it, in which case the money would revert to the Crown. Rocco never contested this, and it is not known what happened to this money.

In the interim, Detective Constable Mathewson had been busy, still looking for new RCMP agents to penetrate the Perri drug empire. On October 24th he reported an important new development. He now felt that the RCMP might be able to get close to Mary Latika, still the Perri maid, and possibly recruit her as an informant. However, there is no follow-up memo in RCMP files regarding the recruitment attempt, which clearly went ahead, so it is impossible to determine whether Mary Latika became an RCMP agent. She continued to work for Perri well into the middle thirties.

Within days of Mathewson's Latika memo (and exactly seven weeks after the inquest), the Toronto gossip magazine *Hush*, the Toronto *Star* and the Sudbury *Star* carried a spate of stories about the possibility that Rocco Perri would "remarry" and about his long affair with a Sudbury woman named Mrs Jessie Leo. On November 1st Mrs Jessie Leo was approached by the Sudbury *Star* for a comment on the rumours. "How should I know whether I am going to marry him or not?" she curtly replied to the reporter on the phone. "He has never asked me yet."

Curiously enough, Mr Joe Leo alias "George Teme," Jessie's common-law husband who had worked for Perri's bootlegging empire, had disappeared in suspicious circumstances in May of 1930, shortly after Rocco had begun his affair with Jessie. He was on a visit to North Bay on mob business, and he never returned. Suspecting foul play he had left a handwritten note behind, which OPP Inspector Stringer later found. In it he stated that he had good reason to believe that Rocco Perri's ally, Domenic D'Agostino of Niagara Falls, New York, "will try to kill me to come into possession of my woman and the money." Sudbury police offered a $3,000 reward for information that would reveal the fate of Leo, and even sent circulars with his picture to every police department in Canada. But nothing ever turned up. It is entirely possible that Rocco, in order to pursue his relationship with Mrs Leo, arranged for that disappearance through D'Agostino, who had been staying with the Leos in Sudbury. This is certainly an angle that the Hamilton police and the OPP actively investigated — without success.

Another detail throws further suspicion on Rocco. On the night of the Bessie Perri inquest, Jessie Leo came down to Hamilton to console Rocco. Rocco also made frequent trips to Sudbury to visit with Jessie at her "palatial Sudbury home" after Bessie's murder. These sojourns "aroused a storm of comment" according to the Sudbury *Star*. Had Rocco disposed of Bessie to pursue his affair with the Sudbury "widow?" Asked about Rocco, Jessie replied, "sure, I know him...I've known him for ten years." She also admitted that Perri had been to see her in Sudbury during the previous few months. But after being asked many other personal questions by the Sudbury *Star* reporter, Jessie "appeared indignant" and said, "Why should I talk to reporters, I don't have to." Then she hung up, and the interview was over.

A few days later, on November 4th, Rocco Perri himself was interviewed by the Toronto *Star* and the Hamilton *Herald* about his relationship with Mrs Leo and about his plans for the future. "I suppose you have heard about my marriage?" Perri playfully asked the reporter. "We are friends," he said of Jessie Leo. "As for marriage, I shall always remain single. I decided many years ago never to marry, and there is no reason why I should now." Asked by another reporter about his rumoured forthcoming marriage to the Sudbury woman, Perri replied, "They know more about it than I do." Asked who killed his wife, Rocco maintained that "the mystery would never be solved."

Hush, which had been the first to publish the rumour of Rocco's impending marriage in October did a gossip exclusive on Rocco's affair with Jessie in its November 13th, 1930, issue. The article also featured a discussion about Bessie's relationship with the late Hamilton Police Chief William Whatley, and others. Headlined, "ROCCO PERRI HAS NOT PROPOSED MARRIAGE/More About Hamilton Police Chief's Tragic End," the *Hush* exclusive opened with Jessie Leo's denial of marriage in the Sudbury *Star*. In the best gossip magazine tradition, without any proof, *Hush* then "broke" one of many "stories" in the piece. Joe Leo wasn't dead; he was alive and well, according to a *Hush* source. Futhermore, the sleuths at *Hush* had ascertained that Jessie Leo had been selling her homes to move to Hamilton.

Interest in the possible matrimonial alliance between Rocco Perri and Jessie Leo, if the latter's husband is really dead, in spite of the fact that both have denied the hope of such an eventuality, is strengthened by the fact that Mrs Leo has just sold her palatial Sudbury home at the corner of College and Baker Sts for $20,000. It is said that she intends moving to Hamilton, where she has many friends. Her properties at Kirkland Lake and Cochrane have also been sold. Friends of Rocco in Hamilton say that marriage with the beautiful and wealthy woman, who has long admired the little Italian, would lead him out of his lonely misery and be the means and impetus for him to become a useful and respected citizen in the city of his adoption. Those qualities that enabled Rocco to rule their bootlegging world in the OTA days could be well employed in constructive political work in Hamilton, which might end in municipal honours. Contrary to *Hush's* belief, according to the Toronto *Star*, Rocco still believes that he too was marked out for assassination on

that fateful night last summer. This may account for the fact that
he is still closely guarded wherever he goes, by members of his
sect, who are ever faithful to their erstwhile king. Sometimes, it
is said, the little man's nervous system gives way temporarily and
he retires to bed for a week at a time to find consolation in his
bible and complete rest.

Hush always felt that Rocco was more sinned against than
sinner. For many years his life was saddened by his wife's sinister
association with the late Chief of Police Whatley and the late
License Inspector Sturdy of Hamilton. What a terrible story it
is. And now Sturdy is in his grave, without disclosing where his
ill-gotten gains are hidden. Whatley, it has been alleged, shot
himself...and his Bessie has been murdered. Truly, "the way of
the transgressor is hard."

And so the exclusive continued, with more lurid tales of how
Bessie (never Rocco) had corrupted Police Chief Whatley
and other more senior officials over the years. Rocco and
the officials were the victims of Bessie's greed, said *Hush*,
and Rocco's entire career to this point was summarized as a
series of criminal acts initiated by Bessie.

The *Hush* report was, of course, exaggerated. Though
Bessie was certainly an asset to him in his criminal career,
Rocco was able to function in crime quite well without her,
and eventually found a replacement for her, who was able to
run his mob and rackets with equal zeal and imagination.

Curiously, the Sudbury "widow" disappeared from
Rocco's life as quickly and mysteriously as she appeared.
Obviously Rocco's relationship with Jessie Leo was a matter
of convenience for them both. It died a natural death when
Rocco moved on to bigger and better things.

The sensational events surrounding the murder of Bessie
had a profound emotional and psychological effect on
Rocco, but he was also being affected materially — by
events in the larger world. When asked by the Toronto *Star*
about the state of bootlegging profits in an interview on
November 4, 1930, Rocco was adamant: "only the little
ones [operate now]....People who go to bootleggers have

little money." For bootleggers in Canada, as for the majority in North America, "times were bad," Rocco told the *Star*. Apart from the economic realities of the Depression, there were other factors that led to Rocco's bleak assessment of the situation.

The whole bootlegging situation had changed dramatically as a result of political action in the United States and Canada in 1929 and 1930. The United States had been pressuring Prime Minister Mackenzie King for years to impose restrictions on the export of liquor from Canada to the United States. King had not been eager to do anything, as his government was collecting $60 million a year on taxing the liquor exports, more than double the amount the government was collecting through income taxes. But finally, on March 4, 1930, after a U.S. threat to increase tariffs on imported Canadian goods, Mackenzie King introduced the Canada Export Act in the House of Commons. (Ironically, the U.S. government raised the tariff on Canadian goods anyway a few months later after the introduction of the Canada Export Act. So much for good faith.) The act banned the export of Canadian alcohol to countries under Prohibition as of June 1, 1930, thus giving rum runners until May 31, 1930, to make their last shipments. Of course, serious bootleggers like Rocco Perri quickly found ways around this legislation, such as routing the booze by way of the Caribbean, but it put a serious crimp in his operations. Perri had been hurt further by Gooderham & Worts' 1927 decision to stop supplying him with their product.

The New York *Times* of June 1, 1930, reported that on the night before the Export Act became law, 5,000 cases of booze went by boat from Canada into Michigan alone, and that from now on "small bootleggers who cannot finance the double bonds required" would be put out of business, allowing officials "to concentrate on the liquor which is coming over by carloads [and train] and by air." Essentially, small bootleggers could not afford to pay the taxes the law now required them to deposit to ensure that the liquor went to a legitimate customer.

Once the Export Act came into effect, distilleries and

breweries would no longer have dealings with bootleggers, and the underworld operators had to manufacture their own brew in illegal stills. Market demand for their product dropped drastically, since the homemade hooch did not measure up to the real Canadian whisky that Americans had come to value so highly. Moreover, the booze had to be manufactured and stored in large quantities if the operation was to be profitable, so the risk of detection was great. Small stills had existed throughout Prohibition, serving local neighbourhoods with the cheap rot gut, or "white mule," for which Rocco had shown such contempt. But business was business, and Rocco's people now had to operate stills themselves. They had to be closed down from time to time — whenever they were discovered by the authorities — but they were also replaced by new ones. Rocco's profits from bootleg booze were now less than 20 percent of what they had been in the roaring twenties.

By June 1930, Rocco had also become deeply involved in the narcotics trade. The Perris' move into drugs in the mid- to late-twenties was a diversification that had been in the works for some time. However, with the RCMP investigation into Perri's drug trade in 1929 and 1930 and with Bessie's death, Rocco was at his wit's end by November 1930. From the time of the murder in mid-August until October, he had remained in seclusion. When he did go out on October 15th, he was arrested for reckless driving. (He had packed four people into the front seat — no doubt bodyguards.) Perri was convicted and fined $10 and stood to lose his driving permit for ten days, but his long-time lieutenant, Frank DiPietro, took the rap by claiming that it was he, and not Rocco, who had been driving. Even on such a minor offence, Rocco was insulated, and as the *Herald* noted in the headlines of a front-page story of October 29, "ROCCO PERRI HAS ESCAPED $10 PENALTY/F. DiPietro Says He Was Driving Perri's Auto/HAS GREAT LUCK/Conviction Quashed; First Fine Imposed on Him Also Cut." The officer was unable to contradict DiPietro's testimony, as he had not actually seen Rocco driving.

Meanwhile, Rocco's business had begun to get seriously

out of hand, and it took him a few months to shake off his depression and put his affairs back in order.

The first public indication of Rocco's business troubles came in a series of lawsuits from people to whom he owed money. The plaintiffs ran the gamut from senior officials of the Hatch & McGuinness Company to Italian tradesmen and even fellow mafiosi in Hamilton. Everyone, it seemed, was after Rocco in the courts in the late fall of 1930. And Rocco was unable to fight back successfully.

On November 3, 1930, just two weeks after the reading of Bessie's will, Hatch & McGuinness filed a major claim against Rocco for debts incurred as far back as the mid-twenties. Their claim was for over $23,000, based on a promissory note undertaken late in 1926 and signed January 17, 1927. At this point, Rocco gave an interview with the Toronto *Star* in which he said he was giving up the liquor game. This aggravated Perri's own precarious situation, as creditors now feared he would not have the money later to pay them for past debts, especially after the Hatch & McGuinness suit. Also, without Bessie to manage the cash flow, former business associates were worried about how the Perri finances would be handled. Within a week of the Hatch & McGuinness filing and Rocco's *Star* interview, another writ was filed against Rocco by one Charles ("Tony") Calarco of Toronto for more than $14,000 (the reason for the claim was not revealed.) To make matters even worse, one of Rocco Perri's own drivers, Andrea Cantanzetta of Hamilton, issued a writ on November 18th claiming $5,636.84 due him on a promissory note signed by Perri on June 19, 1926. Cantanzetta had been jailed in September 1924 with Perri gang member John Russo (also known as John Ross or Rosse) for delivering a load of bootleg booze for Rocco, and the "promissory note" probably represented back pay for several bootlegging jobs. The claims against Rocco now totalled about $43,000, more than the value of Bessie's official estate.

In the meantime Rocco was confined to his bed

"suffering from a severe cold," according to the *Herald* of November 18, 1930.

The Hatch & McGuinness case was put off for a long time by Rocco's lawyer Charlie Bell. On November 2, 1930, Bell's office filed an affidavit with the court, outlining Rocco Perri's legal position on the $23,000 promissory note. In it Rocco's unique defence was that since he was involved in criminal activity on behalf of Hatch & McGuinness, namely selling their liquor for consumption in Ontario before the OTA was repealed, the promissory note was no longer valid: "I deny owing the plaintiffs anything. I say that if I did execute a note in favour of the plaintiffs [Hatch and McGuinness] in the sum mentioned I am not liable to plaintiffs, as the consideration for which the note was given was illegal by statute, and further, that it is illegal in that the note was given for whisky purchased in Ontario for sale and delivery in Ontario in contravention of the provisions of the Customs Act of Canada and also the Ontario Temperance Act and its amending statutes, and was further, in any event, void and unenforceable under common law." This gave the court something to think about, made it certain Rocco would have a trial and helped to delay the case so that he did not appear in court until January 1931. It was a full year later that the matter was finally resolved in a precedent-setting decision. The *Spectator* on November 18, 1930, covering this first phase of the case, ended its short story on Rocco's defence by stating that "the case will no doubt be watched with interest by bootleggers, brewers, distillers, and lawyers." Appropriately enough, on the same day, the *Spectator* carried a front page story entitled, "WAR DECLARED UPON GANGLAND IN THE STATES/ Menace Has Reached National Proportions/ Situation Most Acute in Chicago District/Hoover Moves to Wipe Out Racketeers."

The first judgments to come against Rocco were the Cantanzettta and Calarco claims. Cantanzetta was awarded $5,000 in early December when his lawyer, William Morrison, formerly Rocco's own counsel, successfully argued the claim in court. Calarco was awarded the $14,000 due. It was the ultimate humiliation for Rocco, to be ordered by a court to pay a "debt" to one of his former drivers, whose loyalty obviously did not extend beyond Bessie.

Since Rocco refused to pay the "debt," Morrison arranged for an issuance of an execution against his goods and chattels. The Sheriff of Wentworth County ordered the seizure of a number of Rocco's effects during the first week in December. John O'Reilly, Rocco's attorney for this matter, argued in court on December 17th that the sheriff "wrongfully seized" the Perri goods, as they were part of Bessie Perri's estate, which had yet to be legally passed to Rocco Perri under the terms of her will, for which he, O'Reilly, was the executor. Thus, argued O'Reilly, the seizure order should have been made on him, not Perri, since the executor had up to one year in which to distribute the assets of the estate, after first having advertised for creditors. The court ruled against O'Reilly and Perri, ordering a sheriff's sale of Rocco Perri's chattels on Christmas Eve. It was reported that William Schrieber, the Toronto lawyer for one of Bessie's daughters, had made inquiries at the sheriff's office about the legality of seizing some of the effects, which belonged to his client.

The items listed for the sheriff's sale were: a piano valued at $2,100; the Marmon coupe; two mahogany centre tables, five oriental rugs, four lamps, one fern stand, a chesterfield suite, a dining-room table, six chairs and a liquor wagon. According to the *Herald* of December 17th 1930, Perri's dog, "which failed to warn them in the house of the presence of intruders in the garage who murdered Mrs Perri," was included in the list of things for sale. Rex, of course, *had* barked but this didn't stop the sheriff from including him on the list.

Meanwhile, it was reported, Rocco had developed pneumonia and was confined to his bed. According to the *Spectator*, "a consultation of doctors was held on Saturday," as Perri's condition was considered "very serious." The next day, one of Perri's doctors, Dr Vincent Agro, denied this report, stating that Rocco was "resting...but that his condition was far from serious." As things stood in December 1930, they could not have been much worse for Rocco, especially with a former gang underling publicly humiliating him. Still he made a valiant attempt, in spite of his apparent weakness and deep depression, to turn things around. Somehow he managed to recover from his pneumonia and call off the sheriff's sale by raising the money to pay off his former driver, Andrea Cantanzetta, and by mid-January 1931 he was back in fighting form working on his defence on the suit brought by Hatch & McGuinness and back at the helm of his criminal empire full-time. In a court statement on January 13, 1931, Rocco declared that he would pay all his debts.

The Hatch & McGuinness case continued throughout 1931. On January 24th the venue was changed to Guelph and later, in March, it was moved to St Catharines. But Rocco kept busy in his criminal career, in spite of all the obstacles in his path, while the case continued.

From later court evidence, it appears that Rocco had set up several stills in 1931 to supply points in Ontario and the United States. One still was seized in 1932 in a house on Concession Street in Hamilton that had once belonged to a late local judge. It had the capacity to turn out 26,000 imperial gallons of "white mule" a month. This was more than many small legitimate distilleries, and the weekly profit from the operation was $5,000. Nevertheless, this was a far cry from the profits of the twenties when Rocco and Bessie were able to make more than a million dollars a year bootlegging quality liquor.

Whether Perri re-activated his narcotics trade to the levels of the late twenties is harder to determine, as he was never prosecuted for trafficking. He may have encountered more resistance than in the past, however, since in Hamilton itself a small-scale "war on drugs" was going on in 1931. Magistrate Burbidge was quoted in one news article as saying that "if those convicted [of trafficking] were flogged to death it would be no more than they deserved."

The Hamilton police were also staging a crackdown on all organized crime. There was a feeling in Hamilton, in early 1931, that things had gone out of control, and this kept the heat on Rocco and his gang. The *Herald* of October 28, 1930, carried a front page story about the need to "drive out gunmen and other criminals" from Canada. And in 1931 Toronto *Star* reporter C. Roy Greenaway, in a popular book entitled *Open House*, published in 1931, has an entire chapter on the Perri mob, "Big Shots" in which a profile of Al Capone appeared alongside a portrait of Rocco Perri. Here is a brief excerpt from Greenaway's essay, which helped entrench the legend of Rocco Perri as the Al Capone of Canada.

It is difficult to see much difference between our crime news and that of Chicago. Except for the quantity and spectacular magnitude, it is just as hard to find much intrinsic dissimilarity between its representative human products: Alphonse Capone and Rocco Perri.

The variation seems principally to be between the product of concentrations of 156,000 and 3,300,000 people. Both Capone and Perri are manifestations of the same microbe. But Capone is to Perri as Scarlet Fever is to Scarlatina. Not having had the disease as badly as Chicago, Hamilton recovered quicker, with a temporary immunity.

Both of these Big Shots I have seen lately, and have been struck by the remarkable resemblance between them. Both are far removed from the true moving picture gangster. Neither began life with a bullet-shaped head, nor acquired in later years a broken nose and a cauliflower ear. Neither resembles in the least the stage impersonation of a low-browed person with evilly glinting eye, a plaid cap drawn down over beetlin' brows, and a swagger in itself sufficient to warn the world of a man bent on devilment....

Aptly enough, the French Romantics divided mankind into two classes, the flamboyant and the drab. Among the flamboyants of crime today in these two countries undoubtedly rank Alphonse and Rocco. Flamboyant alone describes the flashiness of Al, with his vaselined handsomeness, Napoleonic exaggeration, infernal cunning, impish humor, rococo villa and diamonds, red leather slippers and silk dressing gowns; his dexterity with the pea-shooter and the grand manner, his theatrical and effective entrances and exits.

Rocco, philosophising, might have been preparing Al's breviary back in those palmy days of 1924 when there was pseudo-prohibition in Ontario and a temporary protective alliance between the King of the Bootleggers and the local police in Hamilton until the attorney-general ordered an investigation.

"I'm a bootlegger," openly boasted Rocco. "I'm not ashamed of it. And a bootlegger I shall remain.... On this text Al enlarges in an alarming manner; "All I ever did was to sell beer and whisky to our best people.... They call me a bootlegger, and some people call bootleggers criminals. I am simply supplying the demand of millions of law-abiding and law-making citizens. I sell liquor to judges, bankers, senators, governors, mayors; and I have preachers I sell wine to. It is no more criminal to supply this liquor than to barter for, possess and consume it. I am willing to be classed in the same category with judges, bankers, senators, governors, mayors and other well-known people, call them what you like."

In this matter of talking at least, so far as I can discover, Rocco even out-Caponed Al. In this land whose proud boast is that one law is supreme and organized crime cannot exist, Rocco outlined a higher law — the law of the Sicilian gunmen. "We do not go to the police to complain," said Rocco. "That is useless. We take the law into our own hands.... We believe that we have the right to inflict our own penalties."

Greenaway now moves to a revealing portrait of Al Capone, the quintessential mobster of the time:

...I talked to him in a Chicago court room for half an hour [on February 25, 1931] while he was waiting to answer a charge of contempt. Already Rocco the Little had suffered for his original ideas in Hamilton. Now even Al the Great, of Chicago, felt occasional qualms of doubt about the result. The problem of meeting him at last had resolved itself by chance into reaching the court-room at what proved to be the psychological moment, 35 minutes before the trial was to begin. As luck would have it, Chicago's "Public Enemy No. 1" was also early. His guards, tricking the crowds, slipping in with the Big Shot half an hour before the doors were open. It was as if Mussolini and his staff had arrived for a review. In fact, as one of Al's courtiers remarked: "If Mussolini came into Chicago on the same day as you, Al, you'd have the bigger crowd."

You fastened your glance at once on Capone because of the irrepressible exuberance of his personality and the sumptuousness of his dress. While he looked exactly like his later photographs, they never even suggest his size, his coloring, and his stylishness. For, above all, Capone is big: bigger than anything I had been led to expect from press clippings.... The Capone that I saw was over six feet tall, with shoulders wider than anybody else's in the court room. Out of a thousand people he would have attracted attention by his animation, his laugh, his raven-black brilliantined hair and eyebrows standing out against the ruddiness of his Miami-tanned face like the patent leather against red paper. His large lips registered in the memory, and the two scars on the left side of his face, one a pink welt a quarter of an inch wide extending from the sidebar almost to the corner of the lip, the other along the line of the jaw-bone.... Every time he smiled three sharp crows feet wrinkled up in the corners of his eyes. They are striking eyes; a bluish-grey, whose pupils dilate until they seem benevolent, then contract, under antagonistic emotion, until they point, motionless, adamant, menacing.

Greenaway asked Capone if he knew Perri:

Questions regarding a possible acquaintanceship between the Perris and Capone at first amused him, then offended his dignity. The final masterpiece of his replies was, "I don't even know what street Canada is on." He showed all the satisfaction of a wit who has spoken something memorable and was gloating over it. But one last question, asked as a joke, had the effect on Capone of a banderillo's dart. "What do you think of 'Bugs' Moran?" His back was turned, and he noticeably stiffened. When he turned around his face had literally darkened, his eyes contracted. Silently he walked away again, then, suddenly, jerked round the second time. "Ask him," he almost hissed back at me.

Greenaway concluded his double portrait of the gangsters with a challenge to the government: "The question must soon be settled — which is the Bigger Shot; the gangster or the state?" He added that the Chicago experience should be a real lesson for Canada in keeping people like Rocco Perri in check.

On August 13, 1931, a year after the murder, Rocco Perri installed a huge stone at the Ohev Zedek Cemetery on Caledonia Road. In an interview with the *Herald,* he said, "I will never forget that day." The magnificent tombstone he had erected, the largest in the Jewish cemetery even to this day, included a photograph of Bessie, a Hebrew inscription and the large engraved name, "BESSIE STARKMAN PERRI." (Recently, according to the caretaker, the name "PERRI" was removed from the stone by her family, but an impression of the original engraving is still clearly visible.) Rocco was also credited with improvements to the cemetery, including a new ornate metal fence and the inclusion of a large tract. He still wore bands of mourning in Bessie's memory, and he placed ornate wreaths upon the grave below the elaborate new tombstone.

There is little documentation of Rocco Perri's life from 1931 through 1934. He stayed in the background except when he gave the occasional newspaper interview and when he was making one of his numerous court appearances over debts. It was a low period for Rocco. His criminal businesses were slow and his prominence as a public and underworld figure was waning.

The police had not forgotten him, however. A memo dated February 24, 1932, written by Hugh Mathewson, now a corporal in the RCMP, detailed an interrogation with a drug dealer named Mickeniewich, who was doing time in Kingston Penitentiary. Mickeniewich maintained that a fellow prisoner in Kingston told him that "Rocco Perri obtained his narcotics from the United States by means of a cable that went under water from a farm house on the Canadian side to another farm house on the American side." Mathewson stated that "the story being that the drugs were placed in a waterproof metal container and when the money had been paid over and the necessary signal given, the container would be hauled across by means of a cable to this side of the river." Mickeniewich also claimed that he personally had delivered "thousands of dollars worth of narcotics for Perri." Mickeniewich later admitted under interrogation by Mathewson that his source was a Perri drug distributor named "Baldy" Nicholson. Mathewson dismissed Mickeniewich's story as just "another yarn," since there was no hard evidence to go on. "Baldy" would undoubtedly deny the confession and, at any rate, Mickeniewich's informer status would be completely compromised if they used his account of Nicholson's confession.

Another opportunity for the RCMP to get Rocco Perri for drugs had been lost, and like the entire RCMP drug investigation itself, the memo is tantalizingly inconclusive, though it does point to Rocco's methodology. The use of underwater cable systems was technically possible and had been used in Windsor for transporting booze. Perhaps Rocco actually did adapt the technology to drug smuggling.

The Hatch & McGuinness case, in which the well-known liquor company was suing Rocco for payment of a promissory note worth more than $23,000 was so sensational that it took over a year for all the arguments to be heard. Charles Bell, Rocco's long-time senior lawyer, along with his law partner, R. Howard Yeates, conceived an ingenious defence, based first on the illegality of the transactions in Ontario under the Ontario Temperance Act. In a later amendment of the defence, he claimed that the transactions amounted to a conspiracy to violate the laws of the United States, namely, the Eighteenth Amendment and the Volstead Act.

H. A. F. Boyde, the lawyer for Hatch & McGuinness, argued that if there had been a conspiracy, Rocco Perri "would be a man of turpitude in the conspiracy." But Bell was able to shoot back, "No more turpitude than the plaintiffs." Boyde had to concede the point, stating, "Perhaps not; they delivered the goods." Boyde's real point was to question the setting up of the "conspiracy" as defined by Bell, who had filed the amended defence including the conspiracy to violate the U.S. laws only a week earlier, nearly a year into the case. Boyde had been caught off guard. Mr. Justice McEvoy allowed the amended defence and Boyde rested his case on Rocco's own admission that he had signed the promissory note.

Bell relied heavily on the information he had received about Herbert E. Hatch. Hatch had no office, but did business wherever he met anyone, keeping no documents apart from promissory notes. Hatch had taken orders for liquor which Perri telegraphed to him from Hamilton and usually paid for in cash. Payment had always been made to him by Mrs Bessie Perri. "She was the financial agent?" asked Bell. "Yes, that's why I wanted her to sign the note," replied Hatch. But things went awry. Hatch testified that Bessie Perri had once given him a cheque for $7,000 which later proved worthless and was uncollectible. After this he asked for everything in writing. The promissory note in this case had been signed by Rocco on January 17, 1927, at his home in the presence of Hatch, Bessie and Larry McGuinness. According to Hatch, Bessie had refused to sign the note, which was why Rocco Perri signed it.

In his decision read on January 7, 1932, Mr. Justice McEvoy dismissed the action. He agreed with Bell's arguments that the transactions were indeed illegal, "being for liquor delivered to Perri for sale in Ontario and the United States contrary to the laws of both countries." He further found that Herbert Hatch and Larry McGuinness had "full knowledge of the whole plan." Rocco's victory was complete.

CHAPTER 16

ANNIE GET YOUR GUN

By fall 1933, Rocco was once again in bad shape. On October 18th he was sentenced to ten days in jail for failing to pay a $20 debt to Arthur F. Dell, a well-known Hamilton tire dealer. Rocco didn't even bother to appear at the hearing, and Judge Henry Carpenter ordered his immediate committal. Clearly, Perri was having trouble handling his own finances. In fact, Toronto's gossip magazine *Hush* said he was finished. In its issue of October 28, 1933, headlined "ROCCO PERRI'S DOWNFALL/Former Underworld Plutocrat in Hamilton Finally Landed in Legal Net," *Hush* said, "Bessie Perri was really the brains and directing force of the whole Perri organization," and without her, Rocco was facing an "ignoble end." As for Perri himself, *Hush* was very sympathetic: "(Rocco Perri) has many good qualities.... When he had money, he was ever ready to help a friend in distress. [This is confirmed by many sources: Rocco, in the true "Godfather" tradition, was always helping people out of difficulties.] Where are those friends today?"

It was a bit premature to be writing off Rocco, for he was far from finished in the winter of 1933. Fortuitously, Prohibition in the United States was ending. On December 5th, the Twenty-first Amendment was ratified and Prohibition ended in the United States. This was to open up a whole new avenue of opportunity for Rocco.

And Rocco was not as lacking in friends as *Hush* suggested. One new friend in particular made all the difference. It was Rocco's new common-law partner in crime, Annie Newman, forty-four. She was his new Bessie, who helped change the gangster's fortunes. While it remains a mystery how the two met (though it seems likely that it was through Bessie), it is clear that Annie Newman was firmly in place in Rocco's life and his mob by the end of 1933. Annie, who became Rocco's second common-law wife and, more importantly, his second-in-command in the rackets, was, like Bessie, a Jewish immigrant from Poland who had settled in the Toronto area in about 1907. She had arrived in Canada at the age of eighteen with her three sisters, Leah, Bina and Rose. Their father had died when they were very young and they had been brought up by their impoverished mother in Poland. All the girls, including Annie, had gone out to work at a very early age. Like Bessie, Annie had worked in the sweatshops in Toronto's Spadina garment district during her first years in Canada.

Annie was certainly a looker. One of her nephews, Harry ("Hushy") Gold, describes her even at sixty as having "the body of a sixteen-year-old, the white hair of a woman of sixty, and the cold, blue eyes of a killer." She was petite, no more than five-foot-three, but very attractive, with a great figure and a perennial tan. She had beautiful grey-blue eyes and a soft, slightly accented voice. Her silver hair was sleek and polished, usually drawn into a bun at the back of her head in what she called a "rat" — not one hair was ever out of place. On special occasions she would wear a full white wig à la Cleopatra. Socially, she was always an elegant dresser — she bought and wore the finest-quality clothes; privately, she loved to sunbathe in the nude. While she rarely drank alcohol and didn't smoke, she loved to dance and play poker. "She became real animated when gambling, and she always liked a good time.... She was a party girl with a great sense of humour," according to "Hushy" Gold. But she had another side.

She was tough, wily and sharp. She knew how to handle

people and was an extrovert who naturally got along with many different types of people, from mobsters and molls to little old ladies. But, according to those who knew her well, "you couldn't put anything past her." One gang member who worked under Annie in the late thirties didn't mince words about how he felt about his boss: "She was a hunk of garbage…a rotten bitch, but I wouldn't mind crawling into her pants.… She was very good-looking but greedy." She had "a shrewdness born out of necessity to accomplish what she had to," according to "Hushy," who adds that "she had an excellent survival instinct, and after survival, came luxury." And while she could neither read nor write in English, she was learned enough to keep Rocco's books and help him run his various illegal enterprises. And, most importantly, she knew how to handle Rocco so that he ran his criminal empire with the maximum efficiency.

But what *was* Perri's new racket, now that Prohibition in the United States was over? Overnight the flow of illicit whisky resumed, but this time in reverse. Moving from one extreme to the other, the United States went from total Prohibition to total access. Suddenly it became a source of inexpensive, quality liquor. The restricted nature of alcohol sales in Ontario created a thirsty market and a source of bountiful profit that Rocco was once again well placed to serve.

The dash and *élan* of the heyday of Prohibition boot-legging had no place in the new arrangements of the 1930s. Smuggling a load across the Niagara River under cover of night had a certain romance, but now it presented too many risks to sustain a business. In this new racket, the modern Canadian highway system became Rocco's ticket to success. Through his mob connections, Rocco Perri got his liquor from underworld sources in Chicago. Specially modified Dodge and Ford coupes, which could carry up to 300 gallons of liquor at a time without showing the load — even upon careful scrutiny — travelled the distance to Detroit. There they confronted the only possible obstacle to a dry market as far east as Montreal: Canadian Customs, but sometimes those paid to notice conveniently looked the other way.

RCMP documents obtained under the Access to Information Act reveal that Rocco Perri controlled not only the Ambassador Bridge that connected Detroit to Windsor but the tunnel nearby as well. Between 1934 and 1940, when the RCMP finally broke up the ring, Perri also ran illegal distilling equipment and gaming tables, across the river.

By early 1934, Annie was acting as liaison for Rocco with elements of the Chicago and Detroit mobs and, more important, she was helping to run the new organization which included many new drivers, as well as some current and former Customs' officials. Later statements of one Perri driver, Milton Goldhart, indicate that he went to Annie Newman for his job, since he knew Annie and Rocco were in the bootlegging business. Annie also paid for Goldhart's fines whenever he was caught. And, representing Rocco Perri, she accompanied the Perri drivers to Chicago, making arrangements with and paying Joe Tarallo and Vincent and Mary Sola, the Chicago bootleggers supplying the alcohol.

Rocco was still encountering some problems with the law. On November 28, 1934, the RCMP raided 166 Bay Street South and charged him with illegal possession of 234 gallons of alcohol. Rocco was slipping. In the twenties, police had been unable to find illegal booze at Rocco's home. In court on January 22, 1935, Rocco's new lawyer, Harry F. Hazell, maintained that while Perri had had a "colourful career," this was "a first offence" under the new Excise Act and that in these "hard times a jail term was not merited." Of course, it was maintained, the alcohol did not belong to Perri. Magistrate Burbidge found that since Perri was vulnerable to "the possibility of another charge being laid," he agreed with Hazell and fined Perri only $500, or three months in jail. Rocco was then taken for fingerprinting and a mug shot over the stringent protests of his lawyer, who claimed that Perri "was a free man" after he paid his fine. Later, on March 13, 1935, Perri was fined again for avoiding the excise tax on booze.

In fall 1936, newspaper readers in Hamilton read that Perri, in one of his rare perfectly legal enterprises, was persuaded to buy a lake freighter for salvage. Rocco was assured that the value of the lead in the bottom of the boat made it an excellent buy at $1,500. However, after the purchase went through and Rocco dismantled the vessel, he found that the weight of the lead had been grossly overestimated and that it had very little value. He had been the victim of a scam. It had cost Rocco over a thousand dollars, but he had learned his lesson and kept away from legitimate enterprises after that.

Apart from the pressures of business and underworld rivalries, the thirties were a happy time for Rocco and Annie. They lived for the most part at 166 Bay Street South, where Annie was clearly mistress of the house. Rocco "liked women who took control," states her nephew "Hushy" Gold, "and she was a very strong personality — but she certainly didn't downgrade him or belittle him in any way." Annie also had a kindly side which her nephews frequently saw. According to "Hushy," "she was always good to the kids — she always gave us little gifts, nothing extravagant."

Rocco, according to "Hushy," was even more generous and kind-hearted around the children: "He was always jovial, always kind — he treated us kids great. He needed power (in the mob) to be able to have things to give. He got great satisfaction out of it.... He used to bring silk stockings to my mother if she was in need.... If you wanted anything, you got it just like that.... Rocco was a giver.... He was good to all children that were around him.... I can't say anything bad about Rocco...." Rocco was also a great cook ("he made the most fantastic spaghetti sauce" according to "Hushy"), and he loved to cook for the children. But for the children, he also had an air of glamour and mystery about him. "We knew he was no angel," states "Hushy." Even when he came to the cottage, it seemed to "Hushy" like "an Italian funeral" when Rocco and his friends arrived in their "big black cars."

During the summers in the late thirties "Hushy" and the family spent a lot of time at the family cottage on Lake Simcoe. "Hushy" developed a leg problem that required weekly medical attention, but his parents did not have a car. So, out of the goodness of his heart, Rocco "used to come all the way from Hamilton to Lake Simcoe every Monday just to drive me to the clinic at the Hospital for Sick Children," reports "Hushy." Rocco was the perfect uncle. Another of Annie's nephews, Harry Romberg, confirms "Hushy's" opinion: "There was a goodness about him — something about him attracted people."

But by the late thirties, all was not domestic bliss. From early 1938 on, Rocco and Annie were besieged by a series of legal and underworld problems that nearly did them in.

On January 14, 1937, the morality squad of the Hamilton police under Inspector Alex Roughhead raided 166 Bay Street South. Two men were arrested and charged with keeping a common betting house. Once again, it wasn't Rocco who was keeping the gambling house, but a Perri underling, John Mostacci of Clinton Street and his associate, John Honigman of Main Street. They were found in a room in the attic with two telephones and racing sheets and a few slips of papers recording bets. Their lawyer was Harry F. Hazell, a lawyer Rocco used from time to time. On February 5, 1938, Magistrate Burbidge found Mostacci and Honigman guilty, sentencing the former to four months in jail and the latter, after pleading guilty to a reduced charge of being a found-in, was fined $20 or 21 days. Once again Rocco was totally insulated.

The first bombing attempt on his life occurred on the evening of Sunday, March 20, 1938, just four days after the Simcoe Street home of Black Hand boss and rival bootlegger John Taglerino had been bombed. (Earlier, in the middle of the twenties, Simcoe Street had been the scene of many Black Hand and gang bombings.) John Taglerino's little baby narrowly escaped death as debris from the blast shot across the baby's bedroom. At the Perri's, a bomb ripped apart the porch of 166 Bay Street South. "BOMB SHAKES CENTRE OF CITY, WRECKS ROCCO PERRI HOME," screamed the headlines of the *Spectator* above a half-page picture of the bombed-out remains of the front of Perri's home and a picture of Perri and his dog.

Rocco and Annie were out when the bomb exploded at

8:00 P.M. In fact, the only occupants of the house at the time were Fifi (the Perris' French poodle) and a litter of kittens. The force of the blast was enough to damage many houses in the area, and the *Spectator* reports that "the dynamite struck terror into the hearts of thousands of citizens whose quiet Sunday evening at home was ruined." Fire trucks and pedestrians filled Bay Street after the blast. The entire front porch of the house had been blown away, the cellar door ripped to tinder and the steps to the house torn to shreds. Ironically, Hamilton RCMP officer Eugene Touchie was out walking with his lady friend near Rocco's house on Bay Street at the time of the blast.

Perri himself, said to have been at the drugstore "sipping an effervescent bromide" for a splitting headache, didn't arrive back at the scene until 10 P.M. as police and spectators waited. This was how the *Spectator* reported his arrival at the bombing scene: "Still the debonair figure whose affairs frequently made him a front-page figure, Rocco Perri appeared suddenly aged when he viewed the evidence of what might have been an attempt on his life. 'The front door is wide open for you,' someone facetiously remarked. He made no reply but walked quickly to the kitchen and put in a telephone call advising other members of the household to return home. He didn't mention the bombing on the telephone, but said some visitors had come in. None of the emotion that characterized events in the same room eight years ago [after the murder of Bessie] was evident in his demeanour. He was utterly stunned but succeeded in keeping cool. 'No, I haven't received any threats,' he told a newspaperman.... We were out of the house all day, came home for supper and then went out again about 8 o'clock, Fifi and the kittens were alone in the house.... A boy ran in [to the drugstore] shouting that my home had been bombed."

At first, the bombing appeared to be part of a feud between Perri's organization and that of John Taglerino and his brother Sam. Police tried to resolve the dispute by bringing Taglerino and Perri down to police headquarters for a peace conference. They talked with Police Chief Ernest

Goodman and Chief of Detectives Joe Crocker, both veteran Perri investigators, for over two hours.

If the bombings were not caused by rivalry between Taglerino and Perri, they were likely attempts against the lives of both Taglerino and Perri, made by a gang with connections to Buffalo's Don Stefano Magaddino. Police Chief Ernest Goodman, in an interview with the *Spectator*, stated that Taglerino and Perri were "friends" who had "jointly offered to co-operate in every way with us in our investigation." Goodman added: "Both men are deeply concerned by the bombings and the fact that other citizens should have been inconvenienced and upset by the attacks directed at them." But no solution came out of the conference between the two gang leaders and the two police officers.

One other explanation for the bombings is possible. By 1938, events in Europe, including Mussolini's aggressive stance towards Great Britain, had created a grass-roots, anti-Italian crusade in Canada. Police did not discount the outside possibility that "an anti-fascist may have made a fanatical attack to relieve pent-up feelings over Italy's position."

It is also possible that the Taglerino bombing was only a smokescreen, an attempt to divert attention away from Taglerino's and/or the Buffalo mob's attempts to get rid of Rocco Perri. Later events seem to support this theory.

After the March bombings, Rocco and Annie moved temporarily, for security reasons, to a new house — the home of gang member Joe Romeo at 498 Hughson Street North in Hamilton. Rocco's insurance covered the costs. However, within months, on the evening of November 29, 1938, a second bombing attempt occurred. This time the bomb was in Rocco's car, a 1938 De Soto Sedan (registered in Annie's name), which was parked in front of his home. Rocco had been attending a card game across the street at the home of one of his drivers, John Russo (also known as John Ross or Rosse), at 499 Hughson Street North. The dynamite exploded as soon as Rocco started the car. Two colleagues, including longtime lieutenant Frank DiPietro as well as Fred Cordello (a.k.a. Ferdinand Condillo) were severely injured, but Rocco, still leading a charmed life, was miraculously thrown clear with only minor scrapes. The car was a total wreck, blown to a thousand pieces, which littered the street for over a block. Frank DiPietro lost three toes. The force of the explosion sent the front wheel of the car through the front door of a neighbouring house. A hole several inches deep was blown into the pavement beneath the car. Fortunately, Rocco had purchased explosion insurance for the newly purchased sedan shortly before the bombing, which, according to the insurance adjustor, was "just a coincidence."

In an interview with police, Rocco described his good fortune: "I was lucky, I guess. I touched the starter. Bang! Then I was under the car and the fire started. I don't know who could have done it." A solemn Rocco Perri, with a bandage on his face, was then whisked from the scene in a police cruiser in the company of Inspector of Detectives (and Acting Chief) Joe Crocker. Perri was offered police protection but he refused, saying, "I don't need it. When you are under fire all the time, you get used to it."

Hamilton Mayor William Morrison, who, ironically, as a lawyer, had represented Rocco Perri and his cousin Mike Serge in a bootlegging case shortly before Bessie's murder, announced that lawlessness "will be curbed in this city." This didn't reassure those in the Italian section, as according to the *Spectator* of December 1st, "fear pervaded the foreign colony last night as conjecture was rife about the reasons for the attacks upon Perri and the likelihood of further violence being attempted. Habitués of the places where night life is enjoyed said to-day they were typical of a deserted village." Hamilton police were reeling, especially since Police Chief Ernest Goodman had died earlier in the week. The RCMP joined Acting Chief Crocker in investigating the incident as rumours of matters over which they had jurisdiction abounded. In one story, carried in the *Spectator*, it was stated that several days before the bombing, threats had come to Perri from gangsters in northern Ontario. But before the RCMP were able to examine the matter closely, events overtook them.

On December 1st, widespread rumours that Rocco Perri had been killed in a traffic accident swept Canadian and American newspaper and police circles. But he was safe. In fact, he had been conferring with Acting Chief Crocker by telephone all that morning. A fiery collison near Ann Arbor, Michigan, took place on Monday, November 30, 1938, the day after the bombing of Rocco's car. Two men in the car were burned beyond recognition, and the car, which proved to be alcohol-laden, was traced to Hamilton, where it was assumed that Rocco was one of the victims. Investigation of the crash in Ann Arbor, however, revealed that the car had been driven by Bill ("The Butcher") Leuchter, a twenty-six-year-old Perri associate and employee (who also owned a butcher shop in Hamilton, hence the sobriquet). The passenger was one of Annie Newman's young recent recruits named Mike Mikoda. The car had smashed into a tractorized, four wheeler truck causing several explosions during which flaming gasoline shot into the air and menaced spectators. One passerby had his hair singed, and a female spectator had her fur coat burned by the fiery spray. "The Butcher" and Mikoda had been literally cremated alive. The inquest determined that their deaths had been accidental, and that the car had contained 250 gallons of alcohol weighing approximately 1,500 pounds.

In 1939 Rocco and Annie had continued legal problems which kept them in court and in the public eye. Hamilton police, under Sergeant Arthur Chamberlain this time, struck again. Another raid on Rocco's house, on January 9, 1939, resulted in police charging Annie Newman with illegal possession of a fully loaded .25 calibre automatic revolver which was found on a table by Detectives Howard Moreau and Herbert Witthun. Annie claimed it was hers, taking the rap for Rocco, since she as yet had no criminal record. Annie was tried and convicted a week later, after an RCMP check by Chamberlain determined that the gun "had not been registered in accordance with the requirements of the law." She was given a suspended sentence and a small fine.

A few weeks later, in February 1939, the RCMP discovered a still worth $10,000 run for Rocco by his old lieutenant Frank Ross (alias Sylvestro). Since police didn't have enough evidence to charge Perri, they tried to charge Ross with conspiracy to evade the excise tax. Ross went underground, and the RCMP offered a $500 reward for information leading to his arrest. But more pressing matters were at hand for the RCMP.

Everyone knew that Perri was in the bootlegging business, and RCMP documents make clear that they suspected Perri's organization was the source of a large part of the illicit alcohol and other contraband in western Ontario. But how was he doing it? A major RCMP investigation of the Perri rackets ensued, both as a result of the car bombing and of the Ann Arbor collision. Six months later, after developing sources inside Perri's organization, including Customs officers, the RCMP struck out against Rocco and Annie.

On August 26, 1939, a memo to the Commissioner of the RCMP entitled "Irregularities of Customs Officials" recommended the immediate arrest of the "principal co-conspirators Rocco Perri and Anne Newman before they go into hiding." The arrests climaxed a six-month investigation by the RCMP.

The Toronto *Telegram*, in an exclusive story on September 1, 1939, published a front page exposé, headlined, "MOUNTIES LAUNCH DRIVE TO CRUSH GANGLAND IN ONTARIO" on the coming RCMP sweep against organized crime in the province. It began, "After years of intensive investigations, methodical planning, and a quiet tying up of pertinent evidence, the Royal Canadian Mounted Police are ready to rip the cover from Ontario's underworld." After covering the arrests of Rocco and his co-conspirators, the *Telegram* exclusive narrated the story behind the arrests:

The *Telegram* has learned that this is but the first step in a concerted drive by the RCMP to bring gangland leaders to justice and strike a crushing blow to the forces of lawlessness.

Startling revelations of the extent of smuggling, bribery, bombings, mysterious disappearances, the drug, white slave, and alcohol traffic in this province, are imminent. And the tentacles of the underworld here reach into the United States....

On the same day as the *Telegram* exposé, the Germans invaded Poland. The RCMP planned attack on the underworld was to be limited, for the time being, to the arrests made in the Perri case. But the information gathered for the planned war on the mob was to prove most useful in the future.

The arrests occurred at 5:15 in the afternoon of August 31, 1939. Rocco Perri and Annie Newman, driving in Annie's car, were stopped and arrested at the corner of St Clair and Bathurst streets in Toronto. They were charged with bribing customs officers and with conspiracy to breach the Customs Act. In Windsor on the following two days, six customs officials, Carl Gough, thirty-six, Norman Lepainc, thirty-eight, Edward Mansell, thirty-six, Wilfred Fletcher, forty-one, Thomas Arthur Smyth, thirty-one and Harry Jarvis Smith, forty-five, were arrested and charged with bribery and corruption in the performance of their duties, along with two of Perri's bootlegging and gambling associates, Sam Motruk and Sam ("Fan") Miller. In addition, an RCMP search warrant was out for René Charron, one of Annie's Montreal partners, whom Annie had introduced to a customs officer on her payroll to get several loads of liquor over the border and who was believed to be hiding out in Montreal. The story of the arrests was carried prominently in all the major newspapers in the country.

Rocco and Annie were taken by train to Windsor under heavy RCMP escort. Rocco was in an unusually jovial mood as he faced reporters at Toronto's Union Station and later on the train. Accompanied by three RCMP officers, Rocco held a mobile press conference during the train trip. According to reporter Douglas Macfarlane, Rocco, while "careful enough to evade touchy subjects," chatted "freely about anything else but the customs case in question." He "seemed far from perturbed at his police escort and the prospect of facing a Customs Act conspiracy charge in Windsor. As a matter of fact, the fifty-year-old swarthy Hamilton bootleg King showed every sign of enjoying the enforced trip from Toronto."

"Let's talk about the war," Perri suggested with a smile.
"The Hamilton war?" countered a reporter.

Avoiding the question, Rocco said he would do the patriotic thing and fight for Britain if war broke out: "Canada is my country. Canada is part of the British Empire. I would fight for it. I left Italy more than twenty-five years ago. I don't remember much about it." According to Macfarlane, Perri's accent "was a dead give-away to the place of his birth as he whipped in the odd 'a' where English folk would say it was unnecessary." The interview continued with Rocco "grinning his Italian grin" throughout the interview:

"What about those bombs, Rocco?" asked one reporter, referring to the many bomb attempts on Perri's life.
"Hell, there aren't any left in Canada. They've taken them all across to Europe. They need them over there."
"How long is it since you've been in Windsor?" asked another reporter.
"Yes, Windsor is a nice place. It's great getting a free ride there."
"What about your arrest, Rocco?"
"The only thing that I am sorry about is that I had a date. A lotta fun, this life."

While Rocco was irrepressibly friendly and ingratiating with the press, "a Canadian 'Little Caesar' if ever there was one," according to Macfarlane, Annie was another story. Unused to publicity, she was not happy with the reporters buzzing around her at the other end of the train. She was extremely embarrassed about being under arrest, and hid her face every time a photographer approached. And, unlike

Rocco, she refused all interviews with reporters. Rocco tried to protect her by promising certain reporters and photographers that he would co-operate fully if they just let Annie alone and out of the picture. This worked up to a point, but as Doug Macfarlane said in his article, Annie Newman was just too alluring a target to let go.

> Her striking features, crowned with snow-white hair, made any display at grab pictures on the train seem definitely out of place. In any case, the forty-seven-year-old Polish Jewess used a newspaper and her handbag to effect in covering her beautiful face when photographers approached. She talked only briefly but sufficiently to express her dislike of anything that had to do with publicity.

Two pictures of Annie, described in the caption as Rocco's "beautiful white-haired companion," appear with the story: one of her, accompanied by a stern-looking RCMP matron, holding a newspaper and purse over her face, and one full-face mug shot of a clearly unamused Annie Newman — if looks could kill, this would have done the job. (In contrast, a picture of a smiling Rocco, joking with one of his captors, a tall handsome young RCMP officer named George Ashley, appeared right next to the grim Annie photo.) The Windsor *Star* headline is "Lady Friend Dodges Camera." Annie is called, variously, Rocco Perri's "housekeeper," "companion," "friend," and, occasionally, even Rocco's, "alleged wife" by the various papers. She does not appear though, as "Mrs Perri."

After spending a day in a Windsor jail, Rocco and Annie were released on $10,000 bail put up by Leah Newman Romberg, Annie's sister, and two of Rocco's Toronto associates. According to the Windsor *Star*, Rocco "appeared none the worse for his night in a police cell.... As a matter of fact, officers revealed that he 'slept like a baby'." Perri was described as "calm, reflective and unperturbed" throughout the bail hearing, while Annie was described as "expressionless." Annie's conviction in 1938 for possessing an unregistered gun was mentioned by their Windsor lawyer Charles Croll as "the only time she had been in trouble."

Croll also told the court that Rocco had had no convictions since 1928. Accordingly, Police Court Judge Brodie granted bail at half the rate requested by William Kelley, the special Crown attorney. Brodie reasoned that there was "no danger of his [Perri] not appearing." And much to Perri's amusement, Judge Brodie added that "in view of the amount of publicity he's getting in the news-papers, I'm afraid there's little hope of his leaving Ontario."

But how had the RCMP finally managed to make the case against Rocco, especially since Perri, as usual, had carefully insulated himself? It was not until three members of Perri's bootlegging ring agreed to become Crown witnesses that the RCMP learned of the huge scope of the operation. The RCMP memo on their statements indicates astonishment that the corruption of Canadian customs officials in Windsor went as far back as 1933 and had possibly even prevailed for a considerable time prior to that date.

The three Crown witnesses were David Michael Armaly, Victor Bernat and Milton Goldhart. All had taken part in the Perri bootlegging business, Armaly as a customs officer and driver and Bernat and Goldhart as drivers. Armaly was the key Crown witness. He had recruited his fellow officials to the conspiracy before he was dismissed from his post for letting through parts for stills. Later he took up driving for the ring. Bernat had always been a driver, and though considered insignificant, he was able to offer some corrobo-rating testimony for Armaly's story. Goldhart's testimony was considered to be the more damaging of the trio because he dealt directly with Annie Newman and had been driving with Rocco and Annie for over two years. All three men were crucial to the successful prosecution of the Perri case. The federal deputy minister of justice admitted in a confi-dential letter to the attorney general of Ontario that "there is little or no direct Police evidence."

But the police were not the only ones aware of the slender nature of the Crown's case. RCMP informers in the underworld reported that Perri's arrest had caused "a violent furor amongst the underworld as far away as Chicago." In an urgent memo marked "Secret," Superintendent Kemp, the commanding officer of "O" Division, advised the commissioner that the witnesses might be tampered with or eliminated:

> It has been strongly intimated from a source believed to be reliable that definite steps may now be expected by those whose interests have been affected, to make some attempt to ensure that certain of the Crown witnesses are not available for the forthcoming trial.... In view of what we know as to foreign elements here and in the United States who are interested in this case, it is felt that the information received is not exaggerated, and should be acted upon.

The RCMP were under no illusions. The two most recent attempts on Perri's life were hardly needed to remind them that people in Perri's league played for keeps. Superintendent Kemp insisted that the chief witnesses/ informers be placed in protective custody in secret locations, with the RCMP picking up the full tab. Armaly and his wife and four children were put in a summer cottage outside Ottawa. Bernat was put up by the RCMP detachment in Amherstburg, Ontario. Goldhart, who was from Toronto, was placed with the Lindsay, Ontario, detachment.*

Cecil Kirby, the RCMP informer of the 1980s, was not the first bad guy to be supported by the Force. Armaly and Bernat were hardly paragons of virtue. Before the end of the trials, Armaly confessed to forgery, illegal gambling, cheating on welfare, taking bribes and fraud, among other illegal

---

*The RCMP commissioner was also worried about keeping down the costs of lodging them. The $3-per-day costs for the witnesses seemed a heavy burden, though the RCMP later paid Crown Attorney Tom Phelan a daily rate of $300 for his attendance at departmental hearings on the trials. As it turned out, the trials did not actually begin until January 1940, thus costing the RCMP many $3 per diems to their informers. The controversy over these payments raged in the press, and the public was up in arms at the generous treatment of the witnesses — which included immunity from prosecution.

acts. He had such a checkered career that Perri's counsel, Joe Bullen, K.C., of Toronto closed his cross-examination of Armaly with one short question: "Is there much short of everything in the Criminal Code of which you are not guilty?" Armaly replied with a lame, "I don't know." Bernat had a long criminal record and was equally disreputable.

But the stories the three informers had to tell were certainly worth the price. For the first time in his long criminal career, Rocco Perri faced the real possibility of ending up behind bars for many years for some very serious crimes. Armaly, Bernat and Goldhart represented a real chink in Perri's otherwise impenetrable armour.

Dave Armaly, originally from Ste Marie, Quebec, had become a customs officer at the age of twenty-one in October 1929 after attending university for one year. He took a job at a shoe store, where he was later caught embezzling store funds. He was immediately dismissed, but the charges of fraud against him were withdrawn to spare the store further embarrassment. Armaly was then fortunate enough to get a job at Canadian Customs at the Walkerville Ferry, which ran between Detroit and Windsor and was, at the time, the major route of automobile traffic between the two cities. Armaly, always a heavy gambler, started gambling in 1931 at a house in Windsor run by Rocco Perri associate Sam "Fan" Miller, a Windsor gambling boss. In order to pay off a gambling debt of $35, he agreed, in 1933, to let a car belonging to Miller go through Customs. It was easy money and Armaly was soon letting cars through regularly for the Perri ring. Warned by a telephone call from Detroit which car to look for, Armaly would let the smuggler know which traffic lane he would be working. Between 1935 and 1936 Armaly claimed to have waved close to two hundred cars through Customs for Perri's associate Sam Miller. But Armaly was observing only part of the flow. Since he could not always be on duty at a traffic lane, Armaly claimed he recruited other officers, including the senior bridge officer, to the conspiracy. It was not until 1936 that Armaly was able to confirm (for himself) that he was actually working for Rocco Perri.

In March of that year, Sam Miller introduced Armaly to Annie Newman. Armaly claimed that he initially refused to work for a woman, until she mentioned that she worked for Perri. Armaly immediately agreed to go on working. His meetings with Annie Newman continued even after he was dismissed from the Customs Service in May 1936 for corruption (appropriately enough, he was letting in some roulette wheels for gambler Max Shapiro of Montreal as well as still parts for Perri), as he served as a liaison between the Perris and the other Customs officers. Most of his meetings were with Annie Newman, some in front of the Norton Hotel in Detroit, but on several occasions, when Perri himself attended, they met at his house. Now unemployed, Armaly managed to keep his family fed by deducting a small fee from the money he delivered to the other customs officials. Annie eventually set Armaly up in a drug store in Windsor, conveniently located just past the Ambassador Bridge, and he soon started to drive for Sam Miller.

During the trial, Armaly testified that he had made over twenty trips to Chicago, occasionally with his wife, to haul liquor to Detroit. At this point the car was usually turned over to another driver to clear customs, in case Armaly was recognized by one of his former colleagues not on the take. The load had been supplied by Chicago mobster Joe Tarallo, the bootlegger associated with the Sola family who also sold to Perri. (Tarallo was later convicted of tax evasion in connection with post-Prohibition bootleg activities in Chicago.)

In Chicago, Armaly loaded five-gallon tins of booze into the specially constructed car at Joe Tarallo's garage at 121 East 123rd Street. The telephone number at Tarallo's establishment was entered as evidence of one of the numbers dialled frequently from Rocco Perri's Hamilton residence. Asked by the Crown where he stayed while in Chicago, Armaly responded, "The Westin and the Alcatraz." Blushing at the laughter from the court room, he realized his mistake and mumbled "The Alcazar."

Armaly continued to drive for Miller until early 1938. At that time he had a run-in with Miller over a car accident that had occurred on the way to Montreal in which several gallons of alcohol had been lost. Miller refused to pay him his fee, and Armaly walked out. Armaly took up with Milton Goldhart, who was running a few cars now himself for Victor Sola, a nephew of Joe Tarallo in Chicago, but Armaly continued to meet with Annie Newman. Armaly sent Annie and Rocco coded telegrams about times of deliveries, which were entered in the evidence. These were usually addressed to "Joe Newman" at both Annie's and Rocco's Hamilton addresses: 166 Bay Street South and 498 Hughson Street North. Armaly claimed to have met with Bill ("The Butcher") Leuchter and his young companion the morning of his fiery demise to arrange for clearance through customs on his return from Chicago. The deaths of the two men coming so close after the recent attempts on Perri's life shook Armaly deeply. He feared for his own safety.

In 1939, after a little red notebook was found in a raid at Sam Miller's gambling establishment, the RCMP dispatched an officer to question Armaly, whose name appeared in the book. To the officer's surprise, Armaly broke down and confessed about an entirely separate issue, namely his working relationship with Rocco Perri and Annie Newman. His confession was totally unexpected, but the RCMP were prepared to make the most of it. He outlined all his criminal dealings with the Perris.

Armaly said he had met Milton Goldhart at Sam Miller's gambling club in Windsor in the early thirties. Goldhart told Armaly that he was working for Rocco Perri and Annie Newman. Early in 1936, Goldhart had proposed that Armaly help him bring in alcohol for Perri. Goldhart then took him to a parked car. In the car was Annie Newman, who took Armaly for a ride. Annie told Armaly that she was working with Perri, "the best man in the alcohol racket." Armaly then recruited many of his colleagues at Customs. He named Edward Mansell, Carl Gough, Wilfred Fletcher and Norman Lepaine as collaborators. As a result of Armaly's confession, the RCMP brought in Frank Zaneth, now an inspector, to take charge of the investigation.

Victor Bernat's testimony identified several of the customs

officers named by Armaly. He had met most of them with another of Perri's Windsor associates, Sam Motruk. Motruk had found Bernat driving a bread wagon. The offer of $75 a week and a fast car to smuggle liquor was too good to refuse, but Bernat was only a minor cog in the wheel. The most sensational of his recollections was his report "that one of the Customs men, Gough, had threatened to take care of anyone who squealed to the police."

During the eight-day trial Rocco Perri maintained an unruffled calm and seemed to really enjoy himself as he had enjoyed almost everything throughout his long career. But Annie clearly did not relish the proceedings, and her anger at one point even brought Rocco into open conflict with reporters. Halfway through the trial, on January 25, 1940, when photographers tried to shoot Annie entering court with him, Rocco, in a rare instance of public hostility, threw several rocks at Barney Gloster, the Windsor *Star* photographer. The headline in the *Star* that day was "ROCCO THROWS ROCKS BUT PHOTOGRAPHER GETS PICTURES." According to the *Star*, "Perri became enraged when Mrs Newman screamed her protests at having her picture taken, and Barney, like a good photographer, ducked for cover, Perri dashing off his hat and throwing two large stones at the fleeing figure. He [Perri] added a few choice cuss words and invited newsmen to come back and fight." Rocco was certainly going all out to shield his common-law wife. It is the only known instance of Rocco Perri's losing his cool in public in his long criminal career.

Part of Perri's arsenal was his defence team, which consisted of Joseph Bullen, K.C., of Toronto and a young Windsor MP, who later became one of the most prominent Liberals and a senior cabinet minister, Paul Martin. (Rocco's long-time senior lawyer, Charles Bell, had died in February 1938, collapsing after giving a passionate summation in a stock fraud trial.) In a recent interview Martin recalls that attacking Armaly's credibility seemed to be the most obvious tack to take right from the start. Even today, Martin does not think Armaly was a very impressive witness on which to build a case. He was an opportunistic rogue, particularly open to attack as a paid informer, a mercenary who would fabricate and say anything to get continued support. At the trial Martin zeroed in on the fact that Armaly was on the RCMP payroll as an informer while he was also collecting welfare from the City of Windsor. Martin made mincemeat out of Armaly in his cross-examination, pointing out his convictions, his criminal activities and, most important, his violations of his oath as a customs officer:

> *Martin.* When was the first time you went to a bookie?
> *Armaly.* Sometime before I joined the Customs Service.
> *Martin.* You knew most of the gamblers in town. You knew the whole racket?
> *Armaly.* Pretty well, I guess.
> *Martin.* Do you recall going to some of these men and saying "Come on, boys, I want some of the money or I am going to squeal?"
> *Armaly.* No, I didn't say that.
> *Martin.* You remember your oath as a Custom's Officer.
> *Armaly.* Yes.
> *Martin.* You violated the oath?
> *Armaly.* Yes, I did.
> *Martin.* And you are under oath now. Aren't you?

In later cross-examination Martin brought up information he had about Armaly's alleged defrauding of the Welfare Department:

> *Martin.* When did you go *off* relief?
> *Armaly.* September 1st last year.
> *Martin.* I suggest that you were on relief until September 26th, all the time you were still being paid by the police.
> *Armaly.* I may have. I don't remember the exact date.
> *Martin.* Then you weren't telling the truth when you stated a moment ago you were not on after September the 1st.
> *Armaly.* I didn't say that.
> *Martin.* Yes, you did! You said September 1st, last year. [pause] Have you been approached by the Welfare Department?...[pause]
> *Armaly.* Ah...
> *Martin.* No...But you expect to, don't you, being a cheat?

Martin then told the court that Armaly was the real criminal. "I suggest to you that the witness not only lied in the witness box here, but he also lied to the police." Martin alleged that Armaly "hoodwinked" the police in an effort to divert them from charging him for his role in alcohol smuggling.

Perri's own lawyer, Joe Bullen, summed up for the jury the defence view of Armaly in this succinct fashion. "I would rather believe a yellow dog grovelling and sniffing for his food in an ash can in the alley than believe this witness."

Armaly was devastated. He had no credibility left. But what concerned the Mounties watching their case being torpedoed was Martin's source of information. He seemed to know minute details about Armaly's interrogation by the RCMP. A worried memo from the RCMP officer assigned to the trial expresses concern about the source of Martin's facts:

> Cross-examination by Mr Martin, MP, disclosed the astonishing fact that Mr Martin was familiar with a certain interview which took place in the office of the writer, many months ago between Armaly, the other witnesses and myself, which was actually for the purpose of clearing up some obvious errors in their statements, and this was what Mr Martin charged. Mr Martin failed to follow up his questioning along these lines, otherwise I would have been forced to testify accordingly. I cannot understand in what manner Mr Martin became possessed of his facts.

In a secret memo to the commissioner, Superintendent Kemp attempted to provide the answer: "I am not aware of how the information referred to came into the possession of Mr Martin. In as much as Goldhart is missing, I can only assume that he was responsible for this."

According to his own account, Milton Goldhart, who today lives in retirement in Miami, had been tricked into co-operating with the Crown by Inspector Frank Zaneth. Goldhart maintains that he was advised that he would go to jail for six months if he did not agree to tell all, though he refused later to sign an affidavit confirming that his confession was true and voluntary. Still bitter about the experience, he says that Zaneth was "a dandy Dan with spectacles....a little shit and a liar. Zaneth called me a rat the first time I met him. I felt like zapping him. No one calls me a rat." Goldhart is also bitter about Armaly, who he says "was a complete shit." As for Rocco, he now states admiringly and without reservation that "Roc was the finest person I met in my life, a prince."

With the help of "Roc," Goldhart had got revenge on Zaneth for his alleged treachery. While he was living under RCMP protective custody, Goldhart managed to get a message to his good friend and one-time boss. Perri gave Goldhart his instructions in a pay-phone-to-pay-phone conversation, and Goldhart then disappeared before the trials began. The worst fears of the RCMP were realized. Although they thought Goldhart had been murdered, he had actually gone to England and joined the RAF, ironically serving his country in a way the RCMP had neither desired nor anticipated. "Roc was the only one who knew where I was. I called him from a pay phone in NYC by pre-arrangement," says Goldhart, maintaining that he "was never a rat" and "only answered questions to get them [the RCMP] to lay off me. My lawyer advised me that I had no choice under the circumstances." (The mounties were never to find out what actually happened to Goldhart.)

Appearances to the contrary, Goldhart could not have been Paul Martin's source, for by the time Martin was preparing the defence for the Customs cases, Goldhart was in England fighting for Britain in her hour of need. Martin's sources were probably within the Customs Service itself. After all, he was the federal MP from Windsor for the governing Liberal party, and there were many customs officers among his constituents. There was a major internal probe of Customs going on at the time in Windsor as a result of the trial, resulting in some major internal shake-ups. There is no doubt that Martin was privy to a lot of inside information because of the chaotic situation in his own riding. Martin certainly had no need for Goldhart's input to demolish Armaly. However, Goldhart's presence might have provided the corroboration the Crown was now desperately seeking to rebuild Armaly's credibility.

Some of the relevant parts of Goldhart's statement to Zaneth, which the jury did not have the chance to see, have been obtained from RCMP files. Goldhart had stated that Annie Newman offered him a job driving alcohol from Chicago via Windsor to Hamilton starting at $25 a trip. Later this went up to $100 a trip plus expenses, which Goldhart says "equals about five grand today [1986]." On many occasions he personally drove with Annie Newman to Windsor and Chicago. On one trip to Chicago, Annie contacted Mrs Mary Sola and her son Vincent. Goldhart then took his car to the Sola garage and filled it up with alcohol. Annie Newman drove with Goldhart as far as Detroit, crossed into Canada by herself, and met Goldhart on the Canadian side. She had fixed things with Customs and Goldhart's car was not searched. The two then drove to Dundas, Ontario, where they met with another car, which took the load of alcohol. On another occasion, Rocco himself had driven Goldhart to Dundas for a meeting with Vincent Sola.

Later, when Goldhart was arrested with Sola in Chatham, Ontario, with a load of alcohol, it was Annie Newman who bailed him out of jail. Goldhart also said that there were "four or five Customs officers who passed the car at different times while I was working for Anne Newman and Perri." He was never nervous when going through Canadian Customs with a load, as he knew that "in each case it had been fixed by Armaly." Goldhart added that "in each instance after passing the Customs, Anne Newman gave me an envelope containing money to deliver to Armaly, which I did."

After his arrest, during late 1937 and 1938, Goldhart, along with his old friend, Toronto bootlegger Louis Beaver, operated independently, but still sold his alcohol to Rocco Perri. "I used to telephone Perri from Paris, Ontario, when I was en route to Hamilton with alcohol, and on his instructions, I would leave the car in the village of Dundas, Ontario, and leave the car keys under the floor mat of the car. This generally occurred between 12 p.m. and 5 o'clock in the morning, when Perri would come out from Hamilton with a driver, who would take over the loaded car. Perri would then drive Louis Beaver and myself to Hamilton, where he paid for the alcohol, at his home, and where we waited for my car, which would be returned to me empty. My arrangement with Perri at that time was that he would take any quantity of alcohol that I could deliver to him, at any time that I could do so, as long as it was at the price we had agreed upon."

In his signed statement to Zaneth, Goldhart had stated that Annie Newman was involved in all aspects of the bootlegging: that she went down to Detroit with him, arranged for the payoff of customs officials, arranged contacts in the United States, arranged for the disposition of the bootleg liquor in Canada and in all things connected with the bootleg trade acted to insulate Rocco. Annie, according to Goldhart, was the principal organizer and front for Rocco Perri. But since Goldhart had disappeared before the trial actually took place, this testimony, unfortunately, could not be introduced.

Without it the Crown's case was seriously weakened, and this explains why Rocco had been so confident on the train to Windsor and throughout the proceedings. He knew that Goldhart would not appear. He had made all the arrangements for the disappearance himself. In the end, Goldhart had been loyal, even though he had been forced by Zaneth to outline for the police the inner workings of Perri's bootlegging operations.

Paul Martin cannot recall how the information on the Toronto meeting at the RCMP headquarters in Toronto came into his hands, nor does he remember Milton Goldhart, but his inside knowledge was crucial for the defence. Victor Bernat's character was quickly discredited by the introduction of evidence that he had been involved in smuggling Chinese into the United States. Bootlegging had romance, but alien-smuggling was despised. Those involved usually looted their desperate cargo of any valuables, and there were rumours that before the voyage the aliens were hidden in weighted bags to keep them out of sight. If the smugglers were spotted by the border patrol, the bags were simply slid overboard.

Bernat defended himself vigorously from the stand, but Paul Martin was unrelenting in his attacks on his credibility. He implicated Bernat in a hold-up for which Bernat's brother had been convicted and sentenced to Kingston. He also tried to establish that Bernat was out to "get at all costs" Sam Motruk, a childhood friend with whom he had had a disagreement. This was why Bernat had offered his information to the RCMP, Martin maintained.

Under the pressure of Martin's cross examination, Bernat revealed that his father had once been charged with alien smuggling. He also told Martin that the alien was actually smuggled in by Sam Motruk and someone called "Black Paul." But Bernat's credibility by this time was non-existent.

The demolition of the Crown's case was complete and the verdict was almost anti-climactic. Rocco Perri, Annie Newman and four of the customs officials, Carl Gough, Wilfred Fletcher, Norman Lepaine and Edward Mansell were acquitted on February 1, 1940, after the jury deliberated for almost twenty hours. There was joy in the courtroom as Mrs Sam Miller rushed over to kiss Annie Newman. Two other customs officers, Thomas Arthur Smyth and Harry Jarvis Smith, were acquitted in a separate trial later. Only Perri's unfortunate Windsor lieutenants, Sam Miller (already in Burwash Reformatory for defrauding the government of $16,000 in excise tax) and Sam Motruk were later convicted in a third separate trial and sentenced to prison terms up to two years. Ironically, a Crown witness, a young friend of Bernat's, Philip Bucheski, 18, was found guilty of perjury in yet a fourth trial on May 20, 1940 for lying in his signed statement to Frank Zaneth. He had told Zaneth what Bernat had told him to say about Sam Motruk's bootleg business, because Bernat had promised him a job and money.

Dave Armaly's name appears one last time as a deadpan aside in a follow-up memo in the RCMP files. "At the moment Armaly is facing charges for defrauding Windsor relief agencies and will probably be sent to jail for at least a month." Within weeks of this memo and after the first three trials, Armaly was indeed convicted of welfare fraud committed while he was a protected RCMP informer. In a real twist of fate, Armaly was the one who ended up going to jail, not the criminal organizers, Rocco and Annie, or the allegedly corrupt Customs officers. On February 16th, 1940 Dave Armaly got three months for fraud.

Other charges against Rocco and members of his gang, including Annie Newman and Tony Moranda as well as Harry Alter (alias "Brams") and Wilfrid Gaudreau, for breach of the Excise Act which came out of the Customs cases were dropped on May 22, 1940 due to the "disappearance" of key witnesses. Co-conspirators in the case were Frank Diclimenti, Tommy Parisi, Sam Hill, Paul Syec, Harry Livingstone and Sammy Vallero. Only five witnesses of fifty-eight potential witnesses had been heard by the grand jury. According to RCMP headquarters and special Crown prosecutor Frank Callaghan, the case could not proceed "as the missing witnesses were our most important, we couldn't have hoped to succeed." The judge, while noting that the evidence to convict "was available at one time," had to agree with Callaghan.

Rocco Perri, still leading a charmed life, had once again successfully frustrated the intense RCMP efforts throughout the thirties to put him behind bars. But the RCMP had not yet played all its cards. The mounties had one more trick up their sleeve.

CHAPTER 17

ANNIE GOES FOR THE GOLD

The RCMP's planned war against the mob in Ontario was never executed. Many of the best in the RCMP went to fight in Europe, and the RCMP had to rethink its strategy. With witnesses disappearing at a rapid rate things looked grim in late May 1940. But on May 27th, anticipating the war with Italy, the RCMP drew up a list of suspected enemy aliens and subversives in Canada amongst the Italian population to be rounded up and incarcerated when war was declared. Rocco Perri appeared on the list as "an important member of the Fascio who are naturalized and whose internment is recommended."

It can now be revealed for the first time that the RCMP had a hidden agenda. They planned to execute a body blow against the Mafia in Canada by arresting the top Italian organized crime bosses across the country under the guise of their supposed Fascist sympathies. Ironically, when this massive interning of Canadian Mafia leaders later became a reality, it created a power vacuum which made it easier for Buffalo's Don Stefano Magaddino to take control of the rackets in Canada.

On June 10, 1940, Mussolini declared war on England. The RCMP, with the prior approval of Norman Robertson, the Secretary of the Privy Council, moved swiftly throughout the country to arrest those on their Italian blacklist.

Simultaneously, with auxiliary support from local police forces, the Mounties raided the homes and offices of Italians across the country. Within forty-eight hours thousands of Italians in seven provinces were interrogated and hundreds were under arrest. Many of those arrrested were totally innocent of any involvement in fascism or seditious activity in Canada. A headline in the New York *Times* of June 12, 1940 is, "HUNDREDS OF ITALIANS ARRESTED IN CANADA." The story reports that Canadian reaction to Italy's entrance in the war is so "bitter" that "Ontario's 3,000 Italian families, now in the category of enemy aliens, have been struck off the relief rolls."

The Toronto *Globe and Mail* of June 12th featured the raid under the headline, "SEVERAL HUNDRED HELD IN MOUNTIES' ROUNDUP OF ITALIANS IN CANADA":

In raids extending over seven provinces, Royal Canadian Mounted Police have arrested "several hundred" Italians in the past two days and placed them in receiving stations opened across Canada.... Police have been preparing for the last three months to swoop down on members of the Fascist Party and other Italian organizations the moment war was declared. The word came yesterday. Prepared instructions were taken out of the headquarter's vaults and wired to the different centres. There are now more Italians in custody in Canada than there are Germans and the number is likely to be increased further. In the raids papers were seized which may incriminate others. While the first police push is over, arrests have by no means stopped.... Italy's declaration of war on the Allies set in motion the largest and most thorough roundup of enemy aliens in the history of Montreal, a roundup that brought scores of persons into custody inside thirty-six hours.... Since late Monday afternoon carloads of men [in Toronto, Hamilton and Windsor] have been taken into custody and transferred to the Automotive Building in the CNE grounds.... It is estimated that several hundred Italians have been arrested in the Toronto area since Monday afternoon. Italian clubs and restaurants were raided and searched from top to bottom. A well-known Italian restaurateur was arrested and speedily interned. An Italian newspaper was closed down.... The prisoners were given no warning of their impending arrest. The police closed in on them in a lightning move and men were taken from their homes to police stations in a daze.... An elderly Italian priest was interned and yesterday a well-known Italian with a criminal record was caught in the police net. The Italian colony on upper Dufferin Street and the "Little Italy" in the College and Clinton Streets sections were the chief targets of the raiding squads [in Toronto].

Seventeen police cars were used in the Hamilton round-up four hours after Mussolini's declaration of war. The *Spectator* states that "the raid was one of the most carefully prepared and methodical in police annals. There were no wailing sirens — like one would expect in a Hollywood roundup — and the police cars were at great pains to obey traffic signals."

At the same time, a feverish anti-Italian sentiment flared up across Canada. Riots against Italians broke out in Toronto, and shops and small factories owned by Italians were stoned. Similar riots were reported in Montreal, Hamilton, Windsor and other major Canadian centres, mostly by mobs of "rowdy" citizens.

All that the public was told was that the government's plan was to detain all known and suspected members of supporters of the Fascist party. Under the stringent provisions of the War Measures Act, even the newspapers were not allowed to print the names of those rounded up and imprisoned.* However, the government, following the plan conceived by the RCMP, allowed the arrests of the leading members of the mob in Canada.

The names of those arrested and later sent for the duration of the war to internment in Camp Petawawa in northern Ontario, made up a "Who's Who" of the Mafia in Canada at that time:

---

*There was one notable exception. The arrest of James Franceschini, the President of Dufferin Shipbuilders Co. was revealed in the House of Commons by C.D. Howe, the Minister of Munitions, and this was reported in the Toronto *Star* of June 15, 1940. A major and important debate in the House of Commons over the continued detention of Mr Franceschini took place on May 4, 1942. The two principal participants in the debate, both future prime ministers, were then Minister of Justice Louis St Laurent and then Opposition MP, John Diefenbaker.

Frank Sylvestro (alias "Frank Ross"), Hamilton bootlegger and Perri lieutenant
Antonio ("Tony") Papalia, Hamilton bootlegger and associate of Rocco Perri
Vincenzo (James) Sacco, Niagara Falls bootlegger allied with Perri
"Black Peter" Sacco, Niagara Falls gambler and bootlegger
Domenic Belcastro, Guelph arsonist and counterfeiter
Calogero ("Charlie") Bordonaro, Hamilton Black Hand bomber and Mafia leader allied with Perri
Domenic Longo, Guelph bootlegger allied with Perri
John (alias "Archie" or "Czar") Saccone, Niagara Falls alien smuggler
Giovanni ("John") Durso, Hamilton associate of Corde and Perri

The list goes on, with names of suspected gangsters known to the RCMP in Toronto, Thorold, St Catharines, Welland, Hamilton, Guelph, Windsor, North Bay, Niagara Falls, Montreal and even Trail, British Columbia.

Moreover, the secret government memos ordering the arrests indicate that senior government officials, including Prime Minister Mackenzie King and Justice Minister Ernest Lapointe, knew the real reason for the many arrests. Norman Robertson, who signed most of the incarceration orders, as chairman of the inter-departmental committee for reviewing RCMP files on enemy aliens and "persons suspected of treasonable or seditious purposes," spells it out directly in several memos. For example, in the document filed on August 1, 1940, for the arrest of Raymond Parisi of Hamilton, Robertson writes that Parisi is to be interned because he "is a member of the Mafia....[and] a constant associate of racketeers and convicted criminals." The Mafia is described as "an Italian secret society." Still, with Parisi, involvement with the Fascists and support of Mussolini was suspected.

In the case of Frank Corde, also of Hamilton, evidence of being in the Mafia was sufficient for internment, and this seems to have been the case for imprisoning other Mafia leaders who had no known Fascist sympathies. Corde's committal document, written by the Commander of "O" Division of the RCMP, makes enlightening reading:

> From the perusal of this file it appears that this subject has a very bad reputation. He has a bold and talkative manner and is a low criminal character. It is considered that he would commit an act of sabotage if the price was high enough as he is unscrupulous and would make money regardless of its sources. He follows the races.... He is suspected of having administered narcotics to race horses under his supervision. When Corde is not training horses, he co-operates with the local bootleggers, alcohol, and narcotics pedlars. His home has been searched on several occasions under the O. & N. D. [Opium and Narcotic Drugs] Act but without results. Ex-S.A. 909 reported that Corde was a member of the Maffia. [sic]....Corde associates with the criminal element of the Italian underworld in Hamilton and has been one of the prime movers and instigators of crime in Hamilton. His association with Italians of the racketeer type is sufficient to cause alarm....Corde is known at the Toronto Division Office for a number of years as one of the "higher-ups" in the Italian underworld of Hamilton. His successful evasion of the law has been solely due to his directive methods. He, himself, has never become, of later years, directly implicated due to his method of directing criminals. Our interrogation of this subject, definitely points to the fact that for a number of years he has never been legitimately employed. His reticence on this subject can only be viewed in the light that he wishes to conceal his real method of livelihood....It is felt that his position in the underworld could be considered a potential source of danger to the State.

A similar line of reasoning is used for the incarceration of Domenic Longo, Anthony Ratiliano, Domenic Belcastro, Thomas Rasso, John Saccone, Frank Sylvestro (a.k.a. Ross), Michael Perri, Vincenzo Romano, and many other suspected Mafia members. In some cases lip service is given to possible fascist or "anti-British" feelings for which there is little or, in most cases, no evidence given.

Of course, Rocco Perri's name was at the top of the RCMP list of those to be immediately put away. Unfortunately, the intelligence backgrounder, similar to the one on Rocco's associate Frank Corde and which must have been prepared for government officials by the RCMP, no longer survives in government files, but it can be safely assumed that the committal reasons were the same, for the RCMP certainly saw Rocco as a Mafia leader who was an habitual and dangerous criminal.

Rocco was arrested on the evening of Monday June 10, 1940, in the very first police raids in Toronto and Hamilton. Simply put, placing Rocco Perri in prison under the War Measures Act was about the only route left for the Mounties in their twenty-year battle to put him behind bars. The beauty of the current situation — from the point of view of the RCMP — was that since it was all done in utmost secrecy, Perri, for the first time, had no recourse to his high-paid mouthpieces or his political allies. There was to be no trial, there would be no disappearing witnesses. Rocco was powerless against the full weight of the federal government operating with almost dictatorial powers. His arrest and internment at Camp Petawawa were not even reported in the newspapers, though everyone in the Italian community knew about it through word of mouth.

Annie Newman tried to push all the levers that might turn the situation around — everything that money could buy. The bereft Annie tried everything to get Rocco out of Camp Petawawa where he was interned with other "enemy aliens," including the German prisoners of war. She used political connections, including a priest in Timmins, an aide to the minister of justice, and others. But the government was unrelenting. Rocco was to stay imprisoned in the northeastern Ontario army base for more than three long years, though his younger brother, Mike, was released on March 12, 1942 on petition and on the recommendation of RCMP Commissioner S. T. Wood and Minister of Justice Louis St Laurent. Unlike his brother Michael, who it was found had supported the Canadian war effort and therefore became a "loyal subject," Rocco was considered too great a threat to the security of the state to be released.

With Rocco out of the way, Annie came into her own, criminally speaking. Before Rocco was interned in early 1940, he and Annie had worked out an elaborate gold highgrading/smuggling scam with a ring that had been operating in Canada for five years from 1935 to 1939. The group, originally led by one Simon Dollinger, involved high-grading gold from Timmins, Ontario — that is, the gold was stolen by Timmins miners and taken out in their lunch buckets and other convenient hiding places. The gold was then smuggled into the United States and sold to jewellers like New York's Jack N. Rubin, head of the London Gold and Gem Exchange. The United States had gone off the gold standard in 1933, and the passage of the Gold Hoarding Act in the United States had made it lucrative to sell gold to Americans illegally. The gang also smuggled American scrap gold and coins *into* Canada, melted them down, mixed the recycled gold with their own highgrade gold, and sold it to the Royal Mint and other places in Canada. Millions of dollars were made by the gang in these schemes. Other members of Dollinger's original group included J.S. Witten-berg, Charles H. Lamothe, Marko Serder, Harry Rotstein, Moses Boxinbaum, and Joseph Shapiro. Dollinger's gang was broken up by Ontario police working with the Secret Service, and Simon Dollinger was sentenced to three years in jail in 1940. Jack Rubin was sentenced to sixteen months in Sing Sing Prison, where he was imprisoned for some months before winning an appeal from a higher court.

Annie Newman used her numerous contacts in the Jewish community in Toronto and New York, especially with Toronto businessman Benjamin Faibish and his son, Sydney Faibish, a licensed optometrist, who had taken over the operations of the Dollinger group, as well as Rocco's contacts in the Italian criminal world in Toronto and Hamilton and new connections with a French Canadian highgrading outfit in Northern Ontario, to become involved in an elaborate and highly profitable international gold scam. It reached from Timmins and Toronto to Buffalo and New York City. With the emergency of the war, gold had become an even more precious substance than usual, and American supplies were less than secure. Tight controls were legislated by the governments of the United States and Canada to regulate the flow, source and price of gold.

Former RCMP Deputy Commissioner Bill Kelly, then a corporal, was detailed for nearly a year (1941-42) to the gold case, which he calls "one of the biggest cases during the war," along with a team of veterans from the U.S. Secret Service, the RCMP and the Canadian Foreign Exchange Control Board. According to Kelly, Sydney Faibish, then twenty-one, was the organizing genius behind the scheme. As an optometrist, Faibish was one of the few people in Canada who were legally allowed to buy gold — dentists and optometrists used gold in their work. Annie was Faibish's key Toronto-Timmins-Buffalo co-ordinator, provider of drivers who ran the gold from the Timmins area to Toronto, and the one who arranged to have the gold re-evaluated so that the Timmins area highgraders couldn't cheat on the price. It was primarily Sydney Faibish, a cousin of the imprisoned Simon Dollinger, who dealt with the American connections that purchased the smuggled gold. This involved three Buffalo men, Charles Abrahams, Harry Julius and David Roth, and two New York City businessmen (Dollinger's old connections), Bernard Kushner, the President of Kushner & Pines Inc., and Jack Rubin, Roth's brother-in-law.

The gold came from the mines of Kirkland Lake, Timmins and other northern Ontario mining centres. The gold was highgraded by the Labreque family of Timmins, refined by others and delivered via twelve runners to Annie who was now living in Toronto. Annie then arranged for Toronto assayers to evaluate the mineral before she had it made into "buttons" for delivery to Faibish's Buffalo and New York City connections. In effect, Annie bought the gold from her Timmins connections and sold it to Sydney Faibish in Toronto, who, in turn, was selling it to American connections.

The joint American-Canadian police investigation into the operation (which involved Bill Kelly, RCMP Constable Edward McElhone, Max Fell, the Head of the Investigations Branch of the Exchange Board, and the Buffalo Secret Service office, headed by Edwin Manning and two agents specially seconded from New York City), began in July 1941 and a massive, four-month long undercover operation ensued, involving the interception of mail and the shadowing of the many suspects for months.

By late September 1941, the investigators were ready to spring a trap. Secret Service reports show that Buffalo suspects were under surveillance for at least a couple of weeks as they were waiting for a shipment. Then police investigators followed Harry Julius and Charles Abrahams as they were driving from the Faibish home in Toronto to cross the Peace Bridge on October 4, 1941, with a load of high-grade gold. The undercover operators notified U.S. customs officials, who found that Julius was carrying a canvas vest hiding six buttons and a bar of gold weighing over twenty-three pounds and worth more than $11,500 in U.S. funds. Julius also had several hundred thousand dollars in American and Canadian currency in his possession. As a result, Harry Julius, 42, of the Bronx, and Charles E. Abrahams, 51, Buffalo, were charged.

Between October 6 and November 3, 1941, Annie Newman, Sydney Faibish, Benjamin Faibish, Willie Franciotti, Albert Mazzuca, Frank Deluca and Alphonse, Lionel, Paul, Albert and Ernest Labreque were charged in Toronto by a preferred indictment with conspiring to export without licence over $850,000 worth of gold over a period of twenty-one months. The charges were not made public until the sensational trial began in Toronto on May 4, 1942. Annie was bailed out once again by her sister, Leah Romberg, who put up $20,000.

Since they were to be charged in the United States anyway for breaking U.S. laws on gold, a deal was made by the Canadian authorities whereby four of the U.S. co-conspirators, namely, Abrahams, Roth, Julius and Rubin were to come up to Toronto and testify against Annie Newman, Sydney Faibish et al. in exchange for not being charged in Canada. Roth and Julius also agreed to testify against Bernard Kushner in his Buffalo trial, and as a result received much lesser sentences than Kushner after pleading guilty to all charges. David Roth got out with only a two-year suspended sentence and was placed on immediate probation. Jack Rubin got a year and a half in Sing Sing. Abrahams received a six-month sentence in the Erie County Penitentiary, and Julius got one year and a day in Sing Sing.

Bernard M. Kushner's trial ended with his conviction on May 2, 1942 on six counts of smuggling over a million dollars worth of gold bullion from 1938 to 1941. On May 11, Kushner was sentenced to four years in prison. Kushner had lamely testified all his records of gold purchases had been accidentally detroyed by acid on the night of October 3, 1941. The stolen Canadian gold seized by police was forfeited to the United States Treasury, and today is stored in Fort Knox.

The month-long trial of Annie Newman, Sydney Faibish and their alleged conspirators began in a packed Toronto court room on May 4, 1942. Because the indictments had been secret and because so many defendants were involved in such a massive and complex international smuggling scam, the trial was widely reported in the Canadian media. One of the lawyers for the defence, the wily, colourful Eddie Murphy, had tipped off certain Toronto newspapermen (including police reporter "Jocko" Thomas of the Toronto *Star*) about the upcoming trial, so it was on the front pages of the papers on May 4th. Murphy was a big, hearty Irishman, who, according to Bill Kelly, "could laugh people out of jail" if he were their lawyer but "laughed you into jail" when he was working on the other side as a Crown attorney. The other defence lawyer was R. H. Greer, who years before had defended Rocco and his friends and criminal colleagues, Ned Italiano, Joe Sottile, and John B. Kerr. The Crown was represented by Bob Fowler and his able assistant, John J. Robinette. Judge Keeler McKay was on the bench.

On the first day of the trial, U.S. Customs officials testified about the October 4th seizures at the Peace Bridge — the vests concealing the buttons of gold on Harry Julius. Several buttons, circular convex pieces of metal of about 3½ inches in diameter and weighing up to 70 ounces each, were introduced as evidence. An assayer evaluated the worth of each button and the gold bar, at a total of well over

$10,000. RCMP officer Ed McElhone then testified that he and Corporal Bill Kelly and two other RCMP officers had raided the Toronto home of Benjamin and Sydney Faibish and found several documents, hidden in basement rafters, connecting the Faibishes with Harry Julius and Charles Abrahams as well as a cash box containing $8,656 in U.S. and Canadian currency and a New York City telephone number.

The gold, according to Kelly, was "bought by Labreque who crudely refined it himself out in the bush or in their basement — wherever it was — it was pretty good stuff, 800/900 fine." The "buttons" would be brought down to Annie's by couriers and weighed at Annie's place (she was now living at her sister's house at 14 Wells Hill Avenue, Toronto) and then brought in to be assayed. Kelly states that the RCMP was "able to trace from the notes we found in notebooks seized, the weights of the buttons and the assays." According to RCMP Corporal Bill Kelly, Annie would often "take the gold to the assay offices in Toronto under assumed names before paying for the metal because she couldn't trust all the people who brought it to her. If she didn't go to the assay office herself, she would listen in on the telephone when the analysis was given to the courier. That was her system. Of course, when the courier came to the assay office and said that his name was 'John Smith' [really John Deluca] — and of course they were using funny names — we didn't know who the hell they were. So we had to make sure we tailed them and took their pictures, so that we could identify them. We followed many people for long distances; we did a hell of a lot of footwork."

On May 11, 1942, Harry L. Romberg, a Toronto lawyer and Annie Newman's nephew at whose parents' home Annie had been staying, was subpoenaed to testify for the Crown to help prove Annie's guilt. J. J. Robinette questioned him on his familiarity with $1,000 bills. Romberg replied that he had seen $1,000 bills "twenty-five times or more." He added that he gave Annie use of an office at a Bloor Street theatre his father owned, and that his aunt frequently had him change $1,000 bills into smaller denominations "as she had no bank of her own." Romberg further testified that he had observed

Annie meeting with Sydney Faibish in his theatre office. Romberg was not involved in the conspiracy, and his testimony against his aunt helped to clear him of any accusation of knowing participation in the smuggling.

On May 15th, the jury heard contents of two September 17, 1941 letters addressed to Annie Newman that the RCMP (Kelly and McElhone) and Postal censors had intercepted after being tipped off by Max Fell of the Foreign Exchange Control Board. The first letter concerned Annie's trip to Timmins to see a priest about getting Rocco Perri out of internment. The letter mentions monies owed and cryptically refers to "test results" anticipated. The second letter contained only figures: "814-7 x 2607 x 12040 x 313880." McElhone testified that he followed Annie up to Timmins on the train and observed her meeting with Alphonse Labreque and a priest, Father Theriault, described later by defence counsel Greer as a "personal friend of the then Minister of Justice" [Ernest Lapointe]. A Toronto bank teller then testified that between May 15 and June 12, 1940, he had exchanged eighteen $1,000 bills for Sydney Faibish. Annie Newman, it was also stated, had arranged to have three people, including her nephew Harry Romberg, exchange forty-four $1,000 bills.

Rocco Perri's name came into the trial during Greer's summation to the jury on May 29th. He contended that Annie Newman went up to Timmins only to help her husband get out of internment camp, not to make a gold deal. Greer went on to state that he had "only known Rocco Perri as a bootlegger. He's regarded by police as a local nuisance, not such a bad man, but one who wants people to think he's a bad man.... Perri at one time, according to the newspaper reports, was regarded as one of the seven wonders of the world. I knew him as anything but the great mental star he was regarded to be.... The fact that Annie Newman or Annie Perri, as she was known then, would be anxious to get Perri out of the internment camp was the most natural thing in the world."

In his final summation to the jury, Crown attorney Fowler maintained that the police had proof that the Timmins trip had as much to do with the gold conspiracy as it did with trying to get Rocco Perri out of internment. Fowler then suggested the conspirators' lack of patriotism: "How many guns or planes would $850,000 buy?" Fowler rhetorically asked, adding up all the money earned on the gold in twenty-one months. "Isn't it perfectly clear," thundered Fowler, "that the Labreques, Mazzuca, Deluca, Franciotti, were all bringing gold and that they converged on Annie Newman and Sydney Faibish, who were in touch with New York?"

The Judge's final address to the jury lasted for a marathon five hours and forty-five minutes. McKay told the jury that they had "too much information." It had been one of the longest cases in the history of the City of Toronto up till that time. He tried to simplify the case by stating that the Crown's contention was that the five Labreques, Deluca, Mazzuca, and Franciotti were engaged in collecting the gold, and that the two Faibishes and Annie Newman were instrumental in getting it to refiner Kushner in New York. Mr Justice McKay also focused the jury's attention on the documents found by the RCMP at the Faibish home and on the ten visits of Harry Julius to Toronto between April and October 1941, during which time testimony was given that over $500,000 in Canadian currency was purchased in New York to pay for the gold. Because of the complexity of the massive evidence, the number of defendants and the many charges against them, McKay ordered that the jury be given hotel accommodation for the night. Because many of the defendants were French Canadians, Italians and Jews, Judge McKay ended his lengthy address by telling the jury that "the law knows no racial distinction" and the jury should "so far as it is possible, divest yourself of all prejudice." McKay defined "conspiracy" for the jury only as "an agreement of two or more persons to achieve an illegal object.... It is not necessary to prove any act after the agreement."

After nearly nineteen hours of deliberations over three days, the jury came in with its verdicts at 1:00 P.M. on June 5, 1942. The afternoon dailies scrambled to get the names of those convicted and acquitted in the late editions. Those acquitted for lack of evidence were William Franciotti, Paul Labreque, Alphonse Labreque (though he was facing a retrial on one of the counts), Albert Labreque, Albert Mazzuca and, significantly, Sydney's father, Benjamin Faibish.

Sydney Faibish was convicted of five counts and received the longest sentence of the eleven: four years in Kingston and a fine of $7,000. Lionel Labreque was found guilty of one count of conspiracy and was sentenced to two years in Kingston and fined $1,000. Ernest Labreque received two years and a fine of $3,000; Frank Deluca, one of Annie's runners, got fifteen months.

Annie Newman, as the principal co-conspirator (with a criminal record), received the next-longest sentence: three years in Kingston and a fine of $5,000 (with the stipulation that she serve another year if she didn't pay the fine; she didn't pay). In sentencing her, Mr Justice McKay called Annie the "prime mover" of the conspiracy. He could not comprehend what could motivate such reprehensible crimes, and bluntly told Newman this before sentencing her: "How the love or the lure of gold prompted you to take such a course with conditions as they are in the world today is hard to understand."

At fifty-four, Annie was to spend over two years in prison. Excluding the internment, this is more than all the time served by Rocco. (Her younger nephews were told that Annie was at school, "studying.") Sydney Faibish served his time and emerged to practise optometry — even today Faibish, now in his late sixties, runs Crown Opticians on Yonge Street near Bloor in Toronto.

ROCCO'S LEGACY

After serving three years and four months in the "city without women" (as one writer has referred to Camp Petawawa in his novel about life there at the time), Rocco was finally released from internment by the special order of Justice Minister Louis St Laurent on October 10, 1943. In a rare public disclosure, Colonel C. W. G. Gibson, the Minister of National Revenue, told the House of Commons on October 16th of the release. With Italy's break with the Axis powers, Canada was now releasing most of the Italian civilians interned.

Rocco returned to freedom in obscurity. Many in the press and public had either forgotten about the legendary "King of the Bootleggers" or found his story considerably less important than the news from the war fronts in Europe and Asia. Though Rocco's release was reported in the newspapers across the country, it was buried in a small column inside most papers. (The Toronto *Star* did publish a picture of Rocco calmly smoking a cigarette along with its modest report, and the Hamilton *Spectator* noted that Perri, "formerly of Hamilton," was "known to most Hamiltonians." But there were no major headlines as in the old days.) A lot had changed in the underworld since his incarceration. When Rocco came home, Annie was still in jail, so he stayed with Annie's sister, Leah Romberg, and her family at their home in Toronto at 14 Wells Hill Avenue.

Under the terms of his release Rocco was required to take a job. Annie had purchased for $35,000 the Metro Theatre, a movie theatre on Bloor Street at Ossington, and, for the record, Rocco Perri became the theatre's part-time janitor and doorman. In fact, this was simply a cover to satisfy government officials.

Rocco was formulating a plan to emerge yet again as the King of the Mob. The Buffalo Magaddino family and their Canadian allies had taken almost complete control of the mobs in southern Ontario, but Rocco aimed to take control again. He went to Hamilton in April to begin his struggle to regain power.

According to his cousin Joe Serge, Rocco arrived at Serge's home at 49 Murray Street East on Thursday, April 20th, where he stayed while he conducted business in Hamilton. Significantly, he hadn't yet reported his presence there to the RCMP (under the terms of his release from internment he was supposed to report any journey outside Toronto). It was his second trip to Hamilton in five days. On Saturday, April 22nd, Rocco accompanied Pat Moranda, Serge's stepson, to the city centre, where Perri sent cigarettes to a soldier overseas. In the afternoon Perri left Moranda to go to his house, at 166 Bay Street South. The home he had shared with Bessie and Annie had been turned into a rooming house. Perri went to examine the property, as he was apparently preparing to either sell the house or re-occupy it and use it as his new base of operations. We know that he instructed Harry L. Romberg to arrange to have the house vacated.

On Sunday April 23, 1944, Rocco complained of a headache. He took two pills and drank a cup of coffee. Between 10:30 A.M. and 11:00 A.M. he told Serge that he was going out for a walk to clear his head. He never returned from his constitutional. Two days later, on April 25th at 1:00 P.M., Serge phoned the Hamilton police and reported him missing. Serge told the police that Rocco was "not worrying about anything.... was in good spirits all the time."

Detective Ernest Barrett of the Hamilton police, who in 1924 had spotted Ukrainian mobster Jack Larenchuk's car behind Perri's house, conducted the police investigation of the Perri disappearance, which seems to have lasted only a few days, according to the few surviving police files.

When Serge had notified the police that Perri was missing, Perri's locked sedan was still parked near the Serge house on Murray Street. Accompanied by RCMP Corporal Martin, Barrett interrogated Joe Serge. Barrett's first report is dated April 25, 1944, "Re: Disappearance of ROCCO PERRI":

At 11:15 P.M. I received a phone call from Tony [sic] Serge, 49 Murray Street East, stating that he had made enquiries and obtained a set of duplicate keys [of Perri's car, License #5 R894] from the previous owner, Morris Steinberg, 87 Victoria Ave. S., if I wish to search auto and call for the keys. With P.C.'s Larson and Chinnery I got the keys and searched said auto. In the glove compartment we found two Easter cards, not addressed. On top of the rear seat we found a pair of black overshoes, size 7½. Concealed among newspapers, we found a note, no signature or address. Same is now in the Detective office.

The description of Rocco at the time of his disappearance also appears in the police report: "Description — age 55 years, 5′ 4½ inches 170 lbs. dark complexion, Italian. Wearing blue striped suit, black Oxfords, light brown spring and fall overcoat, light brown fedora hat."

This is the unedited text of the hidden note in Perri's car as it appears in Hamilton police files. All of the spelling and grammatical errors appear as in the original:

I hope whend you received this parcel you not bee offendet not allarmi to cry and worry your selfe I am doin this for your nefid the reason is may some one see or now I have this parcel and may cause you trobles to lose your happy home and you joub. your worek and your dear sweet heart. is you so much in love whit him.

I soon sacrificed my selfe and not jgive you any worry. you

now that? I am not like you to play 2 game bout you not smart noft for me I not full you try hard to full me and maeks me beleive I was the only one you only care you) care so much for me not to goe one step out side the door because you fred some one see you and thei rapport to you sweet Darling.

I never see any one so fred every murder when dei round way or see some one ron Bank. this is very mistery just to think abouT all the affar.

You nat afred to goo to show whit some one you care you not afred to goo to party or to the Hotel of to Toom. or to office walk the street and you was ready to tell to all the worlds bout our love.

I am very glad i come to my sense coase is I to let you remeind my selfe I pay very deer white mony time and very close whit my life to let you full me bout dont you thing you to smart no i was because you show me you was very much in love with me some time agoe. you was crazy. and you provet to me in may ways and I how to trost you bleeve you and not only dat bout yet to love and more love so whend the time come you could full me betet you now I not deserve what you doing to me if you thing I am just a Freind to you you should come whit truth and tell very thing what has hapen. and nat to tray to fuulll mee and leeeve me in suspenden I was the first love you say bout now I am the last from everyone and you still asking me to marry you maybeee you want me for houspond to cover you sweet heart or because is refuse to marry you and if I marry you you will make me very Happy and I nearly bleeve you because troust you love and you give me wonderful time in 3-way.

In a report from Barrett's colleagues Chinnery and Larson, this mysterious note is called "an unaddressed letter, the text of which disclosed a self-sacrifice was to be made."

If the note was Rocco's, then it appears that he had become involved with another woman, unless, of course, they were letters to be sent to Annie who was still in Kingston Penitentiary. It is possible that Annie had become involved with another man while Rocco was interned. She had, after all, been waiting for Rocco for two years before her own imprisonment. The discussion of marriage is curious, since Rocco never bothered to legally marry Bessie, let alone consider marriage to Annie or other girlfriends such as Olive Routledge. If the writer was Rocco, the concern expressed in the letter about his safety seems reasonable enough. There is also a suggestion that Rocco (or the writer) may have been sacrificing himself to alleviate a difficult situation, possibly a triangle that had evolved between himself, Annie and another man or himself, another woman and another man. Is this Rocco's farewell note?

If Rocco was writing to Annie, then it seems quite likely that she had started an affair with another man in Rocco's absence. If Rocco was writing to another woman, a new girlfriend, then Annie herself may have been the third part of the triangle. But the letter is far from clear, and only adds to the mystery surrounding Rocco's disappearance. Curiously, it was never made public by the police until it was released to the authors of this book by former Deputy Chief Keith Farraway in 1985. He found the Perri disappearance file sadly lacking in completeness and thoroughness, and it seemed to him that the reason for this was "that some of the best police investigators were off in Europe fighting for the Allies."

The second report on the Perri disappearance concerns a lead involving a mysterious Sudbury couple. This was the only serious lead the Hamilton police had at the time. A couple from Sudbury had registered as Mr and Mrs C. W. Smith at the Bayview Hotel (at Bay and Stuart streets, Hamilton) at 1:30 A.M. on April 23rd. They changed rooms three times over the next two days. The proprietor was very suspicious of them because "several people of Italian extraction phoned asking for the Smiths." The Smiths had no luggage except for a parcel carried by the woman. They checked out at 11:30 A.M. on April 26th. According to another police source, a waiter at the Windsor Hotel, Mr C. W. Smith was a Pole called "Farmer" who was a "professional gambler" in Sudbury. Other sources disclosed that "Smith" had been in town "over the week-end past but didn't appear at any games, as his presence was unwelcomed by the local gambling fraternity." It is reported in the *Spectator* of April 26th that there was "a report that Perri was seen in a hotel Monday afternoon with two men believed to be from Northern Ontario."

Mike Perri, Rocco's younger brother, reported that he had not seen his brother since Monday, April 19th, when they had attended the funeral of a mutual friend in Hamilton. Mike, who was now running a grocery store on John Street South in Hamilton, seems to have kept out of organized crime activity (even though he had to serve two years in internment because of the activities of his sibling), and after Rocco's disappearance, he faded into obscurity.

Constable Howard Moreau of the Hamilton police added a note in his report that he and his colleagues made two calls at 166 Bay Street South "to investigate reports of a raid being conducted there by six officers last night [April 26], but no one answered the door. Nothing is known of the alleged raid as it was not conducted by any known Police of Hamilton nor the RCMP of Toronto."

There is no further analysis or clue in the surviving Hamilton police file, and, unfortunately, there are no RCMP files on the disappearance (they did their own disappearing act!) even though under the terms of Rocco's release from internment, which was much like being on parole, it was the RCMP's responsibility to keep tabs on him. On May 2, 1944, the RCMP sent out circulars on Rocco to all police departments throughout Canada, officially listing him as missing. The whole disappearance is still shrouded in secrecy to this day.

It seems clear that Rocco was about to re-assert himself in Hamilton. In a liquor hijack trial later in 1944, the notorious gangster Donald ("Mickey") MacDonald identified Rocco Perri as the "Mr X" who was supplying bootleg booze to Hamilton bootlegger Sam Mancuso in December 1943. Mancuso had refused to name the bootlegger, telling the court that he didn't want a bullet in him.

There are those who believe that Rocco made his escape. Milton Goldhart now declares that Rocco talked frequently of retiring and going to Cuba to live. Other former colleagues and friends report that he may have gone to Mexico. The Chief of Inspectors of Toronto Police, Moses Mullholland, told a reporter in 1946 (and repeated to another reporter as late as 1954) that he, too, had heard that

Rocco was in Mexico. "But if he is alive," Mullholland added, "he will likely stay away from here.... Mexico is a big country."

However, events in the underworld after Rocco's disappearance make it fairly certain that he was taken out by rival gangsters who were probably supported or hired by the Magaddino family of Buffalo. It seems quite clear that the long arm of the Buffalo mob snatched Rocco on the streets near Serge's home and disposed of him.

On January 15, 1945, the body of one of Rocco's former bootlegging, gambling and drug trafficking associates, Louis Wernick, forty-two, of 481 Euclid Street, Toronto, was found by a snow plough team in a snowbank near the Long Branch racetrack in Etobicoke. His body had been riddled with bullets, six in all. An OPP investigation carried out by Inspector Edward Hammond revealed that Wernick had been kidnapped by his killers, one of whom was identified as an Italian by the name of Giuseppe. Hammond's underworld informants and police officers familiar with Wernick indicated that he was "definitely a big-time racketeer" and that he had "apparently taken over Rocco Perri's business." That business was, according to police sources quoted in the Toronto *Star* of January 29, 1945, drug trafficking. Wernick, it was found, was also "definitely a whoremaster, having different women every night." Hammond concluded that the murder had "an international aspect," rather than merely a local one. Apparently, the Magaddino family of Buffalo was solidifying its hold on Toronto by killing yet another trusted colleague of Rocco Perri and taking more control of the drug trade. But this was not the last gangland killing associated with Rocco Perri's criminal empire.

Within days of the Wernick murder, another body was found riddled with bullets, this time in Buffalo itself. The head of the anti-rackets crusade in Buffalo, Edward J. Posphcahal, who had instigated a grand jury investigation into the gambling racket run by Don Stefano Magaddino, had been gunned down in a manner reminiscent of Joe Sotille's bombing of Temperance crusaders in the 1920s.

Three hundred Buffalo detectives searched for his killers, but they found nothing. The hand of Don Stefano was everywhere, but he was not touched. Magaddino had that much power in New York state by 1945.

Later, in December 1945, another Perri underling, Giovanni ("John") Durso, who had been interned with Rocco at Camp Petawawa during the early forties and was involved in Rocco's drug trafficking, went missing. His automobile was found inside the Welland Canal, which, ironically, Rocco Perri had helped to build in his early days. Durso had been taken for the proverbial ride, and, like Rocco, his body was never found.

The Buffalo mob solidified its hold on Rocco's old mob, having taken out Perri, Wernick and now Durso and others. The remaining Perri allies, such as Tony Papalia and Charlie Bordonaro and their families had made an accommodation with Buffalo, an arrangement which survived through the fifties and sixties. In the case of Papalia, the arrangement exists even today under the leadership of Tony Papalia's son, Johnny ("Pops") Papalia. According to the 1985 Report of the Criminal Intelligence Service Canada, which represents all the major police forces in Canada, Papalia is currently "installed [as a] new representative in southern Ontario (Toronto, Hamilton and the Niagara Peninsula) to further the interests of La Cosa Nostra's Buffalo, New York, branch"; that is, the Maggadino family now run by Joe Todaro since the death of Stefano Magaddino in 1974.

Rocco's end somehow seems fitting. He had thrived in the underworld in southern Ontario and northern New York state for over three decades, prospering through his uncanny ability to work with all types of people. While he was charismatic, generous and ingratiating, he was also capable of having people killed when necessary. The old proverb perhaps applies: those who live by the sword, die by the sword. Rocco Perri had spent over three decades in the jungle of the mob. That other elements of that same underworld should have taken him out is hardly surprising. He represented a threat to the new organization that had been built up in the early forties. New men took control of new organizations and new rackets, with Buffalo's Magaddino family pulling the strings.

The age of the King of the Mob and the Canadian independent mobs was over for some time. For the next two decades the mob in southern Ontario was to be fragmented and unable to escape the grip of the Buffalo organization under Don Stefano Magaddino, who later became the long-time chairman of the ruling commission of the American Mafia. When in the 1950s the Quebec crime family of Vic Cotroni came under the control of Joe Bonnano, Magaddino's New York City Mafia cousin, the American Mafia takeover of the Canadian mob's racket was complete.

Rocco Perri was the most successful, colourful and original gangster Canada has ever had.

In his old territory, in the southern Ontario cities of Toronto and Hamilton and in the Niagara region on both sides of the Canada-U.S. border, Rocco is a folk hero. Old-timers actually remember him with affection.

He is unique in the history of organized crime — an Italian mobster whose common-law wives, Bessie Starkman and Annie Newman, both commanded the respect of Rocco's men. Though Jewish, Bessie and Annie helped run Italian-dominated crime families in Canada for close to three decades. They were smarter crooks and operated at a higher level than the three women — all bank robbers — most often listed along with the male gangsters of the twenties and thirties — Bonny Parker of Bonnie and Clyde; Arizona Donnie Clark "Ma" Barker, the so-called Czarina of Crime; and Kate Kelly, the wife of Machine-Gun Kelly.

Rocco was also unique among bootleggers. He outlasted two Americans who called themselves King of the Bootleggers, "Big Bill" Dwyer in New York and George Remus in the Midwest. Among Canadians he was unequalled. Montreal was always open for booze, so there was no need for a major bootlegger there. Vancouver went wet in 1921. In Alberta, there was Emilio "Emperor Pic" Picarillo, but he ended his life on the gallows after the shooting of a police officer. Canadian folklore centres on the adventurous Maritime fishermen who dared to sail to Rum Row.

In Canada, business and government entered a voluntary but unspoken partnership with organized crime to provide alcohol to the United States during Prohibition. Rocco was the point man in Ontario. He delivered the best Canadian product from Ontario's bootleg triangle. In effect, he helped the old respectable firms such as Seagram's and Gooderham's, then still owned by the their founding families and later by the rich new upstarts like Harry Hatch, get the foothold in the U.S. market they still have today. And in doing the dirty work, it could also be said that Rocco kept the brewing and distilling families respectable.

If Rocco's body had been found, there would have been another memorable funeral. As it happened, his disappearance was mentioned only on the back pages; major battles were on the front page. The world outside Hamilton was too busy to pay attention to the search for Canada's Al Capone.

As for Annie Newman, she emerged from jail later in 1944 and she sold Rocco's house at 166 Bay Street, which was in her name, in the mid-forties. She later remarried and moved to Chicago. She returned to Toronto in the fifties and eventually married again — this time Kalman Wagner, husband of her late sister Bina, who died in 1956. She ended her days playing cards at the cottage, a somewhat wild old woman who occasionally surprised her nephews when she brought up the subject of the old days. When she died in 1974 at the age of 85, she was buried in Toronto beside her sisters.

As so often happens in Canada, the legend of Rocco Perri has been overwhelmed by the American mass media. The talkies almost began with gangster pictures. It was no accident that the press later dubbed Rocco "Canada's Little Caesar." But Hollywood's vision was limited; Canadian whisky arrived at the border as if by magic. Even in Rocco's day, the gang wars of Chicago and New York got more ink in the Ontario papers than the killings in their own backyard.

It is only now with the resurfacing of documents after many years, that the significance of Rocco Perri, a cocky little bootlegger who rose to be Ontario's mob boss, can be seen. He established the Calabrian criminal presence in Ontario which is still powerful. He forged the bonds between Canada, the United States and Italy which are still around today. And it was Rocco who made Hamilton, not Toronto, Ontario's mob capital.

As Bessie found in those first days of 1912, and as police chiefs, magistrates, Mounties and provincial premiers and attorney generals later discovered, Rocco Perri had lots of chutzpah and charm. His ingenuous, basically likeable personality is perhaps what made him Canada's popular criminal folk hero in a way that Al Capone and others could never be in the U.S. And it may also explain why, for so long, he got away with breaking all the rules. He defied Italian tradition, Jewish tradition, the pushy American giant and the ideals of the British Empire. Milton Goldhart called him "a prince." Had Perri lived in another century, a Machiavelli might have found his methodology instructive.

Rocco would probably have enjoyed the mystery that still surrounds his disappearance. Several RCMP memos report the word on the street was that Rocco had been "taken for a ride," his body put in a wooden barrel which was then filled with cement and dropped into Hamilton Bay. One source was an associate of the late Louis Wernick, who had heard the story from Wernick shortly before the Toronto gangster's own demise. "We won't find his body," an RCMP officer concluded in a 1954 interview, "until the Bay dries up."

TRACKING ROCCO PERRI:

A NOTE ON SOURCES

If Canada had its own movie industry in the 1930s, there would have been a major movie about Rocco Perri, Canada's self-proclaimed "King of the Bootleggers."

The name Rocco Perri was known across Canada during those years and as time went on, a legend was born. Every so often there was a retrospective newspaper or magazine article, or a few paragraphs in a book, all based on earlier clippings, each repeating the mistakes of earlier reports.

It was Jim Dubro who made the first steps to bring substance back to that legend. While researching *Mob Rule*, his pioneering work on modern Canadian organized crime, he decided that the book needed a chapter on the history of the mob. In early 1984, Jim filed a blanket request for files on Rocco and Bessie Perri under the Access to Information Act with the Royal Canadian Mounted Police and went over all the material that had survived in the files of the Hamilton Public Library. The library provided the basic information on bootlegging in the twenties; the RCMP supplied the previously secret files on Inspector Frank Zaneth's investigation of Rocco's corruption of customs officers in Windsor.

As Jim completed the first draft of the manuscript, he showed Robin Rowland the section on Rocco Perri. To someone who was a childhood fan of the TV series "The Untouchables," it was an eye-opener. Canada had three of the most fascinating figures in the history of gangland: Rocco Perri, Bessie Starkman and Annie Newman.

We wrote a proposal for a radio play and sold it to CBC's "Morningside." "King of the Bootleggers" aired January 27-31, 1986. At the same time, *Mob Rule* became a national best-seller.

We had needed more information to write the play. It was then that we visited the Archives of Ontario and found the files which chronicled the events surrounding the poison liquor deaths in 1926. Undercover reports, until then seen only by policemen in the 1920s, contained reports that helped bring Rocco more alive as a character and to prove that Bessie Starkman was a lot more than a gangster's moll.

In late November, 1985, we visited the Public Archives in Ottawa and there we discovered the key file that contained the dramatic RCMP undercover reports on both Rocco and Bessie's drug activities and the murder of Bessie Perri.

On January 15, 1986, we received files on the poison alcohol investigation we had ordered from the U.S. National Archives in Washington as well as the drug files we had found in Ottawa. Although too late to use in the play, it was immediately apparent that the Rocco Perri story was the tale of a powerful mob boss whose influence reached across Canada and into the United States. From that day, tracking the Rocco Perri story became a full-time job for both of us.

Throughout 1986 and into 1987, research continued. Some files were missing. What was once described as the thick Hamilton police file on Rocco Perri turned out to be very thin, containing just a few reports. Fortunately, Rocco's criminal record up until 1922 was contained in his citizenship file. We obtained more files from the RCMP under the Access to Information Act and at the same time discovered that others, including the RCMP report on Rocco's disappearance in 1944, had been destroyed years ago. Later we were able to look at the OPP files on the 1920s gang war and on Bessie's murder.

Freedom of Information requests to U.S. agencies showed that some files had been thrown out while others, such as the Secret Service file on the gold smuggling case, had survived.

The U.S. State Department's bootlegging intelligence files, held in the Archives, were an untapped resource for the history of organized crime in Canada.

In the meantime, readers of *Mob Rule* contacted us and we added the information they supplied on Rocco to our files. Some, like the Runyonesque Milton Goldhart, had been active members of Perri's organization.

We had compiled a vast amount of once-secret material and realized that the story of Rocco Perri went beyond Rocco, Bessie and Annie. It was also the story of the often confusing labyrinth of Canadian prohibition laws, so different from the simple nationwide 18th Amendment in the United States. Historian Ralph Allen has written, "Ontario's law was the weirdest contraption of all," and the Ontario Temperance Act helped, not hindered, Perri's bootlegging operations. *King of the Mob* is also the story of how a well-meaning law led a nation's establishment into business with gangsters and how government winked at organized crime.

Although Rocco Perri is in many ways a legendary figure, organized crime is not glamourous. It is the hard truth that, charming as he was, Rocco Perri ordered many killings, trafficked in dangerous narcotics for a number of years and caused the deaths of innocent people from alcohol poisoning. It is a fact of history that every country has made certain criminal figures cultural heroes, even though they are cold-blooded killers, such as Jesse James, Bonnie and Clyde, or Al Capone. *King of the Mob* is an effort to put facts to a legend and produce a real character out of a folk hero.

ACKNOWLEDGEMENTS

Special thanks to Tom Cherington and Sid Adilman for their early encouragement, which made this book possible.

To Ontario Provincial Police Commissioner Archie Ferguson for his interest and assistance.

To Inspector Jack Patterson, Sergeant Joe Vertolli, Sergeant Joe Fotia of the Ontario Provincial Police, and Chief Superintendent Dahn Higley, (ret.) OPP historian. Chief Superintendent A. C. Tuttle and the Access office of the Royal Canadian Mounted Police with special thanks to Mike Desserault, Stan Horall, RCMP historian, Staff Sergeant Robin Ward (ret.) and Deputy Commissioner William Kelly (ret.); "Jocko" Thomas and Mike Walton at the *Toronto Star*; Deputy Chief Keith Farraway (ret.) Hamilton-Wentworth Regional Police; Mark Gold, Harold Gold, Harry Romberg, Martyn Burke, Milton Goldhart, Richard Neilsen, Lee Lamothe at the Toronto *Sun*, Bert Kuntz and John Yoannou.

Rob Roy, who did some important initial research.

Doug Gibson, who encouraged the research.

The research and writing of this book was supported by a grant from the Canada Council. We wish to thank the Council and Non-fiction grants officer, Claude Guay.

Archivists who gave invaluable assistance were Richard Ramsey, Archives of Ontario; Rod Young, Jim Whalen and Judy Roberts-Moore at the National Archives of Canada; Sandra Burrows and Franceen Gaudet at the National Library of Canada; Cynthia G. Fox and John W. Roberts, Judicial Branch; Katherine Murphy and Ron Swerczek, Diplomatic Branch, Washington; and Peter Bunce and staff, Chicago branch, U.S. National Archives.

Special thanks to Norma Dainard, Keith Alcock, Jacquie Gill,

Gordon Glasheen, Michael Hunchberger and Joseph Smirles at the microfilm section of the Metropolitan Toronto Reference Library.

Research help also came from Mike Ingrisano, Jr., U.S. Customs Service; John C. Weaver, McMaster University; Janice Neil, Chicago Historical Society; Patrick F. Healy, Chicago Crime Commission; L. B. Sheafe, Deputy Director U.S. Secret Service; E. W. Aumand, Access Co-ordinator, Department of the Secretary of State of Canada; S. Parent, Access Co-ordinator, Revenue Canada, Customs & Excise; Margaret Houghton and Brian Henley, Hamilton Public Library; Tammy Danciu and Cathy Berron, *Hamilton Spectator*; staff of the Canadian Broadcasting Corporation Reference Library; Rabbi Chaim Nussbaum; Margy Chan and Andrew Ross, Addiction Research Foundation, for access to the rare temperance collection, Superintendent K. Hoskisson, Merseyside Police, Liverpool, England; Jane Lodge Smith, the New Brunswick Museum; and Stephen Speisman, Canadian Jewish Congress.

Others who have encouraged or advised us and whom we wish to thank are: Jon Lidolt, Fred Rowland, Kit Vincent, Martha Porter, John Grube, Rick Archbold, Wayne Narcisco, Howard Engel, Doug Webb, James Hamilton, Harry Peterson, Larry Rose, Judi and Tom Christou, Tim MacLeod, Marion Hebb, Peggy Este, Dave Martin and Tom Renner.

And, of course, our editor, David Kilgour, and publisher, Morton Mint of Penguin Books Canada Limited.

SELECT BIBLIOGRAPHY AND SOURCE LIST

Books and Journal Articles

Arlacchi, Pino. *Mafia Business: The Mafia Ethic and the Spirit of Capitalism.* Translated by Martin Ryle. London: Verso, 1983.

Bell, Ernest Albert. *Fighting the Traffic in Young Girls; or War on the white slave trade: a complete and detailed account of the shameless traffic in young girls.* Chicago: G.S. Ball, 1911.

Canada. *Royal Commission Appointed to Inquire into the Immigration of Italian Labourers to Montreal.* Ottawa: King's Printer, 1905.
Royal Commission on Customs and Excise, Reports 1-10. Ottawa: King's Printer, 1927.

Chandler, David Leon. *The Criminal Brotherhoods.* London: Constable, 1975.

Dubro, James. *Mob Rule: Inside the Canadian Mafia.* Toronto: Macmillan, 1985.

Gervais, C.H. *The Rumrunners: A Prohibition Scrapbook.* Scarborough, Ont.: Firefly Books, 1980.

Gray, James H. *Bacchanalia Revisited: Western Canada's Boozy Skid to Social Disaster.* Saskatoon: Western Producer Prairie Books, 1982.

Greenaway, C. Roy. "Big Shots" in *Open House.* Ed. William Arthur Dean and Wilfred Reeves. Ottawa: Graphic Publishers, 1931, pp. 219 - 35.
The News Game. Toronto: Clarke, Irwin, 1966.

Hallowell, Gerald. *Prohibition in Ontario 1919 - 1923.* Ottawa: Ontario Historical Society Research Publication 1972.

Harkness, Ross. *J. E. Atkinson of the Star.* Toronto: University of Toronto Press, 1963.

Harney, Robert F. "Montreal's King of Italian Labour: A Case Study in Padronism." *Labour: Journal of Canadian Labour Studies* 4; no. 4 (1979): 57 -84.

"The Padrone and the Immigrant." *Canadian Review of American Studies* 5, no. 2 (1974): 101 - 18.

ed. *Gathering Place: Peoples and Neighbourhoods of Toronto, 1834 - 1945,* Toronto: Multicultural History Society of Ontario, 1985.

Higley, Dahn. *O. P. P.: The History of the Ontario Provincial Police Force.* Toronto: Queen's Printer, 1984.

Katcher, Leo. *The Big Bankroll: The Life and Times of Arnold Rothstein.* New York: Harper and Brothers, 1958.

Kelly, William and Nora Kelly. *The Royal Canadian Mounted Police: A Century of History.* Edmonton: Hurtig, 1973.

Kobler, John. *Capone: The Life and World of Al Capone.* New York: G. P. Putnam's Sons, 1971.

Landesco, John. *Organized Crime in Chicago, Part III of the Illinois Crime Survey 1929.* Chicago: University of Chicago Press, 1968.

McIntosh, Dave. *The Collectors: A History of Canadian Customs and Excise.* Ottawa: NC Press for Canada: Revenue Canada and Ministry of Supply and Services, 1982.

Nelli, Humbert S. *The Business of Crime: Italians and Syndicate Crime in the United States.* Chicago: University of Chicago Press, 1976.

Newman, Peter C. *Bronfman Dynasty: The Rothschilds of the New World.* Toronto: McClelland and Stewart, 1978.

Oliver, Peter. *G. Howard Ferguson: Ontario Tory.* Toronto: University of Toronto Press, 1977.

Pitkin, Thomas Monroe and Francesco Cordasco. *The Black Hand: A Chapter in Ethnic Crime.* Totawa, N.J.: Littlefield, Adams & Co., 1977.

Rohmer, Richard. *E. P. Taylor: The Biography of Edward Plunkett Taylor.* Toronto: McClelland and Stewart, 1978.

Salerno, Ralph and John S. Tompkins. *The Crime Confederation: Cosa Nostra and Allied Operations in Organized Crime.* Garden City, N.Y.: Doubleday, 1969.

Speisman, Stephen A. *The Jews of Toronto: A History to 1937.* Toronto: McClelland and Stewart, 1979.

Weaver, John C. *Hamilton: An Illustrated History.* Toronto: James Lorimer and National Museums of Canada, 1982.

Wolf, George, with Joseph DiMona. *Frank Costello: Prime Minister of the Underworld.* New York: William Morrow, 1974.

Zucchi, John. *The Italian Immigrants of St. John's Ward, 1875 - 1915: Patterns of Settlement and Neighbourhood Formation.* Toronto: Multicultural History Society of Ontario, 1981.

Newspapers

HAMILTON: *Spectator, Herald*
TORONTO: *Globe, Mail and Empire, Globe and Mail, Star, Telegram*
NEW YORK: *Times, Journal*
GUELPH: *Mercury*
WINDSOR: *Border Cities* |Windsor| *Star*
WELLAND: *Tribune and Telegraph*
SUDBURY: *Star*

Archives

Archives of Ontario
    Records of the Attorney General: Case files
    Records of the Ontario Provincial Police: Case files
Ontario Provincial Police Archives
    William Stringer diaries and scrapbooks
    Case files
National Archives of Canada
    Royal Commission on Customs and Excise: Transcripts
    Records of the RCMP: Case files
    Department of Pensions and National Health: Drug intelligence files
U.S. National Archives
    Department of Justice: Case files
    U.S. State Department: Hamilton Consular files
                Bootlegging intelligence files
                Extradition case files
    Coast Guard: Intelligence files
           Seized Vessel files

INDEX